The Music of Maur

Sketch of Maurice Ohana by the novelist Laurence Cossé
Made during rehearsals for the première of *Office des oracles* at La Sainte-Baume,
August 1974

The Music of Maurice Ohana

Caroline Rae

Routledge
Taylor & Francis Group
LONDON AND NEW YORK

First published 2000 by Ashgate Publishing

Reissued 2018 by Routledge
2 Park Square, Milton Park, Abingdon, Oxon OX14 4RN
711 Third Avenue, New York, NY 10017, USA

Routledge is an imprint of the Taylor & Francis Group, an informa business

Copyright © Caroline Rae, 2000.

The author has asserted her right under the Copyright, Designs and Patents Act, 1988, to be identified as the author of this work.

All rights reserved. No part of this book may be reprinted or reproduced or utilised in any form or by any electronic, mechanical, or other means, now known or hereafter invented, including photocopying and recording, or in any information storage or retrieval system, without permission in writing from the publishers.

Notice:
Product or corporate names may be trademarks or registered trademarks, and are used only for identification and explanation without intent to infringe.

Publisher's Note
The publisher has gone to great lengths to ensure the quality of this reprint but points out that some imperfections in the original copies may be apparent.

Disclaimer
The publisher has made every effort to trace copyright holders and welcomes correspondence from those they have been unable to contact.

Typeset in Times Roman by ICA Music.

A Library of Congress record exists under LC control number: 00061800

ISBN 13: 978-1-138-73162-2 (hbk)
ISBN 13: 978-1-138-73159-2 (pbk)
ISBN 13: 978-1-315-18893-5 (ebk)

For my father and mother

Contents

List of Plates	viii
List of Tables	ix
Preface and Acknowledgements	x

Part 1 From the Garden of the Hesperides

1	Pianist to Composer: Cultural Roots, Life and Influences	1
2	Symbolism and Allegory: Images of the Archetype	31
3	Evolution towards Maturity: The Early and Transitional Works	68

Part 2 The Mature Music: Technique, Style and Structure

4	Growth and Proliferation: *Signes* and the Sigma Series	105
5	The Role of Monody	145
6	Harmony as Colour and Timbre	171
7	Rhythm and Aleatorism	193
8	Symmetrical Structures and Approaches to Form	219
9	Epilogue: Reception and Context	244

List of works	263
Bibliography	291
Index	299

List of Plates

Frontispiece:
Sketch of Maurice Ohana by the novelist Laurence Cossé, 1974

between pages 144 and 145

1   The composer's family home on Boulevard d'Anfa, Casablanca
    (From the collection of Solange Soubrane)

2   The composer at the time of his first public recital aged 11
    (From the collection of Solange Soubrane)

3   The composer aged about 23 at the time of his Paris début recital
    (From the collection of Solange Soubrane)

4   The composer (*c.* 1941, standing, centre back row) shortly after joining the British Army
    (From the collection of Solange Soubrane)

5   The composer (seated at the piano) with Ataulfo Argenta during rehearsals for the first recording of *Llanto for Igancio Sánchez Méjías* (*c.* early 1950s)
    (Phot: J. Desmarteau, from the collection of Solange Soubrane)

6   'Paso'. Drawing by the composer (*c.* 1955) of the Spanish procession of Holy Week
    (From a copy given to the present author by the composer)

7   The composer (front third from the left) with members of his family in Casablanca
    (Photo: Bernard Rouget, from the collection of Solange Soubrane)

8   The composer playing tennis at the Bois de Boulogne
    (From the collection of Solange Soubrane)

9   The composer (*c.* 1985) at his Paris flat, rue Général Delestraint
    (Photo: Dominique Souse, from the collection of Solange Soubrane)

10 The composer (right) with Roland Hayrabedian, *c.* 1990
    (Photo: Michel Dieuzaide, from the collection of Solange Soubrane)

List of Tables

2.1	Extra-musical sources for works of the early and transitional periods	34
2.2	Mythological allusions in Ohana's works from 1960 to 1991	54
3.1	Spanish sources in works of the early and transitional periods	70
3.2	The early published works	72
4.1	Disposition of percussion and timbral character in *Signes*	107
4.2	Structural synopsis of *Signes*	114
4.3	Harmonic schemes in *Signes*	126
4.4	The Sigma Series	129
6.1	The timbral divisions of Ohana's 'Masse Sonore'	173
6.2	Timbre I – Chords T–Ia and T–Ib	180
8.1	Symmetrical schemes in the transitional works	223
8.2	Symmetrical schemes in the mature works	224
8.3	*Cris*, 'Générique': formal scheme	237
8.4	*Livre des prodiges*, 'Cortège des taureaux ailés': formal scheme	238
8.5	*Sibylle*: formal scheme	240
9.1	BBC broadcasts of music by selected French composers 1945–69	245

Preface and Acknowledgements

Maurice Ohana was recognised as one of the leading composers of his generation in France, and much of continental Europe, as long ago as the 1960s. Since his death in 1992, his music continues to be performed, recorded and broadcast and a prize has been established to his memory. Both innovative and forward-looking, he contributed to almost every vocal and instrumental form, his work including three operas, a host of choral and other vocal music, music-theatre, several large-scale works for orchestra, seven concertos, three string quartets, other chamber works for diverse ensembles and much solo instrumental music. His music has been championed by many leading performers and conductors including Rostropovich. Yet, in Britain much of his work still remains to be discovered. Ohana did not follow the serialist path of the years following World War II, nor did he join his contemporaries at Darmstadt. As a result his music, like that of Dutilleux and many others, was excluded from representation at the Concerts du Domaine musical and was not imported to Britain at the time when the programming policies of Boulez and Sir William Glock were at the peak of their influence. Consequently, the British view of French music since 1945 became largely synonymous with the music of Messiaen and Boulez to the exclusion of others who achieved recognition beyond our shores.

My interest in the music of Maurice Ohana began in the early 1980s. Finding some recordings of his music almost by chance in the library of the Maison Française in Oxford, it was clear that here was an innovatory composer who was part of the compositional mainstream, avant-garde but not serialist. Curious to learn more about this intriguing figure who, like Dutilleux, was esteemed in France yet almost unknown in Britain, I approached the late Rollo Myers who not only lent me more recordings but, most crucially, provided me with an introduction to the composer. I first met Maurice Ohana in October 1982 when I went to live in Paris on a French Government Scholarship. Once immersed in the musical life of the city (I was a piano student of Madame Yvonne Loriod-Messiaen at the time) I became aware of two distinct, compositional factions: those who had been students of Messiaen or were involved with IRCAM and received commissions from the Ensemble intercontemporain; and those who were not. Ohana, Dutilleux, Marius Constant and many others, belonged to the latter category. Composers of one group could not be comfortably mentioned in the company of the other. Any frustration Dutilleux may have felt in being overlooked by Boulez must have been tempered by the recognition he achieved in the United States early in his career. Ohana and Constant were not so fortunate.

The music of Maurice Ohana belongs to the French compositional mainstream, yet the complexity of his cultural background prevents him from being described simply as a French composer. A British citizen, born in north Africa of Spanish-Gibraltarian parentage, educated, trained and resident in France, Ohana's bureaucratic nationality did not correspond with his cultural identity. Never a problem in France, where the cultural continuum from which he stemmed was readily understood, his music was accepted as their own. In Britain and the United States, the predilection for nationalistic programming by many concert promoters has prevented Ohana from being placed in a convenient musical pigeon-hole and thus, ironically, the cultural complexity which should be a key to understanding his music has been one of the primary causes of his comparative neglect.

In France and mainland Europe Ohana's music, at the time of writing, has been regularly performed, published and available on commercial recordings for more than forty years. Interviews and critical discussion of his music have appeared in France since the late 1950s, yet his work has received little attention in the English language. The surveys of French music by Rollo Myers and Fred Goldbeck, published in the 1970s, recognised the significance of Ohana's then still growing achievement, but it is necessary for an assessment of his music to be brought up-to-date. Not only Ohana but also Dutilleux have, until recently, been overlooked by many British and American scholars. It is the aim of the present study to rectify this omission.

This book is the first detailed study of Ohana's life and music and is the first study in any language to identify the procedures which characterise his mature, compositional style. It is divided into two parts which reflect the main objectives of the study: to set Ohana's work in its musical and cultural context and to identify and define the main features of his musical language and style. Part One discusses Ohana's cultural origins both as the catalyst for his emergence as a composer and as a resonant source for the symbolical and allegorical allusion that permeates his entire musical output. Part One also gives a biographical account of Ohana's life and career and surveys his work up to 1964. Part Two identifies the chamber work *Signes* both as representing the crystallisation of his mature style in 1965 and as engendering a succession of innovatory works which have here been defined as the Sigma Series. The following chapters of Part Two identify and define the main processes of Ohana's mature compositional language with reference to a range of many of his most important instrumental and vocal works and concludes with an assessment of the reception of his music and its historical context. It is hoped that this critical examination of Ohana's music will lay the foundation for future analytical studies.

I am indebted to Maurice Ohana for the interest and guidance he gave to my research from the outset and until his death. I visited him and corresponded with him throughout the decade when I knew him. Our last meeting took place in April 1992. At his Paris flat we often spent many hours playing and discussing his music, usually at the piano, and always in English. Sometimes he would prefer to discuss the music he had performed as a pianist, and which he felt was close in spirit to his own; for example Chopin, Debussy, Falla and Albéniz.

Ohana devoted many hours to our long conversations which took place over a period of ten years. Although he tended not to volunteer explanation about how his music was put together, he responded to my questioning about the processes I was gradually able to reveal through my own analyses. He read much of my doctoral dissertation (University of Oxford, 1989) on which this study is based. He also gave me access to much of his unpublished, personal archive, including some manuscript scores and sketches, various writings (articles, lectures, poems) and drawings. I acknowledge his permission to reproduce some of this material. Since his death the archive material has been in the possession of Solange Soubrane, President of the Association des Amis de Maurice Ohana. I am grateful to her for continuing to keep me abreast of new recordings, performances and festivals which feature Ohana's music, as well as the founding of the Prix Maurice Ohana which is awarded biennially to pianists and composers and other 'Ohanian' projects. I acknowledge her permission to reproduce photographs from the composer's archive. I am grateful to Maître Henri Dutilleux and his wife Geneviève Joy for their interest in this project and for answering my questions. I also thank Marius Constant for providing me with copies of a selection of his writings and other material. I am particularly grateful to Francis Bayer for providing me with copies of documents which even Ohana no longer had in his possession, as well as for sharing his knowledge of the music of Ohana and, more latterly, of Dutilleux.

During Ohana's life-time his publishers made his scores available to me for an unlimited period. I acknowledge and thank in particular Denise George-Jobert of the Société des Editions Jobert and François Derveaux of Gérard Billaudot Editeur. I also thank in this respect the houses of Amphion (Durand), Salabert and Schott Söhne (Mainz). I also wish to thank Corinne Monceau at the Centre de Documentation de la Musique Contemporaine; Gill Jones at the Music Resource Centre at the University of Cardiff; Neil Somerville at the BBC Written Archive Centre in Reading; the library staff of the Bibliothèque de la Radio France at the Maison de la Radio; the staff of the Bibliothèque Nationale, the Bodleian Library and Maison Française in Oxford. I am grateful to the novelist Laurence Cossé for permission to reproduce her drawing of Maurice Ohana and am also grateful to Paulo Pinamonte of the Università Ca'Foscari di Venezia who made known to me the Ohana-Casella correspondence at the Fondazione Cini in Venice. I acknowledge Dr Nick Fisher of Cardiff University School of History and Archaeology who kindly identified and translated some Latin texts. Quotations are in English, the translations of all French sources being my own (the endnotes specify the original language).

I should like to thank the Music Department, Cardiff University of Wales for funding several research trips to Paris during the 1990s, as well as numerous local visits to London and the BBC Written Archive Centre in Reading. I am grateful to the following individuals: Professor Michael F. Robinson, Dr Mike Greenhough, Professor Adrian Thomas, Richard Langham Smith, Pierre-Albert Castanet, Linda Daniel-Spitz and especially my brother Dr Charles Bodman Rae who has given much advice and encouragement during the long gestation of this book. My thanks are also due to Dr Ian Cheverton, who prepared the musical examples, and to Rachel Lynch my editor at Ashgate. Finally I would like to thank my husband, Peter, and sons, Robert and Charles, for their unending patience and support.

The music examples are reproduced with the kind permission of the Société des Editions Jobert Paris, Gérard Billaudot Editeur S.A. Paris, Editions Amphion (Durand) Paris, Editions Costallat (Durand) Paris, United Music Publishers Ltd., Schott & Company Ltd. (London), Boosey & Hawkes Music Publishers Ltd.

C.A.R.
Machen, March 2000

PART ONE

From the Garden of the Hesperides

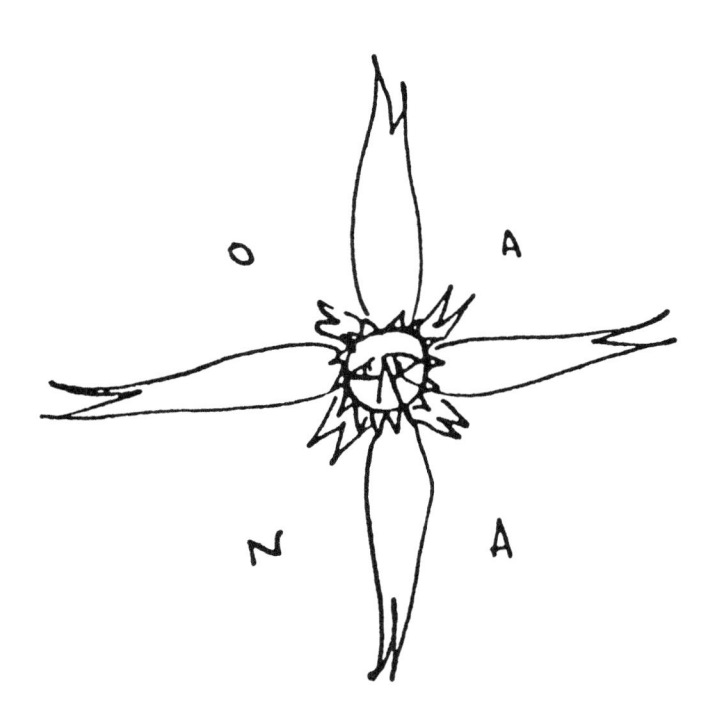

CHAPTER ONE

Pianist to Composer: Cultural Roots, Life and Influences

Maurice Ohana was born in Casablanca on 12 June 1913.[1] By his own declaration he was profoundly superstitious and especially so in any matters involving the number thirteen. Modifying his birthdate to 1914, he suppressed knowledge of the true year of his birth. Writers respected this unusual eccentricity until after his death.[2] An ironic turn of fate proved Ohana's fears well-founded as he died on 13 November 1992. Any biographical discussion of Ohana must, however, begin by considering his cultural origins and nationality which have sometimes been a source of confusion. Recognising the significance of Ohana's cultural roots is the gateway to understanding the composer's creative stimuli. As shall be shown, the Spanish and African influences of his youth and early adulthood provided the raw material which was tempered by his French training, education and environment. Together, these three cultures provided the rich and fertile loam which nourished his compositional growth.

Maurice Ohana was once described by André Gide as a French Joseph Conrad.[3] The intriguing comparison highlighted the issue of nationality as distinct from cultural origin which, in the case of both Conrad and Ohana, did not correspond. Like the Ukrainian-born Pole Józef Korzeniowski, Maurice Ohana's cultural lineage was not defined by his bureaucratic nationality; both, albeit for different reasons, were British citizens. Ohana spent most of his life in Paris, yet was not a Frenchman. He was born and grew-up in Casablanca, yet was not a Moroccan. He was a British subject but could not be described as an Englishman. His parents were of Spanish origin yet Ohana was not simply a Spaniard. The southern culture from which he stemmed reaches beyond the political boundaries of any one country and in his later years he held nationality of more than one state.[4] Maurice Ohana's cultural background is full of contradictions which conspire to make him difficult to place for those who desire the convenience of tidy labelling by nationality. For this reason, Ohana tended to speak more of cultural roots and geographical influence than of nationality. The complexities of nationhood and origin have contributed to the neglect of Ohana's music in the United Kingdom; those who are not readily categorised tend to be excluded. While such complexities are easily understood by those belonging to the same Southern culture, or whose origins were internationalised as a result of the Diaspora, they have represented a source of confusion when viewed from a northern, Anglo-Saxon perspective. In France, where fascination for the exotic and acceptance of the eclectic is almost tradition itself, the issue has rarely been problematic, his country of adoption having always claimed his music as its own.

When describing his cultural origins himself, Ohana liked to identify his birthplace as the 'balcony of Europe', drawing attention to the proximity of southern Spain and north Africa as a meeting point of cultures. The Morocco of his youth, Casablanca in particular, represented a melting-pot of races and creeds with the cosmopolitan mix of Berbers and Arabs together with French and Spanish, both Christian and Jewish. Ohana ignored the political divisions of the modern world, preferring to evoke more ancient civilisations, associating his birthplace with the mythical Garden of the Hesperides, reputed by many scholars to have been sited in north Africa.[5] While Hesperia was for the Greeks the western land of Italy, the Romans called Spain by this name. In earliest legends the nymphs who guarded Hera's famous golden apples, assisted by the dragon Ladon whom Hercules later slew, were the daughters of Atlas's son Hesperus. They lived on the river Oceanus in the extreme west which has been placed by many in the Atlas mountains.[6] As a mature composer he found that such evocations of ancient myth had greater resonance in the context of his music, much of which draws on mythological sources.

> If one asked me to say where I was born, civil states apart, I would refer to this vast area which later I could locate as a place that fascinates me; the Garden of the Hesperides. A certain place with grazing herds of bulls that Hercules had acquired after killing Geryon [mythical three-headed King of Spain]; a place where a great disaster joined the Mediterranean with the ocean. I turn back to this place, I prowl about it in the quest of some memory I know not of, perhaps that of an earlier life, seeking without doubting the forces which feed my music through a metamorphosis whose powers I would not wish to analyse. It is enough for me to perceive that these are the forces that assure, by their diversity, the continuity of a single idea in all that I write.[7]

The youngest in a large family of eleven children, Ohana stemmed from mixed Jewish-Christian lineage, much of his complex cosmopolitanism resulting from his immediate family background and circumstances. The Ohana family was of Spanish origin but resided for a time in London as well as, more permanently, in French colonial Morocco. The composer's father, Simon David Ohana, was of Sephardic, Andalusian-Gibraltarian origin and was born in Casablanca in 1865, the son of Moses and Jamu Ohana who are recorded on the birth certificate as 'subjects of the Moroccan Empire'. Maurice Ohana's mother, Fortuna Mercedes Ohana (née Bengio) was Castillian Spanish and a Roman Catholic, although her family also had Andalusian roots.[8] The family surname, far from being Irish as is often wrongly assumed by some English speakers, is Andalusian, being derived from the village of Ohanes approximately 20 miles north west of Almería on the southern Spanish coast. Although there are historical ties linking Spain and Ireland, there is no known connection in the Ohana family, the name being correctly spelled without an apostrophe.[9]

As with many Jewish families of southern Spain, the Ohanas had close ties with Gibraltar, although the family had been resident in Morocco for many years. Simon David Ohana chose to formalise the family ties with Britain and in 1894, aged 29 and married with four children, he was granted British citizenship by naturalisation.[10] The Home Office certificate, issued in London, is dated 17

July 1894, the Oath of Allegiance 19 July and the registration 20 July. In accordance with the Naturalisation Acts of 1870, Simon David Ohana and his family were required to have lived in the United Kingdom for at least five years within an eight year period prior to the application. The certificate records their address as 236 Queen's Road, Dalston, London.[11] The four children listed at the time of their father's naturalisation were Semtob, Rachel, Albert, and Isaac, aged seven, five, three years and six months, respectively. It is interesting to note that even during this period the Ohana family returned regularly to Morocco; Semtob and Albert were born in Casablanca.[12] Clearly the Ohanas maintained close ties with north Africa, for business as well as for family reasons and despite the regulations of naturalisation requiring an intention to remain in the United Kingdom, they eventually returned to Morocco permanently.[13] When Maurice Ohana was born nineteen years after his father's naturalisation, he was able to claim British citizenship. Surprisingly, his birth was not registered with the British Consul in Casablanca until 27 November 1939, the date recorded on his birth certificate.[14] Two of Maurice Ohana's sisters, born after the family resettled in Casablanca, inherited the estate in the 1940s and remained there until the property was dissolved in 1965 (the family house was sadly later demolished). Semtob remained in Casablanca until his death in 1979 at the age of ninety-two. Members of the family today live in Spain and France as well as in England and the United States of America.

The Ohanas enjoyed a well-to-do, intellectual and cultured family milieu. In Casablanca, they lived in a large villa at 182 Boulevard d'Anfa, the house where Maurice was born. His mother had been a schoolmistress in Gibraltar prior to marriage and his father, described as a commission agent on his naturalisation papers, ran a business in shipping and exports with a British partner. Very much younger than his brothers and sisters, whom Ohana remembered far more as uncles and aunts than as sibling playmates, his childhood in Casablanca was paradoxically a solitary one. While still a young child his older brothers were leaving home to take up careers in business and the professions, settling in different parts of Europe and the United States. He had slightly closer contact with his sisters whom he recalled as being good pianists. Noémi, his closest sibling, was contemplating a career as a concert pianist and gave Maurice his first informal piano lessons when he was five. Her performance of works by Chopin, Albéniz and Debussy, were among Ohana's earliest memories.[15] At the same time he was nurtured into his Spanish culture. His beloved nanny Titi, an Andalusian gypsy woman for whom he maintained a life-long affection, sang him flamenco songs, many in the 'Cante Jondo' style.[16] His mother taught him many old Spanish legends and encouraged his enthusiasm for the re-telling of these tales in family performances of the traditional, comic puppet-theatre, long popular in Spain and also beloved by Falla and García Lorca. In later life these proved important influences on his own approach to theatre music, on the subjects chosen as well as on the means in which they were executed. Ohana's mother also introduced him to many of the dances of Spain and sang Andalusian lullabies (from the flamenco)[17], as well as songs from the Zarzuela:

> My mother, like all Andalusian women of her time sang and loved music. She had a natural voice. Her repertoire went from the medieval 'chansons de geste' to Spanish songs and the Zarzuela.[18]

Ohana never underestimated the significance of the richness and diversity of his Andalusian heritage, itself a mixture of cultures, races and creeds. In later years he formalised his extensive knowledge of Spanish folk music and began a collection of traditional folk songs from the different regions.[19] While he published a number of articles and sleeve-notes during the 1950s and 1960s and gave several talks, most of his ethnomusicological research remains unpublished, his interest being more for compositional than musicological reasons.[20]

> Andalusia was a focus of tremendous civilisation during 10 or 15 centuries. First came what they call the people from the sea, whom I presume came from Crete, the Middle East and Greece. Cadiz was founded over 3000 years ago by the Greeks, and some Roman poets still mention the dancers of Cadiz as being of Greek descent. Then came the Romans who had an influence as well. Then came the Arabs, the Jews and then the Gypsies to crown the whole thing. And the interesting point about Andalusia is that it achieved such a type of civilisation as not to destroy the sediments that were left by the preceding civilisations but just melted with it. That's how we got finally to what is called Andalusian folk art which is the combination of all those influences.[21]

English, as well as Spanish was spoken in the Ohana household, while the family location in Morocco necessitated the speaking of French, although Ohana recalled that this was spoken more among himself and his siblings than by his parents.[22] Exposed to so many languages at an early age, Ohana alarmed his mother by hardly speaking at all until the age of four.[23] Fluent in three languages by the age of seven, speaking each without accent, Ohana undertook his general education in the French schools of Casablanca and took a baccalauréat in Philosophy in 1932 at the Lycée Lyautey, named after the French resident General of Morocco. (That Ohana remained trilingual throughout his life is witnessed by his publications, written in English, French and Spanish.) Although educated in a Roman Catholic environment, Ohana often emphasised that he was brought up without adherence to any specific religious practice. The differing religious backgrounds of his parents may have fostered a flexible approach to formal worship during his formative years. As an adult he was drawn to the Christian liturgy, perhaps as a result of his prolonged studies of plainchant and he completed a Mass for liturgical, as well as concert performance. Vocal music figures prominently throughout his work and he often said his music sounded best in cathedrals, churches or chapels; the Eglise Saint Séverin was chosen as the most appropriate location for his Memorial Service in Paris which included a performance of his Mass.[24]

Ohana spent his first twelve years and much of his youth in Morocco but travelled regularly to Spain, throughout these early years, to visit other branches of the family in Andalusia, Castille and the Basque Country. The Ohana family also spent summers at Granada, San Sebastian and Biarritz. When Ohana was fourteen, part of the family moved temporarily to Biarritz to enable Ohana's sister Noémi to continue her piano studies at the nearby Bayonne Conservatoire. Both she and Maurice enrolled. During this period Ohana journeyed many times the length and breadth of the Iberian peninsula on his way to visit his permanent home in Casablanca and had the opportunity to experience the stylistic diversity of folk music of the different regions. As a teenager, he also began to travel into the Atlas mountains, journeys that he continued to make well into his maturity. He sought out the Berber tribes and took part in their daily activities, experiencing their music at first hand and participating, when allowed, in their tribal ceremonies.[25] In this way, he absorbed much about their means of improvisation and complex rhythmic patterning, learned many of their tribal choral songs and became familiar with their distinctive micro-tonal melodies. Sometimes he would venture into the most remote parts of the Atlas mountains and beyond to settlements bordering the Sahara desert. The tribal music he heard was not always Berber; a visit to Marrakech brought about an acquaintance with a Guyanan drum-team.

> I visited Marrakech where they have an immense square full of all sorts of dancers, musicians story-tellers and so forth. They assemble and make their living out of practising their art. I was struck by the talent and splendid innovation of the black people – from Guyana I think. They played on very carefully tuned drums which are tuned by heating them and even the sticks are of a very refined type. I watched them and listened to them so much that one day one of them, as a sort of token thanksgiving for my faithfulness, offered to let me play one of the drums, so I went on and played what he had played before. He wasn't too pleased to see that his secret had been captured by a foreigner.[26]

In later years he had the opportunity to broaden his experience of black African music. During World War II he was posted to Kenya where he took advantage of non-combatant interludes to visit black African tribes. The experience fused his memory of their music with the drama of the landscape:

> I happened to be posted to Kenya for a while during the war while travelling from Madagascar to the Mediterranean. I stayed there and was lucky enough to visit the tribes round Nairobi and up to Lake Uganda. I heard some most extraordinary performances by village dancers and choirs which melted so much with the landscape that it really remains a whole in my memory. The colours – a sort of reddish brown dust, even the smell of those big bonfires they build in the centre to dance around. I was deeply struck by their art.[27]

It was not only their rhythms which fascinated him but also their choral singing and their ability to create complex polyphonies which function by timbre. He also recalled a particular occasion at the border between Tanganyika and Uganda where he attended a tribal celebration, including such singing, which lasted a whole day and night.[28] The concept of equal-temperament being entirely foreign, he observed that their vocal inflexion incorporated microintervals which were as much the result of timbre and nuance as their own scales. He had noticed similar vocal characteristics in the flamenco, as well as a variety of rhythmic similarities between black African and Andalusian music. Both involve the use of repetitive, rhythmic patterns which are superimposed to create more complex, resultant cross-rhythms. Both also incorporate percussive effects and hand-clapping techniques:

> While in Africa during the war, I heard many of the African tribes' music there and found that many of the rhythms played and sung by these native tribes are really very close to the Andalusian rhythms which basically fed my childhood.[29]

As a mature composer Ohana became fascinated by the myriad cross-fertilisations between Spanish and African folk musics which resulted from the migrations of the indigenous populations caused by the colonisation of the Central and South Americas as well as the slave trade. The blending of these traditions in Cuban music was documented by the novelist Alejo Carpentier with whom Ohana became acquainted in the 1950s.[30] That African and Spanish musics became fused together in the Americas and were subsequently re-imported to Europe led Ohana to view them as sibling traditions, both of which were part of his cultural heritage. For this reason Ohana considered the incorporation of certain jazz idioms in his music as a logical extension of African and Afro-Cuban traditions into a contemporary context. His intimate knowledge and personal experience of these traditions were among the most important musical influences that shaped his mature, compositional language.

The vast expanse of the Atlantic ocean touched the shores of both traditions. Ohana often liked to draw attention to the significance of growing-up on the Atlantic coasts of Africa, Spain and France, which he cited as an important influence not only for its historical associations but also for the shaping of his personality. He described the Atlantic Andalusians as quite different from those of the Mediterranean side; one looks eastward in what he called 'claustrophobic smallness' while the other is 'broad and expansive'.[31] It is interesting to note that Ohana chose a house near Carnac in Brittany as his country retreat from Paris. According to his wishes, his ashes were dispersed in the Atlantic ocean off the coast at Carnac.[32]

> I don't appreciate much the Mediterranean. I think that physically I don't belong to the Mediterranean at all, even if spiritually I sort of loot the Mediterranean treasure here and there, especially the Greek mythology which I very much fancy and which is full of teachings and mysterious signs to me. Of course I descend from the Mediterranean civilisation but I think it's very important that one should be faithful to one's geographical roots. I was born on the Atlantic and I find myself much more at ease with the Atlantic landscape and the Atlantic storms and its sunny days, than in the Mediterranean which is a very restrained field of experience to me. In my seaside house in Brittany when I watch the skies and the sea they convey a sort of permanent lesson, a permanent teaching which concerns music just as much as ordinary living, be it only through the enormous proportions of the Atlantic compared to the Mediterranean.[33]

The Professional Path

Following informal piano lessons with his older sister Noémi, Ohana took formal tuition from the age of nine with a local teacher in Casablanca, May Loftus, who was also Mother Sheila at the Convent of Franciscan Missionaries. At the age of eleven, he gave his first public piano recital for a St Cecilia's Day concert at the Convent; indicating a precocious ability, the programme included the Pathéthique' Sonata op.13 of Beethoven and the op.10 No.5 study of Chopin, the so-called 'black key'.[34] In 1927 aged fourteen, he enrolled at the Bayonne Conservatoire where he, and his sister Noémi, became pupils of the Director, the composer Ermend-Bonnal. (Maurice continued his general education at the Lycée de Bayonne.) Ohana performed regularly at the Conservatoire and in 1930 gave a duo recital at the Casino d'Hossegor with a young cellist who later became Professor of Cello at the Paris Conservatoire.[35] Ohana gave several solo recitals in northern Spain. Ohana's outstanding pianistic gifts were encouraged by Bonnal and before the age of eighteen he had performed all thirty-two Beethoven piano sonatas. As a mature composer Ohana did not recall the experience fondly, remembering the pressure from Bonnal to learn the complete cycle almost as a punishment. Even at this early age Ohana instinctively felt ill-at-ease with music belonging to the Austro-German tradition, a repertoire independent of his own cultural roots.

> My judgement of Beethoven's works is most unorthodox. I dislike many of his works, I think some of them are simply unbearable (for example) some of the piano sonatas which I had to study ... . I think he is a very uneven composer – something which happens with practically every composer with very few exceptions ... . Even in his Quartets which I admire and which fascinate me, there are moments where a sort of rhetoric duty shows its ugly ear and he suddenly becomes a bore. But of course, there again, in those last quartets I think lay some of the most beautiful pages that music ever was rewarded with.[36]

In later life Ohana's conscious distancing of himself from Germanic music was to develop into an almost iconoclastic rejection of the Second Viennese School and its followers. While he admired certain works by Mozart, Beethoven and Schumann, their tradition was not to provide the basis from which his own composition was to develop.

> I was not at all inclined towards the German or central European world, which frankly I detest, not because I dislike the music but because it has been so bossy and so tremendously conquering over minds and geniuses which have been taken out of their course by the too strong will of the German school.[37]

While at the Bayonne Conservatoire, Ohana took private lessons from Jéhanne Pâris, the organist at the Eglise St Eugénie in Biarritz whom he described not only as his most important and complete influence at that time, but also as the catalyst for what he called his 'real birth to music'.[38] Under her guidance he discovered many works which remained important to him in later life, including the string quartets of Debussy and Ravel. They read through scores playing four-hands at the piano. She also made him study solfège as well as Gregorian chant.

> She [Jéhanne Pâris] was a tiny, ugly woman, elegantly dressed and trimmed. She had taught and known all the fabulous names that had made Biarritz a cross-roads of the world, including Prince Yusupov! Her musicianship was unparalleled amongst my teachers.[39]

Ohana's discovery of the writings of Proust, Gide, Dickens and Conrad, to which he was devoted throughout his life, also occurred during this period.[40] He studied at Bayonne until 1931 when he returned to Casablanca to complete his general education. Following the success of his baccalauréat Ohana's father wished him to pursue a more secure profession than that of music. For this reason, Ohana went to Paris in the autumn of 1932 to study architecture. He prepared his entrance exam for the Ecole Nationale Supérieure des Arts Décoratif and, after a brief period at the Ecole des Beaux Arts, enrolled at the Ecole Nationale Supérieure in 1934. He studied there for two years, his teachers including Eric Bagge, for 'décoration', and Professor Genuys for 'architecture'.[41] He met Mallet Stephens and visited the workshop of Le Corbusier (thirteen years before Xenakis). Architectural obligations did not prevent Ohana from continuing his musical training, albeit against his father's wishes, and, in 1932, the same year he arrived in Paris, he became a pupil of Lazare-Lévy. Although encouraged by Lévy to enter the Paris Conservatoire, the constraints of Ohana's father prevented him from doing so. He eventually abandoned his architectural studies in June 1936 on the eve of taking the 'niveau supérieur' and chose not to complete his course at the Ecole Nationale Supérieur des Arts Décoratif. Against his parents' wishes, Ohana committed himself to a musical career.

Musical life in Paris of the 1930s was rich and varied. Ohana attended many concerts including those of the Concerts Colonne, Lamoureux and Pasdeloup and was able to hear all the great pianists of the time, including the young Horowitz, Lipatti, Schnabel, Backhaus, Gieseking (whom he heard perform Debussy) and Fischer whose style Ohana recalled as the greatest influence on his own playing.[42] In 1933 he also heard Paul Wittgenstein's first Paris performance of the Ravel Piano Concerto for Left Hand in 1933, a work which was among the few, select scores Ohana kept permanently beside his piano at his Paris flat, even during the last years of his life. He sought out concerts of American jazz, in particular he remembered the thrill of hearing the bands of Duke Ellington and Louis Armstrong.[43] At the Fêtes de l'Exposition Universelle of 1937 Ohana discovered another work which was to prove a seminal influence; he attended Falla's *Three Cornered Hat* in the production by Massine and Picasso. This discovery not only initiated his investigation into technical aspects of Falla's musical style, including his use of Spanish folk song, use of instrumentation, linear textures and motoric rhythms, but shaped much of his own approach to theatre music in later years.

From 1936 Ohana maintained the career of a concert pianist. His programmes revealed the individuality of his musical taste and always included works by Scarlatti, Chopin, Albéniz, Falla or Granados, while French music was represented by Rameau, Debussy or Ravel. He gave his Paris début recital at the Salle Pleyel in February 1936. Of mammoth proportions, the programme clearly reveals his cultural alignment:

Scarlatti	3 Sonatas
Chopin	Barcarolle, Polonaise-Fantasie, F minor Ballade
	Debussy *L'Isle joyeuse,* 'Bruyères' (*Préludes* II),
	'Poissons d'or' (*Images* II)
Granados	'La maja y el ruiseñor' (*Goyescas*)
Ravel	*Sonatine*
Albéniz	'El Puerto', 'Rondeña', 'Triana,' 'El Albaicin' (*Ibéria*)

This performance was followed by another Paris recital at the Salle Chopin the same year. Becoming dissatisfied with his studies with Lazare-Lévy, Ohana took lessons from Frank Marshall. (Ohana accompanied Marshall to Barcelona and eventually to Casablanca as the worsening political circumstances in Spain necessitated.) Ohana also knew Arthur Rubinstein well at this time and often visited him at his home on the Rue Ravignon; apart from Chopin, Ohana played him, on one occasion, Albéniz's 'El Albaicin' which was apparently received with approval.[44] Although Ohana had performed the notoriously difficult *Fantasía Bética*, dedicated to Rubinstein, the sensitive topic of Falla's music was avoided during his visits; Rubinstein disliked the piece, considering it too long, too cluttered with glissandi and generally badly written for the piano.[45] On matters of technique, Rubinstein's main advice was to explain that security and a singing tone was founded on a straight fifth finger.[46]

Between 1936 and 1939, Ohana gave concert tours in France, Holland, Belgium, north Africa and in Spain (despite the Civil War). During the 1937 and 1938 Paris seasons he performed concertos with the Orchestre des concerts Lamoureux under Eugène Bigot at the Salle Gaveau. His performance of Falla's *Nuits dans les jardins d'Espagne* was met with critical acclaim by both Maurice Imbert and Charles Henry, the latter describing Ohana's interpretation as 'un coup de maître'.[47] Ohana formed a duo with the singer Lotte Schöne with whom he toured during the 1936–37 season and at whose home he met the poet Paul Valéry, an acquaintance of the Schöne family. As Valéry was at that time in the process of developing his new theory of the relationship of music and language, it is tempting to ponder whether this chance meeting may have in any way shaped Ohana's later experimentations with language and text. In 1938 Ohana formed a two-piano duo with Alexandre Hoffstein, their Salle Chopin recital in Paris on 5 May that year including Mozart's K.448 Sonata and Debussy's *En blanc et noir*. Together with the piano *Préludes* and *Etudes*, *En blanc et noir* influenced many of Ohana's later works, most notably *Tombeau de Claude Debussy*.[48]

During the late 1930s Ohana met many refugees of the Spanish Civil War who had fled to Paris, the logical and well-established centre for the northward migration of Spanish composers, performers, writers and artists. Ohana's temporary residence at the Maison d'Espagne in the Cité Universitaire from

1938–1940 brought him into contact with many South American, as well as Spanish writers and intellectuals. By the 1950s the circle had expanded to include Rafael Alberti, Pío Baroja, Camilo José Cela and Sergio de Castro who introduced Ohana to Octavio Paz, José Bergamín and Fernando Pereda.[49] Ohana also knew Alejo Carpentier with whom he often discussed Carpentier's extensive researches into Cuban music and ritual practices.[50] He was also acquainted with Gabriel García Márquez who took several lessons in composition from Ohana in 1955.[51]

The early period of Ohana's life profited from a number of chance encounters which proved significant for his personal development. These fuelled his sense of the superstitious and refusal to believe in mere coincidence. With the greater perspective that the advantage of years can bring, Ohana considered these meetings in later life as 'Signs of Destiny'. The first such meeting took place in October 1936 on board ship crossing the Straits of Gibraltar from north Africa to Spain. He happened to encounter the Argentinean flamenco singer and dancer La Argentinita (Encarnación Júlvez López) who was travelling with her guitarist, the legendary virtuoso Ramón Montoya.[52] La Argentinita (1895–1945) was well recognised as an international star not only for her performances of classical Spanish dance and original choreography of music by Ravel, Albéniz, Granados and Falla, but also for her revitalisation of the traditional folk and gypsy forms of the flamenco.[53] Both La Argentinita and Ramón Montoya had been involved in Falla's Festival of Cante Jondo held at Granada in June 1922.[54] Performing with Antonio Triana and her sister Pilar López she established what later became known, under Pilar's direction, as the Ballet Español. La Argentinita danced the roles of Candelas and Lucía (the latter created for her) in Falla's *El Amor brujo*.[55] Massine choreographed roles for her in Falla's *Three Cornered Hat* (miller's wife) and Rimsky Korsakov's *Capriccio espagnol*.[56]

La Argentinita performed throughout Europe and the United States, as well as in South America and was well-known in intellectual circles of Madrid where her closest friends included the playwright Jacinto Benavente, the composer-conductor Ernesto Halffter and the poet Federico García Lorca with whom she recorded his collection of Spanish folk-songs and founded the Ballet de Madrid.[57] (A close friend of Lorca's family, she was god-mother to his nephew and god-son.[58]) Through Lorca she became an intimate friend of the bull-fighter-poet Ignacio Sánchez Mejías whose death in the bull-ring in 1934 was the subject of one of Lorca's last major poems of which she was the dedicatee (under her real name). Lorca had given La Argentinita the manuscript of *Llanto por Ignacio Sánchez Mejías*, as well as of *Romancero gitan*, these still being in her possession at the time of her meeting with Ohana.[59]

La Argentinita's choreographed versions of the *Iberia* and *Goyescas* of Albéniz and Granados necessitated a pianist, in addition to a guitarist (she had also performed with Rogelio Machado and José Iturbi). Ohana joined forces with La Argentinita's group and toured with them during the 1936–37 season. They performed music by Falla, as well as Albeniz and Granados, and Ohana composed a number of songs for her including an Alborada in the form of a

Jota.[60] He performed with them in Belgium, Holland, England and France including an appearance in Paris at the Salle Pleyel. Their final appearance together was at the Arts Theatre Club in London, a performance organised by Anton Dolin whom Argentinita knew from New York.[61] Through La Argentinita and Dolin, Ohana was introduced to many of the leading figures in ballet of the time. (After the war, Ohana's widening circle of balletic acquaintances resulted in a number of ballet scores which included two collaborations with Maurice Béjart.) Ohana's collaboration with La Argentinita was of enduring significance for his development as a composer. Not only did she encourage him to compose but urged him to look towards his Spanish roots as the source of his compositional identity. As testimony of her confidence in his ability and commitment, she lent him Lorca's manuscripts of both the *Llanto por Ignacio Sánchez Mejías* and *Romancero gitan*. Although Ohana still had these manuscripts in his possession at the time of La Argentinita's death in 1945, and when he composed his own setting of the *Llanto* in 1950, they were subsequently returned to her estate.[62]

In the autumn of 1937 Ohana returned to Paris. Wishing to develop his compositional skills and extend the scope of his musical training, he enrolled at the Schola Cantorum. Studying chiefly with Daniel-Lesur, with whom he took counterpoint, he remained at Schola for almost three years.

> I was lucky enough to meet some masters, Daniel-Lesur in particular, who taught me much on a technical level without ever trying to influence my style.[63]

With many musical interests in common, particularly plainchant, early contrapuntal forms and folk music, Ohana and Daniel-Lesur developed a lasting friendship. After the war they worked together on several combined projects; they formed a two-piano duo and collaborated on Lesur's incidental music for *Don Juan* (1947). Lesur's *Sérenade* for string orchestra (1954) incorporates a Spanish folk-song made known to him by Ohana.[64] The nature of musical training at the Schola Cantorum, with its emphasis on the study of plainchant, counterpoint and the Medieval and Renaissance vocal repertoire, proved a decisive influence for Ohana. He spent much time in the analysis of plainchant, not only Gregorian but also Mozarabic which he had heard at Toledo and Santo Domingo de Silos. He found that this music was much closer to his musical tastes and intuition than conventional diatonic structures. His education at Schola led him to discover the technique and craft which enabled him to mould the musical ingredients inherited from his cultural background:

> In order to send into battle all those deep instincts and unconscious learnings of childhood one needs a very strong métier .... My writing was built entirely upon plainchant in Paris, where I studied at the Schola Cantorum, and by meditating and observing my own folk music.[65]

While at Schola, and still in his twenties, Ohana completed his first essays in orchestral writing; a ballet based on an episode from Don Quixote entitled *La Venta encantada* and a suite, *Les fêtes nocturnes* extracted from his incidental music for a play by Ives Regnier, *La Joie et le bonheur*.[66] These works are among those the composer later destroyed. He also composed a five movement Suite for piano of which only the final movement, a Toccata, survives.

Ohana's real beginnings as a composer were interrupted by the outbreak of war. Despite volunteering to join the British forces soon after war was declared in September 1939, he was required to clarify his national status with the British authorities as well as to fulfil necessary requirements for registration in accordance with the new National Service Act.[67] Leaving Paris on 12 June 1940 (his twenty-seventh birthday), the British withdrawal at Dunkirk forced him to travel to England by a dangerous and circuitous route via Biarritz and Spain before he was able to embark from Portugal. He eventually arrived in London several months after his departure from Paris and joined the British Army in November 1940. His war-time years are interesting for the unusual advantage that chance circumstance offered for personal, artistic development. Following initial training in artillery, his fluency in three languages resulted in transferral to the Intelligence Corps at Winchester. Subsequently he was seconded to a landing brigade of Royal Marines, Royal Scots Fusiliers and Argyll and Sutherland Highlanders. After further training at Winchester and Matlock, he was posted to Scotland for nine months with the 29th Independent Brigade, where he undertook special training in commando and assault at Melrose, Inverary and Scapa Flow. In early 1942, towards the end of his time in Scotland, he gave a recital in the Wednesday Programmes series at the National Gallery of Scotland in Edinburgh. Another huge programme, it comprised three Scarlatti Sonatas, the Chopin Barcarolle, Debussy's *L'Isle joyeuse* and 'Clair de lune' (*Suite Bergamasque*), Albéniz's 'El Albaicin', Granados' Girl and the Nightingale' (*Goyescas*) and Falla's *Ritual Fire Dance*. A local critic described Ohana as 'an interesting young pianist… with fine technical equipment and excellent accomplishment who may go far'.[68]

Ohana first saw active service during a six-month campaign in Madagascar, where he landed from HMS Southampton at Diégo-Suarez on 5 May 1942. He took part in several commando raids (from HMS Southampton and unusually also from HMAS Napier) and was envoy and interpreter with duties in interrogation and counter-espionage with the Field Security Forces. Although not affiliated with the Entertainments Corps, Ohana performed in a Franco-British Gala Concert in aid of the French Red Cross in Tananarive on 4 July 1942; in the presence of the Commander in Chief of the British Forces in Madagascar, Admiral Tennant, he played works by Chopin, Debussy and Falla. In 1943 he was posted to Africa and, spending three months in Kenya, took advantage of non-combatant interludes to search out black African tribes and experience their music. On the way from Kenya to north Africa Ohana became acquainted with the South African poet Roy Campbell. Considering the meeting another of the 'Signs of Destiny' which drew him towards composition, Ohana and Campbell discovered they had much in common: they had both left their country of origin and were serving in the British Army; both had lived in France and Spain; both were drawn to the poetry of Federico García Lorca, Campbell being one of the first to translate Lorca's poetry into English (curious, given that he had fought in the Spanish Civil War on the side of the Nationalists). Campbell made Ohana the dedicatee of his translation of the *Llanto por Ignacio Sánchez Mejías* and, like La Argentinita before, encouraged him to reflect on the legacy of his Spanish roots as the source of his compositional style.

In June 1943 Ohana was posted to Cairo and shortly after saw further active service in Greece where he was wounded during a campaign in the Cyclades. Following a period of hospitalisation in Cairo, he met by chance the son of the then Governor of Gibraltar, General Smith-Dorrian, who obtained Ohana's transfer to the Officer Training School at Algiers, (another of Ohana's 'Signs of Destiny'). After further active service during the invasion of Sicily, Ohana received his Commission on 3 March 1944, still holding the badge of the Intelligence Corps.[69] Posted to Naples during the spring of the same year he was liaison officer with the French Maquis. Following the liberation of Monte Cassino in May 1944, he was sent to Rome where his duties at Intelligence HQ required him to learn Italian. He was promoted to full Lieutenant in September 1944 and held the additional promotion of Acting Captain.

Throughout the war, Ohana managed to carry with him five scores which he kept with him in his kit-bag at all times. Studying and assimilating these scores during periods of military inactivity, his selection, like that of the hypothetical marooned sailor on a desert island, is revealing of taste and aesthetic alignment: two works of Debussy, *Prélude à l'après-midi d'un faune* and *Nocturnes*; two works of Falla, the Harpsichord Concerto and *El Retablo de Maese Pedro*; the Piano Concerto for Left Hand of Ravel.[70] These scores are among the select few (plus some of Stravinsky and Bartók) which remained permanently beside Ohana's piano at his Paris flat.

> All through the war I had in my kit-bag ... 5 scores which are still on my piano, on my table every day now. I remain faithful to them because much as I go on interrogating them and trying to find their secrets they escape me completely. And I find this most exciting ... they act as an incentive.[71]

Remaining in Rome to the end of the war, Ohana took advantage of increasingly long periods of inactivity at Intelligence HQ and was able to devote much of his time to composition (another of his 'Signs of Destiny'). In the autumn of 1944, still a serving officer, he enrolled in Alfredo Casella's piano class at the Accademia di Santa Cecilia.[72] Although Casella was already in failing health, the contact was nevertheless timely and useful; Ohana played with Casella on two pianos and believed they may have given the first Italian performance of Ravel's Piano Concerto for Left Hand.[73] Casella's dual roles of pianist-composer and personal acquaintance with Debussy and Ravel should have made him an ideal teacher for Ohana, although Ohana recalled often being in disagreement with Casella who was fascinated by the serialism of other composers then at the academy, Dallapiccola and Petrassi in particular. Although Ohana's first important works date from this period, *Enterrar y callar* and the *Sonatine monodique*, his attraction towards non-serial structures did not impress Casella.[74] The year of Casella's death in 1947, Ohana published a short, commemorative article in *The Music Review*. Ohana recounts Casella rising from his bed, despite all the sufferings of ill-health to take his piano class three times a week. He drew particular attention to Casella's tone colour, interpretations of Debussy and, perhaps more surprisingly, also of Beethoven.

> We were often amazed during his lessons by the quality and orchestral variety of his tone, seldom attained at the piano, especially in his renderings of the last Beethoven Sonatas or the Debussy Preludes.[75]

During Ohana's period in Italy another 'Sign of Destiny' proved to have lasting consequences. In December 1945 Ohana visited Naples to give a recital at the Conservatoire San Pietro a Maiella. While there, he was invited to give a private performance at the home of the Director of the local Institut Français in order that he might meet André Gide who was breaking his journey there for a week while awaiting passage to Egypt. Gide recorded his first meeting with Ohana in his *Journal* :

> Naples, 17 December 1945 ... yesterday, at the home of Pasquier, the Director of the French Institute, an excellent dinner in the company of Maurice Ohana who, after the meal, played some Bach, Scarlatti, Albeniz, Granados and the Barcarolle and fourth Ballade of Chopin quite remarkably.[76]

Their initial meeting led to a lasting friendship. During Gide's stay in Naples Ohana met with him each day for intensive rehearsal and prolonged musical discussion of Chopin. Regular contact and correspondence ensued (chiefly concerning Chopin), lasting until Gide's death in 1951.[77] Ohana collaborated with Gide on the *Notes sur Chopin* (Paris, 1948), choosing and preparing the musical examples, and was among the close circle of friends with whom Gide celebrated the receipt of his Nobel Prize in 1947. They also collaborated on a series of radio programmes on Chopin for the French radio, although this project did not come to fruition. Several of Ohana's visits to Gide's Paris home in the Rue Vaneau, their discussions of Chopin and Mozart, and playing of duets (including the Mozart Fantasy), are recorded in the 'Cahiers de la Petite Dame', *Cahiers André Gide*. It is perhaps remarkable that Ohana and Gide found as many areas of musical taste in common as they apparently did. While Ohana shared many of Gide's views about Chopin, their opinions must have diverged on the subject of Debussy. Ohana already felt closely aligned to the French anti-symphonic tradition and recognised Debussy as one of the most influential composers of the twentieth century. Gide in dramatic contrast, considered Debussy to represent "the quintessence of the worse shortcomings of the French spirit".[78] Although Gide had known Debussy, his friendship with Ohana was certainly closer and, unlike his acquaintance with Debussy, more seriously reciprocated.

Ohana was demobilised in 1946 and resettled permanently in Paris. Intending to wind-down his pianistic career and devote himself to composition gradually, he gave a number of recitals in the immediate post-war period. Following a recital at the Wigmore Hall, London on 15 June 1947, he gave a short tour in the English south and midlands. He made several recordings and gave a short

WIGMORE HALL
WIGMORE STREET, W.1

LYNFORD-JOEL PRESENTATION

Sunday JUNE 15th at 3 o'clock

MAURICE O'HANA

Pianoforte Recital

TICKETS: 9/-, 6/-, 3/-

May be obtained at the Box Office, Wigmore Hall, (Wel. 2141), Chappell's Box Office, 50 New Bond Street, (May. 7600) and the usual agents.

LYNFORD-JOEL PROMOTIONS LTD., 17 CAVENDISH SQUARE, LONDON, W.1 (LAN. 1539)

For Programme P.T.O.

Programme

Two Sonatas	Scarlatti
E major — B minor	
Gavotte and Variations	Rameau
Ballade in F minor	Chopin
Sonatine -	Ravel
Moderato — Menuet — Finale	
Pastorale Variée [1st performance]	Daniel Lesur
Three Preludes	Debussy
The Interrupted Serenade	
Bruyeres	
Feux D'Artifice	

— INTERVAL —

The Girl and the Nightingale	E. Granados
Prelude	M. O'Hana
Scherzo [from the "Sonatine Monodique"]	M. O'Hana
Rondena	Albeniz
El Albaicin	Albeniz
Ritual Fire Dance	De Falla

PRESS NOTICES

"Exceptional musicianship." — CLAUDE BERARD (PARIS)

"Maurice O'Hana—a young pianist with remarkable gifts." — LA SEMAINE MUSICALE (PARIS)

"Profound musicianship." — (ROME)

VAIL & CO. LTD., Ogle Street, W.1

Ex. 1.1: Ohana's 1947 Wigmore Hall Recital Programme.

broadcast recital on the BBC Home Service on 22 September 1947 (Ravel *Sonatine* and three pieces of Albéniz from *Iberia*). (He had rehearsed these programmes with Gide.) The Wigmore Hall programme was characteristically large, and included not only the first British performance of Daniel-Lesur's *Pastorale variée*, but two works of his own; Prelude (presumably from the piano suite which he later destroyed) and Scherzo from the *Sonatine Monodique*. (see Ex. 1.1) Drawn between the demands of a pianist and composer, Ohana's postwar years were not an easy period in his personal life. His 1939 marriage to Léa Schulmann was in difficulties, a situation aggravated by his war-time absence. They eventually divorced in 1959.

The period immediately following the end of World War II represents a watershed in the main-stream of European music and was no less so for Ohana who had reached a turning-point in his creative development. At the end of the war, he had a portfolio of less than a dozen pieces (most of which he later destroyed) and despite the 1938 Parisian concert performance of *Les fêtes nocturnes*, was effectively unknown as a composer. By the time of his return to Paris his younger contemporaries were already becoming established; even during the darkest years of the Occupation concert life in Paris had been far from inactive. Absent from the Parisian musical milieu throughout the war, Ohana was forced to carve out his position anew. As a composer of Spanish origin educated into and instinctively part of the French tradition, seeking to develop a musical language based on his cultural roots and a reassessment of the Medieval and Renaissance vocal repertories, Ohana was in an isolated position. Considering the new serialism of his contemporaries involved at Darmstadt to stem fundamentally from the Austro-German tradition which had long felt remote to him both culturally and aesthetically, Ohana naturally felt these techniques to be irrelevant to his own creative promptings. Although Ohana received much practical help from his former teacher Daniel-Lesur, who held an important position at French Radio, he needed to find a means of both announcing his presence as a composer and establishing his independence from the predominant trends of the time. To this end, in 1947 Ohana was the motivating force in bringing together a group of like-minded composers who promoted concerts of their music under the name Le Groupe musical le Zodiaque.

Coming together as a body of composers aiming to rival those of the Darmstadt School, their prime objective was to illustrate that integral serialism represented only a part of the compositional mainstream. The Groupe Zodiaque initially comprised only three composers, Ohana, Alain Bermat and Pierre de la Forest-Divonne. All had been pupils of Daniel-Lesur, Forest-Divonne having left Messiaen's classes at the Conservatoire in favour of the Schola Cantorum. Despite their association with former members of La Jeune France, the Zodiaque composers did not seek to rekindle the ideals of the older group, although some of their aims parallel many of Daniel-Lesur's own interests, folk music and plainchant in particular. The educational atmosphere at the Schola Cantorum with its quite different traditions from that of the Conservatoire, may well have fostered, albeit indirectly, a sense of confidence in their own non-alignment. In 1948 the Groupe Zodiaque was joined by Stanislaw Skrowaczewski, then studying with Nadia Boulanger, and Sergio de Castro, a former pupil of Falla who was hesitating between the vocations of composer, painter[79] and poet (he also became a friend of Dutilleux.)[80] They saw themselves as crusading knights defending freedom of musical expression against what they considered to be the tyranny of serialism. Some years later Ohana described post-Webern serialism:

> Mere academic sterility ... as intimidating and terrifying as the propaganda systems of the Nazis ... . These systems destroy more in music than they create – they remove all the art of risk.[81]

The iconoclastic rejection not only of serialism but all aesthetic dogma was primarily a rejection of Germanic musical thinking (not for the first time in France); while the political structure of the Third Reich had been defeated militarily, Ohana in particular feared Austro-Germanic traditions to be conquering culturally. Such vigorous opposition to contemporary trends may also have been in part associated with the cultural origins of the Zodiaque group members, their aversion to serialism being one of geography as well as of musical taste. While Skrowaczewski is Polish and thus has a tradition of kinship with France, Poland having long considered itself independent from Germanic culture (a feeling which, after the war, was particularly strong), the remaining four members belonged to Latinate cultures. Like Ohana, de Castro was of Spanish origin (son of the Argentinean Ambassador to Geneva) and Bermat and Forest-Divonne were French. The group was unified as much by their diversity as by their similarity of purpose. Considering the music of Latinate and Mediterranean countries to be under threat of annihilation by the all-conquering powers of Teutonic musical thinking, they sought to defend the virtues of their respective cultures. (A similar fear of Teutonic domination is also expressed by Federico García Lorca in many of his lectures.)[82] Although the Zodiaque composers did not publish their ideas as a manifesto, Ohana served as the group representative and spokesman to explain their aims and purpose.

Existing initially more as a compositional protest group, the Zodiaque composers only gradually developed more positive aims. Avoiding the creation of their own dogma, they promoted an organic musical language that should emerge spontaneously from the material itself without recourse to elaborate pre-compositional systems. They set about a reassessment of their respective folk-music traditions and aimed in so doing to restore what they considered to represent a natural and true line of development from their most ancient cultural roots. At the same time they looked towards plainchant and the Medieval and Renaissance vocal repertories, both sacred and secular. Many of these aims reflect the traditions of the Schola Cantorum which, from its beginnings, had promoted the study not only of the early contrapuntal masters but also of folk music. In the *Cours de composition* even d'Indy, renowned for his rigid academicism, had argued that musical form should be a consequence of musical material, rather than a superimposed scheme.

The title of the group is as esoteric in French as it is in English and refers to the division of the heavens into the twelve equal parts which included all the positions of the sun known to ancient man. (No dodecaphonic allusion was intended, unless ironically!) Superficially, the group name appears to associate the four compositionally active group members with the four categories to which the twelve signs of the zodiac belong; earth, water, fire and air. (Sergio de Castro's commitments as a painter and writer placed him more as a sympathetic associate.)[83] The real logic underlying the group name is even more curious and is based on a visual cipher which emphasised the equality of all five members; it is geometric and owes its origin to Ohana's years as an architect. The twelve parts of the zodiac may be represented visually as a dodecahedron, a solid figure of twelve faces, the construction of which is based upon the five-sided regular pentagon. As the Zodiaque composers intended their compositional point of departure to stem from what they considered to be the primary sources of music, folksong and plainchant, they chose a name which would allude to the primary forces of nature, the primitive beliefs of pagan man, the representation of which was known in the ancient world.

They mounted their first concert in October 1947 for an invited audience at a private hall in Neuilly (Paris). The following works of Ohana's were performed: the *Sonatine monodique*, *Sarabande* for two pianos, and two pairs of songs for female voice and piano, *Les amants du décembre* a setting of two poems by Claudine Chonez, and two settings of poems by Federico García Lorca in French translation, '*Chanson de la goutte de pluie*' and '*Nana*'. The concert was not without success as soon after, a second Zodiaque concert was broadcast on French radio by the resident orchestra under André Girard and included a performance of a Concerto for brass, percussion and strings by Ohana (a work later destroyed by the composer). A third concert took place in January 1948. The review in the Paris *Spectacle* records 'remarkable' performances of music by this 'interesting new group' and cites *Assemblage*, a trio for violin, piano and double bass by Forest-Divonne for its 'austere counterpoint' and a violin and piano Duo by Ohana (also later destroyed) for its 'dialogue of percussive effects'.[84] Following another French Radio broadcast in March 1948 which included Ohana's setting for baritone and orchestra of three poems (in French translation) from *The Rose Garden* by the medieval Persian poet Shekh Muslihu'd-Din Sadi, the Groupe Zodiaque mounted another invitation concert on 12 June 1948, Ohana's thirty-fifth birthday. The programme included his Suite for piano (later destroyed), *Enterrar y callar* and several chamber works already performed at earlier Zodiaque concerts. In danger of losing some of their original impetus, ten months elapsed before their sixth concert on 29 April 1949 (see Ex. 1.2). An orchestral concert at the Salle Gaveau, again conducted by André Girard, it was well attended by the press (including *The New York Herald*) and received enthusiastic reviews from Marcel Landowski, Maurice Imbert and Marc Pincherle as well as the critic of *The New York Herald*.[85]

Ex. 1.2: Leaflet for the Groupe Zodiaque Concert at the Salle Gaveau, 29 April 1949

The programme included:

Rameau	Concert IV
Roussel	Sinfonietta op.52
Bermat	Prélude
Skrovatchevski	Symphonie for string orchestra
Forest-Divonne	De Profundis
Ohana	La Venta Encantada.

(The unorthodox spelling of Skrowaczewski's name is in accordance with French practice, it appearing thus on the concert programme of 29 April 1949.) The inclusion of two works not composed by members of the group again suggests the spectral influence of the Schola Cantorum. Not only was Roussel Daniel-Lesur's predecessor at Schola but he had been a pupil of D'Indy who was largely responsible for pioneering the Rameau revival in France. (It is interesting to note that the inaugural concert of La Jeune France also included a work by a composer who was not a member of the group.)[86] As Rameau featured in concert programmes during the Occupation, in particular those of the Concerts de la Pléiade, it is likely that his inclusion here represented a clarion-call for the revival of French national pride in the face of foreign, Austro-German serialism.

The presence of Daniel-Lesur, as well as Henri Dutilleux, in senior positions on the music staff at French Radio almost certainly helped promote the music of the Zodiaque composers. Although neither became affiliated to the group, both were sympathetic to their aims. Despite being only three years Ohana's junior and sharing a non-serialist compositional stand-point, Dutilleux has always preserved his independence from any group or manifesto.[87] The pluralist atmosphere prevalent in Paris at time, especially at the recently liberated French Radio where the influence of Henry Barraud, Pierre Capdeville, Roland-Manuel, Désormière and Rosenthal was keenly felt, resulted not only in the enthusiastic promotion of a wide variety of new music by the young generation of French composers, but also a flood of broadcasts of music which had been suppressed under the Occupation. This included works not only by Schoenberg, Berg and Milhaud but Stravinsky, Dukas, Prokofiev, Bartók and of course Mendelssohn.[88] Keen to promote its new-found cultural and aesthetic freedom, the pluralist policies at French radio resulted in commissions from such diverse figures as Ohana, Prey, Nigg, Malec, Philippot, Semenoff, Delerue, Jarre, Petit, Saguer, Szalowski, Castérède, Constant and Jolas, as well as Boulez.[89] Dutilleux was directly responsible for many of these commissions.[90] It was Daniel-Lesur who engineered the meeting of Dutilleux and Ohana at his Paris home in 1948, feeling they would have much in common. A warm friendship was thus engendered. They were particularly close during the 1950s and 60s and remained in regular contact over more than forty years. (Dutilleux was among the small circle of close friends who attended Ohana's private cremation service at Père Lachaise cemetery in November 1992.) Dutilleux commissioned several works from Ohana during his time at the radio, and in 1962 Ohana dedicated his *Tombeau de Claude Debussy* to Dutilleux. The pianist Geneviève Joy,

Dutilleux's wife, performed and recorded Ohana's early piano music and commissioned him to write a new piece, *Sorôn-Ngô*, for the twenty-fifth anniversary of her celebrated two-piano duo with Jacquéline Robin in 1970. The other composers commissioned were: Milhaud, Jolivet, Mihalovici, Auric, Daniel-Lesur, Petit, Constant, Louvier, and of course Dutilleux.[91] In his last published interview, Ohana affirmed his admiration for the work of Dutilleux:

> I saw the work of my friend Henri Dutilleux grow over the years and found within it a steadfast presence which encouraged me to pursue my own work with increasing exactitude ... his music continues to send me signals, like two ships would exchange passing in the night, at the same time enigmatic and comforting.[92]

Inevitably short-lived, the Groupe Zodiaque began to disintegrate by the end of 1949, their last broadcast taking place in March 1950. While Skrowaczewski, de Castro and Ohana succeeded in establishing their respective positions, Bermat and Forest-Divonne gradually abandoned their careers in music. Despite broadcasts and concerts, the group was not able to fund more frequent performances and could not achieve the level of publicity accorded their more widely acclaimed contemporaries. In comparison to the ever widening circle of composers attracted to the teachings of René Leibowitz, both at Darmstadt and in Paris, the Groupe Zodiaque lacked a figure-head who already enjoyed international recognition. Boulez' Concerts Marigny, later the Concerts du Domaine musical, enjoyed greater financial support as well as a more permanent location. While the music of the avant-garde serialists was brought into prominence, this was at the exclusion of other composers, including Ohana, Dutilleux, Constant and many others, whose work did not follow a similar aesthetic path.

Although Boulez later conducted one work of Ohana in January 1954 (incidental music for a play produced by Jean-Louis Barrault's theatre company at the Théâtre Marigny), he has not yet conducted a work by Dutilleux.[93] Boulez never commissioned a work from Ohana. In 1989, Boulez eventually commissioned Dutilleux to write a piece for the Ensemble intercontemporain, although this was abandoned due to a disagreement over the soloist. (Dutilleux was offended that Boulez took so long to offer any commission.)[94] Dutilleux and Ohana were among the composers excluded from representation at the Domaine musical and as a result did not figure among the exports of the Parisian avant-garde abroad. As the influence of Boulez's programming policy was particularly strong during the Glock era at the BBC, as well as long afterwards, the reception of the music of Ohana and Dutilleux suffered significantly in Britain. Any frustration Dutilleux may have felt through being ignored by Boulez was tempered by the championing of his music by Charles Münch during the 1950s; the Koussevitsky Foundation commission for the Second Symphony (premiered by the Boston Symphony Orchestra in 1959) established his international reputation early on in his career. Ohana's music took longer to become known in the United States and was until the 1980s largely overlooked in Britain. Despite the relative success of the Zodiaque concerts and the exposure accorded Ohana's music, it was the première in 1950 of his setting for baritone, female chorus, harpsichord and orchestra of Lorca's monumental poem *Llanto por Ignacio Sánchez Mejías* (the result of a commission from the Cercle Culturel du Conservatoire in 1949) which truly established his compositional presence. A commission for another choral work in 1954, this time from the Norddeutscher Rundfunk, resulted in *Cantigas* and made his music known in Germany. Since that time Ohana's music has been widely performed throughout western Europe and regularly available on commercial recordings. New recordings of his music have continued to be released since his death.

During the 1950s Ohana became increasingly involved with French radio. He spent a short time working with Pierre Schaeffer at the Groupe de Recherche de Musique Concrète and received commissions for incidental music, as well as for concert works. While electro-acoustic techniques were never of central importance in Ohana's music, three works of the 1960s and 1970s and one work of the 1980s require a pre-recorded tape: *Syllabaire pour Phèdre, Sibylle, Autodafé* and *La Célestine*. The position Marius Constant held at French radio as co-founder and director of France-Musique from 1954 to 1966, further aided the promotion of Ohana's music. Founding the Ensemble Ars Nova in 1963 in an attempt to revive the traditional pluralism associated with French music broadcasting in the immediate post-war years, Constant premièred a number of Ohana's important new works of the period, including *Signes* (1965) for flute, zither, piano and percussion, and the chamber opera *Syllabaire pour Phèdre* (1967). Constant was also involved in the commission for Ohana's First Cello Concerto *Anneau du Tamarit* and conducted its première with Alain Meunier and the Orchestre des Concerts Colonne in December 1977.

Some of Ohana's early radio commissions originated from Dutilleux who, in his position as controller of 'Productions d'Illustrations Musicales', sought to develop a new form peculiar to the radio in which words and music were combined.[95] More closely integrated than a broadcast stage-play with incidental music, these radio productions were described as 'musique radiophonique'. Ohana completed three such commissions in 1956: *Les hommes et les autres*, based on a play by Elio Vittorini, *Images de Don Quichotte* based on Cervantes with original text by Alexandre Arnoux, and *Le Guignol au gourdin* based on the play by García Lorca. Ohana completed other scores in this form during the 1960s.[96] These early commissions provided a valuable opportunity for stylistic and technical experimentation, particularly in the use of microintervals (third and quarter tones), electronically inspired sound-textures and unconventional vocal techniques.

The 1950s witnessed another musical discovery which helped shape Ohana's music, in particular his approach to writing in a theatrical context. In 1953 and 1954 he attended performances at the Palais Chaillot of the Peking Opera which happened to be visiting Paris at the time. Ohana described his discovery of the Chinese theatre to be as significant for him as the discovery of the Gamelan was for Debussy.[97] Long dissatisfied with the conventions of western theatre, opera in particular, he discovered in the oriental theatre-form a type of music which could successfully combine musicians with puppets, actors, acrobats and dancers, as well as mime and shadow theatre. Together with his knowledge of traditional Spanish Puppet Theatre which, as a natural eclectic, Ohana considered to have much in common with Chinese theatre, this form provided the catalyst for the development of his own approach to music-theatre. The European and particularly French fascination for the Orient may be considered a well established tradition; like many others, during the 1960s and 1970s Ohana extended his interests towards Japanese music and theatre.

By the 1950s Ohana had wound down his pianistic activities and was able to devote himself entirely to composition becoming, as a result, one of the most prolific composers of his generation. (Ohana still performed extracts of his own piano works on various French radio programmes about his music, even in the 1980s.) Some years later, Dutilleux also made the successful decision to live from his composition (with additional support of his wife, the pianist Geneviève Joy). Aware of the risks involved, Dutilleux remarked of Ohana that 'he knew how to avoid the constraint or security of a second profession.'[98] Although Ohana chose not to accept any permanent teaching position, he taught at various times for limited periods, usually deputising for friends and colleagues. He took the composition class at the Ecole Normale in 1966 and in 1970, each time replacing Dutilleux whose continued eye problems also resulted in Ohana taking over his composition classes at the Paris Conservatoire from 1972–73. Together with Jolivet and Marius Constant, Ohana gave instrumentation classes at the Paris Conservatoire, and took over completely for a short time after Jolivet's death in 1974. Ohana described his teaching as rather subjective, concentrating chiefly on the analysis of works which had a personal significance and which might otherwise be neglected. Typically this included Falla's Harpsichord Concerto and *El Retablo de Maese Pedro*, as well as Debussy's *Etudes* for piano. Although there is certainly no 'Ohana school', as there is no 'Dutilleux school', (such a concept being profoundly alien to the independence of position that both composers have fostered), Ohana maintained a close interest in the work of a number of younger composers known in France whose orientation has revealed an affinity with his own. These include Francis Bayer (also a student of Dutilleux), Edith Canat de Chizy, Hugues Dufourt, Guy Reibel, Jean-Louis Florentz, the Vietnamese Ton-That Tiêt and the Basque Félix Ibarrondo. Ohana also identified closely with the careers of some pianists whom he liked to rehearse and give musical guidance. In the later years of his life these included Jean-Efflam Bavouzet, Laurent Cabasso, as well as Paul Roberts[99], Jay Gottlieb,[100] and Michel Dalberto.[101]

One of Ohana's other main involvements was the founding of the so-called 'Pool de Percussion' in 1961 in collaboration with French Radio. Subsequently the responsibility of the Délégation Régionale de L'Ile de France, the project was designed to gather together the largest possible collection of percussion instruments from anywhere in the world, these to be stored as a reserve of quality instruments for performers and composers. Although still expanding, Ohana's contribution produced diverse instruments from a variety of countries:

drums from Morocco and various Saharan and black African tribes; Cuban M'tumbas and other Latin-American instruments; Chinese cymbals and gongs; and Andalusian bells. While this collection represents an invaluable resource for ethnomusicological research, it also reflects Ohana's own travels and personal interests. Ohana's attraction to unusual instruments precipitated the development in the early 1960s of a new guitar of 10-strings built in collaboration with the luthier Ramirez of Madrid and the guitarists Narciso Yepez and Alberto Ponce. Performers of this instrument are still comparatively rare as an unusually large left hand is required to negotiate the wide neck and finger-board.

Since 1950 the regularity of Ohana's commissions, recordings and broadcasts is testimony to his position as one of the leading composers of his generation in France. His music has also been represented at all the leading festivals of music in France since the 1970s. Ohana's many official involvements reflected his status and recognition in the musical life of France, his memberships including the Commission de la Musique Symphonique de la Société des Auteurs, Compositeurs et Editeurs de Musique (SACEM.); the jury of Les Grands Prix de la SACEM.; the Conseil Supérieur de nomination de professeurs du Conservatoire National Supérieur de Paris; and the Commission des Commandes du Ministère des Affaires Culturelles. In 1962 he was a jury member of the International Flamenco Competition at Cordoba and served on the jury of the Concours de Composition at the Paris Conservatoire from 1966. He was President of the jury of the Concours international de Claude Debussy from 1976 to 1984 and for many years presided at the Académie de Ravel at Saint-Jean-de-Luz. Ohana received many distinctions for his services to French music: he was awarded the Prix Arthur Honegger in 1982 and in 1983 received the Grand Prix de la Ville de Paris and was made Commandeur des Arts et Lettres; he was awarded the Prix Maurice Ravel in 1985; became a Chevalier de la Légion d'Honneur in 1990; and in 1991 received the Grand Prix de l'Académie Française. Together with Olivier Messiaen, Iannis Xenakis Sir Yehudi Menuhin and Mstislav Rostropovich, he was appointed to the 'comité d'honneur' of Musique nouvelle en liberté, founded in 1991 by Marcel Landowski, with the support of the French Ministry of Culture, to promote the programming of new music with standard repertoire. In a career which spanned more than forty years, Ohana's many awards bear witness to his position as one of the major figures in French music since 1945.[102]

Although technically not a French citizen until 1976, when he took French nationality following his marriage to Odile Marcel[103] (daughter of the film director Jean Marie Marcel and grand-daughter of the philosopher Gabriel Marcel), Ohana was always keen to acknowledge his indebtedness to his country of adoption:

> There's no means anywhere else I think of having your personal gifts brought to bear on a real scale of creation outside of towns like Paris where the disciplines are very strict and incentives are very numerous. Without France I would not have been a composer. Whatever my roots and however dominating, for instance, Spanish trends have been in my musical feelings, I could not have

been armed to achieve the synthesis of all those roots without that enormous quality of French teaching that leave a great amount of freedom bringing, at the same time, very strict disciplines but undogmatic disciplines ... .[104]

Ohana inhabited the same apartment in the southern section of Paris's 16th arrondissement at 31 rue du Général Delestraint for more than thirty years. He told me that he chose to live there for four important reasons: it was a quiet area of the city; it was a convenient location for the Radio France building; although small (only two rooms), it was large enough to accommodate his beloved American Model 'D' Steinway; the fourth reason was not a musical one – hew was a keen tennis player and the flat was only a short walk to the tennis courts at the Bois de Boulogne. Arranged simply, Ohana's flat recreated the rustic atmosphere of Andalusia or north Africa while the few decorative objects stood out as ciphers of his creative world: Saharan drums lay under the piano; a miniature, ceramic Chinese dragon and an oriental temple bell hung from the ceiling; an African mask scowled from the wall and by his work-desk hung a Berber mirror under which he kept his writing tools in an eighteenth century Persian box. In his last published interview, Ohana said of these objects: '... they create calm and familiar surroundings. They do not count the passing of time but are soothing and anonymous.'[105]

It was in his Paris flat that Ohana died on 13 November 1992. He was cremated at Père Lachaise cemetery and his ashes dispersed in the sea at Carnac. Throughout his life Ohana remained sympathetic to his ties with British culture. Unusually for someone who had otherwise absorbed French customs, certain habits were preserved from his parental home, as well as his British Army days. Disliking the French predilection for a large lunch at mid-day as too much of a disruption, Ohana preferred to take a large English breakfast and work continuously until 3.00 or 4.00 p.m. when he would break for consultations with his performers, conductors, young pianists or composers over a very English afternoon tea, often Earl-Grey and fruit-cake. His war-time service with the Argyll and Sutherland Highlanders fostered an affection for all things Scottish, also long popular in France. A tall man who had obviously been attractive in his youth, Ohana was renowned throughout Paris for sporting tartan trews and a tartan scarf. While there are many examples of composers, performers, writers, and artists who suffered enforced emigration as victims of political circumstance. Ohana's case was different. Born in a country which was not his homeland, he was an expatriate from the beginning and left out of choice. Although parallels may be drawn with the many Spaniards and South American Spanish who flocked to France to exploit their natural heritage, Ohana's move to Paris was the logical outcome of his French education; he was already as much a part of French as his inherited Spanish culture. It is for this reason that it is fair and accurate to describe Ohana as a French composer, albeit of Spanish origin. His Spanish roots and north African birthplace, tempered by his French training and environment, were the decisive factors in the development of his musical identity.

Notes to Chapter One.

1. Most studies state 1914 as the year of his birth, respecting this unusual eccentricity of the composer. C. Prost correctly cited Ohana's year of birth as 1913 in her dissertation (U. of Aix-en-Provence 1981), although this remains unpublished. She cites 1914 in all her published material. French publications and most sleeve-notes continue to indicate 1914, erroneously.
2. Including the present author.
3. 'Les Cahiers de la Petite Dame', *Cahiers André Gide* No. 7 p. 159 (November 5, 1949).
4. Ohana was granted French nationality following his second marriage in 1976.
5. Falla described the western coastal areas of Spain as the Garden of the Hesperides in his unfinished project *Atlántida* which concerns the lost country of Atlantis, reputed to have sunk off the west coast of Spain.
6. *Oxford Companion to English Literature* (Oxford, 1967), pp. 386–7; W. King, *Heathen Gods and Heroes* (London, 1965) pp. 35–6; W. Smith, *The Concise Classical Dictionary* (reprinted London, 1988) p. 204.
7. M. Ohana, interview (in French), A. Grunenwald (1975) p. 60.
8. Maurice Ohana always described his father's family as Gibraltarian but his mother sometimes as Castillian, sometimes as Andalusian. The author in conversations with the composer in Paris 1982–92.
9. Ohana's name appears erroneously with an apostrophe (O'hana) in some of his British records, on British concert programmes and in his *Music Review* article (1947). In Britain he always emphasised his Gibraltarian connections, although many wrongly assumed that the name was Irish.
10. Certificate of Naturalisation A 7943, 19 July 1894. It is possible that Simon David Ohana was married twice. The name of his wife is not recorded on the Naturalisation certificate but the birth certificate of one of Maurice's sisters, Olga (born Casablanca 1897) records the name of her mother as Mazaltob A. Ohana, formerly Benggio. It has not been possible to obtain further clarification in either British, Moroccan or French records.
11. Dalston falls on the north eastern border of Islington, south of Stoke Newington, between Hackney and Camden Town. According to the current A–Z of London a Queen's Road in Dalston appears no longer to exist. There is, however, a Queensbridge Road.
12. Their British death certificates record Casablanca as their place of birth. Semtob's birth predated the family's move to London.
13. It should be noted that birth certificates for only some of the children of Simon David Ohana can be traced in British records. This is in part due to the complex national status of the Ohana family who lived mainly in Casablanca. It would appear that not all the children of Simon David chose to register their birth with the British Consul (even later in life) and thus may not have asserted their claim to British citizenship. Some emigrated from north Africa to live in Spain, France and the USA, as well as in Britain. Members of the family still live in these countries.
14. While one may presume that the French-Moroccan authorities were given record of the birth in 1913, it is likely that Maurice Ohana required proof of his British citizenship when he volunteered to join the British Forces at the outbreak of the Second World War.
15. C. Prost, 'Formes et thèmes: essai sur les structures profondes du langage musicale de Maurice Ohana', (diss. de troisième cycle, U. of Aix-en-Provence, 1981) p. 14.
16. Literally meaning 'deep song' the Cante Jondo is a particular repertoire of the traditional Flamenco which is characterised by great intensity of vocal

expression. See C. Schreiner, ed., *Flamenco Gypsy Dance and Music from Andalusia*, Eng. trans. M.C. Peters (Amadeus Press, Portland, Oregan, 1990); Falla, 'The Cante Jondo', *Manuel de Falla on Music and Musicians*, Eng. trans. D. Urman and J.M. Thomson (London, 1979) pp. 99–117; M. Cunningham and A. de Larrea Palacín, 'Spain II: Folk Music', *The New Grove Dictionary of Music and Musicians* Vol. 17 (London, 1980) pp. 790–805; I.J. Katz, 'Flamenco', *The New Grove Dictionary of Music and Musicians* Vol. 6 (London, 1980) pp. 635–730; J.B. Trend and I.J. Katz, 'Cante Hondo', *The New Grove Dictionary of Music and Musicians* Vol. 3 (London, 1980) p. 719.

17 A useful chart of the repertoire of traditional songs and dances of the Spanish flamenco is reproduced in I.J. Katz, 'Flamenco', op. cit. (1980) p. 628.
18 Letter (in English) from Maurice Ohana to the present author (8 December 1985).
19 Some of these (for mezzo soprano and piano) have been collected by C.Prost under the title *Huit chansons espagnoles*. Although premièred after Ohana's death, they remain, at the time of writing, unpublished.
20 The most significant of these articles is 'La Géographie musicale de l'Espagne', *Journal musical français* (March–April, 1956).
21 M. Ohana, interview (in English), R. Langham Smith (1993) p. 123. Ohana's article 'La Géographie musicale de l'Espagne' includes a more detailed examination of Andalusian music and its sources, secular and sacred.
22 The present author's correspondence with the composer, January–February 1987.
23 Ibid.
24 18 December 1992. The choice of the *Eglise Saint Séverin* may also have been due in part to the involvement of the composer Félix Ibarrondo, a former pupil of Ohana as well as of Dutilleux, whose clerical affiliations enabled him to officiate. (Ibarrondo and Ohana share the same birthday, although not the same year.)
25 The present author's correspondence with the composer, January–February 1987.
26 M. Ohana, interview (in English), R. Langham Smith (1993) p. 124.
27 Loc. cit.
28 M. Ohana, interview (in French), J.C. Marti (1991) p. 11.
29 M. Ohana, interview (in English), M. Oliver (1984).
30 Alejo Carpentier, *La Música en Cuba* (Mexico City, 1946), trans. L.F. René-Durand (Paris, 1985). Carpentier's article on Ohana, 'Revelación de un compositor', is reproduced in *Ese músico que llevo dentro, obras completas alejo carpentier* Vol. 10 (Mexico, 1987) pp. 215–17.
31 The present author in conversation with the composer in Paris, April 1985.
32 The present author in conversation with Madame Solange Soubrane (the inheritor of Maurice Ohana's estate and Présidente of the Association des amis de Maurice Ohana) in Paris, September 1996.
33 M. Ohana, interview (in English), R. Langham Smith (1993) p. 124.
34 Documents from the composer's archive.
35 C. Prost, 'Notice Biographique', 'Formes et thèmes: essai sur les structures profondes du langage musicale de Maurice Ohana', (diss. U. of Aix-en-Provence, 1981). The name of the cellist is not recorded and it has not been possible to establish his identity from the composer's archives.
36 M. Ohana, interview (in English), R. Langham Smith (1993) p. 126.
37 M. Ohana, interview (in English), M. Oliver (1984).
38 The present author's correspondence with the composer, January–February 1987.
39 Archives of the composer made available to the present author.

40 The present author in conversation with the composer in Paris, March 1983.
41 See C. Prost, (1981).
42 Ibid.
43 The present author in conversations with the composer in Paris, 1982–92.
44 The present author in conversation with the composer in Paris, April 1985.
45 This is substantiated by Rubinstein's remarks in *My Many Years* (London, 1980) pp. 111, 200 and 228–9.
46 The present author in conversation with the composer in Paris, February–March 1984 and April 1985.
47 Newspaper cuttings from the composer's personal archive. The name of the paper has not been preserved.
48 C. Rae, 'Debussy et Ohana: allusions et références', *Cahiers Debussy* Nos 17–18 (1993–1994) pp. 103–20.
49 S. de Castro, 'Pour Maurice Ohana', *L'Avant scène opéra* No. 3 (October 1991) p. 80.
50 See A. Carpentier, *La Música en Cuba* (Mexico City, 1946) trans. L.F. René-Durand *La Musique à Cuba* (Paris, 1985), *¡Ecué-Yamba-O!* (Madrid, 1933) and other novels.
51 The present author in conversation with the composer in Paris, Spring 1990.
52 Ramón Montoya was the uncle of another well-known flamenco guitarist, Carlos Montoya; see C. Schreiner, ed., *Flamenco Gypsy Dance and Music from Andalusia*, Eng. trans. M.C. Peters (Portland, Oregon, 1990) pp. 130–31.
53 Argentinita's most famous choreographies include Ravel's *Bolero* and Granados' *Goyescas*.
54 See Falla, 'The Cante Jondo', *On Music and Musicians*, Eng. trans D. Urman and J.M. Thomson (London, 1979) pp. 99–117.
55 Rita Vega de Triana, 'Antonio Triana and the Spanish Dance; A Personal Recollection', *Choreography and Dance Studies* Vol. 6 (London, 1993) pp. 23–4.
56 L. Massine, *My Life in Ballet* (London, 1968) p. 211.
57 *The Concise Oxford History of Ballet*, ed. Horst Koegler (Oxford, 1982) p. 20.
58 Correspondence between La Argentinita and F. García Lorca is reproduced by D. Gershator, *Selection of Letters of F. García Lorca* (London, 1983).
59 The present author in conversation with the composer in Paris, Spring 1990.
60 Ohana did not release these songs for publication but some have been collected by C. Prost under the title *Huit chansons espagnoles*. These include an 'Alborada' 'in memoriam La Argentinita.
61 There are many references to La Argentinita in the Anton Dolin autobiography *A Volume of Autobiography and Reminiscence* (London, 1960).
62 The present author in conversation with the composer in Paris, Spring 1991.
63 M. Ohana, interview (in French), A. Grunenwald (1975) p. 60.
64 J. Roy, *Présences contemporaines, musique française* (Paris, 1962) p. 352.
65 M. Ohana, interview (in English), M. Oliver (1984).
66 *La Venta encantada* is described as a ballet in J. Roy (1962). It has not been possible to establish the details of the first staged performance which took place in 1940. The first concert performance took place in 1947.
67 A National Service Act permitting liability for service with the Armed Forces was passed on the same day that war was declared. The first Proclamation was signed on 1 October 1939 and applied to men of 20 to 21 years of age. Subsequent proclamations extended the liability to successive higher age groups until by June 1941 all men up to the age of 40 had been registered. H.M.D. Parker, 'Manpower A Study of War-time Policy and Administration', *History of the Second World War*, ed. Sir Keith Hancock (London, 1957) p. 150.

68 Edinburgh newspaper review (1942) from composer's archive. The name of paper has not been preserved.
69 Army Lists July, October 1944 Vol. 2 and January 1945.
70 C. Prost (1981) op cit. p. 18.
71 M. Ohana, interview (in English), R. Langham Smith (1993) p. 129.
72 The Ohana-Casella correspondence is deposited at the Fondazione Cini, Venice.
73 M. Ohana, intervew (in French), J.C. Marti (1991) p. 6.
74 Loc. cit.
75 M. Ohana, 'Alfredo Casella' *The Music Review*, viii (1947) p. 145 (written in English).
76 A. Gide, *Journal 1939–1949 Souvenirs* (Paris, 1954) p. 286.
77 The Ohana-Gide correspondence is edited by Francis Bayer, *Bulletin des Amis d'André Gide*, No. 71, xiv (July, 1986). Selections and further commentary is included in the *Revue Musicale* Nos 391–3 (Paris, 1986) pp. 161–9.
78 F. Bayer, 'André Gide et Maurice Ohana', *Bulletin des amis d'André Gide*, Vol. xiv, No. 7 (1986) pp. 14–15, cited in C. Rae, (1993–4) op. cit. p. 104.
79 Among Sergio de Castro's most well-known works are the stained-glass windows for churches in Caen, Hamburg, and Romont (Switzerland), and the series of murals for the Siège Social d'Atochem at La Défense in Paris in 1988. The covers for many of Ohana's recordings reproduce paintings by Sergio de Castro.
80 C. Potter, *Henri Dutilleux his Life and Works* (London, 1997) p. 122.
81 M. Ohana interview (in French), P. Ancelin (1964), cited in C. Rae, 'Maurice Ohana: Iconoclast or Individualist?' *The Musical Times* (February 1991), p. 70.
82 F. García Lorca, *Deep Song and Other Prose*, trans. and ed. C. Maurer (London, 1980).
83 There is no record of Sergio de Castro's music having been programmed in any of the Zodiaque concerts.
84 Newspaper reviews from Ohana's personal archive.
85 Ibid.
86 Tailleferre's *Ballade* for piano and orchestra was included in the inaugural concert of La Jeune France, 3 June 1936.
87 The present author in conversation with the composer in Paris, March 1998.
88 Henri Dutilleux, *Mystère et mémoire des sons: entretiens avec Claude Glaymann* (Paris, 1997) p. 48.
89 H. Dutilleux (1997) op. cit. p. 68.
90 Dutilleux commissioned the first version of Boulez's *Soleil des eaux*. Noted in C. Potter (1997) op. cit. p. 188.
91 H. Dutilleux (1997) op. cit.p. 54.
92 M. Ohana, interview (in French), J.C. Marti (1991) p. 15.
93 Dutilleux's incidental music for the Jean-Louis Barrault theatre company was conducted by Jolivet at the Comédie Française, prior to Boulez' appointment. Boulez' successive snubs of Dutilleux are recorded in Potter (1997).
94 C. Potter (1997) op. cit. p. 22.
95 Ibid. p. 7.
96 *La route qui poudroie* 1960; *Histoire véridique de Jacotin* 1961; *Hélène* 1963; *Les Héraclides* 1964; *Iphigénie en Tauride* 1965; *Hippolyte* 1966.
97 The present author in conversation with the composer in Paris, June 1988.
98 H. Dutilleux (1997) op. cit. p. 188.
99 The dedicatee of Ohana's first book of *Etudes d'interprétation*.
100 Together with his brother Gordon (a percussionist), the dedicatee of the second book of *Etudes d'interprétation*.
101 The present author was also able to benefit from Ohana's pianistic advice.

102 1956 Prix de la Critique (for Prométhée); 1961 RAI Prize (Italy) (*for Histoire véridique de Jacotin*); 1966 Marzotti Prize (for *Synaxis*); 1968 Grand Prix de l'Académie Charles-Cros (for *Syllabaire pour Phèdre* and *Signes*); 1969 Grand Prix de l'Académie Charles-Cros (for *Cantigas* and *Cris*); 1969 Prix du Président de la République (for *Cantigas* and *Cris*), Prix Italia and Prix Collectif de la Production Contemporaine (for *Silenciaire* and *Sibylle*); 1971 Grand Prix de l'Académie Charles-Cros (for *Silenciaire, Sibylle and Quatre improvisations*); 1974 Prix du Président de la République (for *24 Préludes*) and Grand Prix de la Musique Symphonique de SACEM; 1975 Prix National Français; 1978 Prix 'Florence Gould' de l'Académie des Beaux Arts; 1982 Prix Arthur Honegger and Prix de l'Académie Charles-Cros (for *Lys de madrigaux* and *Messe*); 1982 Ritmo Prize (Madrid) for Contemporary Music; 1982 Prix du Disque Lyrique (Paris); 1983 Grand Prix de la Ville de Paris; 1985 Prix Maurice Ravel; 1986 Laurent de Medici Prize (Florence); 1991 Grand Prix de Musique de l'Académie des Beaux Arts; 1992 SACEM prize for the best new work (for *In Dark and Blue*).

103 Odile Marcel and Maurice Ohana married on 5 May 1976. (He has no children from either his first or second marriage). They collaborated on several works for which Odile prepared the text. They divorced in 1986.

104 M. Ohana, interview (in English), R. Langham Smith (1993) p. 124.

105 M. Ohana, interview (in French), J.C. Marti (1991) p. 12.

CHAPTER TWO

Symbolism and Allegory: Images of the Archetype

All music exists fundamentally as pure sound. Yet, while still satisfying the demands of absolute music, the work of some composers weaves a web of allusion to certain non-musical sources which enhances the essentially abstract nature of the musical material itself. This chapter examines the component images, symbols and allegorical themes that play a substantial role in the music of Maurice Ohana and establishes, for the first time in a discussion of the composer's work,[1] these non-musical themes as representing an important influence on the development of his musical identity.[2] The persistent appearance of these recurrent themes and images in the composer's writings and interviews, as well as in his music, suggests an underlying network of symbolic and allegorical allusion. Just as to ignore the importance of Christian symbolism in the music of Messiaen would be to omit consideration of a non-musical, inspirational source central to his reason for composing, to approach a discussion of the work of Ohana without drawing attention to his symbolic, allegorical and mythological images would be to exclude a part of the composer's creative persona essential to a deeper understanding of his music. The music of Ohana creates an enigmatic world of primeval archetypes where dreams and the imagined are made momentarily concrete.

Parallels can be drawn between the symbolic allusions in Ohana's music and those found in the work of other composers. While such relationships suggest common but independent interests, they may imply a direct cross-fertilisation of ideas or reflect a fascination for such matters in France. Berio turned to Claude Lévi-Strauss's anthropological study *Le cru et le cuit* as the source for much of his ethnological reference in *Sinfonia*. Symbolic and pagan mythological allusions are also found in the work of Messiaen, *Harawi* and *Cinq réchants* in particular, in addition to the Christian symbolism central to his work as a whole. Varèse and Jolivet shared a common interest in pagan mythologies, as well as more esoteric mysticism and magic. Their instinctive attraction to such sources may have been precipitated by their mutual acquaintance with the Cuban novelist Alejo Carpentier[3] whose writings placed him at the vanguard of the Magic-Realist movement in literature and whose early investigations into the primitive ritual practices of the Caribbean were already familiar to the Parisian intellectual élite in the 1930s.[4] Through recourse to pagan symbols Jolivet aimed to restore music to its 'ancient, original sense'.[5] Both Jolivet and Ohana sought to recreate the incantatory atmosphere of primitive, tribal ritual. Although the two composers were well acquainted, Ohana refuted the idea that the music of Jolivet had influenced his compositional interests, despite his admiration for many of Jolivet's early works, including *Mana*. Ohana's acquaintance with Carpentier during the 1950s may have encouraged the deepening of his interest in symbolic and mythological allusion. That Ohana had been familiar with the Spanish-speaking literary and artistic community of Paris since the 1930s would certainly mean he would have been aware of Miguel Angel Asturias's translations of the Quiché Maya *Popul Vuh* and other legends.[6] The understanding of the symbolic and mythological allusion can be traced in the work of Jolivet, Berio, Varèse and Messiaen, as in Ohana, may be enhanced through an awareness of the importance of such stimuli in the broader literary context of the Spanish Magic-Realists, many of whom resided for a time in Paris. Detailed discussion of relationships goes beyond the scope of the present study, although has explored in other writings.[7]

The network of symbolic allusions underpinning work of all these composers represents a recourse to the ancient, collective images of the human imagination.[8] Whether pagan, pre-Christian or Christian, reference to these images may be considered a conscious (for some a subconscious, or even unconscious) attempt to restore an aura of numinoscity and spirituality to music which they considered devoid of any real meaning. This was certainly a conscious aim of the composers of La Jeune France (of which Daniel-Lesur, Ohana's teacher, had been a member) but also underlies many of the ideas proposed by the Groupe Zodiaque (cf. Chapter 1). While these Parisian movements of consecutive decades represent aesthetic standpoints which are not entirely dissimilar, the spiritual archetypes to which they turned were individual for each composer. La Jeune France sought to register their disassociation from what they saw as increasingly impersonal and mechanical trends of French music between the wars. Thirteen years later, the Groupe Zodiaque declared their opposition not only to the intellectualism of serialism, but also, perhaps paradoxically, to what they considered the neo-romanticism of La Jeune France, Messiaen in particular. In the aftermath of World War II, the desire to restore a human and spiritual quality to art, to return to ancient cultural roots in a contemporary world beset by the psychological and political trauma of war, in which a newly rationalised population had been disinfected of superstitions and dehumanised by their own technical progress, could well have been in the air. The Greek writer Nikos Kazantzakis completed *Zorba the Greek* towards the end of World War II and may even have had the music of serialism in mind when he equated arid intellectualism with the end of civilisation:

> ... cerebral acrobatics and refined charlatanism! That is how it always is at the decline of a civilisation. That is how man's anguish ends – in masterly conjuring tricks ... . The last man – who has freed himself from all illusions and has nothing more to expect or to fear – sees the clay from which he is made reduced to spirit, and this spirit has no soil left for its roots from which to draw its sap ... . Everything having turned into words, into musical jugglery, the last man goes even further: he sits in utter solitude and decomposes music into mute mathematical equations.[9]

In Kazantzakis' novel, it is the unselfconscious Zorba who rekindles a sense of spirituality and creative spontaneity in the initially supremely rationalised protagonist narrating the tale. Thanks to Zorba the protagonist is saved from exploring possibly worthy but essentially sterile intellectual processes. Although Ohana was not aware of Kazantzakis' work in the late 1940s when he founded the Groupe Zodiaque, a sense of spiritual dissatisfaction combined with the desire to restore human values to a world in chaos and seemingly devoid of meaning or purpose, was certainly prevalent at the time. If Kazantzakis' image was intended as a reference to serialism, his views of the intellectual processes involved were certainly negative, as indeed were Ohana's. Alternatively, the development of total-serialism itself could be interpreted as a reassertion of intellectual and therefore spiritual satisfaction through its rigorous processes of imposing order, to an almost infinitesimal degree, on a controllable medium when politically most of Europe was in a state of profound turmoil.

At the beginning of his composing years Ohana did not consciously aim to imbue his music with evocative, symbolic images. Rather the additional layer of meaning that became characteristic of his mature work grew naturally from a combination of his instinctive attraction to subject matter already rich in symbolic associations and contemplation of the natural inheritance of his cultural roots. While Ohana's web of allusive symbolism is most prominent in his works from the middle 1960s onwards, similar preoccupations can be traced in earlier works. Many of the early and transitional works are based on a variety of non-musical sources and include subjects drawn from literature and mythology, non-Spanish as well as Spanish. Art also provided a compositional stimulus; several works owe their point of compositional departure to the engravings of Goya, a painter for whom Ohana maintained a life-long affinity. Symbolic and allegorical imagery, verging at times on the surreal, is a common feature of many of these sources, the majority of which belong to the pool of Spanish culture. While the underlying themes may be serious, neither the sources themselves, nor Ohana's treatment of them precludes the presence of a comic dimension which often enhances discourse on the archetypal problems of the human condition. Although many of Ohana's early works were withdrawn, destroyed, or simply remained unpublished, their choice of subject matter reveals much about Ohana's compositional identity and aesthetic alignment. His fascination for subjects drawn not only from Spanish, South American and African legends but also Classical mythology represents a theme which can be traced throughout his composing life. Table 2.1 lists the early and transitional works and the divers, extra-musical sources on which they are based.

Of the works listed in Table 2.1 those based on literary sources represent the largest single group. Ohana's settings and adaptations of Federico García Lorca, Cervantes, Lope de Vega, Tirso de Molina and Shakespeare, as well as of Schéhadé, Sadi and Camus, are testimony to his instinctive seeking out of material rich in allegorical, symbolical and even comic themes all of which in some way present a discourse on the problems of the human condition. The propensity of works based on the acknowledged masters of Spanish literature is revealing not only of Ohana's cultural alignment but his declared intention to reflect upon his cultural roots, particularly in his early period. Although Persian, Shekh Muslihu'd-Din Sadi belongs to the wider pool of Spanish culture as his poems were known in medieval Spain. (Ohana's setting in French, rather than Spanish translation, was presumably for the convenience of performance.) In this context, Ohana's adaptation of Shakespeare's *Midsummer Night's Dream* might appear surprising. Forming part of his broad admiration for the Golden Age drama of the Renaissance (Spanish and English) which established itself in his early works, Ohana's attraction for Shakespeare reappears briefly in *Autodafé* (which includes a setting of part of a sonnet), in *Stream* (which makes reference to *King Lear*) and more than thirty years later in his opera-setting of Fernando de Rojas' dramatic dialogue-novel *La Celestina*; King Lear's soliloquy on the death of Cordelia (in English) is interpolated at the lamentation of Mélibée's father Pleberio who enters, similarly with his daughter dead in his arms.

Table 2.1: Extra-musical sources for works of the early and transitional periods

Source types : L – Literature, P – Painting, M – Mythology

Date	Title of Work		Source
1940	*La venta encantada*	L	Cervantes: *Don Quixote*
1944	*Enterrar y callar*	P	Goya: *Los Desastres de la Guerra*
1947	*Don Juan*	L	Tirso de Molina: *El burlador de Sevilla y convidado de piedra*
1947	*Deux mélodies*	L	F.García Lorca poems: *Cancion del gota de Lluvia, Nana*
1947	*Trois poèmes de Sadi*	L	Shekh Muslihu'd-Din Sadi: *Jardins des roses*
1948	*La Peste*	L	Camus' novel
1948	*Le damné par manque de confiance*	L	Tirso de Molina: *El condenado por desconfiado*
1950	*Llanto por Ignacio Sánchez Mejías*	L	Lorca's poem
1950	*Sarabande*	P	Goya: engravings (various)
1951	*Les représentations de Tanit*	M	Carthaginian and Phoenician goddess of fertility and destruction
1951	*Monsieur Bob'le*	L	Schéhadé's play
1951	*Suite pour un mimodrame*	L	Schéhadé's play *Monsieur Bob'le*
1954	*Cantigas*	L	Medieval and Renaissance Spanish texts
1954	*Tableaux de l'héroïne fidèle*	L + M	Andalusian Romancero
1954	*La chanson du marin*	L	Schéhadé's play
1954	*Soirée des proverbes*	L	Schéhadé's play
1954	*Trois caprices*	P	Goya: *Los Caprichos, Los Desastres de la guerra*
1956	*Les hommes et les autres*	L	E. Vittorini: *Uomini e no*
1956	*Médée*	L + M	Seneca adapt. J. Bergamín
1956	*Images de Don Quichotte*	L	Cervantes: *Don Quixote*
1956	*Le Guignol au gourdin*	L	Lorca's play
1956	*Prométhée*	L	Classical mythology – Prometheus myth
1957	*Fuenteovejuna*	L	Lope de Vega's play

Date	Title of Work		Source
1957	*Tiento*	P	Goya: engravings (various)
1957	*Trois graphiques*	P	Goya: engravings (various)
1958	*Le Romancero du Cid*	L	Spanish hero El Cid – text adapt. A. Arnoux
1958	*Récit de l'an Zéro*	L	Schéhadé's poem
1959	*Songe d'une nuit d'été*	L	Adaptation of Shakespeare
1959	*Homère et Orchidée*	M	Classical mythology
1960	*Quatre improvisations*	M	Classical mythology – evocation of Pan / Syrinx
1960	*Chanson de toile*	M	Teutonic legend: Tristan and Isolde
1961	*Histoire véridique de Jacotin*	L + M	Text by Camilo José Cela
1962	*Tombeau de Claude Debussy*	M	Pagan Sun mythologies (selected movements)
1963	*Cinq séquences*	P + M	Goya – *Caprichos* Mythical rites eg. of Cybele (Tympanum)
1963	*Hélène*	L + M	Euripides and Classical mythology
1964	*Si le jour paraît...*	P	Goya – *Caprichos*
		M + L	Myth: Marsyas (classical) Maya (Buddhist) Troubadour poetical forms
1964	*Les Héraclides*	L + M	Euripides and Classical mythology
1965	*Iphigénie en Tauride*	L + M	Euripides and Classical mythology

The mythological sources of the early and transitional works are also indicative of Ohana's later interests. He provided radiophonic music for adaptations of Euripides, as well for Seneca's tragedy on the theme of Medea. The latter conveniently combines Classical and Spanish cultures; not only was Seneca born in Cordoba, but the French adaptation was undertaken by the Spanish writer José Bergamín.[10] Mythological and historical Iberian themes are also combined in the ballet *Les représentations de Tanit*, a collaboration with Maurice Béjart. The statues of the two-faced Phoenician-Carthaginian Goddess of fertility and destruction were discovered in Ibiza; it is well known that both the Carthaginians and Phoenicians established themselves in southern Spain for reasons of trade before the Roman conquest became fully effective under Augustus. The other Ohana-Béjart collaboration of the 1950s, *Prométhée*, draws on the story of the more familiar figure of Classical mythology. *Quatre improvisations*, a concert rather than theatrical work, is not programmatic in the same sense as the ballets but, like Debussy's *Syrinx*, evokes the God Pan through the incantatory musical material and timbral associations of the flute itself. Ohana's recourse to Teutonic myth in *Chanson de toile* is unusual and even uncharacteristic. Tristan and Isolde appear only in one other work, the opera *La Célestine* and then simply as silent figures among a procession of lovers drawn from legend and history whose love-drama, like that of Calyx and Mélibée, ended in tragedy. The mythological reference in *Cinq séquences* is implicit rather than direct; the third movement 'Tympanum' is not only concerned with rhythm as texture but the title may be an allusion to the drums of ancient Greece and Rome[11] (tympan is a stretched sheet or membrane) which accompanied the ancient and orgiastic rites of worship to the earth Goddess Cybele.[12]

The sources which provided the point of compositional departure for *Si le jour paraît...* are more complex. On the threshold of Ohana's mature style, the work draws on literary and visual sources in addition to its incorporation of mythological allusions. The third movement entitled 'Maya-Marsyas' makes a two-fold allusion; it refers both to the Buddhist Queen Maya, whose dream of miracles made musical instruments play on their own and brought about the birth of spring as well as her own son, and to the unfortunate satyr Marsyas of Classical mythology who unsuccessfully challenged the musical supremacy of Apollo. The fifth movement, 'La chevelure de Bérenice', refers to the dedication by Queen Berenice, wife of Ptolemy III Euergetes, of a lock of her hair, in fulfilment of a vow of hope that her husband would return safely from war; although the hair was lost from the temple it magically reappeared as a constellation in the night-sky.[13]

The work of the Spanish painter Francisco Goya provided Ohana with one of his most enduring extra-musical sources. *Enterrar y callar* ('to bury them and say nothing') borrows its title from Goya's eighteenth etching in the collection *Los Desastres de la Guerra*. The illustration depicts a monstrous pile of mutilated corpses overlooked by two figures in hopeless despair. The sombre mood of Ohana's short piece, composed in 1944, echoes the tragic atmosphere of Goya's etching and his own experiences of war. The Goyesque reference was continued in the title of the set of pieces to which *Enterrar y callar* belongs; *Trois caprices* refers to Goya's collection *Los Caprichos*. Debussy's familiarity with the work of Goya is well known.[14] The title of *En blanc et noir* was inspired by the *Caprichos* of Goya, the original title being *Caprices en blanc et noir*. The white and the black of Debussy's title suggests not only the structure of the piano keyboard but the technique of engraving and its visual austerity. Of the sombre second movement of *En blanc et noir*, Debussy said it had become 'too black' and nearly 'as tragic as a *Caprice* of Goya'.[15] It must be said, however, that Debussy also compared the 'greys' of his three pieces to those of another Spanish painter, Velasquez.[16] Goya's original title-page for *Los Caprichos*, 'The sleep of reason produces monsters', (subsequently moved by Goya to number 43) provides another clue for Ohana's attraction to Goya's work. The nightmare images released from the unreal world of dreams links the rational world with the unconscious mind, providing a spontaneous and fertile pool of creative ideas. Goya's etching is accompanied by lines of text: 'Imagination abandoned by reason produces impossible monsters: united with her, she is the mother of the arts and the source of their wonders.'[17] In drawing on the work of Goya, Ohana returned to images belonging to his cultural background which had already affected him deeply.

> I knew Goya from childhood. I have always been haunted by Goya; his drawings, his paintings, but especially his general attitude to society ... .[18]

Through recourse to Goya, Ohana found a ready-made representation of social organisation disintegrating into a soulless moral decay. It is understandable that he should have found Goya's nightmare world, beset by the tortures and agonies of war, not unlike some of his own war-time experiences. There are other works which Ohana described as Goyesque in character; *Tiento* for solo guitar and the concertos *Trois graphiques* (for guitar and orchestra) and *Sarabande* (for harpsichord and orchestra, originally for two pianos and which was reworked in the guitar concerto). Their sombre mood and austerity of instrumental colouring reflects the darks and greys of Goya's etchings. The title of the guitar concerto refers to the general body of Goya's drawings and sketches, known in Spanish as *gráficos. Si le jour paraît...* borrows its title from the seventy-first *Capricho* and, according to the composer, is imbued with a Goyesque atmosphere throughout. Goya's title translates to mean 'When day breaks we shall go' (*Si amanece; nos Vamos*). Ohana does not use the full title, the dots of his incomplete citation enforcing the sense of doubt inherent in the original Spanish. According to the composer, *Cinq séquences* opens a window to the world of Goya in the sombre fourth movement 'Déchant' which, in Ohana's preface to the score, is described in terms of '... slow scrolling spirals ... shadows and sudden bursts of light, recalling the *Caprices* of Goya, so dear to this author.'

Some of Ohana's mature works (not included in Table 2.1) have also been described as Goyesque by the composer. Without making reference to specific etchings, the connection is intended to provide an interpretative clue. 'Mémorial 44', the fourth movement of *Cris*, recounts the horror of the German concentration camps and lists them by name to the accompaniment of vocal glissandi suggesting the sound of warning-sirens, whistling, sighs and cries of agony. Ohana's suggestion of Goyesque atmosphere in his *24 Préludes* which pay homage to those of both Chopin and Debussy, is more esoteric.[19]

> The 24 Preludes of Chopin will always remain for me an enigma. I find them Goyesque, violent, full of hatred and tenderness, images of terrible demonic power and extraordinary liberty, while their form is that of an immediate bursting forth of raw substance.[20]

This description reveals as much about Ohana's approach to his own *Preludes*, as well as to his highly individual interpretation of those of Chopin. Ohana's mature Goyesque works are closely related to their earlier cousins not only through their predominantly sombre musical character but also through a similarity of instrumental texture. With the exception of *Cris*, Ohana's Goyesque works tend to be composed for the guitar or instruments traditionally associated with its evocation, such as the piano, harpsichord or strings. Many of these works also make use of characteristically Spanish musical features. The rhythm of a slow sarabande dominates *Enterrar y callar* and *Tiento* while the latter also includes a distant memory of Falla's *Homenaje*. The techniques of 'rasgueado' and 'tambora' (cf. Chapter 3), traditionally associated with flamenco guitar playing, are used in *Tiento* and *Si le jour paraît...* which also incorporate melodic fragments suggesting the tragic laments of the Cante Jondo (literally meaning 'deep song', a repertoire of flamenco song-types, characterised by their profound seriousness). Similar allusions occur in the *24 Préludes* as well as *Kypris*.

Ohana's Goyesque allusions are of course highly personal and enigmatic; far from representing any exact musical transliteration, they aim to evoke the spirit of Goya's grotesque fantasy, a primitive world of the unconscious populated by evil demons, monsters and nightmare images in which sometimes even a cynical, black humour reveals itself. Ohana develops this last attribute in his dramatic vocal work *Autodafé* which presents a succession of historical tableaux depicting different scenes of tyrannical dictatorship. The seventh scene, 'Leçon des ténèbres' portrays a Goyesque image of the Inquisition, with the ubiquitous, demonic, grinning donkey of the *Caprichos* leering on in sneering approval. Ohana's attraction to Goya stems not only from the painter's bitter critique of contemporary society but from the attraction of both to the archetypal Spanish fascination for the surreal world of dreams which takes shape in such grotesque and primitive images. In the twentieth century this feature is particularly associated with the work of García Lorca, Salvador Dali, and film-director Luis Buñuel, and is also a feature of certain works of Camilo José Cela with whom Ohana was well acquainted.[21] Nightmarish images of anguish and suffering can also be found in the work of Picasso, the raging brutality of *Guernica* being one of the supreme examples.

Ohana's stylistic watershed of the middle 1960s affected his treatment of symbolism as much as the technical aspects of his musical language (cf. Part Two). Whereas in the early works symbolic allusion was associated primarily with the source on which the work was based, in the mature works Ohana began to develop a symbolic language of his own. With *Signes*, he began a series of works which signalled the growth and proliferation of his mature style, the Sigma Series (cf. Chapter 4). He drew attention to the series by using a secret cipher; their esoteric titles all begin with the letter 'S' which, according to the composer, was derived from the reversed Greek 'sigma' symbolising 'evolution'.[22] For Ohana these works symbolised the evolution of his mature style into his second half-century: 1965 coincided with his fifty-second birthday.

The first work of the Sigma Series, *Signes*, introduces a new approach to symbolic allusion. The work takes its title from the ciphers or 'signs' drawn by the composer at the head of each movement, these representing graphic rather than verbal subtitles (see Ex. 2.1). In the original programme note, Ohana described the graphic symbols as 'having an archetypal value which generates the variants and act as a catalyst for the colour' of each of the six movements.[23] The devices are derived from the programmatic theme of the work which Ohana's original programme note explains as 'the contemplation of the life of a tree'. The six movements depict the tree in various states and conditions: 'at night', 'alive with birds', 'drowned with rain', 'imprisoned in gossamer' (spiders' webs), 'beaten by the wind', and 'burnt by the sun'.[24]

While the ciphers for the first, second, third and sixth movements are representational, those for the remaining movements are more abstract. When Ohana was asked why the sign heading the fourth movement is merely an asterisk, the composer explained that he simply could not draw a tree covered in

SYMBOLISM AND ALLEGORY 39

Ex. 2.1: Graphic subtitles of *Signes*

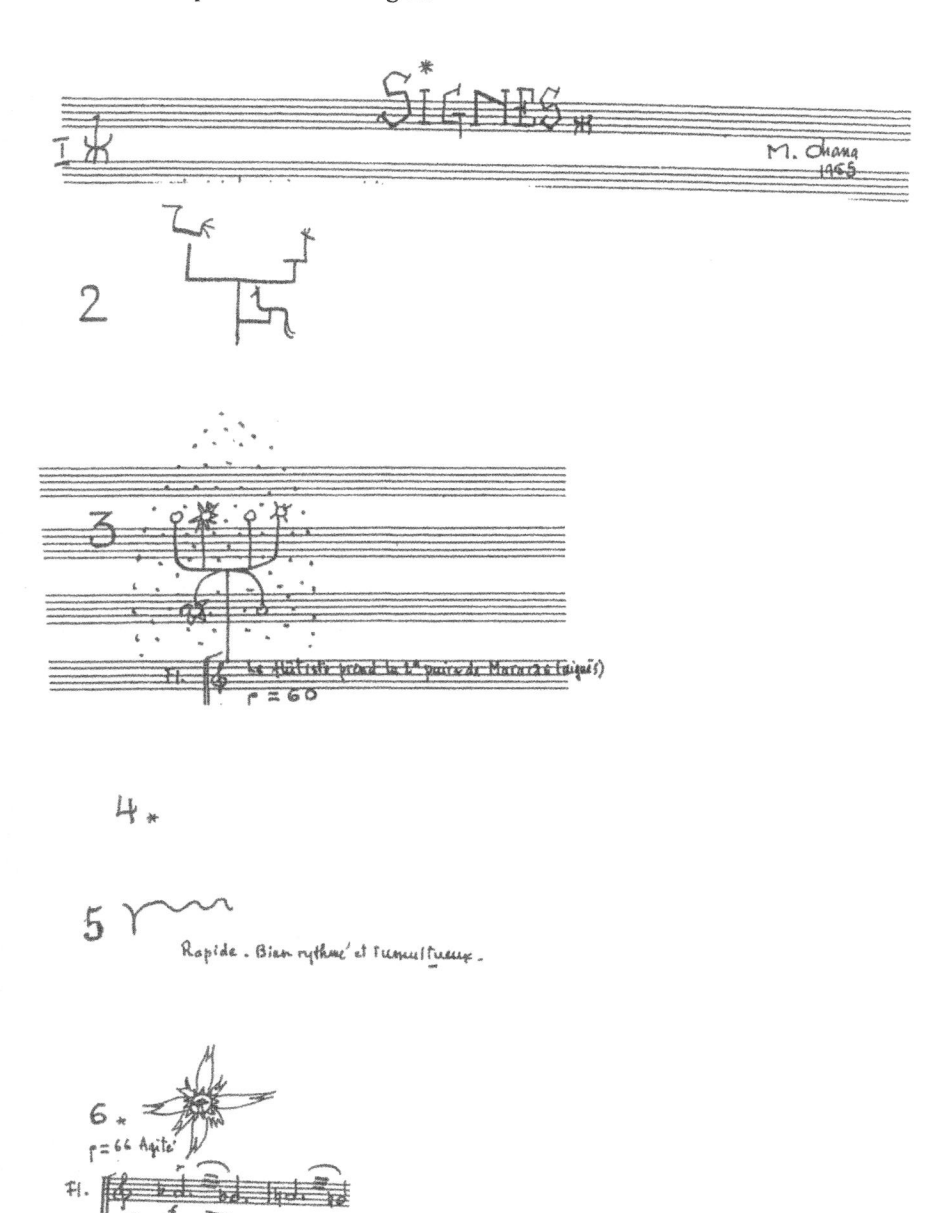

Reproduced by kind permission of Editions Amphion, Paris / United Music Publishers Ltd.

spiders' webs in any satisfactory manner![25] The ability to conceive symbolic ideas in visual terms was an enduring legacy of Ohana's years as an architect. (His manuscripts are also notable for their many drawings.) The use of visual ciphers may stem from Ohana's war-time service in Intelligence where his duties involved work in code-breaking. Apart from the graphic symbols, the score of *Signes* bears no other explanation for Ohana's declared theme of the tree, the image being a personal symbol which he chose to reveal in interviews and programme notes.

The choice of the tree-symbol to indicate maturity is a resonant one. It occurs in a work which the composer himself designated as representing the crystallisation of his mature style, and is the first of his evolutionary Sigma-Series.[26] In *Signes*, as in a tree, his composition has taken root, will grow and proliferate. Ohana's tree-symbol has long being of importance to him:

> The tree is the theme of my life; it has always been my madness. As a child, I once struck my mother because she had a tree felled ... . There is a Celtic legend that says: if one looks at a tree in a certain manner, there is a soul within which is thus released from its prison.[27]

Ohana would seem to be comparing the tree-symbol to his own composition, the 'certain manner' in which the soul may be liberated suggesting his creative processes. On being questioned as to what this 'certain manner' might be, Ohana characteristically remained enigmatic replying that 'it will remain a mystery'.[28] Ohana's mystical ideas echo those of the Renaissaance artist Michelangelo who, it is said, considered his sculpture to lie already hidden within the marble and that his work was simply to make it visible.

The tree-symbol is an ancient one, reaching back to the origins of many cultures and is often associated with physical growth and psychological maturation. In the ancient world it was one of the symbols of Zeus, although after Christ it was used to represent both the Crucifixion and Resurrection.[29] It is the pre-Christian symbolism which is of greatest significance in Ohana's work. In primitive tribes of West Africa some trees are ascribed magical powers and are named spirit, or 'Ju-Ju' trees. In many primitive cultures the tree played a vital role, serving as both a psychic identity and external representation of an individual's soul and voice; tribesmen considered their lives and fate to be intimately bound with that of their chosen tree.[30] In resuscitating this ancient symbol, Ohana sought to colour his music with a halo of psychic association by reference to an archetype that already holds an instinctive and special spell. Wishing to escape from modern rationality, he attempted to rekindle the vitality of unconscious association still present in the conscious mind of what to most modern, industrialised nations would be considered a primitive tribesman. This magical aura gives a colourful and fantastic aspect to the world of the primitive and is a link between the rational world of consciousness and the world of instinct.

Of the graphic symbols heading the individual movements of *Signes*, that for the sixth movement, the sun-burst indicating the tree 'burnt by the sun', is one of the most esoteric and intriguing. This cipher appears in many of Ohana's manuscript scores and was often used as a form of personal signature (see Ex. 2.2). Representing the face of the sun, Ohana's sun-burst is drawn with observing eyes, surrounded by glowing rays, four of which are long and reach out to each point of the compass. Ohana inscribes his name between the four longest rays. (The letter 'h' is not aspirate in French and is therefore conveniently omitted by the composer for the purpose of these insignia.) Ohana identifies himself with the sun in the context of his own composition; it is he, in accordance with ancient, cosmogonic myth, who is the creator of all within his own musical universe, as the sun is the source of all life. In *Signes* the sun-burst is all the more potent and has a deeply spiritual implication; the tree, Ohana's chosen symbol for psychological and musical maturity, is burnt by the sun, the archetypal symbol for the life-force.

Ex. 2.2: Ohana's 'sun-burst' signature (reproduced from the *Piano Concerto*)

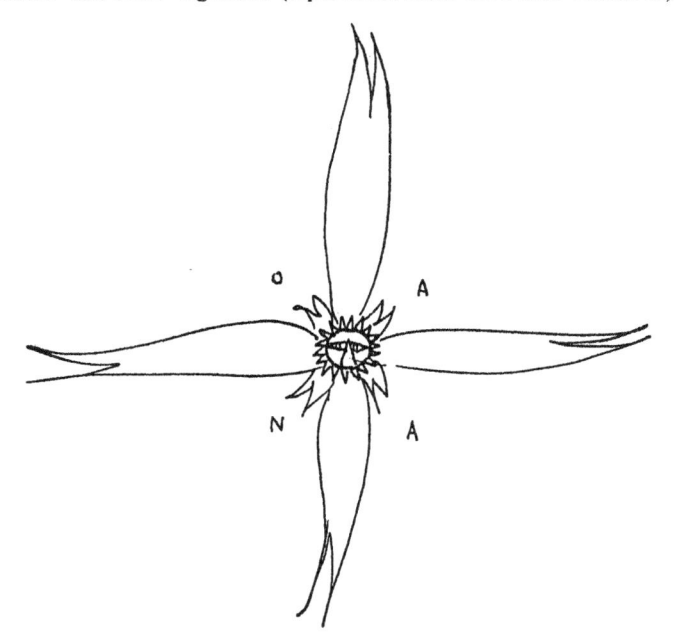

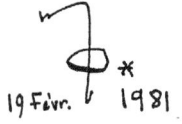

Reproduced by kind permission of Société des Editions Jobert, Paris / United Music Publishers Ltd.

Like all archetypes, the sun-symbol is a familiar image, often associated with cult-worship, which appears in many cultures of the world from the most ancient history to the present day. It is closely related to the symbol of the circle which, in the form of a mandala, is associated with the Jungian concept of 'wholeness'.[31] A sun-burst motif of extraordinary similarity to that of Ohana is the Macedonian symbol of Royalty found on the sarcophagus presumed to be that of King Philip II. Ohana's use of the symbol pre-dates the Macedonian excavations of the 1970s and is therefore unlikely to have been adopted directly from this source. Ohana's sun-burst symbol appears in a variety of contexts throughout his scores. As well as incorporating the letters of his name, it sometimes appears with the mystical Latin inscription 'nox et dies sum', as on the manuscript scores of the sixth *Etude d'interprétation*, *T'Harân-Ngô* and *Nuit de Pouchkine*[32] (see Ex. 2.3).

Ex. 2.3: Ohana's 'Nox et dies sum' signature

a) 'Troisième pédale', *Etudes d'interprétation* (I)

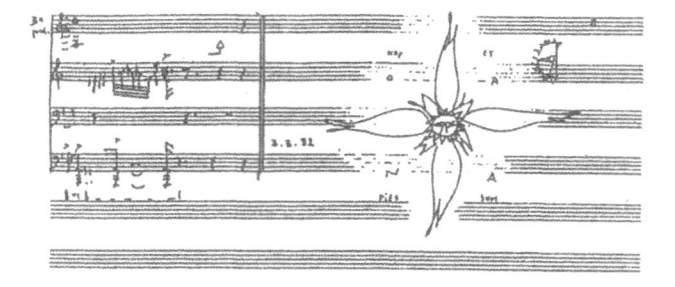

b) *T'Harân-Ngô*

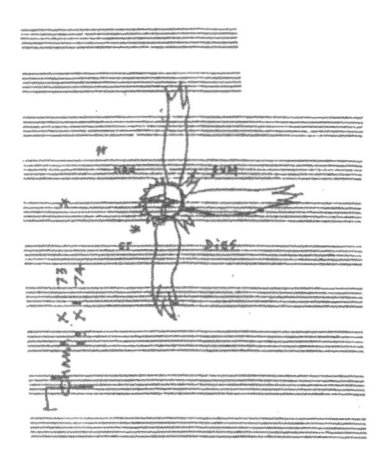

Reproduced by kind permission of Société des Editions Jobert, Paris / United Music Publishers Ltd.

SYMBOLISM AND ALLEGORY 43

c) *Nuit de Pouchkine*

© 1992 Gérard Billaudot Editeur S.A. Paris. Reproduced by kind permission.

While there is no explanation why Ohana chose to include this inscription on some insignia and not on others, it may suggest that the works in question held some special significance for the composer alone. To echo the meaning of the added text, Ohana's cipher, in these cases, is often altered to include a representation of the moon; either the moon is shown separately at the side of the sun in the company of several stars or, as in *T'Harân-Ngô*, a single face becomes simultaneously that of both the sun and moon. Extending ancient, cosmogonic myth to include the moon as well as the sun, both become omnipresent observers, overseeing all that passes under their respective skies. This is in keeping with Ohana's vision of an imagined world where music simply exists in a timeless universe, created by an unknown, ageless author. This theme underlies *Anonyme XX siècle* and 'Epitaphe' in *Swan Song*, both of which were completed in the last years of his life, and echoes Debussy's image of music as the history of the world told by the wind.

> If by chance my music should survive, I would like it to blend anonymously into a forest of music for all man-kind in a world of distant but imaginable listeners. This music may only have a single author, without name, but who is omnipresent and without age.[33]

The complete realisation of what may be called Ohana's Sun-Moon symbolism appears in the choral diptych *Lux noctis – Dies solis* (Light of night – Day of sun), a spiritual hymn to love and life. Both sections of the work set an adaptation of lines by Catullus, drawn freely from several poems,[34] while *Dies solis* also includes an anonymous Latin text found by Ohana in a Roman ruin in southern Spain. Abounding in learned, Classical allusion (Venus, Hymen, Hesperus, Queen Berenice's hair, the west wind Zephyr and Ariadne), the text of *Lux noctis*, much of which is taken from love poems to Lesbia, celebrates the passion of love, equating it with the eternal light of the heavens. *Dies solis* contrasts the eternity of the rising and setting sun with the brevity of human existence.

> Day of sun / Sun in splendour / Give us eternal light (of your spirit) on this Day of yours [from the Spanish Roman ruin] / Suns can set and rise again / when once our short day is set / we must sleep one endless night.[35]

Other references to sun and moon imagery occur in *Trois contes de l'Honorable Fleur*, a music-theatre work based on three allegorical tales written by the composer. The sun is associated, unusually, with the destructive powers of the Apocalypse of the third tale (and is drawn in the score in several places); burning relentlessly it destroys life rather than creates it. The moon, on the other hand, is associated with eternity and is present throughout the work (represented musically by a chorale) as a more peaceful and benevolent overseeing deity. Given the Japanese associations of the work as a whole (cf. Chapter 4),[36] the personification of the moon as a deity suggests the oriental Goddess Kwan-Yin. *Cadran lunaire*, for guitar, also involves sun and moon imagery. The title itself is a play on words; while 'cadran solaire' means literally 'sun-dial', Ohana's playful substitution of 'lunaire' suggests a similar instrument to be used for calibration of the night hours by the light of the moon. The nocturnal character of the work recalls the tranquillity of Bartókian night music, tinged with the colourism of Debussy. Three of the movement titles make Classical, hellenic references, two of which are associated with night-time activities: the first movement 'Saturnal' evokes the mid-winter festivals of ancient Rome in honour of Saturn; the third movement 'Sylva' refers to the God of fields and forests often associated with Pan and believed to be the son of Saturn. The final movement 'Candil' (derived from the Latin 'candeo') makes an enigmatic reference to the warmth and brilliance of the sun, and thus reaffirms the vital forces of life. (The remaining movement 'Jondo' refers to the Spanish flamenco.)

Sun-moon imagery is a symbolism of opposites. Such archetypal symbolism has been suggested by C.G. Jung to be an important part of the inner life of modern man, as well as that of the ancients.[37] The real life of man in all ages consists of a series of associations with opposites: night and day; birth and death; good and evil; Heaven and Hell; happiness and misery; the Yan and Yin; the male and female principles of the 'animus' and 'anima'; and even the former political division of Europe into East and West. (The male and female principle is also inherent in the two Japanese scales 'ryo' and 'ritsu'.[38]) Through his mystical 'nox et dies sum' insignia, Ohana's own symbolism may be one of reconciling these archetypal opposites and suggesting the existence of some utopian world, or Garden of Eden where, like the poetic images of William Blake, there is no more inner conflict – where the 'lion shall lie down beside the lamb'.[39]

Ohana's sun-moon imagery, sun-burst signature and tree-symbol are all archetypal images associated with nature. This broader theme is one Ohana claimed as one of the primary elements of his music:

> The great lessons of music were not given to me by musicians. I received them solidly from the sea, the wind, the rain on the trees and from the light, and even more from the contemplation of certain landscapes that I seek out because they seem to belong more to the origin of the world than to any civilised place.[40]

Again suggesting Debussy's image of the history of the world told by the wind, Ohana's preoccupation with nature as an underlying theme in his work results in a certain amount of descriptive impressionism. The fifth movement of *Signes* evokes an impression of the wind's tumultuous strength and is, by the composer's own declaration, intended as a commentary on Debussy's 'Ce qu'a vu le vent d'ouest' (*Preludes* I).[41] Further examples of Ohana's impressionist 'wind-music' appear in the sixth movement of *Si le jour paraît...*, 'Jeu des quatre vents', and in the second of the *Trois contes de l'Honorable Fleur*, 'Le Vent d'Est enfermé dans un sac'. These descriptive evocations are of contrasted character. While 'Jeu des quatre vents' aims to suggest the awesome power of nature's forces, the more light-hearted *Trois contes*, presents a comic personification of the rumbustiuous but playful East wind, represented musically by a succession of disjointed rhythms on percussion. Not only is the wind depicted in Ohana's scores but also the rain. Impressionist 'rain music' appears in *Trois contes*, the *Etudes d'interprétation*, *T'Harân-Ngô* and the third movement of *Signes*, where persistent repeated notes, superimposed in rhythmic ostinati on unpitched percussion, are intended to suggest the pattering of falling rain (cf. Ex. 4.5). The eighth of the *24 Préludes* for piano exploits the highest tessitura of the piano, with cascades of tremolandos, repeated notes and glissandos to suggest rainfall. In the pianistic context, this piece represents an extension of similar descriptive impressionism found in Liszt's *Jeux d'eau à la Villa d'Este*, Ravel's *Jeux d'eau* and Debussy's *Jardins sous la pluie*.

While the 'rain-music' in *Trois contes* is certainly descriptive and evocative, it also takes on an additional, symbolic role. In the third tale, 'La Pluie remontée au Ciel', the return of rainfall one thousand years after the Apocalypse symbolises not only the restoration of life after destruction, but also forgiveness. The particular imagery of 'La Pluie remontée au Ciel' has close parallels with the rain and water symbolism in *The Waste Land* of T.S. Eliot, as well as with Death and Resurrection symbolism. Other works of Ohana take the theme of nature further and equate the primary elements of sun, rain, wind and fire with the creative force of all life. These ideas underlie the two large orchestral works of the 1970s, *T'Harân-Ngô* and *Livre des prodiges*, as well as the *Etudes d'interprétation* of the 1980s. The allusions create an atmosphere of primitive ritual in a manner owing much to Stravinsky. *T'Harân-Ngô* derives its title from Taranis, a Celtic god of thunder, and is a celebration of the primary forces of nature; it bears the sub-title 'conjuration, contemplation, glorification des forces premières de la nature '. Although the work is performed without a break, the four, titled sub-sections reinforce the primeval, ritualistic associations: 'Astres – lumière et nuit' (Stars – light and night), 'Le feu – la terre' (Fire and earth), 'Les moissons et les arbres' (Harvests and trees), 'L'air et l'eau – le silence et l'absence' (Air and water – silence and absence). *T'Harân-Ngô* includes many references to *The Rite of Spring*, these being achieved in a variety of ways: through the primordial subject matter itself; the size and treatment of the orchestra; the paraphrase of certain melodic fragments and superimposition of ostinati recalling Stravinskian processes. Composed five years later, *Livre des prodiges* includes similar allusions but takes the process further; intended as a commentary on *The Rite of Spring*, its bi-partite structure is borrowed directly from Stravinsky. Ohana's textual allusions are subtly woven into the substance of his musical material and function according to the parameters of his own language (cf. Chapter 5). Without succumbing to the dangers of mere collage, it is a process of allusion not unlike that found in certain works of Varèse and Berio. There are other aspects of Ohana's mature and late works which reveal an affinity with the ritualistic aspects of Stravinsky; most notably in *Signes*, the first tale of the *Trois contes*, the *Piano Concerto*, the *Etudes d'interprétation* and *Kypris*, all of which either include quotation or paraphrase distinctive melodies from *The Rite of Spring*. Although none of the quotations or parodies are indicated in the score, their recognition depending on the listener's familiarity with Stravinsky's score, they signal the importance of Stravinsky's influence for Ohana, one which he rarely indicated publicly.

Ohana was drawn to Stravinsky not only for technical, compositional reasons (he kept a number of Stravinsky's scores permanently beside his piano at his Paris flat, including *The Rite of Spring*, *Les Noces* and *Symphony of Psalms*) but in Stravinsky, Ohana discovered many preoccupations similar to his own. Drawing on his experiences of African music, north and south of the Sahara, Ohana consciously sought to rekindle the energy of tribal ritual. In some works he alluded to *The Rite of Spring* while in others he incorporated rhythmic procedures derived from African drumming (cf. Chapter 7). Ohana signalled his evocations of African, or Afro-Cuban ritual in certain esoteric titles, some of which are derived from African words.[42] Such work or movement titles usually incorporate the suffix 'ngô'. This serves as a verbal clue to the presence of material intended to create the atmosphere of ritual incantation and primitive ceremonial: *T'Harân-Ngô, Sorôn-Ngô, Koro-Ngô, Son Changó, Farân-Ngô, Iya-Ngô*. The last four examples occur in *Livre des prodiges, Office des oracles*, the Second String Quartet and *Avoaha*, respectively. Ohana's Third String Quartet bears the sub-title *Sorgin-ngô*. The 'ngô' suffix appears in many African languages and is similar to the Swahili 'ngu', as in 'mungu' meaning Allah, or God.[43]

> The suffix 'ngô' is found in a certain number of words describing dances of African origin and sometimes also in the name of instruments accompanying these dances. Such examples, in popular Andalusian art, are Tango, Zorongo, Fandango, likewise the Bongo, an instrument often used in our percussion. The ideophone 'ngô' seems, furthermore, to characterise incantatory dances which come from ancient tribal ceremonies.[44]

The connection of the 'ngô' suffix with God has an intriguing parallel in Spanish folk culture. Performers of the traditional, Andalusian flamenco are often heard to proclaim 'Olé' at moments when the music or dance has achieved a special magic. According to superstition this exclamation is made as a form of blessing; Olé is derived from Allah. In evoking the name of God, the performers protect themselves from supernatural spirits, or 'Duende', who have been summoned by the magic of the performance (cf. Chapter 3). Performers and observers can often be seen to cross themselves at these points.

A constant source of inspiration for Ohana was the internationalism of his cultural background. His Andalusian heritage, discussed in his study of Spanish music 'Géographie musicale de l'Espagne', itself represents a melting-pot of many diverse races and cultures.[45] While these may appear disconnected from the Anglo-Saxon perspective they are closely related in an Iberian context. Spanish and black African cultures further cross-fertilised as a result of myriad transatlantic migrations. In the South Americas, they blended not only with each other but also with the indigenous populations. These cross-currents are central to understanding the relationship between Spanish, black African, South American and French musical traditions. Through his friendship with the writer Alejo Carpentier Ohana was able to learn much about Cuban music which involves a particularly fertile blend of these rich musical traditions. (Carpentier embarked on extensive study of Cuban music and ritual for his early Magic-Realist novel of 1933, *¡Ecué-Yamba-O!*, and also published a history of Cuban music.[46]) Afro-Cuban rhythms became an important feature of Ohana's musical vocabulary from the middle 1960s onwards.

Ohana's fascination for the blending of African and Spanish musical traditions found in the New World of South America is revealed in the operas *Autodafé* and *La Célestine*. It culminated in his last completed work *Avoaha*. Here Ohana brought together these most important strands of his creative world in the celebration of what he described in the preface to the score as an imaginary, syncretic rite. This work aims to synthesise not only these diverse musical traditions but also their respective mythological beliefs and attendant, ritual ceremonial. The movement titles are clues to their cultural origin and are explained in the composer's preface to the score. 'Iya-Ngô', of Afro-Cuban origin, calls together participants of the ceremonial in the opening movement, while 'Igvodou' is the name of a sacrificial rite of the West Indies. Deities of Afro-Cuban origin are described in the third and fifth movements; the blue Goddess of the sea 'Yemaya' and the Universal Mother 'Iya', are equated through text in English with the black Virgin Mother. Various un-named, primeval deities are invoked in the eighth movement 'Aux Dieux de la Foudre et du Vent', in praise of the Gods of Thunder and Wind. A black God of Love is celebrated in the sixth movement 'Eros noir' which is described as an 'Alleluya' and incorporates rhythms of the South American Rumba (cf. Ex. 7.1b). The plight of the slaves imported from Africa by the Spanish is remembered in the fourth movement 'Refrain d'esclaves' and an eulogy to their heroes and ancestors is the subject for the tenth movement 'Eloge des héros et des ancêtres'. The eleventh movement, 'Tiger Moon', includes melodies paraphrasing Negro spiritual songs which are also found in the fifth and twelfth movements. The text of many movements invokes the African God Changó who is associated with the mythical, sacred forest of western Africa, as well as with wind and thunder. The ninth movement, 'Imprécations au Dieu Changó sourd aux sortilèges', is intended as the principal obsecration to the God. The work as a whole includes many African words, Ohana's preface indicating Bantu, Dahoman and Yoruba as languages which can be found in the text. Neither the meaning of these words nor their precise location are revealed due to their sacred character, a condition of the ethnologist who made them known to the composer. Like many earlier works of Ohana's, *Avoaha* is a polyglot work including not only African languages but English (used in the several Gospel and Negro spiritual melodies), an old form of Spanish and, in the seventh movement, Seneca's prophecy of the discovery of the New World is set in its original Latin. While musical elements of Spanish popular music are subtly embedded throughout the score, the Iberian apogee occurs in the final movement which refers to the mythical 'El Dorado'. The European fantasy of another Eden or Paradise-world, fecund, inhabited by noble savages and overflowing in gold and unimaginable riches, is here described in an imaginary report to Queen Isabella. The clue to Ohana's musical internationalism is given in a quotation from the French ethnologist and anthropologist, J. Mauss which heads the preface to Ohana's score: 'European music, however great, is only one music. It is not all music.'

Like *T'Harân-Ngô* and *Livre des prodiges*, *Avoaha* is ritualistic and includes evocations of primitive ceremonial. In some works where such evocations either

SYMBOLISM AND ALLEGORY   49

dominate the main argument of the work as a whole, as in *T'Harân-Ngô*, or where there is some special, personal significance, Ohana sketched images associated with the ritual or the ceremonial concerned in the manuscript. At the end of *T'Harân-Ngô* he drew the sun-burst as prime source of all life, the tree-symbol decked with birds, a stick of wheat representing fecundity, primitive man dancing under storm-clouds and added his 'nox et dies sum' signature (see Ex. 2.4a and Ex. 2.3b). The *Etudes d'interprétation* include more complex drawings in the manuscript: 'Mouvements parallèles' depicts a tribal dance accompanied by drums, surrounded by the sacred elements of nature, sun, fire and water (see Ex. 2.4b); 'Main gauche seule', shows primitive man and his animals at the mercy of nature, the elements in their most un-benign form as a raging tempest (see Ex. 2.4c). Both these *Etudes* incorporate African and Afro-Cuban rhythms as does *T'Harân-Ngô*. In contrast, the fifth of the *Etudes d'interprétations*, 'Quintes', is calm and reflective; the frenzy of primitive man's ceremonial over and nature at peace, Ohana illustrates two, mythical centaurs courting by the light of the all-seeing moon (see Ex. 2.4d).

Ex. 2.4: Sketches at the end of selected manuscript scores

a) *T'Harân-Ngô*

Ex. 2.4 (*continued*)
b) 'Mouvements parallèles', *Etudes d'interprétation* (I)

c) 'Main gauche seule' *Etudes d'interprétation* (I)

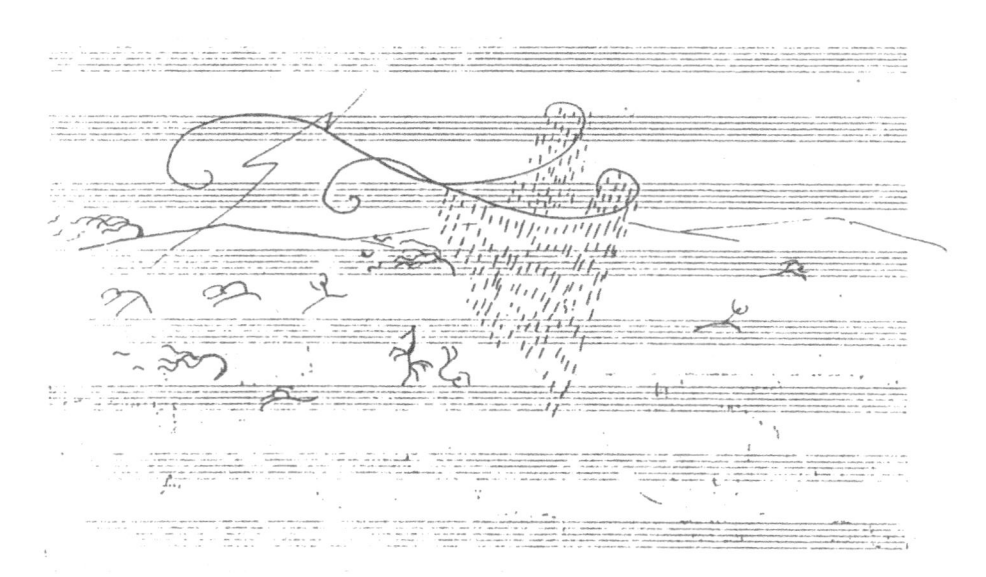

d) 'Quintes', *Etudes d'interprétation* (I)

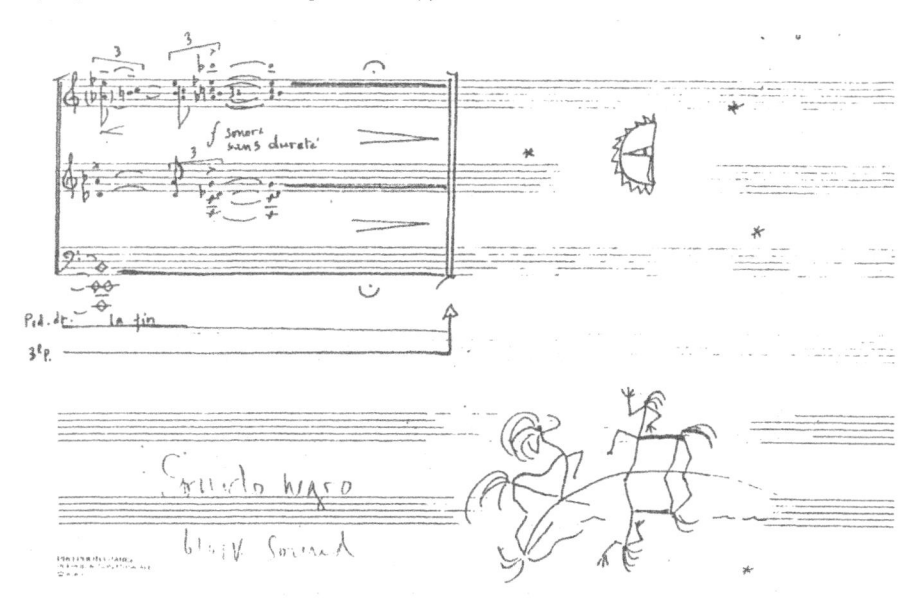

Reproduced by kind permission of Société des Editions Jobert, Paris / United Music Publishers Ltd.

All the images are archetypal in their associations. The extension of these images into a music which aims to recreate the energy of primitive man's ritual was, for Ohana, a logical development. Other objects also were given special properties. Even stones became fetishes imbued with primitive powers and associated with sacred rites in many ancient tribes. It is not insignificant that, when away from Paris, Ohana chose to live at Carnac on the Atlantic coast of Brittany; given that he was steeped in ancient mythology he could not have been unaware of the well-known Druid stones only a few kilometres away. Ohana's researches into the mythology of his own cultural heritage led him towards a rediscovery of ancient symbols whose potency for modern man has either been forgotten or pushed aside into unconscious memory. Primitive man has been described by C.G. Jung as being more aware of the power and energy of these archetypal images than modern man whose reliance on mythological belief has been more or less dissolved by his cultural civilisation:

> We [modern man] have learned to discard the trimmings of fantasy both in our language and in our thoughts, thus losing a quality that is still characteristic of the primitive mind. Most of us have assigned to the unconscious all the fantastic, psychic associations that every object or idea possesses. The primitive on the other hand, is still aware of these psychic properties; he endows animals, plants or stones with powers that we find strange and unacceptable ... . It is exactly this halo of unconscious association that gives a colourful and fantastic aspect to this primitive's world.[47]

In making recourse to images rich in such association, however diverse, Ohana in effect drew on what Freud called the 'archaic remnants' of the human mind, and Jung 'collective images', or 'archetypes'.

> Just as the human body represents a whole museum of organs, each with a long evolutionary history behind it, so we should expect to find that the mind is organised in a similar way ... the experienced investigator of the mind can see the analogies between the dream pictures of modern man and the products of the primitive mind, its collective images and its mythological motifs ... fantasies and symbolic images – these are what I call the archetypes ... archetypal symbols arise from the psyche's age-old collective basis ... and are without known origin, they reproduce themselves in any time or any part of the world.[48]

Through creating a network of allusive symbolism in his mature and late works, Ohana drew continually on these spontaneous images in his music. Drawing attention to what he described as his 'immemorial memory' in an interview, Ohana would seem to have acknowledged the existence of such archetypes, or archaic remnants.

> A very important element for me is memory, an immemorial memory. It is a memory that ... engages with a certain type of imagination. I am also convinced to have lived in extremely distant epochs. Understand who can, in any case I do not understand.[49]

Ohana's 'immemorial memory' may also be a cultural memory. He drew freely on images and symbols interrelated through a common, cultural background and cross-migrations of peoples. These allusions embraced his Spanish as well as African heritage, in addition to other cultures associated historically with these regions. He considered his attraction to jazz, appearing most markedly in works from the 1970s onwards, to belong to the same cultural continuum and therefore a natural extension of his incorporation of Spanish, African and Afro-Cuban elements into his music. For Ohana this was not mere eclecticism. His attraction to Japanese and Chinese oriental cultures could, however, be seen to be more simply eclectic, although in much of their theatre he recognised the spontaneous appearance of similar archetypes already familiar to him. This latter association is explored chiefly in *Trois contes de l'Honorable Fleur*.

Contemplation of his cultural roots, his Spanish origins and upbringing in north Africa, led Ohana towards these particular geographical regions for the source of much of his later attendant symbolism. The location of his birthplace had, for Ohana, a convenient mythological resonance which he liked to emphasise in explaining his cultural origins. Avoiding the bureaucratic complications of his quasi-expatriate status he preferred to associated his origins with the explanations of Classical mythology (cf. Chapter 1). Born in what was to the ancients the 'balcony of Europe', Ohana cited as his place of origin the Garden of the Hesperides, where the goddess Hera was reputed to have kept her famous trees bearing golden apples, guarded by the Dragon Ladon. This region is also associated with the legends of Hercules who temporarily relieved Atlas from his burden of the heavens and later slew not only the dragon but the mythical three-headed King of Spain, Geryon. In this context, Ohana's cultural complexity ceases to be an obstacle to approaching his music but becomes an important key to its understanding. His life-long preoccupation with subjects from Classical mythology, spawned by the location of his birth place, sustained his creative impetus throughout his compositional career. Such allusions could be interpreted as his quest for an 'immemorial' and cultural memory.

In Ohana's mature and late works, this mythical garden becomes equated with the ancient dream of a Golden Age or Paradise. In the last movement of his last work it becomes 'El Dorado'. The garden is both the primeval forest, analogous to that found in the paintings of the Douanier Rousseau, and a sort of Garden of Eden existing in an imagined Golden Age. It is here where Ohana's symbolism of opposites is reconciled. Another Paradise garden bathed in the symbolism of a Golden Age is the real Garden of Tamarit at Granada. Taking Lorca's last collection of poems *Diván del Tamarit* as a starting point, the first cello concerto *Anneau du Tamarit* is set against a background of Arcadian allegory. According to Ohana's preface to the score, the Garden of Tamarit becomes 'a universe in a solitary dream reaching the shores of the eternal presence'. Through the poetry on which it is based, the work suggests an imagined world of peace and plenty where peoples of different cultures and beliefs lived harmoniously. In a highly unconventional view of Spanish history, Ohana considered the period before the Fall of Granada the true utopia where Jews, Christians and Arabs could live together without fear or persecution in a civilised society of exemplary learning. The more conventional view is to consider the Golden Age of Spain to be the period of world domination after the Fall of Granada.

> It was a prodigious time when the Arabs, having invaded Spain, created a synthesis of refined and fertile civilisations. We owe them much: gardens and fruit, architecture, trigonometry and algebra, the third and quarter tones, poetry, court music and philosophy. A period of civilisation of exemplary tolerance was destroyed by the Catholic Kings ... .[50]

Ohana's nature symbolism belongs to this same imaginary perfect world, as do the pagan men and animals which populate his primeval forest. The Golden Age, for him, was the ancient pagan world, energised by the vitality of its ritual practices. Ohana's most enduring imagined Paradise was that of Arcadian perfection exemplified by Classical mythology. A large number of his works are freely based on, or allude to Classical legends. Others are intended as portraits of certain characters, heroes, gods or even monsters drawn from these myths. Some works, not surprisingly aim to recreate the atmosphere of ancient rites, such as those associated with Cybele or Bacchus, while others are, more simply, intended to evoke the peace and tranquillity of Arcadian landscapes through instrumental association and allusive titles. It has already been shown how Ohana's instinctive attraction to mythological subjects was beginning to emerge in his early period. His first important works based on mythological subjects did not appear until the middle 1960s in the works of his Sigma Series. Again these legends embody collective symbols that have not been consciously invented but are archetypes originating in the immemorial memory, or archaic remnants of the psyche.

Table 2.2 lists Ohana's works based on mythological subjects or including references to mythical characters or themes. It should be noted that all but one of the Sigma Series are based on mythical subjects. Starting in 1960 there is some overlap with Table 2.1 in order to show the development of this preoccupation following the period of refinement which took place during the early 1960s. During a period of more than thirty years it can be seen how Ohana's fascination with these subjects was almost continuous. While the majority of subjects are drawn from Classical mythology, a few of the works listed include references to legends of a wider ethnological origin. Myths associated with creation or the worship of nature can be traced in Classical legends and are also associated with the rites of many primitive societies in Africa and South America. References to non-classical, cosmogonic myths have been included.

Table 2.2: Mythological allusions in Ohana's works from 1960 to 1991

Date	Title	Description	Mythological allusion
1960	4 Improvisations	flute	Pan/Syrinx myth
			Arcadian landscape
1962	Tombeau de Claude Debussy	sop. pno., zither, orch	
	'Soleils'		Sun mythologies
	'Autres soleils'		Sun mythologies
1963	Cinq séquences	string quartet	
	'Monodie'		Classical lament
	'Tympanum'		Rites of Cybele
	'Hymne'		Sacred ode 'imnos'
1963	Hélène	incidental music	Euripides' play
1964	Si le jour paraît...	10-string guitar	
	'Maya-Marsya'		Ovid, Aztec myth
	'La Chevelure de Bérénice'		Classical myth – Berenice
	'Jeu des quatre vents'		Nature worship
1964	Les Héraclides	incidental music	Euripides' play
1965	Iphigénie en Tauride	incidental music	Euripides' play
1965	Neumes	oboe and piano	Aulos, Arcadian landscape
1965	Signes	instr. ensemble	
	'alive with birds'	flute	Pan / Syrinx myth
	'drowned with rain'	percussion	Nature worship
	'imprisoned in gossamer'	zither	Kithara – Greek music
	'beaten by the wind'	piano	Wind mythologies
	'burnt by the sun'	tutti	Sun mythologies
1966	Synaxis	2 pianos, perc, orch	
	'Diaphonie'		Ancient Greek music
	'Tympanum'		Rites of Cybele
	'Sibile' [sic]		Sibylline myth
	'Maya'		South American Aztec myth
1966	Hippolyte	incidental music	Euripides' play

Date	Title	Description	Mythological allusion
1967	*Syllabaire pour Phèdre*	chamber opera	Euripides
		Soprano	Sibylline myth
		Form: Greek Tragedy	Parados, Stasimon, etc.
1968	*Chiffres de clavecin*	hpchd, orch	
	'Etoiles – Nuées'		Nature worship
1968	*Sibylle*	soprano, perc, tape	Sibylline myth
1969	*Silenciaire*	perc. and strings	Cosmogonic myth
1970	*Sorôn-Ngô*	2 pianos	Nature worship
1970	*Syrtes*	cello and piano	Syrtós: ancient Greek dance
1971	*Autodafé*	chamber opera	(Includes mythical animals)
		Form: Greek tragedy	
	'Saturnale interrompue'		Bacchanal
	'Mayas'		South American Aztec myth
1972	*Sarc*	oboe	Aulos, Arcadian landscape
1974	*T'Harân-Ngô*	orchestra	Taranis: Celtic Thunder God
			Cosmogonic myth
			Ritual nature worship
1974	*Offices des oracles*	Music-theatre	
	'Dragon à trois têtes'		Monsters: Hydra, Cerberus etc.
	'Minotaure aux miroirs'		Minotaur – labyrinth myth
	'Son Changó'		African God of the forest
	'Pythié'		Pythia Priestesse of Dephi
1975	*Sacral d'Ilx*	hpschd, oboe, horn	Arcadian landscape
1976	*Anneau du Tamarit*	cello and orchestra	Arcadian landscape
1976	*Satyres*	2 flutes	Pan/Syrinx myth
1976	*Lys de madrigaux*	female chorus	
	'Calypso'		Odysseus: nymph of Ogygia
	'Circé'		Odysseus: witch of Aeaea
	'Parques'		Parcae – The Fates
	'Tropique de la Vièrge'		Sibylline myth/Virgin mother
	'Miroir de Sapho' [*sic.*]		Portrait of Poetess Sappho
1978	*Trois contes de l'Hon. Fleur*	music-theatre	Mythical animals
	'Prologue'	Moon personification	Moon mythologies
	'Ogre mangeant des jeunes ...'		Ogre myth reversed
	'Vent d'Est enfermé ...'	Personifications of Nature	Wind mythologies
	'La Pluie remontée au Ciel'	Personifications of Nature	Death & Resurrection
1979	*Livre des prodiges*	orchestra	Cosmogonic myth
	'Cortège des taureaux ailés'		Andalusian mythical animals
	'Hydre'		Monsters
	'Conjuration des sorts'		The Fates
	'Soleil renversé'		Cosmogonic myth
	'Alecto'		The Furies
1980	Second String Quartet	–	
	'Sagittaire'		Cheiron myth
1982	*Cadran lunaire*	10 string guitar	Moon mythologies
	'Saturnal'		Roman Festival of Saturn
	'Sylva'		God of Woods (Faunus / Pan)
	'Candil '		Sun mythologies

Table 2.2 (*concluded*)

Date	Title	Description	Mythological Allusion
1982	Etudes d'Interprétation (I)	piano	
	'Mouvements parallèles'		Ritual nature worship
	'Main gauche seule'		Ritual nature worship
	'Quintes'		Arcadian landscape
1985	Kypris	instr. ensmble	Goddess of Love (Crete)
1987	La Célestine	opera	
	Characters incorporated:		Sibyl, Fates, Furies, Pluto, Pan, various mythical monsters, witches, Arcadian myth –Arcadia destroyed
1987	Quatre choeurs	Children's choir	
	'Nuées'		Nature worship
1988	Lux noctis-Dies solis	4 choral groups	Sun & Moon mythologies Hymn to Love References include – Hymen, Venus, Hesperus, Ariadne, Orion, Hair of Berenice
1989	Trois prophéties de la Sibylle	2 sops, pno, perc	Sibylline myth
1991	Avoaha	chorus, pnos, perc	African, Afro-Cuban & Spanish mythologies

The years spent in writing incidental music for the Euripides' plays gave Ohana the opportunity of becoming familiar with the structure and forms of Greek tragedy. This experience enhanced his developing interest in Classical mythology with a detailed, technical knowledge of their theatrical structure which he was subsequently able to incorporate into his own work. Such adaptations appear most strikingly in his chamber operas *Syllabaire pour Phèdre* and *Autodafé*, both of which are articulated according to the traditional divisions of Greek tragedy. Both works are enclosed by a Prologue and Epilogue with internal Episodes separated by Parados and Stasimon sections. A female, vocal soloist plays an important role in both works, acting as leader of the chorus, or Choryphée. Although Ohana adapts the function of this singer to his own dramatic ends, her conventional position in alternation with the chorus is preserved. The opera *La Célestine* also borrows certain Classical, theatrical conventions. The Sibyl and Parques remain outside the main action of the tragedy but comment upon it in a manner not unlike a Greek chorus. In this way they prevent too close an involvement with the main protagonists and keep the focus of attention on the destiny of tragedy rather than on individual characters. This function is further enhanced by the presence of a narrator who announces and explains the action before it takes place. A similar technique is employed by Stravinsky in *Oedipus Rex*.

In addition to associating a work or movement with a particular character or myth, Ohana evokes Classical, Arcadian landscapes through instrumental association. In several works, the flute and oboe are intended to suggest instruments of ancient Greece, the syrinx and aulos, respectively. While the syrinx is thought to have been a wind instrument played without a reed, the aulos is considered to have been a generic description for reeded wind instruments.[51] Such associations with the flute appear in the *Quatre improvisations*, *Signes* and *Satyres*, while similar allusions using the oboe occur in *Neumes*, *Sarc* and *Sacral d'Ilx*. The traditional incantations associated with magic and spell-weaving of the syrinx, particularly, are exploited by Ohana in works where the flute appears as a soloist. The works including the oboe as soloist are not only incantatory in melodic style, but their dramatic quality and greater intensity of expression may, in turn, be intended to suggest the great laments with which the aulos is reputed to have been traditionally associated.[52] A more enigmatic instrumental allusion is associated with one of Ohana's favoured solo instruments, the zither which, in some contexts, can be taken to suggest the Greek kithara.

Most of Ohana's works indicate their mythical references either directly through their titles or, in dramatic works, through the inclusion of particular characters. (This applies to movement titles as well as to entire works.) Other works create an aura of Classical allusion more indirectly as in *Anneau du Tamarit* or *Sacral'd'Ilx*. The latter combines its ritualistic mood with a reference to the area of Elche in southern Spain, known in ancient times as 'Ilx'. In the late nineteenth century a pre-roman bust of a young woman, the 'Lady of Elche' was discovered there. Ohana's use of the original place name helps evoke the atmosphere of an ancient, perhaps forgotten world populated with pagan peoples and fantastic animals. The first string quartet *Cinq séquences* has already been shown to incorporate different layers of allusion (the Goyesque undertones of the fourth movement have been discussed earlier). Its title is quite abstract and functional, indicating the succession of the five movements. Although the main compositional focus for the work centres on the adaptation of techniques derived from plainchant and early polyphony, some of the movement sub-titles also refer to features of ancient Greek music. The second movement, 'Monodie' evokes both a classical lament, or 'threnody', as well as the monody of plainsong. The third movement, 'Tympanum', suggests the ancient percussion instrument (a hand-drum without jingles) used reputedly in the rites of Cybele and Dionysus, as well as the medieval dulcimer, or psaltery. The final, fifth movement, 'Hymne', suggests the sacred ode or 'imnos' addressed to a God or Hero.[53] 'Tympanum' is a movement title which is also to be found in *Synaxis* which, like *Cinq séquences* composed three years earlier, explores compositional techniques of the early medieval period. In both works 'Tympanum' denotes a music of frenetic and percussive character and has much in common with Ohana's ritual music designated by the 'ngô' suffix.

Other work titles make more general Classical allusion. *Neumes*, for oboe and piano, is taken from the Greek 'pneuma' and refers not only to the notation of plainchant, but to the breath by which it is thought the player of the aulos (or other wind instrument) could modify the pitch. *Synaxis* means literally 'concentration', 'meeting' or 'collection' and is described by Ohana in the preface to his score as 'the name given to a primitive liturgy of the second century.' *Synaxis* itself contains among its movements 'Diaphonie' from the Greek 'diaphonia' meaning discord, or the refusal of two sounds to combine or unite, so grating on the ear. Its third movement, 'Sibile' (later corrected to 'Sibylle' by the composer) is a reference to the prophetic woman of classical mythology. *Syrtes* for cello and piano, is derived from the Greek 'syrtós', a dance-form found in the north African realms of the Greek empire, as well as the Greek mainland. *Satyres* for two flutes, is a celebration of sensuality. While the instruments themselves and their incantatory material evoke the magical powers of Pan's syrinx, the title suggests the work to be a portrait of his cloven-footed, horned and tailed cousins and their Bacchanalian woodland antics. Through such exotic allusions, Ohana places his music in a setting outside our own time and experience, and opens a window to his supernatural world of pagan mythology.

In a number of Ohana's mythologically allusive works, certain characters not only reappear in different guises but are central to his language of imagery. One of the most important of these recurrent figures is the Sibyl who was given the power of prophecy by Apollo. Although granted eternal life she forgets to ask for eternal youth and is condemned to the perpetual torment of ever increasing decrepitude without the escape of death. In Ohana, she makes her first tentative appearance in *Synaxis* but comes into full prominence in the work of her own name, *Sibylle*, for soprano, percussion and electronic tape. There are many legends associated with the Sibyl, but in Ohana she appears as the mystical prophetess who, despite her great gifts, is profoundly tragic. In Ohana, the vocal music associated with her is always composed for a female voice. Characterised by an intensity of expression, it represents some of his most personal declarations. The Sibyl appears by name only in one other work, the opera *La Célestine,* where she is represented by two sopranos whose vocalisations prophesy the unfolding tragedy of the lovers Calyx and Mélibée. (Ohana extracted the Sibyl's prophecies from the opera in an arrangement for concert performance by coloratura soprano, mezzo soprano, piano and percussion, cf. Ex. 5.1)[54]

The Sibylline character appears elsewhere in a variety of guises. In *Autodafé* she is equated with the Coryphée of Episode II 'Vitrail'. In *Lys de madrigaux*, for female chorus which is a commentary on the feminine anima, she appears three times: as the nymph Calypso; as the magic sorceress Circé; and as the tragic, lyric poetess Sappho. In *Office des oracles* she appears as 'Pythié', the priestess of Apollo's Oracle at Delphi (cf. Ex. 8.2). Due to the association of the Sibylline character with expressive, quasi-improvisatory vocalisations, she can be recognised musically in other works, although is un-named: in the third movement, 'Debla' of *Cris*; in the solo sections for female voice of the Mass, 'Kyrie', 'Agnus Dei' and 'Trope'; and in the anonymous coloratura soprano role of *Syllabaire pour Phèdre*. The female voice had for Ohana a special association with his most personal expression. In this context, it should be noted that the composer's own Epitaph, the third movement of *Swan Song*, gives prominence to the soprano, and the final section of his last work *Avoaha* concludes with an unaccompanied mezzo soprano describing the 'crazy, forgotten land of promised joy', 'El Dorado'. It is also interesting to observe that Ohana once equated the flamenco singer *La Niña de los Peines* with his tragic Sibyl. In so doing, he revealed many other symbolic images, linking the Classical character with the out-pourings of personal grief, quintessential of the Andalusian Cante Jondo.

> La Niña! ... who emanates a calm and strangely luminous power. When she intones her song, night and day are illuminated together ... . Taking one by surprise there is the black sound, deep and irradiating ... and *duende*. Lorca has compared her to ... the darkness of Goya ... . Both Pythie and Sibylle, ancient one who weeps or dangerous priestess, greeting the balcony of heaven, this apparition of divine-woman ends her worship in a melodic line of a single thread in one whole sob.[55]

While associated primarily with the female voice, Ohana's 'Sibylline' qualities are not exclusive to the vocal music. The vocal characteristics and expressive lyricism of Ohana's Sibyl are translated into an instrumental medium in *Kypris* whose inspirational source is related to the female anima. In the composer's programme notes for the first performance of this work, Ohana describes *Kypris* as 'a nocturnal poem to the Cretan and Cypriot Goddess of Love'.[56]

Other more ominous figures of classical mythology to reappear in Ohana's scores include the three Fates who determined the destiny of men by spinning, weaving and cutting the thread of life. Under their French name *Parques*, they appear in *Lys de madrigaux* and the opera *La Célestine*. In both works they are musically characterised by a distinctive and rhythmically decisive, repetitive homophony which, in the opera, assumes the role of a quasi fate motif (see Ex. 2.5). A female chorus representing the Fates enters the stage at each point in the action where the web of destiny draws tighter about the lovers Calyx and Mélibée. The rhythmic ostinato of the Fates, described in the score as 'the measuring of Time', pulls the tragedy inexorably to its fatal conclusion.

Ex. 2.5: 'The Measuring of Time', *La Célestine*, refrain of the Parques, 'Le jardin des délices' (reduction, fig. 58)

© 1993 Gérard Billaudot Editeur S.A. Paris. Reproduced by kind permission.

There are other allusions to supernatural powers able to affect the fate of men. The three avenging Furies, perhaps the most feared goddesses of classical mythology dreaded by gods and men, appear briefly in *Autodafé*. Both *Livre des prodiges* and *La Célestine* contain invocations to 'evil spirits of darkness' in their respective 'Conjuration des Sorts'. In *Livre* this invocation is followed by the appearance of the Fury named 'Alecto' from the depths of Tartarus, said to be as far below Hades as Heaven was above the earth. Her presence, following the calling on powers of evil, is one of the supernatural 'wonders' suggested by the title, *Livre des prodiges*. Ohana's preoccupation with supernatural deities is developed further in *La Célestine*. In order to fulfil her promise to Calyx, the witch Celestine evokes the powers of darkness in a call to evil spirits, not unlike that of the witches in *Macbeth*. (The Shakespearean reference is reinforced elsewhere in the opera.) As a result of her magic, Pluto the King of Hades, appears and the lovers Calyx and Mélibée consummate their passion in a 'Night in the Garden of Delights'. With such match-makers at work, the lovers' fate could only be tragic!

Mythological persons are not the only characters who make their appearance in Ohana's scores. Mythical animals, particularly monsters, are also subjects for musical portraits. The associations of the Pan-Syrinx myths of the *Quatre improvisations* and *Satyres* have already been mentioned, as has the same nocturnal, cloven-footed god evoked in 'Sylva', the third movement of *Cadran lunaire*. Sylvanus, reputed by some to be the son of Saturn, by others the son of Faunus, was closely associated with Pan and believed by the Romans to be the god of fields and forests, promoting the fertility of all nature.[57] *Offices des oracles* contains several references to mythical creatures of varying types. A three-headed dragon is portrayed in the third movement, the three heads being depicted by the three independent layers of aleatory counterpoint in the three instrumental groups into which the ensemble is divided. The Cretan minotaur makes an appearance in the fifth movement 'Minotaure au miroirs', its actual presence in the labyrinth being represented musically by the introduction of a cantus firmus on trumpets and trombones, and visually by the drawing of a bull's head in the score. The bull image appears in other works. The minotaur appears again in the fourth Episode of *Autodafé,* although here it is one of many monsters and tyrants of history which, at the end of the work, are finally destroyed in a purifying immolation. (*Autodafe* was the sentence of execution by fire, administered on heretics by the Spanish Inquisition.) In *Livre des prodiges* a procession of winged bulls, 'Cortège des Taureaux ailés' is represented at the opening, while a hydra is depicted in the fourth movement. The hydra appears again, together with another winged bull in *Trois contes de l'Honorable Fleur*. A symbol of man's animal persona, the bull is an archetypal image of virility, recurring in the myths and religions of many ancient Mediterranean cultures. It still persists most potently in the Iberian peninsula, where the ritual slaughter of the bull-fight approaches a form of worship.[58] As in the ancient rites of Dionysus and Mithras, the bull is a creature condemned by its hidden symbolism to eternal sacrifice.

The presence of mythological allusion in both subject and character represents a form of allegorical symbolism which generates much of Ohana's mature and late work. This, however, is not the only way in which his allegory is manifest.

There are some notable instances where allegory is central to the argument and subject matter of a work. The three most striking examples all intended for dramatic production, *Autodafé*, *Office des oracles* and *Trois contes de l'Honorable Fleur*, present contrasting discourses on the archetypal problems of the human condition. All three works are examples of Ohana's playful, tongue-in-cheek humour. Through a series of satirical episodes depicting various dictators of history and man's oppression through combinations of tyranny and intolerance, *Autodafé* is intended as an allegory of the twentieth century. Through the course of history, Ohana aims to show that the human race has learned nothing from its mistakes and that, as a result, the modern world, devastated by two world wars is in a state of profound, cultural decay. At the end of the opera, Ohana asserts his own will over the centuries of human oppressors; in the 'Epilogue' we are shown that the various monsters and tyrants of the preceding 'Episodes' are nothing but huge puppets and childish toys. They are thrown into the air and destroyed in the inferno of the autodafé. In the tradition of all great comedy, the humour of Ohana's score serves to underline the more serious moral. Over the flames of the fire, a narrator intones, in English, lines from a Shakespeare sonnet: 'So shalt thou feed on Death, that feeds on men, And Death once dead, there's no more dying then.'[59]

Completed three years after *Autodafé*, *Office des oracles* is less bitter in its satire. For three choral groups and orchestra, with mimes and dancers, *Offices* was originally intended as music-theatre. In the manner of a pseudo-liturgy, the ten main movements pose the same question to ten different 'oracles' (the first and twelfth serve as a prologue and epilogue). While remaining implicit, the question demands clarification of the direction, purpose and meaning, if any, of musical art. The work is an allegory of the compositional problems of contemporary music. The composer consults oracles from 'Alpha' to 'Omega' and although his question is serious, the oracles, as might be expected, answer only in riddles, some of which are more comic than solemn. After a short introduction the composer consults the oracle of his own dreams in the second movement, 'Oniracle' (a title which compresses 'onirique' and 'oracle') but quickly passes on to address two mythical monsters, a dragon and a minotaur. Instead of inspiring fear, the three-headed dragon of the third movement is made to look merely ridiculous, producing mocking laughter (in the choral groups) through the uncoordinated movement of its heads (achieved musically through superimposition of layers of aleatory counterpoint). Similarly the minotaur of the fourth movement is unable to produce an answer, remaining trapped in its labyrinthine, Cretan prison. In the fifth movement, 'Son Changó', the composer seeks a solution from the African god Changó whose forest is reputed to possess magical attributes; the replying riddle suggests that ritual and magic may provide a possible answer. Still inconclusive, the composer wonders, in 'Météoracle', if a weather forecast might enlighten him, but the oracle of the sixth movement warns only of an approaching storm. In 'Tarots' the seventh movement, he consults gypsies to seek his future and compositional fortune in the cards, but to no avail.

The following movements suggest a more cynical criticism of the paths found by other composers. In a playful jibe at Messiaen, the eighth movement 'Interrogation aux oiseaux' parodies bird-song, not a feature of Ohana's own language. He may well be questioning the validity of such paraphrases as the way forward for musical composition. Another unusual technical procedure, an open aleatory form, is used in the ninth movement 'Ecriture automatique' which merely caricatures the process. Alluding to the divination technique of automatic writing, the movement comprises several blocks of material which can be performed in any order or freely superimposed; the blocks include a section satirising Tartini's famous 'Devil's Trill' sonata and the tenth movement 'Oroscope' which borrows text from the horoscopes of a French tabloid newspaper. Passing from oracle to oracle only the penultimate movement reveals the closest suggestion of a solution to the perennial problem of composers. In more serious vein, the eleventh movement referring to 'Pythié', Apollo's priestess at the oracle of Delphi, contains a lyrical, Sibylline solo for female voice (cf. Ex. 8.2). This is the spiritual heart of the work and the end of the composer's quest. The oracle of the God of the Muses has presented an answer to the question in the expressive lyricism of the human voice; a positive and humane future for musical expression is offered which the composer, through the movement's position at the end of the work, appears to accept. Matching 'Alpha' as a prologue, 'Omega' is a contemplative epilogue in which more than thirty chant-like melodic fragments are superimposed in a web of pianissimo aleatory counterpoint.

Perhaps the most enigmatic of Ohana's allegorical works is *Trois contes de l'Honorable Fleur*. Music-theatre for soprano and ensemble, based on three fairy-tales by the composer (libretto by his second wife Odile Marcel), this work consciously aims to translate the magical and symbolic world of the painter, le 'Douanier' Rousseau into musical terms and combine it with the ritual, simplicity of the Japanese Noh. Ohana explained that as a result of being given a volume of Japanese poetry by a student, he was at once drawn to consider imagery in the manner of Rousseau: 'where the mysterious and supernatural blur together with magic and where a universe of allegory is reduced to its most simple expression.'[60] The same student also informed Ohana that his name transliterates phonetically to mean 'honorable flower' in Japanese, hence the composer's playful choice of title.

The three humorous fairy-tales make use of familiar images which are subtly reworked to produce an unexpected twist in the anticipated symbolism. The first tale concerns an evil ogre, son of an ogress and a dragon, who eats young girls caught out at dusk. A young girl duly arrives (soprano), leading a goat, but is not only disbelieving of the ogre's existence, which she supposes to be 'une légende de vieille femme', but is far from being afraid when confronted by the monster. In the manner of a composite Jack-and-the-Beanstalk and Red-Riding-Hood, she admires the ogre's sharp teeth and impressive size. She tricks him into dancing with her, certainly not the personification of innocence, and having flattered him into a vulnerable position, cuts his throat with a knife. Rather than representing the conventional figure of purity who, through her honest courage, cleanses the world of a manifestation of evil, the young girl herself becomes wicked and becomes transformed into an ogress, assuming the evil role of terrorising late-night passers-by. A succession of quotations from Stravinsky's *Rite of Spring* underline the twist in the symbolism (cf. Chapter 5). Contrary to the victim in Stravinsky, this young girl is far from representing an innocent maiden sacrificed to a pagan god.

The imagery of the second tale is more complex and concerns the East and West winds as symbols of male, sexual desire. The East Wind (percussion) appears as an undisciplined, wild creature who teases and torments all with his playful advances, in particular one 'Honorable Lady' (soprano). Despite her rebukes, the East wind persists and she is compelled to call upon the Tribunal of the Gods to assist in the 'defence of her honour'. They provide a magic bag into which he is trapped. At once seeing the East Wind's sadness and recognising his repentance upon his imprisonment, the 'Honorable Lady' begs the Gods for their clemency. The East Wind is finally released but severely punished; he is condemned to inhabit distant regions of ice and snow. The West Wind, on the other hand, is portrayed as a warm wind, 'Lord of the Earth, Fire and Water' (instrumental ensemble). He recognises the 'Honorable Lady's attentions, seizes his opportunity now that his rival is banished, and cruelly seduces her. The Gods are seen to disapprove, but the Lady is willing. She exits with the West Wind. When the East Wind is allowed to return, his youthful playfulness gone and wearing his mantle of snow, he learns of his rejection. It turns out that his love was the greater and the purer.

Finally, the third tale concerns the archetypal Christian and pre-Christian Death and Resurrection symbolism. It portrays the destruction and restoration of the utopian dream of the Garden of Eden. Primeval earth is peaceful and verdant, abundant with life and nature. All is nourished by the rain (soprano). One day monkeys descend to the earth and destroy the trees and flowers by constructing a massive city. In so doing, they release the powers of evil (not unlike Pandora's box). The world is polluted and becomes populated by monsters. The rain, in the Sibylline personification of the soprano, laments the destruction of the earth and eventually disappears behind the Gates of Heaven for a thousand years. In the meantime drought takes hold and Eden is burnt into a desert by the 'Suns of death'. In the ensuing Apocalypse all life is destroyed. One thousand years later the rain decides to return and life is reborn, although this time the monkeys are captured and imprisoned in a cage by the noble eagles. An Epilogue describes the Arcadian, primeval forest restored with the beauty of flowers and trees, where tigers are free to roam. The symbolism of rain as restorative of human spirituality and salvation is a well-known archetype recalling the imagery not only of T.S. Eliot's *The Waste Land* but that of the mystical Fisher King who, in addition, has parallels in the character of Amfortas in the legends of the Holy Grail, and with Arkel in *Pelléas et Mélisande*.

As in the symbolic, dream paintings of Rousseau's late works, Ohana's fairy-tales are set in a mythological world, or primeval forest, existing in a timeless age of purity and innocence before history began. Certain images in *Trois contes* are specific in their relation to some of Rousseau's so-called jungle paintings: the primeval forest itself; the tiger and the monkey, as well as other mythical creatures; the exotic flowers suggesting an intoxicating perfume; the surveying sun or moon; and an overall sense of timelessness and magical enchantment. The moon in each of the tales assumes an important symbolic role; the only common character to each of the allegories, she (a spoken part for soprano) describes herself as 'illuminating the sleeping earth and knowing of all secrets of which the day is ignorant; of watching over the sleeping earth under the stars and seeing lovers stretched out in her shadow.' (The moon is also represented musically by a chorale on the piano, first heard in the 'prologue'.) Given the borrowings from the Japanese Noh which are incorporated into the structure and staging of this work, the personification of the moon would appear to suggest the Oriental Moon-goddess, Kwan-Yin. The composer dedicated *Trois contes* to the Japanese singer Michiko Hirayama, who gave the first performance and has recorded the work.

The characterisations of these allegorical tales are fully in keeping with the Japanese models upon which Ohana chose to base *Trois contes*. They include many features typical of Noh and other Japanese theatre plays: personifications of nature, references to agricultural ritual, and rain-seeking ceremonies. Whereas a traditional performance of the Noh would contain a Prologue followed by five tales, Ohana's work contains a Prologue followed by three. The music-theatre setting with its costumes, masks, puppets, shadow theatre and dances echoes Noh, Kabuki and Bunraku forms. Furthermore, narration by a female character is also in keeping with Japanese tradition, as is the incorporation of deities, monsters, animals and the blending of comic and serious elements. Ohana's choice of instrumentation aims, intentionally, to paraphrase traditional oriental sound-textures: the flute evokes the Bamboo flutes; the zither suggests the Koto and Shamisen; and as in Japanese theatre Ohana's percussion, subdivided into component metal, skin and wood sections, articulates the progress of the overall ritual.

Both the primeval forest of Rousseau and the mythical, pagan world of Ohana are manifestations of the human longing for a lost Garden of Eden. In what may be seen by some as a hugely optimistic view of the human condition, it is perhaps not without significance that both Rousseau and Ohana sought to restore their respective Arcadias in the late years of their lives. In the work of Rousseau, Ohana recognised the common desire to restore a spirituality to a crumbling and decadent epoch, through a conscious return to the collective, impersonal roots of the human imagination, where contradiction and impossibilities are dissolved. In this respect, Ohana's symbolic and allegorical language appears to have parallels with the 'Magic Realist' movement of contemporary South American literature. Although he rejected what he considered to be a somewhat ready label associated with this group of writers, of which Alejo Carpentier, Miguel Angel Asturias and Gabriel García Márquez are considered the vanguard, there are parallels which may be drawn.[61] Márquez *Cien años de solidad* is accepted as one of the leading examples of this symbolic and surreal style where circular time and magic are commonplace; the imaginary Colombian town of Macondo is an island enclosed by the primeval forest and the arrival of ice for the first time is recorded as prodigy. Ohana knew many South American, as well as Spanish writers including not only Carpentier but also Márquez whom he first met during the writer's first visit to Paris in the 1950s.[62]

The sum of Ohana's very personal use of symbolism and imagery may appear superficially to be luxuriant indulgence, or mere eclecticism. Such a view would represent a cruel oversimplification. Ohana justified, if a composer ever needs to justify, his instinctive responses to his particular form of enigmatic mysticism in the cultural background of his geographical and genealogical heritage. In this sense, as Cocteau said of poets in general, Ohana sought to 'sing in his genealogical tree'.[63] With the passing of the twentieth century, it may now be acceptable to consider eclecticism in a light far from negative, particularly since attraction to the exotic has more or less been a characteristic of the French creative mind for over one hundred years and Ohana, although not French by birth, was quite certainly French by education and adoption. The fascination with allegorical themes is not uncommon in much of the French literature and painting which has been so influential on the present century. To account for this would represent another study in its own right. Ohana's symbolism is not only akin to that of the painter Rousseau, as he pointed out himself, but also close to the apparently childish, but quite un-childlike, imagery of Albert Jarry's *Ubu Roi* and Antoine de Saint-Exupéry's *Petit Prince*. Indeed *Ubu Roi* is one of the tyrants portrayed in *Autodafé*. In keeping with the original aims of the Groupe Zodiaque, Ohana sought to lend his music a halo of numinoscity through allusion to archetypal symbols and images which, still in an age of apparent supreme rationality, have not altogether lost their psychic energy.

Notes to Chapter Two.

1 A selection of these themes have been examined in C. Rae, 'Le symbolisme et l'archétype du mythe européen dans l'oeuvre de Maurice Ohana', *Cahiers du CIREM*, Nos 24–25 'Musique et Europe', (Tours, 1993) pp. 115–30.
2 S. Jarocinski discusses the definition of symbol, as opposed to allegory in 'The Symbol in Art', *Debussy Impressionism and Symbolism*, Eng. trans. R. Myers (London, 1976) pp. 22–60.
3 Carpentier left Cuba for France in 1928 with the help of the poet Robert Desnos. (Carpentier's father was French.) Although he returned to Cuba in 1939, he finally settled permanently in Paris in the 1960s and remained there until his death in 1980.
4 Jolivet became acquainted with Carpentier through Varèse. Carpentier was a close friend of both Hilda and André Jolivet.
5 A. Jolivet, 'Réponse à une enquête', *Contrepoints* No. 1 (1946) p. 33 cited in S. Gut, *Le Groupe Jeune France* (Paris, 1984) p. 55.
6 One of the leading figures of the Magic-Realist movement, Asturias studied at the Sorbonne with Georges Raynaud in the 1930s. (Raynaud had already translated the *Popol Vuh* into French.) He returned to Paris in the 1960s and

was appointed Guatemalan Ambassador to Paris shortly before winning the Nobel Prize for literature in 1967.
7   These parallels have been explored in the following articles: C. Rae, 'Myth and Mysticism in Jolivet: Musical Magic Realism?', *Nation, Myth and Reality: Music in the 1930s* (forthcoming at the time of writing with CUP) and C. Rae, 'Magic and Music – Alejo Carpentier and Maurice Ohana: Cross-Connections in 20th Century French Music and the South Americas', *Des Amériques impressions et expressions* (Paris, 1999) pp. 222–30; J. Martin and K. McNerney, 'Carpentier and Jolivet: Magic Music in *Los pasos perdidos*', *Hispanic Review*, Vol. 52 (1984) pp. 491–7.
8   C.G. Jung ed., *Man and his Symbols* (London, 1964); C.G. Jung, *The Undiscovered Self* (London, 1958).
9   N. Kazantzakis, *Zorba the Greek*, trans. C. Wildman (London, 1972) p. 138 1st publ. Athens 1946. 1st English edn. Oxford 1959 trans. C. Wildman.
10 Following the Spanish Civil War José Bergamín went into exile in Mexico. His work was denied publication in Spain for many years and is still better known in France.
11 D. Randel, *The New Harvard Dictionary of Music* (Cambridge, Mass., 1986) p. 890. 'Tympanum' as 'frame' can also refer to several plucked instruments of the Middle Ages, including the dulcimer and psaltery.
12 W. Smith, *The Concise Classical Dictionary* reprinted (London, 1988).
13 Commemorated in a poem by the Alexandrian poet Callimachus of the mid third century BC. Ohana later used lines from this poem in the choral diptych *Lux noctis - Dies solis*.
14 Although Granados was also inspired by the work of Goya, his dramatic impressions of Goya's paintings in the *Goyescas* (1911) tend towards the more picturesque and romantic. As a pianist Ohana used to perform at least one piece from the collection, but as a composer was attracted to the more nightmarish world of Goya's engravings. The *Goyescas* did not, therefore, provide a compositional model for Ohana.
15 Letter to Jacques Durand 14 July 1915 in *Correspondance 1888–1918*, ed. François Lesure (Paris, 1993) p. 351.
16 Letter to Robert Godet 4 February 1916 in *Claude Debussy, Lettres à mes deux amis* (Paris, 1942) p. 149.
17 F. Goya, *Los Caprichos* introduction by Philip Hofer (New York, 1969).
18 M. Ohana, interview (in English), M. Oliver (1984).
19 Ibid..
20 M. Ohana, 'Ecrire aujourd'hui pour le piano', *Panorama de la Musique* (March–April 1980) p. 13.
21 Ohana and Cela also had British connections in common; while Ohana inherited British citizenship from his father Cela's mother was English.
22 In mathematical terms the '$\sum$' also represents summation.
23 Ohana, programme note (in French) for *Signes* reproduced in C. Prost, 'Catalogue raisonné, *La Revue musicale* (1986) p. 201.
24 Loc. cit.
25 The present author in conversation with the composer in Paris, March 1991.
26 The present author in conversation with the composer in Paris, February 1983 and March 1984.
27 M. Ohana, interview (in French), F.B. Mâche (1978) pp. 114–15.
28 Loc. cit.
29 C.G. Jung, 'Approaching the Unconscious', *Man and his Symbols* (London, 1979), pp. 18–103.
30 Ibid.

31 A. Jaffé, 'Symbolism in the Visual Arts', *Man and his Symbols* (London, 1979) pp. 240–9.
32 The published scores of *T'Harân-Ngô* and *Nuit de Pouchkine* are not yet engraved but are reproduced from Ohana's final manuscript.
33 M. Ohana, interview (in French), A. Grunenwald (1975) p. 59.
34 Catullus, poems Nos 4, 5, 6, 7,62 and 66. Poem No. 66 is a translation of a poem written by the Alexandrian poet Callimachus, of the third century BC. who was influential on poets of the generation of Catullus, as well as later generations.
35 Text of *Dies solis* trans. Dr Nick Fisher, Cardiff University, School of History and Archaeology.
36 C. Rae, 'Music-Theatre and the Japanese Noh', 'The Music of Maurice Ohana' (diss. U. of Oxford, 1989) pp. 270–88.
37 See C.G. Jung, (1964).
38 E. Markham, 'Japanese Music' *New Oxford Companion to Music* ed. D. Arnold (Oxford 1983) Vol. i, p. 973.
39 W. Blake symbolism of opposites in 'Songs of Innocence and Experience' (Oxford, 1970) and 'The Marriage of Heaven and Hell' (Oxford, 1975).
40 M. Ohana, interview (in French), A. Grunenwald (1975) p. 59.
41 The present author in conversation with the composer in Paris, March 1983.
42 According to the composer.
43 C.G. Jung, (1964) op. cit. p. 81.
44 M. Ohana, programme notes (in French) for *Sorôn-Ngô* reproduced in C. Prost, 'Catalogue raisonné, *La Revue musicale* (1986) p. 207.
45 M. Ohana, 'La Géographie musicale de l'Espagne' *Journal musical français* (March and April, 1956).
46 A. Carpentier, *La música en Cuba* (Mexico City, 1946) Fr. trans. R.F. Durand (Paris, 1979).
47 C.G. Jung, (1964) op. cit. pp. 43–5.
48 Ibid. pp. 67–9.
49 M. Ohana, interview (in French), M. Cadieu (1980) p. 42.
50 M. Ohana, 'Sud-Nord' (in French), *20ème Siècle: images de la musique française* (Paris, 1986) p. 164.
51 A. Barker, *Greek Musical Writings*, Vol i *The Musician and his Art* (Cambridge, 1984).
52 Ibid. p. 15.
53 S. Michaelides, *The Music of Ancient Greece* (London, 1978) pp. 212, 344–5.
54 *Trois Prophéties de la Sibylle* (1989).
55 M. Ohana, record sleeve notes (in French) for 'La Niña de los Peines', *Grands Cantaores du Flamenco*, Vol. 3, Le Chant du Monde LDX 74859 CM340 (no date on disc).
56 M. Ohana, programme notes (in French), for *Kypris* (MS).
57 W. King, *An Historical Account of the Heathen Gods and Heroes* (London, 1965); W. Smith, *The Concise Classical Dictionary* (reprinted London, 1988).
58 F.G. Lorca, 'Play and Theory of the Duende' and 'Sun and Shade' in *Deep Song and other Prose*, trans. C. Maurer (London, 1980) pp. 50–8.
59 Shakespeare Sonnet No. CXLVI. 'Poor soul, the centre of my sinful earth ...'.
60 M. Ohana, interview (in French), B. Massin (1978).
61 Ohana did not like the term 'Magic Realist' as he felt it was too glib. The author in conversation with the composer in Paris, March 1992.
62 The present author in conversations with the composer in Paris, 1982–8. Gabriel García Márquez won the Nobel Prize for literature in 1982 for *Cien años de solidad* (Buenos Aires, 1967).
63 J. Roy, *Présences contemporaines, musique française* (Paris, 1962) pp. 386–7.

CHAPTER THREE

Evolution towards Maturity: The Early and Transitional Works

Although Ohana's first important compositions date from 1944, it would be misleading to suggest either that he came to music late in life or was a late developer. His pianistic gifts led him first towards the career of a concert pianist and only following the interruption of World War II, and the opportunity for personal reassessment that his war service provided, did he discover his real vocation to lie in composition. By the end of the war he had made the decision to wind-down his pianistic activities and devote himself to composition. His aptitude for improvisation and extemporisation, traditional attributes of a composer, had emerged in his collaborations with internationally known performers of Spanish folk music, as well as in his knowledge and practical experience of African tribal music.

Beginning the process of synthesising musical language that could draw on his cultural roots and reflect an aesthetic alignment independent of the Austro-German tradition, Ohana was not attracted to the serialism of his contemporaries. Encouraged to look towards his Iberian heritage by La Argentinita, Roy Campbell and Sergio de Castro, Ohana's Spanish sources figure prominently during the period of his first creative thrust up to 1960 and are fundamental to his first large-scale work *Llanto por Ignacio Sánchez Mejías* in which the influence of Falla is particularly pronounced. Embarking on a compositional career in his thirties, Ohana's first works do not represent juvenilia but may be considered early in the larger context of his overall output. In 1960, Ohana's music entered a phase of more intensive refinement; not only did he develop new techniques and sound-textures but moved away from the Iberianism which had dominated his work up to that point. Although the seeds of this change in compositional direction were sown during the early period, particularly in the choral work *Cantigas* and the ballet for solo percussion *Etudes chorégraphiques*, 1960 defines Ohana's readiness to begin the process of fusing the wide range of his inherited traditions into a more unified, less obviously derivative whole. Owing more to the influence of Debussy than of Falla, the works composed between 1960 and 1964 represent a transitional period of technical exploration and development. The explorations of the early 1960s came to fruition in *Signes*, the work the composer himself declared to be the first of his mature compositional style,[1] and were developed further in the ensuing works of the Sigma Series (cf. Chapter 4). The present chapter will therefore examine Ohana's works up to 1964.

Ohana embarked on his career as a composer at a time when many were engaged in a reassessment of musical language, or experimentation with new compositional method. Not only had Stravinsky and Messiaen arrived at their respective technical and stylistic watersheds, but Lutosławski and Carter, the same generation as Ohana, were absorbed in a reappraisal of compositional direction. The younger generation, inspired by the teaching of Leibowitz, looked towards the newly rediscovered Second Viennese School for their point of compositional departure, Boulez later hailing Webern as the 'threshold' for new music.[2] Against such a background of wide-spread review of method, style and technique, it is not surprising that Ohana only began to produce his first important works in his late thirties. Dutilleux, on the other had, had announced his compositional presence before the war through winning the coveted Prix de Rome in 1938 while still in his early twenties and had continued to fulfil commissions, as well as receive performances, even during the dark years of the Occupation. Ohana was, in a sense, less fortunate. His war service with the British Army necessitated his absence from Paris until demobilisation in 1946 when he was forced to carve out his position anew. Ohana's compositional output is therefore synchronous with that of many of his younger contemporaries. Like Dutilleux, however, his compositional maturity flowered during the 1960s, *Tombeau de Claude Debussy* and *Signes* being in this respect comparable with *Métaboles*.

Throughout Ohana's early period (1944–59) many works resulted from commissions as a result of the success of *Llanto por Ignacio Sánchez Mejías* in 1950. A large number of these commissions were for incidental scores for stage, radio and film, and stemmed from the necessity of living from composition. Many of Ohana's radio scores resulted directly from commissions by Dutilleux who developed an innovative form of radio play in which words and music could be combined in a new and different way from the more traditional broadcast stage-play. Described as 'musique radiophonique' they were part of Dutilleux's series of 'illustrations musicales'.[3] Ohana continued to accept such commissions until the middle 1960s. The opportunity for technical experimentation under the relative anonymity that the writing of incidental music allows was invaluable for the development of his musical language; new techniques could be explored in the incidental music before being exposed and developed further in concert works. One of the most characteristic features of Ohana's work as a whole that was to emerge from such experimentation was his use of microintervals; not only quarter-tones but third-tone intervals which he used for the first time in the radiophonic music *Les Hommes et les autres* of 1956.[4]

Within the context of continued stylistic exploration, Spanish sources provided the compositional catalyst for the majority of Ohana's early works; his knowledge and personal experience of Spanish folk music represented the raw material that could be tempered by the 'métier' of his French musical training. The point of departure for concert, theatre works and many radiophonic and incidental music projects, the influence of Spanish sources dominates the early period and is manifest in a variety of guises. Ohana drew on the folk music of different regions, often but not exclusively the Andalusian flamenco and Cante

Jondo,[5] incorporating many of the rhythmic and melodic features of these styles. He looked towards the vocal repertoire of the Medieval and Renaissance periods not only because this music had attracted him at the Schola Cantorum but as many Spanish folk melodies are themselves derived from plainsong. He studied the music of Falla for solutions to many technical and stylistic compositional problems, most notably the Harpsichord concerto and *El Retablo de Maese Pedro* which were among the scores kept in his pack throughout the war. He drew on his knowledge of ancient Iberian mythologies and was attracted to literature of the great Spanish writers, as well as the art of the great Spanish painters. Far from any colouristic recourse to the picturesque, or mere impressionist exoticism, Ohana's Iberianism is akin to the nightmare-world of Goya's etchings, the violent suffering of Picasso's *Guernica* and the dark surrealism of Federico García Lorca's poetry. It combines the grotesque alternations of tragedy and comedy, a common feature of much of the Spanish literature on which Ohana drew and, like the sharp contrasts of light and shade which symbolise the eternal play of life and death in the bull-ring, reflects what Lorca described as the essential characteristics of the Spanish personality.[6] Table 3.1 lists Ohana's Spanish inspired works of his early and transitional periods and includes incidental music in addition to concert works. (His setting of three poems from *The Rose Garden* by the medieval Persian poet Shekh Muslihu'd-Din Sadi have been included here as they were known in Moorish Spain.)

Table 3.1: Spanish sources in works of the early and transitional periods

Date	Title of Work	Description	Source
1940	*La venta encantada*	orchestra	Cervantes: Don Quixote
1944	*Enterrar y callar*	piano	Goya
1945	*Sonatine monodique*	piano	Folk music, including flamenco
1947	*Sarabande*	2 pianos	Spanish courtly dance
1947	*Don Juan*	incid. music	Traditional legend
1947	*Deux mélodies*	songs	Lorca poems
1947	*Trois poèmes de Sadi*	songs	Moorish Spain – Sadi poems
1948	*Le damné par manque de confiance*	incid. music	Tirso de Molina
1948	*Paso*	piano	Flamenco, Cante Jondo
1950	*Llanto por Ignacio Sánchez Mejías*	'oratorio'	Lorca, Cante Jondo, Falla
1950	*Sarabande*	concerto	Spanish courtly dance,
1951	*Les représentations de Tanit*	ballet	Ibizan myth
1952	*Concertino pour trompette et orchestre*	concerto	Folk music, including flamenco

Date	Title of Work	Description	Source
1954	*Cantigas*	choral	Medieval and Renaissance texts and vocal repertoire
1954	*Tableaux de l'héroïne fidèle*	radio score	Andalucian romancero, Falla, folk music
1954	*Hommage à Luis Milán*	piano	Spanish Renaissance lutenist
1954	*Paso, Solea*	ballet	Flamenco, Cante Jondo
1954	*Tiento, Farruca*	percussion	Flamenco
1955	*Trois caprices*	piano	Goya, Cante Jondo
1956	*Médée*	radio score	Seneca adapt. J. Bergamin
1956	*Images de Don Quichotte*	radio score	Cervantes, Falla, folk music
1956	*Le Guignol au gourdin*	radio-score	Lorca, flamenco, Falla
1957	*Tiento*	guitar	Flamenco
1957	*Fuenteovejuna*	incid. music	Lope de Vega, Castillian folk music
1957	*Trois graphiques*	guitar concerto	Goya, flamenco
1958	*Farruca*	harpsichord	Flamenco
1958	*Le Romancero du Cid*	incid.music	Castillian legend, folk music
1961	*Histoire véridique de Jacotin*	radio score	Camilo José Cela, folk music
1964	*Si le jour paraît....*	guitar	Goya

The emphasis of Spanish models in Ohana's early works has sometimes resulted in him being described rather too simply as a 'Spanish' composer (although this does not apply to the studies by Prost, Bayer or Halbreich).[7] While this is not untrue in the context of the early period, the rather over simplistic label does not account for the stylistic changes which took place in the early 1960s, or for the presence of African influences which emerged for the first time in the *Etudes chorégraphiques* of 1955. That Ohana did not entirely abandon Spanish sources in his mature music is witnessed in the operas *Autodafé* and *La Célestine* as well as in the first Cello Concerto *Anneau du Tamarit* (composed in memory to Federico García Lorca), but the greater breadth of musical material in his works of the 1960s and beyond resulted in a less obviously derivative style. Iberianism became one of many inspirational sources, rather than the predominant stylistic ingredient.

The Early Works

Ohana's initial compositional output was prolific; the combined sum (including incidental and 'radiophonic' scores) totals more than forty works composed from 1938 to 1959. During the period of progressive technical and stylistic refinement which took place in the 1960s, Ohana became dissatisfied with many of his early works which he no longer considered representative and, as a result, much of his initial output was either withdrawn, destroyed or simply remained unpublished.[8] He allowed only eight works from the early period to remain in publication, this representing less than a third of his initial production. The early published works are listed in Table 3.2. (As the constituent movements of *Trois caprices* for piano were composed at different times, they have been listed separately. Although counted as a single work they will be discussed individually.) Although these works provide the focus for the present discussion, consideration will be given to their context in Ohana's early period as a whole.

Table 3.2: **The early published works**

Date of completion	Title	Publisher
1944	Enterrar y callar, *Trois caprices* no.1*	Billaudot
1945	*Sonatine monodique*	Billaudot
1948	Paso, *Trois caprices* no.3*	Billaudot
1950	*Llanto por Ignacio Sánchez Mejías*	Billaudot
1954	*Cantigas*	Billaudot
1954	Hommage à Luis Milán, *Trois caprices* no.2*	Billaudot
1955	*Etudes chorégraphiqes*	Schott
1957	*Tiento*	Billaudot
1957	*Trois graphiques*	Amphion-Durand
1958	*Recit de l'an Zéro*	Billaudot

(* Although composed separately, these three pieces were published together as the *Trois caprices* in 1955 and have therefore have been calculated as a single work.)

As a pianist-composer begins to synthesise a musical language, it is not unusual for his first works to be written for his own instrument. While the works for piano do not represent Ohana's main compositional preoccupation in either his early or mature periods, the piano music as a whole includes some of the composer's most personal statements. Some of his earliest works are for piano: the pre-war Toccata[9], the *Trois caprices*, the *Sonatine monodique* and a Sarabande for two pianos (later revised as a one movement concerto for harpsichord[10]). 'Enterrar y callar' (To bury them and remain silent) became the first of the *Trois caprices* and is the earliest of Ohana's works to remain in public circulation. Composed in Rome in 1944 while at the Accademia di Santa Cecilia, the title is borrowed from the eighteenth of Goya's etchings 'Disasters of War' (cf. Chapter 2). Depicting a pile of corpses awaiting burial, the brutality of Goya's etching provided a poignant parallel for Ohana's own experiences of war.[11] The prevailing mood throughout the short piece is of unrelenting melancholy and is in many ways akin to the outpouring of personal grief expressed in Falla's *Homenaje, le tombeau de Claude Debussy* for solo guitar, a work which Ohana knew well and admired. Like Falla's *Homenaje*, the material is built from slow, repetitive patterns which enforce the evocation of a funerary lament. In bar 12 an ostinato pattern emerges to suggest the tolling of bells which is not unlike the bell-tolling in 'Le Gibet' of Ravel's *Gaspard de la nuit*, also slow and lugubrious.[12] Another repetitive rhythmic pattern characteristic of the piece is first heard in the opening bars; the dotted rhythm with its emphasis on the second-beat, is borrowed from the Sarabande, but is here expanded into a slow-motion 6/4. (The same rhythm is found in Ohana's *Tiento* for guitar, which also presents a mood of sombre lamentation.) A short introduction is followed by successive variants of the two thematic ideas which first appear in bars 5 and 6 (see Ex. 3.1).

Ex. 3.1: *Trois caprices*, 'Enterrar y callar', (bars 1–7)

© 1967 M.R. Braun, Gérard Billaudot Editeur S.A. Paris successeur.
Reproduced by kind permission.

Two fortissimo statements reminiscent of the Andalusian 'saeta' (flamenco song-type belonging to the repertoire of the Cante Jondo[13]) interrupt the main body of the piece and are heard again as faint echoes in the final bars. (Literally meaning 'arrow', the saeta is a short unaccompanied song chanted in religious processions called 'Pasos', during Holy Week in Andalusia. It is usually associated with a spontaneous eruption of sentiment and is addressed to the religious statues of the Virgin Mary or Jesus which, typically, are processed. The stanzas of the song are usually punctuated with interpolations on trumpets and drums which follow the procession.) Harmonically, the emphasis of minor ninths, major sevenths and tritones set against combinations of perfect intervals and major seconds anticipates the harmonic processes of Ohana's mature language (cf. Chapter 6). Another feature of this piece also characteristic of later writing is detailed pedal notation; he makes clear distinctions between the use of the 'third' (sostenuto) pedal (which sustains selectively) and the sustaining pedal (which sustains indiscriminately) and also provides instructions for the use of the 'una corda'. He also indicates passages where neither sustaining nor sostenuto pedal are to be used (senza pedale). A particularly unusual pedalling effect is required in some fortissimo passages where he specifies the 'una corda' to create a distinctly nasal sound, possible on large, resonant instruments. Ohana's experience as a concert pianist would have made him profoundly aware of the need for precise pedal notation, as well as the range of resonant, harmonic and timbral effects that can be achieved. His work with Alfredo Casella at the time of composing 'Enterrar y callar' may have emphasised this point further. Ohana admired the unusual range of pianistic sonority Casella was able to obtain, even during the war and already in deteriorating health.[14]

Composed at the same time as 'Enterrar y callar', the *Sonatine monodique* was intended as a jocular, tongue-in-cheek, compositional study; no note should be sounded with any other, unless in unison. The result, as the title indicates, is an essay in monody as the means for generating all musical material. Owing much to the extrovert virtuosity of the 1940 Toccata, each of the four movements explores a different approach to monodic texture, any possibility of monotony in the alternation of recitativo melodic lines versus guitar-like, broken-chord figurations being avoided through recourse to a variety of rhythmic patterning, accentuation, tempi, resonance (through pedal indications) and mood. The musical character of the work is Spanish but, unlike 'Enterrar y callar', is essentially light-hearted. The incisive triple meter and syncopation of the ternary first movement 'Allegretto con moto' is intended to suggest the rhythms and character of various Spanish folk dances, notably the bulería, jota and fandango. (While the 'bulería' belongs to the flamenco repertory, the 'fandango' and 'jota' are widely performed throughout Spain and transcend regional classification.[15]) It is only the second movement, 'Vif', where Ohana specifies a jota by name, this example recalling Falla's jota in the *Siete Canciones populares Españolas*. (A jota is usually in rapid triple time with four bar phrases.[16]) Here Ohana changes the meter from the more conventional 3/8 to a 6/8, unusual for this dance-type.[17] The ensuing Andante represents an amalgam of the Andalusian gypsy 'debla' (a flamenco song-type) and the 'soleá' (belonging specifically to the Cante Jondo repertory of the flamenco[18]), with arpeggiated figurations paraphrasing the vocal melisma characteristic of the original models. As in all improvised forms, changes of tempo and nuance are numerous. The final, dance-like 'Animé' is the most virtuosic and extrovert of the toccata-like movements with syncopations and hemiola alternations of 3/8 and 2/8 characterising the rhythmic fabric. Towards the end of a movement two entries of a brief fugal exposition emerge but quickly disintegrate back into the guitar-like figurations of the opening section as the form is humorously debunked and the fugue, that most Austro-German of formalised structures, is, as the composer said, 'mise à plat'.[19]

The seven concert works completed between 1947 and 1948 which follow the *Sonatine monodique* are among those later withdrawn by the composer or for which he simply did not seek publication. All but one was premièred at the Concerts du groupe Zodiaque. Although suppression of these works suggests that Ohana considered them unrepresentative of his subsequent development, these works illustrate an extension of compositional activity beyond that of writing for piano. They include a Concerto for Brass, Percussion and Strings, a Duo for violin and piano, as well as several songs of which one is a setting of Lorca. The only work of the late 1940s to remain in publication is the 'Paso' which later became the third of the *Trois caprices* for piano. The title refers to the solemn processions of Holy Week in which the Andalusian saeta figures prominently.

> The Saeta achieves the synthesis of all the spiritual currents of the Mediterranean world which are represented in twenty centuries of Andalusian culture. Musically it is one of the most sombre and most complex types from the treasury of Andalusian folk music. Byzantine and Muezzin chant and the Delphic hymn have each contributed to the birth of the Saeta and have no doubt merged together with other sources more ancient and more mysterious still. As with all Andalusian music, the gypsies have tempered the whole with their interpretative genius ... it is in essence pagan.[20]

Like the Holy procession itself, the short piano piece is slow and sombre, fortissimo, percussive interpolations alternating with expressive, melismatic or declamatory material. Improvisatory in character, the harmonic emphasis of perfect intervals and major seconds and the melodic inflections of the augmented second, suggest the modal scales of the flamenco. The many effects of resonance achieved through a combination of careful pedalling instructions and the use of the full range of instrument echo many similar effects in the concluding section of Albéniz's *Fête-Dieu en Seville* which also refers to the processions of Holy Week and which Ohana knew well and had frequently performed. Ohana later explored the theatrical, as opposed to purely musical, aspects of the *Paso* in a ballet of that title commissioned for the Opéra de Lyon in 1954.[21] (The score was later withdrawn.)

In 1949, Ohana accepted a commission from the Cercle Culturel du Conservatoire to compose a large work for chorus and orchestra.[22] He chose for his text one of Federico García Lorca's last poems, *Llanto por la muerte de*

Ignacio Sánchez Mejías. The poem, one of Lorca's most important works, is an elegiac ballad lamenting the death of his bull-fighter friend Ignacio Sánchez Mejías who was gored in the bull-ring at five in the afternoon on 11 August 1934 at Manzanares.[23] The death of Ignacio, who was also a playwright, caused widespread lamentation among the intellectual circle in Spain at the time, including both Rafael Alberti and José Bergamín. Ohana was well acquainted with Alberti and Bergamín at the time of writing his setting of the *Llanto*; they also figure among the dedicatees of *Cantigas*. Ohana had been encouraged to set the *Llanto* by La Argentinita, Ignacio's lover, owner of Lorca's manuscript and dedicatee of the poem.[24] Ohana worked directly from the poet's manuscript which had been given to him by La Argentinita some years before. Describing his setting rather incongruously as an 'oratorio', Ohana reflects the aura of mysticism approaching religious fervour that is typically associated with the bull-fight in Spain. Lorca described the 'corrida'[25] as both a 'Liturgy of bulls' and an 'Office',[26] while the Cuban-born novelist Alejo Carpentier described both Lorca's poem and Ohana's setting in terms of a cantata, a liturgy and a Passion, likening death of Ignacio to the descent of Christ from the Cross.[27] While such analogies may be blasphemous, parallels have been drawn in modern Spanish literature between the ritual sacrifice of the bull and the Passion, the suffering of which is said to be particularly emphasised in some forms of Spanish Catholicism. According to Lorca, the contemplation of death and sacrifice, in whatever context, is one of the manifestations of the 'duende':

> The *duende* does not come unless he sees that death is possible. In Spain, where dance is religious expression, the *duende* has unlimited range over the bodies of dancers, over the breasts of singers, and in the liturgy of bulls, an authentic religious drama, where, as in the Mass, a God is sacrificed to and adored.[28]

Literally meaning 'ghost' or 'demon', 'duende' is the term used by flamenco musicians to describe the manifestation of a particular magic in a performance, provoked by what they also refer to as 'black sounds'.[29] They often exclaim 'Olé' at these points and cross themselves as a protection from the supernatural powers which they believe are released. Ohana described the 'black sounds' which announce the presence of the mysterious 'duende' as '... this magic enclosed in sound which strikes one down when it appears but which can be defined by no one.'[30]

Without cutting any of Lorca's original text of the *Llanto*, Ohana's setting adheres to the four-part structure of the poem: 'La cogida y la muerte' (The Tossing and the Death); 'La sangre derramada' (The Spilled Blood); 'Cuerpo presente' (The Laid-out Body) and 'Alma ausente' (Absent Soul). The text is shared between a baritone soloist, narrator and chorus; while the first movement is entirely sung, the remaining three divide the text into sections of accompanied and unaccompanied vocalisations, accompanied parlando recitation and unaccompanied recitation with intervening instrumental commentaries. In this way Ohana not only accelerates progress through the text itself, preventing the work from being too long, but draws attention to the musical properties of the poetry itself, generally recognised as one of Lorca's main achievements. Clearly Ohana considered much of the text too rich in its own sonority to be appropriate for musical setting in its entirety. Much of the recitation occurs at points of the most intense and violent imagery. The chorus of twelve female voices (mezzos and contraltos) is used only in the first section 'La cogida y la muerte' which is poetically constructed as an alternation of narrative and refrain. Ohana's setting takes the form of a quasi-responsorial psalmody with the vocalisations of the solo voice being answered by the choral interpolations of the refrain which reiterates the time of the fatal goring, 'a las cinqo de la tarde' (at five in the afternoon). The refrain material suggests the melodic contour of plainchant, as does much of the vocal material in the *Llanto* (see Ex. 3.2).

Ex. 3.2: *Llanto por Ignacio Sánchez Mejías*, 'La cogida y la muerte' (bars 88–92)

© 1966 M.R. Braun, Gérard Billaudot Editeur S.A. Paris successeur.
Reproduced by kind permission.

The musical style of the *Llanto* represents a synthesis of Spanish influences. That of Falla is revealed not only in the use of baritone as the solo voice but in the choice and economy of instrumentation which resembles more the brittle aridity of the *Retablo de Maese Pedro* and Harpsichord Concerto, than the luxuriant sonorities of the *Sombrero de tres picos* or *Noches en los jardines de España*. Included in Ohana's orchestra of single woodwind, two horns and strings are a harpsichord, trumpet in C and timpani. Although the harpsichord is sometimes used as a soloist, its main function is to provide an allusive, guitar-like texture in the many ostinato figures which dominate the work. In the second movement 'La sangre derramada', it introduces the slow, march theme which is designed to recall the processional music of the Andalusian 'Paso' (see Ex.3.3). The broken-chord figuration which immediately precedes the march theme is reminiscent of those of Falla's Harpsichord Concerto, as are many figurations of the *Llanto*.

Ex. 3.3: *Llanto por Ignacio Sánchez Mejías*, 'La sangre derramada' (bars 184–8)

© 1967 M.R. Braun, Gérard Billaudot Editeur S.A. Paris successeur.
Reproduced by kind permission.

The trumpet also plays an important role throughout the *Llanto*. This stems both from its significance in the ritual processions of Holy Week and in the bull-fight where it announces the main stages of the kill and death of the bull. In Ohana's score, this role is reflected in its association with what has here been called the 'lament theme' which unites the work as a whole (see Ex. 3.4).

Ex. 3.4: First statement of the 'Lament Theme', *Llanto por Ignacio Sánchez Mejías*, 'La cogida y la muerte' (bars 18–23)

© 1967 M.R. Braun, Gérard Billaudot Editeur S.A. Paris successeur.
Reproduced by kind permission.

(C. Prost has suggested that the theme symbolises death.[31]) An important feature of the theme is its emphasis of the descending minor third which becomes an intervallic feature, characteristic of much ensuing material, as well as the basis of the instrumental interpolations in 'Cuerpo presente'. Drums, like trumpets, feature in the rituals of procession and the bull fight; Ohana accords the timpani, side drums and other skin percussion special prominence throughout.

The other main stylistic influences are those of the flamenco, in particular the repertory of songs of the sombre, Cante Jondo style.[32] While Ohana is careful to avoid too obvious a statement of the clichéd phrygian cadential formula associated with this repertoire (the A–G–F–E descending pattern), the stepwise, descending fourth is nevertheless often embedded within the vocal or instrumental line, although frequently transformed either into a descending diminished fourth or into a tritone.[33] The improvisatory vocalisations, ornamentations and modes of attack of the baritone soloist are characteristic of these intensely expressive songs. The first utterance of the baritone in 'La cogida y la muerte' (bar 66) paraphrases the characteristic 'ay' exclamations associated with many of the tragic lamentations of the Cante Jondo, this also providing the melodic and rhythmic cell which generates much of the ensuing vocal line and many of the ostinati (see Ex.3.5).

Ex. 3.5: Generative cells in *Llanto por Ignacio Sánchez Mejías*, 'La cogida y la muerte'

a) bar 66

b) bar 81

c) bar 102

© 1967 M.R. Braun, Gérard Billaudot Editeur S.A. Paris successeur.
Reproduced by kind permission.

The principle of variation is not only essential to the compositional process in this work but is the basis of many of Ohana's later techniques (see Part Two). It is a variation process which follows the spirit of improvisation, rather than any formalised pattern. The vocal line itself is simple and spontaneous, following, in declamatory fashion, the natural, syllabic pattern of the text. The subtlety of rhythmic nuance enhances the effect of improvisation despite being measured even in unaccompanied sections. Interchanging with the instrumental ensemble in the manner of a *Cantuor* with his guitarist, the vocal line incorporates a number of effects derived from the flamenco, including glottal attacks, chest and throat resonances, senza vibrato or 'voix détimbré', florid ornamentation and the use of an unusually high tessitura. The narrow interval compass (the melodic line rarely exceeds a sixth) and orientation towards certain pitches are also features of the Cante Jondo. Ohana makes careful use of enharmonic notation to suggest the microintervals which would occur naturally in a flamenco performance. (He does not actually notate microintervals in this work.) Harmonically, the work is chiefly modal, although chromatic substitutions result in considerable emphasis of the tritone, major seventh and minor ninth. The superimposition of tritones within chord-aggregates that span major sevenths is a feature of his harmonic vocabulary. (The 'Llanto' chord is discussed in Chapter 6.) Structurally, Ohana's forms are varied, as are the forms of the original poem: the first movement conforms to an overall binary scheme, while the third and fourth movements are essentially strophic; the second is more unusual as it combines an internal strophic format with an overall arch structure, the central point being identified by a climax of orchestral tremolos and a variant of the 'lament' theme on the horns ('La sangre derramada', bars 179–84.)

While many seeds of Ohana's later style were sown in the *Llanto*, Lorca's poem providing a natural stimulus for Ohana's recourse to his Spanish roots, the effect of the work as a whole tends towards the almost exhaustively austere. Eschewing the instinctively humorous side of Ohana's creative persona which was able to flourish in his stage and radio music, the unrelenting melancholy of the *Llanto* is untypical of his early music. While the Goyesque *Trois caprices* are certainly sombre, their more subtle harmonic vocabulary yields greater colour and nuance and indicates more clearly the way in which his language was subsequently to develop. Inspired not only by Lorca but also his association with La Argentinita, Ohana's *Llanto* belongs to the great era of revitalisation of Spanish folk music that was initiated by Felipe Pedrell, developed by his pupils Albéniz, Granados and Falla and culminated with the Festival of Cante Jondo held at Granada in 1922 over which Falla and Lorca presided.[34] Composed towards the end of the period when the Spanish classical dance companies, including those of Pilar López and 'Antonio',[35] as well as the great singers such as La Niña de los Peines, were at their peak of popularity, Ohana's *Llanto* may represent a fond farewell to an era.

After completing the *Llanto*, Ohana made sketches for a guitar concerto (into which the Sarabande for harpsichord and orchestra was reworked). He further exploited the ritualistic sonorities of the trumpet in a Concertino for trumpet and orchestra which he completed in 1952. Returning to the more traditional forms of the *Sonatine monodique*, commentators of the time suggested Ohana to be ill at ease in the quasi-classical environment that the Concertino inhabited. Such criticism may have encouraged the composer's subsequent withdrawal of this work during the 1960s, despite the second movement being described as 'of rare beauty, the muted trumpet evoking Andalusia, the blues and Negro music.'[36] At the same time, Ohana began to explore even older Iberian traditions in the orchestral suite *Les représentations du Tanit*. Inspired by a series of Ibizan statuettes representing the Phoenician-Carthaginian Janus-like Goddess of Fertility and Destruction, this work aims to evoke the ancient, erotic rites of initiation over which, according to legend, Tanit was meant to have presided. The individual statues correspond to each musical 'representation'. The incantatory atmosphere of primitive magic and rhythmic vitality of the work attracted the attention of Maurice Béjart who later choreographed the suite as a ballet to provide a companion to the other 1956 Ohana-Béjart collaboration, *Prométhée*. Parallels can be drawn between Ohana's developing fascination for myth and magic and similar preoccupations in the music of Jolivet (cf. Chapter 2).

In 1953–4 with the composition of *Cantigas, Tableaux de l'héroïne fidèle,* and *Hommage à Luis Milán,* Ohana turned to sources from Medieval and Renaissance Spain for his point of compositional departure. The *Cantigas* are based on Medieval and Renaissance Spanish texts; the *Tableaux* are based on tales from the Andalusian Romancero, a form of folk ballade dating from the Renaissance; the *Hommage* commemorates the work of the early sixteenth-century Aragonese composer Don Luis de Milán, who wrote for the lute and vihuela. The *Cantigas* and *Hommage* are among the works which most clearly indicate the direction of Ohana's future compositional style.

The result of a commission by the Hamburg Norddeutscher Rundfunk, *Cantigas* is scored for a mixed chorus (from which soloists periodically emerge) and an ensemble of wind, percussion and piano. Revealing a far more lyrical side of the composer's musical personality, the six-movement work borrows its title from the thirteenth-century mystic poems and monodies of King Alphonso X 'the Wise', known as the *Cantigas de Santa Maria*. The fourth of the six movements, 'Cantiga del azahar' (Song of the Orange Blossom), amalgamates text from three of Alphonso's poems and incorporates a monody directly attributed to him. The remaining five movements use texts by four Medieval and Renaissance poets: 'Cantiga de los Reyos Magos' (Song of the Magi), attributed to José de Valdivielso; 'Cantiga del destierro' (Song of Exile) and 'Cantiga de la Noche Santa' (Song of the Holy Night) attributed to Fray Ambrosio Montesino; 'Cantiga de Vela' (Song of the Vigil), attributed to Gonzalo de Berceo; and 'Cantiga del Nacimiento' (Song of the Nativity), attributed to Juan Alvarez Gato. The literary and artistic friends to whom Ohana dedicated five of the six movements are also worthy of mention: José Bergamín, Sergio de Castro, Rafael Alberti, Octavio Paz and Isabel and Fernando Pereda. With the instrumental ensemble playing a subsidiary role, the work explores a vocal style which owes much to the Medieval and Renaissance vocal repertories Ohana studied at the Schola Cantorum. Much of the internal movement structure follows responsorial and antiphonal patterns, this being particularly notable in the fifth movement which alternates contemplative, unmetred vocalisations of a contralto soloist with more extrovert, metred, homorhythmic material of the chorus and ensemble. Many of the contrapuntal textures suggest the character of renaissance polyphony, although the borrowing of certain technical procedures associated with this repertoire (trope, conductus and cantus firmus) are explored only in his later music, most notably *Chiffres de clavecin, Silenciaire, Office des oracles* and the Mass (cf. Chapter 5).

Reflecting the musical character of King Alphonso's original monodies on which *Cantigas* is based, Ohana drew on the melodic properties of Mozarabic, Gregorian, Sephardic and Muezzin chant-types, all of which are associated with the Iberian peninsula and which profoundly influenced the melodic shapes of Spanish folk music.[37] Although organum-like textures are not exploited as much here as in his later vocal music, particularly the Mass, parallelism is a feature of many of the homophonic textures. As in the *Llanto*, a distinction is implied between enharmonically notated pitches in an attempt to depart from the conventions, even restrictions of modern temperament. Although here actual quarter-tones are notated in some of the unaccompanied solos, many of which are unmetred to suggest the spontaneity of improvisation. Almost wholly unaccompanied, 'Cantiga del azahar' is the most personal and expressive of the six movements and represents the emotional heart of the work; an unmetred, improvisatory melody migrates through the vocal parts, descending from a solo child soprano, through the contraltos to the basses of the chorus. Ex. 3.6 illustrates the beginning of the movement. The slow, solemn beauty of the melody, whose text in praise of the Virgin, creates an atmosphere of purity and poetic contemplation. That it is the only movement not to bear a dedication may suggest a particularly personal meaning for the composer. While the harmonic environment of the *Cantigas* as a whole is chiefly modal, certain harmonic features anticipate procedures of the mature works. Many chord-aggregates are constructed to give aural emphasis either to tritones or to perfect intervals in a process which anticipates his later harmonic processes (cf. Chapter 6).

Ex. 3.6: *Cantigas*, 'Cantiga del azahar' (opening to fig. 1)

© 1975 Gérard Billaudot Editeur S.A. Paris. Reproduced by kind permission.

Like *Cantigas, Hommage à Luis Milán* (the second of the *Trois caprices* although the third to be composed) explores a harmonic vocabulary based on the differentiation of intervallic timbre; tritones, minor seconds (and their inversions) are contrasted with chord-aggregates based on perfect intervals and major seconds (and their inversions). While this is indicative of the way in which Ohana's later harmonic language was to develop, the early works investigate the process in a far less developed way than the mature works (cf. Chaper 6). Don Luis de Milán was himself noted for an innovatory approach to harmony particularly in his *Tientos* for vihuela.

> His [Milán's] works for voice and lute, and for lute alone, are striking for their exquisite harmonic discovery, for a refinement combining a vigour that is both haughty and luminous.[38]

Ohana's *Hommage* is also notable for its exploration of effects of resonance and use of clusters, some of which juxtapose black and white keys (a technique fully developed in the later piano music, notably the *24 Préludes*). The pianist is also required to use a felt-covered ruler (forearms are, however, more convenient) to depress a white-key cluster spanning a major ninth over two octaves which is sustained by the sostenuto, or third-pedal. Against this harmonic background, contrasting chord-aggregates are superimposed, resonances being cleansed with each new chord by sostenente pedal. Marked 'Andante libero', the improvisatory character of the piece is further enhanced by the lack of metred bars. While the musical content of the *Hommage* does not draw on the Renaissance vocal repertories in the manner of the *Cantigas*, the reference to Milán reflects Ohana's fascination for the period.

Composed originally as a radiophonic score but adapted for theatrical production, *Tableaux de l'héroïne fidèle* draws on a Renaissance source for its subject matter, but its musical influence owes more to the twentieth century, in particular Falla. Ohana wrote his own scenario based on the Andalusian Romancero.[39] Set in Cordoba at the time of the Moors, the tale concerns a young girl sentenced to death on a false charge of perjury. She is being tortured when the people of Cordoba revolt and save her from execution although she subsequently dies. Rosemary and orange trees appear on her tomb, symbolising both her innocence and the miraculous deliverance of Andalusia.[40] A series of static scenes, rather than continuous action, this work represents a curious hybrid form, part incidental music, part music-theatre owing once again much to Falla's *Retablo de Maese Pedro*. With only two singing roles, the 'faithful heroine' and the 'treacherous minister', the remaining characters are spoken parts which, in the theatrical production, were mimed by puppets.[41] Although later destroyed by the composer, the work indicates Ohana's attraction to a dramatic form whose origins stem from the Spanish Puppet theatre of which both Falla and Lorca were also fond. Ohana had the opportunity to pursue this interest further two years later in his radiophonic music for comic episodes from Cervantes' *Don Quixote* and for Lorca's comic puppet-play for children, *Le Guignol au gourdin* of 1956. Both scores owe much not only to Falla, not least in the use of the harpsichord but also to the Stravinskian textures characteristic of *Histoire du*

Soldat. In 1958 *Le Guignol* was extended and revised (he added a soprano, baritone and male chorus and slightly expanded the instrumental ensemble) as a music-theatre production to be programmed with *El Retablo de Maese Pedro* at the Festival de Carcassonne.[42] Ohana produced and directed both works in collaboration with Yves Joly. Fascinated by the Chinese Peking Opera which he had seen in Paris in 1953 and 1954 and which he described as a profound influence on his own approach to music-theatre,[43] additional mimes, puppets, actors, acrobats and children he incorporated into both productions. The fusion of the Classical and Spanish subjects represented in Lorca's comic play for children were also ideally suited to such a production.

From as early as 1947 with the *Concertino pour cuivres, percussion et cordes*, Ohana had been experimenting with extending the role of percussion, his fascination stemming not only from his knowledge of Spanish folk music but also his experience of African tribal music (cf. Chapter 1). While the role of percussion in the *Llanto* is largely conventional, it nevertheless requires three players and an array of African toms in addition to a large selection of side-drums, xylophone and tam-tam. The *Suite pour un mimodrame* demands a larger than usual percussion group and even *Cantigas* requires four percussion players, with pitched and unpitched skins and wood (toms, bass-drum, timpani, and xylophone) as well as pitched and unpitched metal (glockenspiel, various cymbal-types, gongs and tam-tam). In 1954 Ohana rearranged the incidental music to *Soirée des proverbes* for flute and percussion and completed his first work for solo percussion, the two flamenco dances *Tiento* and *Farruca*. Although subsequently withdrawn these two works provided the opportunity for experimentation which came to fruition in the *Etudes chorégraphiques* of 1955, a more substantial work for solo percussion. Part of his attraction for writing for solo percussion stemmed from a growing desire to escape the conventions of equal temperament:

> I think percussion is something important in my music because it has escaped equal-temperament. Rather than any intellectual acquisition, the percussion has been something that I have known my whole life, and has become an extension of my means of expression. Despite an ear that is trained to hear primarily melody, I wanted also to develop a means of writing pure rhythm, but soon discovered that one can suggest melody in an abstract sense through the use of percussion. This is what I did in the *Etudes chorégraphiques*, particularly in the second movement.[44]

The first version of the *Etudes chorégraphiques* (four percussionists) was the result of a joint commission from the Norddeutscher Rundfunk and the Hamburg State Opera. Intended as a ballet for Dore Hoyer, one of the leading German dancers and choreographers of her generation,[45] the original plan was for the percussionists to be positioned on the stage, their physical movements to be part of the choreography itself. Unhappy with many of the choreographic and musical arrangements involved, Ohana did not allow the work to be premièred in this version. In 1963 he revised the work for six percussionists to fulfil a commission from Les Percussions de Strasbourg, to be staged with choreography by Manuel Parrès for the Ballet Municipal de Strasbourg. Enhancing sound-texture without significantly changing the musical substance, the four movement structure of the work remained unchanged, the alterations mainly involving an expansion of instrumental timbre. (It is the second version which is recorded and often performed as a concert work.) Each of the six percussion groups is individually characterised by its own combination of instrumental timbre, the overall ensemble including: two vibraphones, glockenspiel, six pitched crotales, seven Thai gongs (pitched), four Chinese cymbals (pitched); four suspended cymbals (high and low), five cymbals (medium and large) triangle, two gongs (medium and low), three tam-tams (two medium and low), anvil; xylophone, marimba, woodblock, temple blocks, maracas; eight toms (pitched); two Afro-Cuban M'Tumbas (high and low), five side-drums (with and without snare), tambourine and bass drum. While Varèse's *Ionisation* was admired by Ohana,[46] his real musical sources were those of African origin:

> I lived in Africa. I heard the percussionists of Guinea ... the Berbers who have a remarkable use of percussion to accompany their tribal choirs ... . The hazards of war took me to Kenya, Uganda and Tanganyika. I witnessed tribal celebrations, some in quite remote areas, and even heard a tribe of Pygmies ... . Some of the music that has brought me the most is that of the black Africans of Guinea and the Berbers, the ancient inhabitants of Africa who have a highly developed instinct for the percussion.[47]

While the rhythms of Spanish folk music played an important role in the development of Ohana's musical language, it was the adaptation of African rhythms and drumming techniques which shaped his approach to rhythm in his mature music (cf. Chapter 7). This process began in the *Etudes chorégraphiques* which combines Spanish rhythms with African derived procedures and rhythmic patterns, most notably the asymmetrical quintuplets which, according to the composer, are characteristic of black African tribal music.[48] Although less sophisticated in its technical vocabulary than his mature works, the *Etudes chorégraphiques* explore many types of superimposed ostinati (cf. Ex. 7.6), including the layering of metred and unmetred rhythms in a brief passage in the second movement (cf. Ex 7.7). They also investigate the pseudo-melodic, as well as rhythmic capabilities of the percussion, although this is more developed in the percussion concertos of the 1960s, *Synaxis* and *Silenciaire*. The *Etudes chorégraphiques* represent Ohana's first, albeit tentative, movement away from the Spanish influences that otherwise dominate the works of his early period.

With the *Tiento* for solo guitar, one of his most frequently performed and recorded works, Ohana returned to the more sombre side of his Spanish persona. Literally meaning 'touch' or 'feel', the title refers not only to the flamenco form of the same name,[49] but to the traditional form common in the Iberian peninsula of the sixteenth to the early eighteenth centuries, in which the player would 'try out' the instrument, often in the manner of a toccata. Not unlike Falla's *Homenaje* and the first of the *Trois caprices*, the mood of the *Tiento* is Goyesque, brutal, melancholic and grief-stricken, as are the most emotionally charged songs of the Cante Jondo. The opening material suggests the theme of the *Folias de Espagna,* while the piece as a whole features the stately rhythms of the Sarabande, hemiola-like juxtapositions of triple and duple metre, together with alternations of binary and ternary rhythmic patterns (see Ex. 3.7). Ohana has described these as not only characteristic of the 'tiento' but as closely associated with other flamenco forms. According to Ohana, these rhythms were derived from a Greek pattern known as the 'epitrite' rhythm (cf. Chapter 7).

> It would seem that the rhythmic structures of the tiento, like those of the Andalusian tango and its derivative, the tanguillo, have stemmed from the epitrite rhythm known to the ancient Greeks.[50]

Ex. 3.7: Rhythmic patterns in the *Tiento*

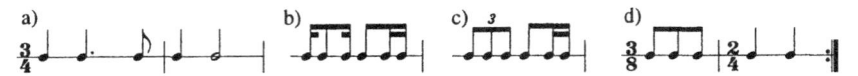

Ohana makes occasional use of quarter-tones to enhance the expressiveness of the melodic line, while the chordal structures exploit the resonant capacity of the low strings. The work ends with a ghostly 'tambora' (striking of the wood of the guitar).[51] Other examples of 'tientos' in Ohana's work include the first movement of *Si le jour paraît...* and the third movement of the guitar concerto *Trois graphiques,* although the latter is of a more extrovert character. Both the *Tiento* and *Trois graphiques* have been arranged to enable performance on the ten-string guitar which Ohana developed during the early 1960s in collaboration the guitarists Narciso Yepez and Alberto Ponce.[52] As in Falla, the textural relationship between the guitar and harpsichord in Ohana is very close. The guitar *Tiento* exists in a version for harpsichord and in 1958 Ohana composed a *Farruca* intended for performance on either instrument.

Following his incidental music to Lope de Vega's play *Fuenteovejuna* (one of the acknowledged masterpieces of Spanish Golden Age drama), Ohana re-worked his earlier sketches for the guitar concerto which finally appeared in 1957 entitled *Trois graphiques.* Like *Trois caprices,* the title of the guitar concerto refers to the etchings of Goya. The work is based on the forms and performance style of the flamenco guitar but is designed for performance on a classical instrument. (The construction of the flamenco guitar is slightly different.) The concerto not only incorporates microintervals, but periodically requires specific techniques which include: playing near the bridge to create a harsh, or rasping tone quality; the pushing of the string downwards towards the sound-board (in classical playing it is pulled parallel to the sound-board); the specified use of finger tips and finger nails; the dampening of strings with an outstretched finger of the left hand (apagado); the playing of the wood of the instrument (tambora); certain rhythmic accentuations (golpe); and the dramatic 'rasgueado' (meaning stroking) in which all strings are strummed rapidly and often violently (sometimes with the nails) up or down the instrument to produce a particularly strident and percussive sound. That Ohana knew and had performed with Ramón Montoya (1880–1949), one of the acknowledged masters of the flamenco guitar,[53] provided him with an invaluable insight into the art of the performance style (cf. Chapter 1):

> In contact with Montoya ... I was able to observe the resources ... and range of technical means at the disposal of such a great and real flamenco guitarist ... . It does not just concern the degree of virtuosity but also the essence and musical conception of his style ... . It is a bitter, percussive guitar playing; ornamentations are barely harmonically analysable, the rasgueado melting into a metallic or wooden resonance and the absence of a tempered scale overwhelms the modern ear with percussive effects. It becomes a play of rhythm, timbre and sound-density.[54]

Dedicated to Narciso Yepez who gave the first performance, the concerto conforms to a three movement fast (with a slow introduction)–slow–fast scheme; 'Graphique de la Farruca et cadences', 'Improvisation sur Graphique de la Siguiriya', 'Graphique de la Bulería et Tiento'.[55] The lively, rhythmically incisive first movement is articulated by three guitar cadenzas, although there are many sections where the soloist plays with the ensemble. There are many allusions to the *Llanto,* on which Ohana was working when be began drafting ideas for the concerto, throughout the first movement. The final cadenza also makes reference to Falla's *Homenaje.* The more reflective second movement alludes to the expressive Cante Jondo[56] and includes a quotation from the *Llanto* in the solo part (fig. 3). The movement is characterised by the alternation of contrasting sections of tension and relaxation, the soloist improvising on the orchestral interpolations. The referential note 'E' is given particular prominence, melodically and harmonically (not uncommon in guitar music due to the tuning of the instrument). The virtuosic third movement incorporates techniques of 'tambora', 'rasgueado' and the percussive effects of strings striking the fingerboard. While the timbrally 'harsh' intervals of tritones and major sevenths (and their inversions) abound in the outer movements, the expressive Siguiriya emphasises 'softer' perfect intervals and minor sevenths (and inversions), often in sections of melodic parallelism, again anticipating the harmonic procedures of his mature style. Occasional use is made of quarter-tones as well as third-tone microintervals to intensify the expressive range of melodic lines. The use of percussion and trumpet throughout the concerto recalls the *Llanto.*

Completed immediately following the guitar concerto, *Récit de l'an zéro* is the first work, other than incidental music, to incorporate the zither tuned to third-tone microintervals which had been introduced to Paris by Juan Carrillo in 1955. Already experimenting with quarter-tones in *Cantigas* which preceded his discovery of the new instrument, Ohana was keen to find a means of developing a coordinated system for notating and performing the microintervals accurately. The zither was not only easy to tune to either quarter or third-tones but convenient for training singers to pitch the relatively unfamiliar intervals.[57] Having used third-tones for the first time in the incidental music to *Les hommes et les autres* Ohana began to use them increasingly, gradually abandoning quarter-tones altogether. He refined his use of the third-tone zither in *Récit* and much of the subsequent incidental music, prior to using the instrument as a soloist in *Tombeau de Claude Debussy*.

> There is a difference of tone between the two instruments. The zither in thirds of a tone is much sharper and has a crystalline quality which is lacking in the zither tuned in quarter-tones ... . The use of these new intervals seems to me to be a natural step towards the conquest of one more of the harmonics coming next after Debussy's ninths and Ravel's elevenths and thirteenths. The only new thing is that they are deliberately played and thus enlarge the possibilities of the melody to an immense extent.[58]

Although one of Ohana's many commissions from French radio, a project which dated back to 1954, he was never entirely happy with *Récit de l'an zéro* which has not been performed since 1961. (His setting of George Schéhadé's allegorical Nativity play can be staged or performed as a concert work.) The work is significant for the opportunity it gave Ohana to develop his approach to theatre music, the juxtaposition of spoken dialogue with sung text (solo and choral) and for the incorporation of the third-tone zither, piano and large percussion group into the instrumental ensemble. His dissatisfaction with the work may have resulted from a sense of musical frustration: practical necessities required the completion of a commission already delayed for several years when he wished instead to explore different aspects of his language. The instrumentation of some of the incidental and radiophonic music which followed *Récit* indicates the beginnings of such exploration: the score for Bronislaw Horowicz's *Homère et Orchidée* was for an unaccompanied third-tone zither, while that for Pierre Barbier's *La route qui poudroie* combined the zither with woodwind, percussion, piano, strings. The radiophonic score for Camilo José Cela's *Histoire véridique de Jacotin* also combines the third-tone zither with wind, percussion and strings, as well as solo voices, thus anticipating some of the instrumental and vocal colouring of *Tombeau de Claude Debussy*. Ohana's music for Edmond Lévy's film *La Blessure* explores relationships between the unusual combination of flute, third-tone zither, percussion and piano which anticipates the scoring of *Signes* (cf. Chapter 4). Between the late 1950s and the middle 1960s Ohana's music underwent a profound stylistic change.

The Transitional Works

The early 1960s represented a turning-point in Ohana's compositional direction and heralded the emergence of his mature style. He ceased to draw as intensively on Spanish sources as in his early works, and looked instead towards his French musical ancestors, most importantly Debussy.[59] Although the works composed between 1960 and 1964 contain many features which are characteristic of his compositional maturity, only from the middle 1960s onwards, with *Signes* and the works of the Sigma Series, did all the techniques of his mature style become fully established. It is for this reason that the works of the early 1960s have been described as transitional. While *Carillons pour les heures du jour et de la nuit* and the *Quatre improvisations* stand at the threshold of his new compositional path, *Tombeau de Claude Debussy, Cinq séquences* and *Si le jour paraît...* reveal a new refinement which shows Debussy as Ohana's true musical and spiritual father. Although much of Ohana's writing for harpsichord was initially close to that of Falla, his writing for the instrument from *Carillons* onwards is dramatically different and owes far more to ideas first explored in *Hommage à Luis Milán*. In *Carillons*, as the title suggests, the harpsichord is investigated as much for its resonant and percussive qualities as for its melodic capabilities. It exploits a range of effects including extensive use of cluster-chords (arpeggiated and non-arpeggiated) and the juxtaposition of extremes of register and dynamics. Improvisatory in character, *Carillons* develops the rhythmic flexibility found in the first movement cadenzas of the guitar concerto and unaccompanied vocalisations in *Cantigas*; apart from one short section, it is almost entirely unmetred. A much richer harmonic vocabulary than hitherto, a chord-aggregate system contrasts tritone-based chords with others based on softer sounding perfect intervals or minor sevenths. Sections of note-for-note organum-like parallelism serve to thicken the vocal character of the melodic lines in the outer sections. A small-scale collage, the sectionalism of the piece is suggestive of some of Debussy's piano *Etudes*. Given the forward-looking nature of this piece and the timbral explorations suggested by the title, it is interesting to note that some years later Ohana completed a commission for the carillon of bells at the *Eglise Saint-Germain-l'Auxerrois* in Paris. The resulting work was subsequently transcribed for harpsichord as *Wamba*, the name given both to the Visigoth king of seventh century Toledo and to some of the great bells of Spanish cathedrals.[60]

The *Quatre improvisations* for solo flute, composed also in 1960, are similarly forward-looking. Suggesting the incantations of primitive ritual, not unlike Jolivet's *Cinq incantations* of 1936, these four short pieces seek to recreate the spontaneity of improvisation within a composed score. They also explore a more organic approach to melodic structure which anticipates Ohana's later process of continuous extension by variation and addition (cf. Chaper 5). While the seeds of this process are to be found in the baritone vocalisations of the *Llanto,* their context in the *Quatre improvisations* is quite different, the improvisatory nature of the process being entirely explicit. The musical substance is also liberated from the constraints of text. Like *Carillons*, the *Quatre improvisations* are largely unmetred but sectional. Each of the four short movements is freely constructed from successions of melodic units which pivot about certain referential notes: in the first movement, 'D♭' and 'E', but ending on 'B♭'; in the second, 'E' and 'D', but ending on 'C–plus–2-third-tones'; in third and fourth movement, 'C'. The *Improvisations* make systematic use of third-tone microintervals to the exclusion of quarter-tones. While Ohana's instinctive attraction to different traditions of monodic vocal music, whether flamenco, African tribal chant or plainsong, helped to formulate his melodic style, the *Quatre improvisations* represent one of the first manifestations of a melodic style in which individual features have coalesced into a more homogeneous, less obviously derivative whole. Similarly, the rhythmic structures are less derivative, although individual units can be traced to their African, Spanish or, as in the last of the *improvisations,* Afro-Cuban roots.

Although *Carillons* and *Quatre improvisations* reveal Ohana's new compositional direction, the limitations of writing for the solo instruments inhibit the further technical experimentation and timbral refinement that the larger forces of his next important work could allow. Commissioned by French radio, *Tombeau de Claude Debussy* was originally intended to be one of three works designed to commemorate the centenary of Debussy's birth. The other contributors were to have been Messiaen and Dutilleux.[61] Only Ohana completed something for the occasion; an orchestral work in seven movements with three soloists, which he dedicated to Dutilleux. The influence of Spanish music, so conspicuous in his earlier scores, is barely evident, having here been absorbed into a more unified language. The work clearly illustrates Ohana's alignment with the French tradition and reveals an approach to instrumentation evoking a Debussian colourism that is more typical of his subsequent works than of those which preceded it. A small string section, single wood-wind, horn and trumpet are enhanced by a large percussion group (requiring six players) that is divided into three timbral groups: pitched and unpitched metal; pitched and unpitched wood; pitched and unpitched skins, the pitched section including eight African toms whose role is entirely melodic. The three soloists, soprano, piano (alternating celesta) and third-tone zither (two instruments are required to achieve the necessary range of pitch), merge with the ensemble as much as they are juxtaposed against it. Due to Ohana's predilection for clusters and effects of resonance, the pianist is required to make use of felt-covered rulers as in *Hommage à Luis Milán* and *Carillons*. Originally intended to include a text by Raphaël Cluzel (from which some of the movement titles are drawn), the soprano line unfolds in a quasi-improvisatory, but composed, vocalisation without text. Although later vocal works make use of phonemes and morphemes to articulate the vocal line, the wordless vocalisations in *Tombeau* evoke the magical atmosphere of Debussy's sirens of the *Nocturnes*. Used purely as a sound-texture, the voice appears in only three movements; the first 'Hommage', the fourth 'Autres soleils', and the seventh 'Envoi', and underpins the structural symmetry of the work as a whole. (The central axis is represented by the solo piano cadenza of the fourth movement 'Autres soleils', cf. Chapter 8). The vocal writing is also notable for its extensive and systematic use of third-tone microintervals, these being constructed from third-tone scales which are themselves based on the very Debussian whole-tone scale (see Ex. 3.8).

Third-tone intervals are found in the orchestral parts as well as in the soprano and zither, and although their function is largely colouristic, extending the expressiveness of melodic lines, they also occur in a harmonic context. Associated with the whole-tone scale from which they are constructed (cf. Chapter 5, Ex. 5.4), they often occur as cluster-chords within sections of thickened monody as an added harmonic colour within a chord-aggregate that is otherwise based on equal-temperament. Such chord-aggregates tend to include

Ex. 3.8: *Tombeau de Claude Debussy*, 'Hommage'
(reduction – soprano, third-tone zither, fig. 5–6)

Reproduced by kind permission of Editions Amphion, Paris / United Music Publishers Ltd.

tritones and major seconds, characteristic features of the whole-tone scale. Ohana considered the use of third-tones a means of developing Debussian harmonies. In the preface to the score of *Tombeau* he indicated that one of the objectives of the work was to 'make concrete some of Debussy's intentions, principally in the harmonic sphere'. It is interesting to note that in Debussy's conversations with Ernest Guiraud he reflects on the possibilities of an 'octave divided into eighteen degrees' and proposes that 'other scales should enrich the tonal scale'.[62] As the third-tone scale divides the octave into eighteen degrees, it is tempting to ponder whether Debussy may have been considering third-tone microintervals.[63]

Ohana takes as his compositional point of departure certain rhythmic and melodic fragments from the piano music of Debussy. In the preface to the score, he indicates 'borrowings' from the *Préludes*, *Etudes* and *En blanc et noir* but specifies that these represent only a point of compositional departure. Some commentators have suggested the *Tombeau* to include quoted phrases from *Pelléas et Mélisande* (Arkel, Act IV), as well as 'Nous n'irons plus au bois' from *Jardins sous la pluie*.[64] As none of these allusions, or near citations are indicated in Ohana's score, they are purely subjective and depend for their recognition on the listener's familiarity with the Debussian source. The opening of the first movement, 'Hommage' is characteristic of Ohana's allusive technique. The opening phrase of the movement simultaneously evokes two

Ex. 3.9a: *Tombeau de Claude Debussy*, 'Hommage' (bars 1–6)

Debussy preludes; the harmonic structure contains characteristics of the first chord of 'Feuilles mortes' (the simultaneous sounding of dissonance and resolution), while the phrase as a whole paraphrases, in slow-motion, the opening phrase of 'La terrasse des audiences du clair de lune' (see Ex.3.9a and Ex. 3.9b). The melodic parallelism of the opening of Ohana's score is a feature of the work throughout and is not only a typical trait of Debussy but is a texture also common in Dutilleux as well as in Messiaen.

Ex. 3.9b: Debussy, 'La terrasse des audiences du clair de lune', *Préludes* (II) (bars 1–2)

Reproduced by kind permission of Editions Costallat, Paris / United Music Publishers Ltd.

The most intriguing Debussian allusion occurs in the third movement, 'Ballade de la Grand Guerre', which draws much of its material and structure from the second movement of *En blanc et noir* of which François Villon's *Ballade contre les ennemis de France* is the principal starting point.[65] Ohana alludes to Debussy's repeated note motif, as well as to the passage marked 'sourdement tumultueux'. Like Debussy, he evokes the rumble of distant canons, fanfares and makes reference to the Marseillaise (see Ex. 3.10). Both Ohana's movement and the Debussian model are constructed in an arch-form which embraces a central more rapid and intense section. While Debussy composed *En blanc et noir* against the background of the World War I,[66] Ohana's experiences in World War II must have provided a poignant parallel.

Ohana's first string quartet, *Cinq séquences* follows, as the title suggests, a five movement plan. Further developing the structural symmetry explored in *Tombeau de Claude Debussy* although less Debussian in musical content, the quartet pivots about the central movement 'Tympanum' which stands out from the surrounding movements through its treatment of rhythm as a texture independent of other musical parameters. In 'Tympanum' Ohana makes use of layering techniques first tentatively explored in the *Etudes chorégraphiques* but which are here developed to a far greater level of sophistication and textural subtlety. Two sections of metred homorhythm at the opening and close of the movement (the first very brief, the second longer and more climactic) enclose an extended, unmetred section where each of the four parts play repetitive rhythmic patterns independently of each other. With some parts governed by different metronome markings, the technique is one of superimposing contrasting patterns to create complex, resultant cross-rhythms where the vertical coincidence of parts is undefined and left to chance (see Ex. 3.11). All parts being strictly notated, Ohana described this linear process as 'combinatoire' rather than 'aléatoire' (cf. Chapter 4). Making use of percussive textures including playing with the wood of the bow and using different pizzicati (open and stopped strings, on the fingerboard, near the bridge, with and without glissandi), the effect is one of intense rhythmic activity, evoking the atmosphere of drums. Although the individual rhythmic units are often articulated on a single repeated note, some units involve two pitches, like tom-toms, to clarify the rhythmic outline and pattern rather than to introduce any sense of melody. The title enforces the textural allusion: 'Tympanum' refers to the drums of ancient Greece and Rome, as well as to several plucked, zither-like instruments of the Middle Ages.[67] The section also incorporates third-tone microintervals. While many aspects of *Tombeau de Claude Debussy* presage Ohana's mature style, it is not until *Cinq séquences* that he first incorporates this new 'combinatoire' technique.

Ex. 3.10: *Tombeau de Claude Debussy*, 'Ballade de la Grande Guerre' (fig. 5–6)

Reproduced by kind permission of Editions Amphion, Paris / United Music Publishers Ltd.

The remaining movements support the overall symmetry of the work, while their individual titles allude to Ohana's recourse to medieval vocal music, further developing ideas explored in *Cantigas*. 'Monodie' and 'Déchant' involve different approaches to writing that is essentially monodic. The former aims to evoke the atmosphere of improvisation with unaccompanied melodies descending from the first violin through each instrument to the cello, articulated by brief homophonic interpolations from the remaining instruments and concluding with a thickened monody in note-for-note parallelism, senza vibrato. The latter, recalling Medieval discant, includes much organum-like parallelism where all voices move at the same speed, in different instrumental combinations and is again senza vibrato. The outer movements 'Polyphonie' and 'Hymne', as the titles suggest, explore contrasting polyphonic textures; the former contrapuntal and linear, the latter involving organum-like parallelism in four or more parts throughout. Although sometimes involving octave displacements and transpositions, the melodic lines of all movements suggest the contours of plainchant. The quartet also involves third-tone microintervals in addition to conventional temperament in semitones. Ohana writes in the preface to the score: 'strings, like the human voice and percussion, offer among non-electronic means of expression the greatest possibilities for exploring the sound-world contained between the notes of equal-temperament.'

Ex. 3.11: *Cinq séquences*, 'Tympanum' (figs. 3–4)

Reproduced by kind permission of Société des Editions Jobert, Paris / United Music Publishers Ltd.

The final work of Ohana's transitional period, *Si le jour paraît...* for 10-string guitar, borrows its title from one of Goya's etchings of the *Caprichos*, 'Si amenece vamos' (If day breaks, we shall depart). Ohana's title indicates that the quotation of Goya's title is intentionally incomplete (cf. Chapter 2). Although Spanish in terms of its artistic allusion and its sombre mood (which recalls *Trois caprices* and the *Tiento*), the sound-world of *Si le jour paraît...* is Debussian; a feature which is placing by the appearance of the movement titles at the end of each piece, in the manner of Debussy's *Préludes*, rather than at the beginning. (The later work for 10-string guitar, *Cadran lunaire*, also adopts the same procedure..) Despite the incorporation of certain performance techniques and rhythmic patterns derived from the flamenco, *Si le jour paraît...* is far less overtly Spanish than his earlier guitar works; these idioms have become colours and textures in a broader musical vocabulary that has been fused into a stylistically unified whole. Like *Tombeau de Claude Debussy* and *Cinq séquences*, the movement structure conforms to a symmetrical plan, although is here expanded to seven movements. The central, fourth movement about which the work pivots, 'Vingt avril (Planh)', is the expressive heart of the work. A funerary lament based on the Provençal Planh of Troubadour poetry, the movement commemorates the execution on 20 April 1962 of an unnamed political prisoner in Franco's Spain.[68] The larger symmetry is reflected in the inter-relationships of the first three movements which incorporate a range of performance techniques derived from the flamenco, while the last three movements draw their inspiration from Debussian references to nature.

The individual movements balance each other through contrasting subject and musical character. The third and fifth movements 'Maya-Marsya' and 'La chevelure de Bérenice', allude to mythological matters. The former is a celebration of light, the powers of winds and the renewal of nature in Spring. It is an extrovert, virtuosic display, rhythmic and metred, and is dedicated to the memory of the flamenco guitarist Ramón Montoya. Referring to the constellation, the latter evokes the peace and tranquillity of the night-sky. It is slow, reflective, improvisatory and unmetred, and is dedicated to the composer Ivo Malec.[69] The second and fourth movements explore contrasting forms of monody. 'Enueg' borrows its title from the Troubadour songs of Protest and is slow, largely unmetred and explores a violence of percussive expression, enhanced through glissandi, the use of 'rasgueado', string snapping, fortissimo tremolo 'tambora' and the harsh sound-textures of playing at the bridge or beating of the strings with a metal ruler. 'Jeu des quatres vents' is rapid, extrovert and percussive, recalling Debussy's *Prelude* 'Ce qu'a vu le vent d'ouest'. It is dedicated to Manuel Ruiz Pipó. The outer movements act as prologue and epilogue. The first movement provides an introductory prelude presenting a range of material and instrumental textures and is dedicated to Alberto Ponce.[70] Borrowing its title from the flamenco, 'Temple' refers to the preparation or tuning-up of a singer's voice prior to commencing the melismatic improvisations of the Cante Jondo. Alluding to the Troubadour song describing the parting of lovers, the final movement 'Aube' suggests the day-break implicit in the title of the work as a whole. Slow, expressive but senza vibrato, the movement evokes a pessimistic mood; the pain of separation and impending solitude, the greys of black and white of Goya's etchings (and of Debussy's *En blanc et noir*, cf. Chapter 2) which are reflected in the restrained instrumental timbre. Third-tone microintervals are used throughout.

Si le jour paraît... was the first of Ohana's works for the 10-string guitar, an instrument which he developed in collaboration Alberto Ponce and Narciso Yepes (for whom the work was originally intended) and the Spanish maker Ramirez.[71] While preserving the conventional tuning of the upper six strings, the additional strings greatly enhance not only the resonant capacity of the instrument but also the range of harmonic possibilities. From bottom to top the order of strings in Ohana's scordatura is as follows: G♭–A♭–B♭–C (low) –E–A–D–G–B–E.[72] Ohana's enthusiasm for the instrument resulted in providing alternative versions for *Tiento* and the concerto *Trois graphiques*, to enable performance on the new instrument. Although *Si le jour paraît...* remains one of Ohana's most effective works, it is rarely performed as few players are able to manage the increased girth of the neck and larger dimensions of the instrument overall. (The composer has provided ossias to enable performance on a conventional instrument of six strings.)

The progressive broadening of Ohana's compositional interests during his transitional phase is indicated not only by his recourse to Debussy, and techniques borrowed from Medieval and Renaissance vocal repertoire, but by a growing attraction for Classical subjects. Like many aspects of his music, the seeds of this interest were sown in the early period; he completed an incidental music score for an adaptation of Seneca's Medea by José Bergamín and collaborated with Maurice Béjart on the ballet *Prométhée*. In the 1960s Ohana undertook a series of collaborations for radiophonic scores on adaptations of Euripides by Gabriel Audisio: *Hélène* (1963), *Les Héraclides* (1964), *Iphigénie en Tauride* (1965) and *Hippolyte* (1966). The technical and stylistic explorations of these scores are reflected not only in the transitional works themselves, but came to fruition in the later 1960s with his own adaptation of Euripides for the Choeur Maurice Ravel and Ensemble Ars Nova in the chamber opera *Syllabaire pour Phèdre* (1967). All of these scores require either vocal soloists or chorus. Ohana's predilection for writing for the voice dominates his catalogue from the early period up to and including his last completed work *Avoaha*. Vocal traditions, whether improvised folk music of Spain and Africa, or composed music of the Medieval and Renaissance repertories, provided the continuity of creative inspiration in Ohana's instrumental works, as well as those for vocal forces. The incorporation of the microinterval scales of third-tones, progressively refined during the later 1950s and into the transitional period, is derived from the natural intonations of monodic vocal traditions from plainsong to Spanish folk melodies. After 1966, incidental music no longer figures in Ohana's catalogue, the necessity for intense stylistic experimentation in the synthesis of an effective, and unified musical language having subsided. The number of commissions for concert and theatre works increased sufficiently for Ohana to be able to continue to live from composition, a feat for which he won the admiration of Dutilleux:

> He [Ohana] knew how to avoid the constraints or security of a second skill, of a subsidiary occupation. It is a choice full of risks which I was only able to make later.[73]

Throughout his early and transitional periods, Ohana moved from a language that was essentially derivative to one where individual, inspirational sources were able to blend into a more homogenous whole, fused through his continued reflection on the musical common denominators which unite them. Clearly Ohana's compositional approach is eclectic but can be seen in a light far from negative. If the early works are unified by the predominance of Spanish influence, the transitional works are characterised by increasing exploration with independence of rhythmic and melodic parameters. *Carillons*, *Quatre improvisations* and *Tombeau de Claude Debussy* point the way towards Ohana's mature style. *Cinq séquences* introduces the new technique of 'combinatoire' counterpoint (cf. Chapter 4) and develops an essentially linear approach to harmonic density. *Si le jour paraît...* illustrates a more developed approach to internal structures which reveals the composer's indebtedness to the sectionalism of Debussy, particularly that of the *Etudes* for piano.

Notes to Chapter Three.

1 The present author in conversations with the composer in Paris, February 1983 and March 1984.
2 P. Boulez, 'Incipit' originally published in English as 'Note to Tonight's Concert: Webern's Work Analysed', in *New York Herald Tribune* (28 December 1952) (S. Walsh trans. *Stocktakings From an Apprenticeship* (Oxford, 1991) p. 215.) Published in French, text of the *Domaine musical* No. 1 (1954), in German in *Die Reihe* Vol. 2 'Für Anton Webern (Wien, 1955) pp. 45–6. Reproduced in *Relevés d'apprenti* (Paris, 1966) 273–4.
3 C. Potter, *Henri Dutilleux his Life and Works* (London, 1997) p. 7.
4 J. Roy, *Présences contemporaines musique française* (Paris, 1962) p. 400.
5 See C. Schreiner, *Flamenco Gypsy Dance and Music from Andalusia*, Eng. trans. M.C. Peters (Amadeus Press, Portland, Oregan, 1990); Falla, 'The Cante Jondo', *Manuel de Falla on Music and Musicians* Eng. trans. D. Urman and J.M. Thomson (London, 1979) pp. 99–117; M. Cunningham and A. de Larrea Palacín, 'Spain II: Folk Music', *The New Grove Dictionary of Music and Musicians* Vol. 17 (London, 1980) pp. 790–805; I.J. Katz, 'Flamenco' *The New Grove Dictionary of Music and Musicians* Vol. 6 (London, 1980) pp. 635–730; J.B. Trend and I.J. Katz, 'Cante Hondo', *The New Grove Dictionary of Music and Musicians* Vol. 3 (London, 1980) p. 719.
6 Federico García Lorca equated the sharp contrasts of light and dark, night and day, with the life-death symbolism of the bull-ring in 'Sun and Shade', *Deep Song and Other Prose,* trans. C. Maurer (London, 1960) pp. 57–8. Picasso drew on the same themes in a series of etchings of the 'Corrida'.
7 A detailed study of the Iberian issue of Ohana's music has been written by Odile Marcel, the composer's second wife, 'L'Ibérisme de Maurice Ohana', *La Revue musicale* Nos 351–2 (Paris, 1982) pp. 11–26.

8   A number of works were withdrawn as a result of a dispute with his then publisher Pierre Noël. Several of these were later reinstated with Billaudot, although no performances have taken place since the 1950s. Some hitherto withdrawn and unpublished works were deposited with his two main publishers (Jobert and Billaudot) during the last years of his life.
9   The Toccata is the only surviving movement of Ohana's *Suite pour piano* but remains unpublished.
10 Much of the one movement harpsichord concerto was reworked in the guitar concerto, *Trois graphiques*.
11 The relationship between Ohana's references to Goya and those of Debussy is discussed further in C. Rae, 'Debussy and Ohana: allusions et réferences', *Cahiers Debussy* Nos 17–18 (1993–4) pp. 109–10.
12 Although during his years as a concert pianist, Ohana performed more Debussy than Ravel, *Gaspard de la nuit* was of course well-known to him. Ohana felt that in comparison to Ravel, Debussy's piano music had been unfairly neglected by the young virtuosi of the Conservatoire.
13 I.J. Katz, 'Flamenco', *The New Grove Dictionary of Music and Musicians* Vol. 6 (London, 1980) p. 628.
14 M. Ohana, 'Alfredo Casella', *The Music Review* viii (1947) p. 145 (Original in English).
15 I.J. Katz (1980) op. cit. p. 719; M. Cunningham and A. de Larrea Palacín (1980) op. cit. p. 798.
16 Ibid.
17 M. Ohana, 'Notes du quelques formes du folklore espagnole', copies of the composer's MS in the author's personal archive.
18 The 'Cante Jondo', meaning literally 'deep song' is a special sub-group of flamenco song characterised by a particular seriousness of expressive intensity.
19 Conversations with the composer in Paris, March 1984.
20 M. Ohana, 'Los Gitanillos de Cadiz', sleeve-notes, *Club français du disque* G4188 (1955) p. 11.
21 Ohana's drawing of the *Paso* is reproduced as Plate 6.
22 Ohana dedicated his setting of the *Llanto* to Alain Bermat, a fellow member of the *Groupe Zodiaque*.
23 He died in Madrid on 13 August 1934, *Oxford Companion to Spanish Literature* ed. P. Ward (1978) p. 331.
24 Under her own name, Encarnación Júlvez López.
25 The Spanish term for the bull-fight
26 Lorca, 'Play and Theory of the Duende' and 'Sun and Shade', respectively, in *Deep Song and other Prose*, trans. C. Maurer (London, 1980) pp. 50–51, 51–8.
27 A. Carpentier, 'Revelación de un compositor', *El Nacional*, Caracas, 29 April, 1956, reproduced in *Ese músico que llevo dentro I, Obras completas de Alejo Carpentier*, Vol. 10 (Mexico, 1987) pp. 214–17.
28 Lorca, 'Play and Theory of the Duende', op. cit. pp. 49–50.
29 C. Schreiner (1990) op. cit.
30 'La géographie musicale de l'Espagne', *Journal musical français* Nos 47–8 (Paris, April 1956) p. 8.
31 C. Prost (1981) p. 119.
32 The following songs types are among those most typically associated with the Cante Jondo style of the flamenco: caña, debla, martinete, polo, saeta, serrana, siguiriya, solear and toná. (J.B. Trend and I.J. Katz, 'Cante Hondo' *The New Grove Dictionary of Music and Musicians* Vol.3 (London, 1980) p. 719.
33 C. Prost (1981) has suggested that the Andalusian modal scale of the flamenco provided the basis for these transformations.

34	Falla, 'El Cante Jondo', *Manuel de Falla on Music and Musicians*, Eng. trans. D. Urman and J.M. Thomson (London, 1979) pp. 99–117.
35	See H. Koegler, *The Concise Oxford Dictionary of Ballet* (Oxford, 1982) pp. 18 and 261.
36	J. Roy, (1962) op. cit. p. 393.
37	M. Cunningham and A. de Larrea Palacín (1980) op. cit. p. 0
38	M. Ohana, 'La géographie musicale de l'Espagne', *Journal musical français* (March 8, 1956) p. 8.
39	Spanish ballads of folk origin. See P. Ward ed., *The Oxford Companion to Spanish Literature* (Oxford, 1978) pp. 507–8.
40	J. Roy, (1962) p. 394.
41	Loc. cit.
42	M. Ohana, 'La marionette à l'opéra', reproduced in *La Revue musicale* (1982) p. 75.
43	M. Ohana: 'Théâtre musicale', *c.* 1970 (MS in the possession of the present author) p. 1.
44	M. Ohana, interview (in French), C.Paquelet (1987) pp. 56–7.
45	H. Koegler (1982) op. cit. p. 207.
46	Ohana admired much of Varèse's work. The author in conversation with the composer in Paris, April 1992.
47	M. Ohana, Interview (in French), C.Paquelet (1987) p. 56.
48	A.M. Jones, *Studies in African Music*, 2 Vols (Oxford, 1959).
49	I.J. Katz (1980) op. cit. p. 628.
50	M Ohana, 'Los gitanillos de Cadix' op. cit. p. 2.
51	The score incorrectly indicates the tambora over the last two bars. According to the composer it applies only to the final bar.
52	The additional strings extend the instrument to a low C. Ramirez of Madrid was one of the first to build the 10-string guitar.
53	C. Schreiner (1990) op. cit. p. 130–1. Contemporary masters of the flamenco guitar include Paco de Lucía, Paco Peña and the Romeros family.
54	M. Ohana, Interview (in French) P. Bolbach (1982). p. 6.
55	Farruca, Siguiriya, Bulería and Tiento are all song and dance forms of the flamenco.
56	The Siguiriya belongs to the Cante Jondo repertory of the flamenco.
57	The third-tone zither is based on the whole-tone scale, the quarter-tone zither on the chromatic scale. In the third-tone scale, every third string is tuned a tone apart, the intervening strings being tuned equidistantly to the third-tone microinterval. The third-tone scale precludes the existence of semi-tones or quarter-tones.
58	M. Ohana, 'Micro-Intervals, Experimental Media II' *Twentieth Century Music*, ed. R. Myers (1968) pp. 149–50 (Original in English).
59	M. Ohana, Interview (in French), J.C. Marti (1991) p. 9.
60	'Wamba' is the first of *Deux pièces pour clavecin* (1980–82).
61	A letter from Messiaen to Dutilleux dated 16 August 1961, now housed in the Paul Sacher Stiftung, Basel. Cited by C. Potter (1997) pp. 14–15.
62	Debussy-Guiraud conversations, collected by Maurice Emmanuel, reproduced in E. Lockspeiser *Debussy his Life and Mind*, Vol. 1 (London, 1962) pp. 173–4.
63	That the third-tone scale precludes the existence of semi-tones, distinguishes Ohana's scale from that envisaged by Busoni.
64	C. Prost, 'Catalogue raisonné', *La Revue musicale* Nos 391–3 (Paris, 1986) p. 198.
65	These allusions are examined in detail in C. Rae, 'Debussy and Ohana: allusions et réferences', *Cahiers Debussy* Nos 17–18 (1993–4) pp. 103–20.

66 Debussy dedicated the second movement of *En blanc et noir* to Lieutenant Jacques Charlot who was killed in action on 3 March, 1915.
67 *The New Harvard Dictionary of Music* ed. Don Michael Randel (HUP, 1986) p. 890.
68 C. Prost is contradictory about this point. She suggests the lament commemorated the assassination in 1962 of a political prisoner of Franco's Spain in 'Catalogue raisonné' (*La Revue musicale*, 1986) p. 200, but refers to the Spanish Civil War in her booklet notes to CD-Astris Auvidis E 8513,1993). It is likely that Ohana was commemorating the more recent event which only shortly predated the composition.
69 Ivo Malec, like Ohana, was among the composers commissioned by Dutilleux to write scores for his 'illustrations musicales'.
70 Alberto Ponce gave the first performance (complete) of *Si le jour paraît...* and completed the fingering for the published score.
71 It was not the first 10-string instrument ever constructed. An earlier instrument with a different scordatura was invented in the early nineteenth century for which Ferdinando Carulli provided a method in 1927.
72 The same scordatura is used in Ohana's later work for 10-string guitar *Cadran lunaire*.
73 H. Dutilleux, *Mystère et mémoire des sons - Entretiens avec Claude Glaymann* (Paris, 1997) p. 188.

PART TWO

The Mature Music: Technique, Style and Structure

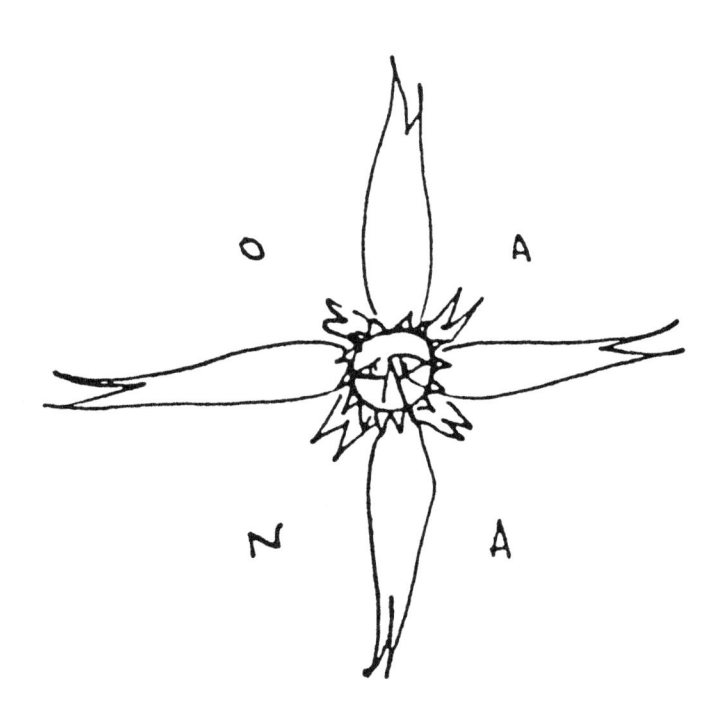

CHAPTER FOUR

Growth and Proliferation: *Signes* and the Sigma Series

Signes, for instrumental ensemble, was declared by Ohana to be the first of his works to contain all the main features of his mature compositional language.[1] Completed during the spring of 1965, *Signes* is central to an understanding of the development of the composer's technique, style and structure and will therefore be examined in detail in the present chapter. It is also the first of a series of works composed over a period of eleven years, here described as the Sigma Series, which bear witness to the growth and proliferation of his mature language into a range of other genres. Although the process of stylistic evolution began in Ohana's transitional works of the early 1960s and was accelerated by the innovations of *Tombeau de Claude Debussy* and *Cinq séquences*, the stylistic synthesis of *Signes* defined, for the composer, a new creative starting-point. It is for this reason that *Signes*, rather than *Tombeau de Claude Debussy*, represents the burgeoning of his compositional maturity. That the middle, rather than the early 1960s represent the birth of Ohana's mature style is further supported by another change in his compositional habits; after 1966 he ceased to accept commissions for incidental music or radiophonic scores, presumably as he no longer sought the opportunity for experimentation that these commissions presented. (Dutilleux's departure from French Radio in 1963 may also have precipitated Ohana's decision.) Ohana's approach to symbolic reference also changed during the middle 1960s (cf. Chapter 2). Associated with the resonant symbolism of the tree, as well as being the first of the Sigma Series, *Signes* indicates the beginning of a deeper evolution; as a result of the discoveries of the transitional period, Ohana's compositional process had not only taken root but could grow and proliferate into his second half century.

Drawing its title from the ciphers, or signs, which appear at the head of each of the six movements, and which represent esoteric allusions to nature (cf. Chapter 2), *Signes* has much in common with Debussy. The themes of nature evoked in the six portraits of the tree ('at night', 'alive with birds', 'drowned with rain', 'imprisoned by spiders' webs', 'beaten by the wind' and 'burnt by the sun') generate the musical character of each movement. In this sense, the work can be described as impressionist in that it is pictorial and descriptive. Like Debussy's often enigmatic titles for the piano preludes which appear at the end of each piece, the allusions inherent in Ohana's ciphers serve to enhance the purely musical substance. The Debussian associations are further underlined in the fifth movement which evokes the tempestuous forces of the wind; featuring the piano, this movement pays homage to Debussy's prelude 'Ce qu'a vu le vent d'ouest'.[2] Although there are no quotations from the Debussy prelude, the allusion is achieved through similarity of mood, pianistic gesture, figuration and texture; both pieces make use of repeated notes, arpeggiation, rapid juxtapositions of register and extremes of register, resonant chordal writing, and exacting pedalling techniques. Both Ohana's movement and the Debussy prelude are sectional and contain similar musical indications; while the Debussy is marked 'animé et tumultueux' Ohana's is marked 'rapide, bien rythmé et tumultueux'. Ohana's movement bore an additional, personal significance for the composer; following the innovation of the central piano cadenza in *Tombeau de Claude Debussy*, *Signes* confirmed Ohana's rediscovery of the piano as a solo instrument.

The unusual instrumentation of *Signes* (comprising flute doubling piccolo, piano, two concert zithers and a large percussion group for four players), enabled Ohana to consolidate his distinctive approach to timbral interplay, first explored in *Tombeau de Claude Debussy*. (Some of the incidental music of the transitional period, notably *La Blessure,* reveals earlier experimentations with this unusual combination.) The subtle inter-relationship of instrumental timbre represent one of the most crucial aspects of Ohana's musical language and one which consolidated his colouristic approach to a harmony (cf. Chapter 6). The purely melodic dimension of *Signes* is represented primarily by the flute (and piccolo), whose solo monodies are a feature of the work in general and of the second movement in particular. A combination of melodic and harmonic functions is carried out by the two zithers which figure in many of Ohana's instrumental and vocal ensembles dating from 1956. His use of the third-tone zither in *Tombeau de Claude Debussy* extended its role from that of a supporting accompanist to a fully-fledged soloist. In *Signes,* two matching zithers of forty-eight strings are required to be tuned differently; one chromatically, the other in third-tone microintervals (see Ex. 4.1).

Ex. 4.1: Range and tuning of zithers in *Signes*

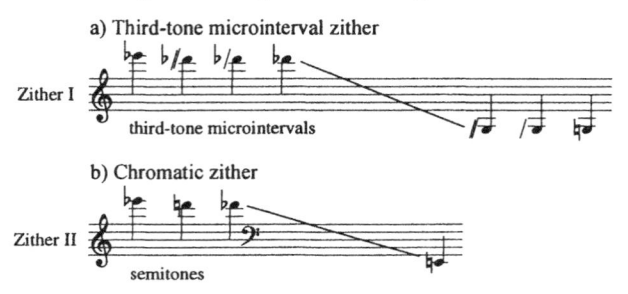

While the middle and upper pitch-registers of both instruments correspond, (the highest string of each instrument is tuned to the same pitch), the zither in semitones has a greater range than the zither in third-tones; the former requires two strings for each step of a major second, the latter requires three. Each zither is to be played with a variety of different sticks (metal, wooden and felt-covered)

in order to produce a range of timbres as well as dynamics. For the same reason, there are some instances where the strings are required to be plucked. The third solo instrument of the group, the piano, fulfils a combination of rhythmic, as well as harmonic functions. While the chordal facility of the piano is convenient for thickening-out harmonic densities, the use of extremes of the piano register to obscure exact pitch recognition allows it to be identified with percussion; the effect in the high registers often suggests metal percussion, while the low registers evoke drums. As in all Ohana's works for piano, a modern concert piano with the additional third pedal is specified. The pianist is also required to make use of three felt-covered rulers of exact lengths to depress certain chord-clusters on either black or white keys (see Ex. 4.2).

Ex. 4.2: Range of the felt-covered rulers required by the pianist in *Signes*

The three main solo instruments are combined with a large percussion section which provides resonant enhancement. The percussion also plays an important rhythmic role and is given prominence, in this respect, in the third movement. Pitched percussion is sometimes used in a melodic context and frequently doubles the main soloists in sections of monodic parallelism. The section as a whole comprises pitched (including approximate pitch) and unpitched instruments of each main timbral group (metal, skins and wood) and includes several instruments of African, Afro-Cuban and South-American origin. Requiring four players, the percussion is sub-divided into four distinct but contrasting timbral groups which are summarised in Table 4.1. While the four groups each have an individual character, there is inevitably some overlap, not unlike the sub-divisions of the *Etudes chorégraphiques* for solo percussion.

Table 4.1: Disposition of percussion and timbral character in *Signes*

P = pitched (incl. approximate pitch); U = unpitched (susp.= suspended)

Timbral character	Group I	Group II	Group III	Group IV
Metal	P + U	U	P + U	P
Skins	P	P + U	P+U	–
Wood	–	P + U	U	U

Table 4.1 *(concluded)*

Timbral character	Group I	Group II	Group III	Group IV
Metal: P	5 Chinese cymbals 3 gongs (high, medium, low)	–	vibraphone glockenspiel* 2 gongs (high, low)	celesta crotales
Metal: U	3 susp. cymbals (high, medium, low) tam-tam (medium)	1 susp. cymbal (low) tam-tam (large)	1 susp. cymbal (low) pair of cymbals	–
Skins: P	2 Saharan drums	5 African toms	2 bongos (high, low)	–
Skins: U	–	2 snare drums 1 side-drum 1 bass-drum	2 side-drums tarole (no snares) tambourine (large with jingles)	–
Wood: P	–	xylorimba	–	–
Wood: U	–	2 temple blocks (high, low)	temple block	maracas claves guero rasp

Note: (*) The glockenspiel is sometimes incorporated into Group II to allow combinations with the vibraphone as a timbral alternative to the xylorimba.)

Thus Group I contains only metal and skins, with a predominance of pitched (including approximately pitched) instruments. (Due to their respective acoustic properties, gongs have been considered as 'pitched', while cymbals and tam-tams are 'unpitched' percussion.) Group II contains unpitched instruments of all three types and also representatives of pitched skins and wood, with the xylorimba playing the most important role of its section. (Although designated 'high' and 'low', the temple blocks have no definite pitch.) Group III, like Group II has unpitched instruments of all types, while its pitched metal plays a prominent role in the percussion as a whole. Group IV contains only pitched metal and unpitched wood. In the pitched percussion, a variety of timbres is achieved through differing combinations of celesta, glockenspiel, vibraphone, xylorimba, crotales and Chinese cymbals. These instruments are also combined periodically with the piano or zithers. Certain combinations of percussion effect a subtle timbral transition between pitched and unpitched instruments of the same type: the xylorimba is related to temple blocks and claves; African toms and Saharan drums to bongos and bass and side drums (without snare); celesta and crotales to suspended cymbals and tam-tam played pianissimo. The pitches indicated in the preface to the score for Chinese cymbals, gongs, Saharan drums and African toms are revealing as they indicate Ohana's concern for creating timbral associations with certain harmonic colours (cf. Chapter 6). The gongs tend to be reserved for emphasising the timbrally soft intervals of minor and major thirds and perfect intervals, often in music of a more reposeful character, while the

Saharan drums are associated with the aurally angular minor seconds in music of a more rhythmically active character. The pitch selection for the Chinese cymbals and African toms enables them to give emphasis to either aurally soft or harsh-sounding intervals and therefore blend or contrast with the other instruments of their timbral group (see Ex. 4.3). The acoustic properties of certain metal percussion prevents the perception of pitch in terms of exact intonation, although in the preface to the score, Ohana indicates how Chinese cymbals and gongs may be struck at specific positions to achieve the desired pitch as closely as possible. The approximate pitch of Chinese cymbals and gongs is juxtaposed with the contrasting timbre of the other pitched metal instruments, glockenspiel, crotales, celesta and vibraphone. As African toms and Saharan drums are able to be tuned precisely, Ohana is able to make use of exact pitches in all three timbral groups of the percussion. At times, the piano is also used in its lowest register to suggest the sound of drums, an effect which is exploited in the fifth movement.

Ex. 4.3: Non-chromatic pitched percussion in *Signes*

a) Chinese cymbals — Timbres I and II

b) Gongs (approximate) — Timbre II

c) Saharan drums — Timbre I

d) African toms — Timbres I and II

In terms of instrumental timbre, although not in terms of delineation of pitch, parallels can be drawn between *Signes* and *Le Marteau sans maître*. While the differentiation of instrumental timbre in each movement is not as rigorous in Ohana as in Boulez, there is some correspondence of sound-colour between the two works: both include the flute (although that of Boulez is the alto instrument); Ohana's zithers in some respects take the place of Boulez' guitar and viola (when plucked); and although *Le Marteau* requires only one percussionist, as opposed to Ohana's four, the disposition of percussion in both works owes much to the Gamelan, beloved as much by Messiaen as by Debussy. The combination of flute and metal percussion at the end of *Signes* recalls similar sonorities at the closing section of *Le Marteau*. There are also decisive differences which distinguish the timbral characteristics of the respective works; *Le Marteau* does not include piano and *Signes* does not include a voice or bowed stringed instrument.

The Gamelan textures of *Signes* stem in part from the composer's description

110   THE MUSIC OF MAURICE OHANA

of the work as an 'oriental landscape'.[3] In addition to the percussion, other instruments are intended to suggest certain oriental instruments to enhance an atmosphere of ritualistic stasis. In the second movement, the rapid repeated notes of the piccolo recall the Chinese clay-whistle or 'xuan' (see Ex. 4.4a),

Ex. 4.4: Oriental allusions of the piccolo in *Signes*

a) 'alive with birds' (second movement, fig. 12–13)

Reproduced by kind permission of Editions Amphion, Paris / United Music Publishers Ltd.

while in the fourth movement, the microintervals, glissandi, wavering and pinching of notes suggest the melodic embellishments associated with the bamboo flute or 'kagura-bue' of Japan (see Ex. 4.4b). There are other examples of similar stylistic paraphrase on flute, as well as piccolo, including fluttertonguing.

The zithers are particularly rich in timbral allusion, evoking both the Japanese 'shamisen' and 'koto' as well as the Chinese 'qin' and 'zheng' groups of instruments. The tuning in third-tone microintervals permits approximation to oriental scales which are not based on the conventions of Western equal-temperament. The zither also equates with the function of the Japanese 'sho'; although the 'sho' belongs to the group of wind-instruments, the zither fulfils a similar role when doubling piano or pitched percussion in chord-cluster combinations designed to thicken-out the texture to create harmonic densities. The emphasis of metal percussion in certain sections of *Signes* suggests both the Gamelan and the ceremonial function of Chinese and Japanese bells, gongs and cymbals, while the xylorimba equates to the Chinese 'muquin', or xylophone.[4] Although the skin and wood percussion is largely drawn from African, Afro-Cuban and South-American types, Ohana's use of these instruments in *Signes* belies their origins; the effect of skin or wood percussion (pitched or unpitched) in sections including repetitive patterns on a single note suggests the ritualistic role of similar percussion in traditional oriental music. Even when a certain process is drawn from African principles, such as the superimposed layering of rhythmic counterpoint in which vertical coordination is undefined, as in the opening of the third movement depicting the gentle pattering of rainfall, the sound-world evokes the serene delicacy of the orient (see Ex.4.5).

Ex. 4.4 *(concluded)*: Oriental allusions of the piccolo in *Signes*

b) 'imprisoned in spiders' webs' (fourth movement, fig. 21–22)

Reproduced by kind permission of Editions Amphion, Paris / United Music Publishers Ltd.

The nature-symbolism generating each movement of *Signes* recalls the pictorial impressionism of traditional Chinese and Japanese music. A chamber work of fourth century China entitled *Three Transpositions on Plum Blossom* includes among its ten sub-sections, 'evening moon over the mountains', 'blue-bird calls the soul' and 'plum blossoms dancing in the wind',[5] while much music of traditional Japanese theatre includes supplications to the gods of wind and rain or draws on subjects from agricultural ritual. *Signes* further enhances the oriental associations through incorporating characteristic stylistic features: heterophony; the use of microintervals to suggest an intonation not based on Western equal-temperament; cluster-chords; chains of stylised melodies of limited interval range, many of which are modal; parodies of the sound, function and performance style of particular oriental instruments; and an overall atmosphere that is predominantly static and ritualistic. In terms of texture and sound-world, *Signes* is to Ohana as *Sept Haïkaï* is to Messiaen, although the works themselves are different and individual to each composer.

Ex. 4.5: *Signes*, 'drowned by the rain' (third movement, fig. 16–17)

Table 4.2: Structural synopsis of *Signes*

Percussion: M = metal, S = skins, W = wood; p = pitched, u = unpitched.
Metrical Type: m = measured, u/m = unmeasured

Section & Figure		Texture	Instrumentation	Character	Metrical Type
			Movement I – night		
1	0–1	thickened monody	ziths., pf., perc. (M–p/u)	assez lent	m
2	1–2	incantatory monody	fl.,1/3-tone zith.	libre	u/m
3	2–3	homophony	ziths., pf., perc. (M–p/u W–p)	libre	m
4	3–4	thickened monody	fl., chr.zith., pf. perc. (M p/u)	calme	m
5	4–end	ostinato	zith., pf.	très mesuré	m
			Movement II – birds		
1	to bull*	incantatory monody	fl., perc. (M–p/u)	très mesuré	m
2	bull–7	'combinatoire counterpoint' (rhythmic and monodic layering)	fl., perc. (M–p S–p/u)	animé	m & u/m
3	7–8	layered monodies	fl , 1/3-tone zith.	in tempo	m
4	8–10	'combinatoire counterpoint' (rhythmic and monodic layers)	fl., 1/3-tone zith., pf., perc. (M–p/u)	animé, un peu libre	u/m & m
5	10–11	incantatory monody	fl., perc. (M–p W–p)		m
6	11–12	'combinatoire counterpoint'	fl., 1/3-zith., pf., perc. (S–p W–p)	librement très mesuré	u/m & m
7	12–13	'combinatoire counterpoint'	picc., 1/3-tone zith., perc. (M–p S–p/u)	librement	m & u/m
8	13–14	heterophony	picc., pf., perc. (S–p/u)	très mesuré	m
9	14–15	incantatory monody	fl., perc. (M–p/u)	lent, libre	u/m
10	15–end	thickened monody	fl., 1/3-tone zith., perc. (S–p W–p)	lent	m
			Movement III – rain		
1	16–17	'combinatoire counterpoint'	perc. (M–p/u S–p W–u)	librement	u/m & m
2	17–18	thickened monody and heterophony	perc. (M–p/u), zith., pf.,	tenu	
3	18–19	'combinatoire counterpoint'	pf., perc. (M–p/u S–p/u W–u)	librement	u/m & m
4	19–end	heterophony and monodic layering	fl., 1/3-tone zith., perc. (M–p W–p)	sonore, léger	m
			Movement IV – spiders' webs		
1	to 20	monody	chr. zith., pf., perc. (S–p)	tenu	m
2	20–21	monody	1/3-tone zith., pf.	librement	u/m & m
3	21–22	heterophony	1/3-tone zith., picc., pf., perc. (M–p.u)	lent mesuré	m
4	22–end	monody	1/3-tone zith., perc. (M–p)	libre, souple	u/m

Section & Figure		Texture	Instrumentation	Character	Metrical Type
			Movement V – wind		
1	to 23	rhythm	pf.	bien rythmé tumultueux	m
2	23–24	rhythm	pf., zith., perc. (S–p/u W–u)	bien rythmé tumultueux	m
3	24–25	rhythm	pf., perc. (M–p/u)	agité, éclatant	m & u/m
4	25–26	rhythm	pf., perc. (M–u S–p)	libre	u/m
5	26–27	thickened monody	pf.	mesuré	m & u/m
6	27–29	monody v. rhythm	pf.	vif, rythmé percutant	u/m
7	29–end	thickened monody	pf.	mesuré, clair lent	u/m
			Movement VI – sun		
1	to 30	heterophony	fl., 1/3-tone zith., pf., perc. (M–p)	agité	m
2	30–31	'combinatoire' counterpoint	fl., 1/3-tone zith., pf., perc. (M–p S–p)	agité	m & u/m
3	31–32	'combinatoire' counterpoint	fl., perc. (W–p)	léger, libre	u/m
4	32–33	thickened monody	fl., ziths., pf., perc. (M–p/u)	lent	m
5	33–34	thickened monody	fl., 1/3-tone/chr. zith., pf., perc. (W–p)	très mesuré	m
6	34–35	monody	fl., 1/3-tone zith., pf., perc. (M–p W–p)	cadence, rapide furieux	u/m
7	35–end	monody	fl., 1/3-tone zith., pf., perc. (M–p/u)	libre	u/m

Note: (*) Movement II: the second section substitutes a figure number for a drawing of a bull's head.

Although divided into six movements, *Signes* is intended to proceed without a break, a preference emphasised by the through-numbering of figure numbers in the score. (As many sections of the work are unmeasured, *Signes* is articulated in terms of figures rather than bar numbers.) This is another idea first explored in *Tombeau de Claude Debussy* and which subsequently became a feature of his mature style. Ohana shares his preference for musical continuity between movements with Dutilleux whose dislike of breaks between movements is also a feature of his music dating from the middle 1960s. The overall structure of *Signes* reveals an underlying symmetry through instrumentation and movement duration. While the outer movements utilise the ensemble members as a group, the four inner movements accord particular prominence to an individual instrument (or combination of instruments in respect of the percussion): the second movement features the flute; the third features the percussion; the fourth features the third-tone zither; the fifth features the piano. Despite this broad division, other members of the ensemble are not excluded but support the featured instrument in a variety of combinations; although particularly prominent in the second movement, the flute also plays an important, if supportive, melodic role in five of the six movements (it is tacet in the fifth movement). The internal movement structure is sectional with the sub-divisions delineated by contrasts of texture, instrumentation, or material. Many sub-sections present a variant of what has gone before, although others introduce material which is entirely new. In this way the internal structure revealed in *Signes* is a paradoxical hybrid combining the sectional and the organic. While the sectionalism owes much to that of Debussy's piano *Etudes*, the variation principles have parallels with certain processes in Dutilleux. Non-developmental in any traditional sense, *Signes* is essentially static, the variation process being more akin to the contemplation of an object in still-life viewed from a variety of perspectives; the object itself is unchanging but each new angle presents a different interpretation, background and context. Processes of continual variation are developed further in later works, as well as in those of the Sigma Series. The main articulations of movement structure throughout *Signes* as a whole are summarised in Table 4.2.

Although the second movement contains the largest number of sub-divisions with ten internal sub-sections, it is of equivalent overall duration to the fifth movement which contains only seven. This is due to the nature of the material itself which, in the fifth movement, is constructed from more complex, individual units than in the second. The sixth movement also contains seven internal sub-sections but is much shorter than the fifth, again due to the differing character of the musical material. Despite its seven sub-sections, the sixth movement is of equivalent length to the first. The outer movements balance each other in terms of instrumentation and basic character; both are shorter than movements two and five but longer than the shortest movements three and four around which the work pivots. The weight of the work is focused on its two longest and most complex movements. The beginning of the second sub-section in the second movement is the only instance where internal subdivisions do not correspond with the figure numbers. Instead, the division marking the end of the introductory solo flute monody and the entry of new material is defined by an additional graphic, or 'sign', a bull's head, drawn in the score by the composer. While this is the only occurrence of a less conventional definition of sub-sections in *Signes*, such illustrations appear at important structural points in the manuscripts of several other works, most notably in *Autodafé* and *Office des oracles*. In *Signes*, several figure numbers designating important structural subdivisions are decorated with abstract designs, some of which suggest the rays of the sun and flower-like images.

The incantatory monodies characteristic of *Signes* are revealing of Ohana's approach to melody as a whole. Associated chiefly with the flute, they owe much to the incantatory style of his earlier *Quatre improvisations*. Within an overall style that can certainly be described as 'Ohanian', certain features recall melodic characteristics of both Stravinsky and Bartók. As Ohana kept a number of Stravinsky and Bartók scores close to his piano and composing-table at his Paris flat (including *The Rite of Spring, Les Noces, Symphony of Psalms* and *Music for String Percussion and Celesta*) and as the score of *Signes* indicates that it was composed in Paris, it is possible that he may have turned to these composers for solutions to compositional problems. Ohana's attraction to the music of Stravinsky and Bartók, particularly at a time when his own language was undergoing the refinement of the transitional years, may have resulted in a subconscious assimilation of certain stylistic traits. Although in his writings and interviews Ohana cited Stravinsky and Bartók as stylistic influences far less frequently than either Falla or Debussy, he made no secret of his admiration of their music. A number of Ohana's later works include quotations from *The Rite of Spring*, most notably *Trois contes de l'Honorable Fleur*, the Piano Concerto and *Kypris*, while *T'Harân-Ngô* and *Livre des prodiges* were designed as musical commentaries on that great icon of the twentieth century. Allusion to Bartók is less immediately obvious, although Ohana acknowledged indirectly his significance for his own music in 'Septièmes' the seventh of the *Etudes d'interprétation*, which is dedicated to Bartók's memory and which parodies a mid-European folk-song in its closing section (cf. Ex. 5.9). Although Ohana was instinctively attracted to Stravinsky and Bartók, as much as to Falla, through their use of folksong, it was the deeper aspects of their melodic style into which the folksong was absorbed that influenced him. It is not without significance that Ohana equated the work of these composers:

> In the case of Bartók, as with Falla, what results from this research [into folkmusic] is not a recourse to the picturesque but an identification of the archetypes of musical thought. Bartók, Falla and Stravinsky, in his early years, were able to penetrate the secrets of an art that has taken generations to develop. They each had the necessary gifts combined with the correct geographical place of birth, in order to be able to evolve and absorb their traditions.[6]

In *Signes* the incantatory monodies of the flute clearly illustrate the influence of both Stravinsky and Bartók. Section '2' of the first movement includes the first appearance of one such incantatory monody (see Ex. 4.6a). It demonstrates a melodic line which is generated by the persistent return to the referential note 'E', its initial and lowest note. The articulation and use of *acciaccature* grace-notes recall the wind parts in the Introduction to Part One of *The Rite of Spring* (see Ex. 4.6b and Ex. 4.6c). The grace-notes are used in three distinct ways: as part of melodic and rhythmic units (the divisions being self-evident) in the manner of Stravinsky; as a means of throwing the rhythmic accentuation onto the pitch of the note immediately following the grace-note, onto which it is slurred; and as a means of achieving octave displacement of certain notes in the melodic line, as Stravinsky very frequently does. (This latter characteristic is a feature not only of *The Rite* but also of the introductory section of *Les Noces*.) Although the monody is pivotal and static, it is combined with a gradual ascent in pitch of one octave. This melodic ascent is revealed more clearly by allowing for the effect of octave displacement and compressing the monody within one octave.

Ex. 4.6a: *Signes*, 'at night' (first movement 'section 2', fig. 1–2)

Ex. 4.6b: Stravinsky, *The Rite of Spring*, Introduction to Part One (bars 28–38)

Stravinsky extract © Copyright 1912, 1921 by Hawkes & Son (London) Ltd.

Ex. 4.6c: Stravinsky, *The Rite of Spring*, Introduction to Part One (bars 48–51)

Stravinsky extract © Copyright 1912, 1921 by Hawkes & Son (London) Ltd.

Ohana's incantatory monody also illustrates his predilection for melodic oscillation, which in Ex. 4.6b occurs between the 'F#' and 'F', against the pivot note 'E'. These three notes (E–F#–F) form an intervallic cell that is characteristic of Bartók, consisting of interlocking tone and semitone. Such cells abound in *Music for Strings Percussion and Celesta*, as well as in the *Divertimento*, both of which Ohana knew well (see Ex. 4.7a and Ex. 4.7b). Similar features occur in

Lutosławski[7] whose music Ohana admired, although did not discover until some years after the completion of *Signes*.[8]

Ex. 4.7: Bartókian three-note cells
a) *Divertimento*, second movement (bars 2–5)

Three-note intervallic cells of tone / semitone

Bartók extract © Copyright 1940 by Hawkes & Son (London) Ltd

b) *Music for Strings, Percussion and Celesta*, first movement (bars 1–3)

Cells of interlocking semitone / tone

Three-note cells of interlocking semitone / minor third

Although unmetred and marked 'un peu libre', the rhythmic values of Ohana's melodic line in Ex. 4.6a are strictly notated and accorded the tempo indication ♩ = 100. In Ohana, the absence of metred divisions is characteristic of this type of incantatory monody which aims to evoke the spontaneity of improvisation. It is not entirely unaccompanied; a chord-cluster is sustained by the piano (denoted by the asterisks) and third-tone zither (see Ex. 4.8).

Ex. 4.8: Chord-cluster, *Signes*
(first movement, fig. 1–2)

Although the cluster primarily provides timbre and resonance (as well as some continuity with the sub-sections before and after section '2'), the pitches Ohana has chosen to notate are significant. Although the outer notes of the cluster achieve only slightly greater aural prominence than the inner pitches which combine semitones and third-tone microintervals, the notated pitches spell a chord which belongs to a specific harmonic colour, emphasising minor seventh, tritone and major seconds (the diminished third between C♯ and E♭ is aurally equivalent to a major second). Ohana's predilection for contrasting harsh sounding tritones with softer sounding perfect intervals has already been observed in the early and transitional works. In his mature music, this instinctive process was developed into a more coordinated (although not systematic) technique of alternating and juxtaposing two, contrasting harmonic schemes; one comprising harsh intervals, the other comprising softer ones. (This colouristic process is discussed in detail in Chapter 6.) The chord underpinning the incantatory melody is equivalent to Chord T–Ib of the harmonic scheme designated as Timbre I (the 'F', which would make Chord T–Ib complete, occurs in the notes of the added-cluster). The cluster-notes and third-tone microintervals are added-colour devices which serve to obscure the quasi-tonal properties inherent in the chord-aggregate itself.

A more extended incantatory monody occurs in Section 1 of the second movement, which features the flute as the leading solo instrument (see Ex. 4.9). The appearance of a monody at the opening of the movement, almost wholly unaccompanied except for two isolated chords on zither, piano, crotales and gong (a timbral allusion to the 'bells' in the closing section of *Les Noces*), suggests the character and function of the Japanese 'fue-ondo' monodies which introduce the main sections of the Gagaku. Like Ohana's introductory monody, the 'fue-ondo' is usually played on a flute and is unaccompanied in order to allow the soloist a certain rhythmic flexibility.[9] This example also illustrates Ohana's predilection for paraphrasing rhythmic and melodic characteristics of *The Rite of Spring* (Ex. 4.6b and Ex. 4.6c), the Stravinsky also revealing similar underlying oscillating and pivotal characteristics.

The contours of this incantatory monody are more complex than in the earlier example. In what is a 'pivotal' melodic type, it demonstrates the use of the referential-note 'D' up to the end of its first sentence at Fig.5. The second sentence is more dynamic: while maintaining the referential-note, the monody is extended to effect a gradual descent of a major sixth (from the referential note) to 'F'. Through the use of octave displacement and *acciaccature,* the third sentence effects a return to the original referential-note via the successive pulling 'E♭'. Thus, while the monody gives an impression of activity from cell to cell and sentence to sentence, it is fundamentally static. As in Ex. 4.6a, many of the *acciaccature* result in a Stravinskian type of octave displacement in the melodic line. In Ex. 4.9, the annotations below the flute stave compress the melody within an octave, thus illustrating the repetitive, intervallic cells. These are self-evident due to their rhythmic articulation. Between figs. 5 and 6 the monody also incorporates Bartókian three-note cells; those contained within a group of

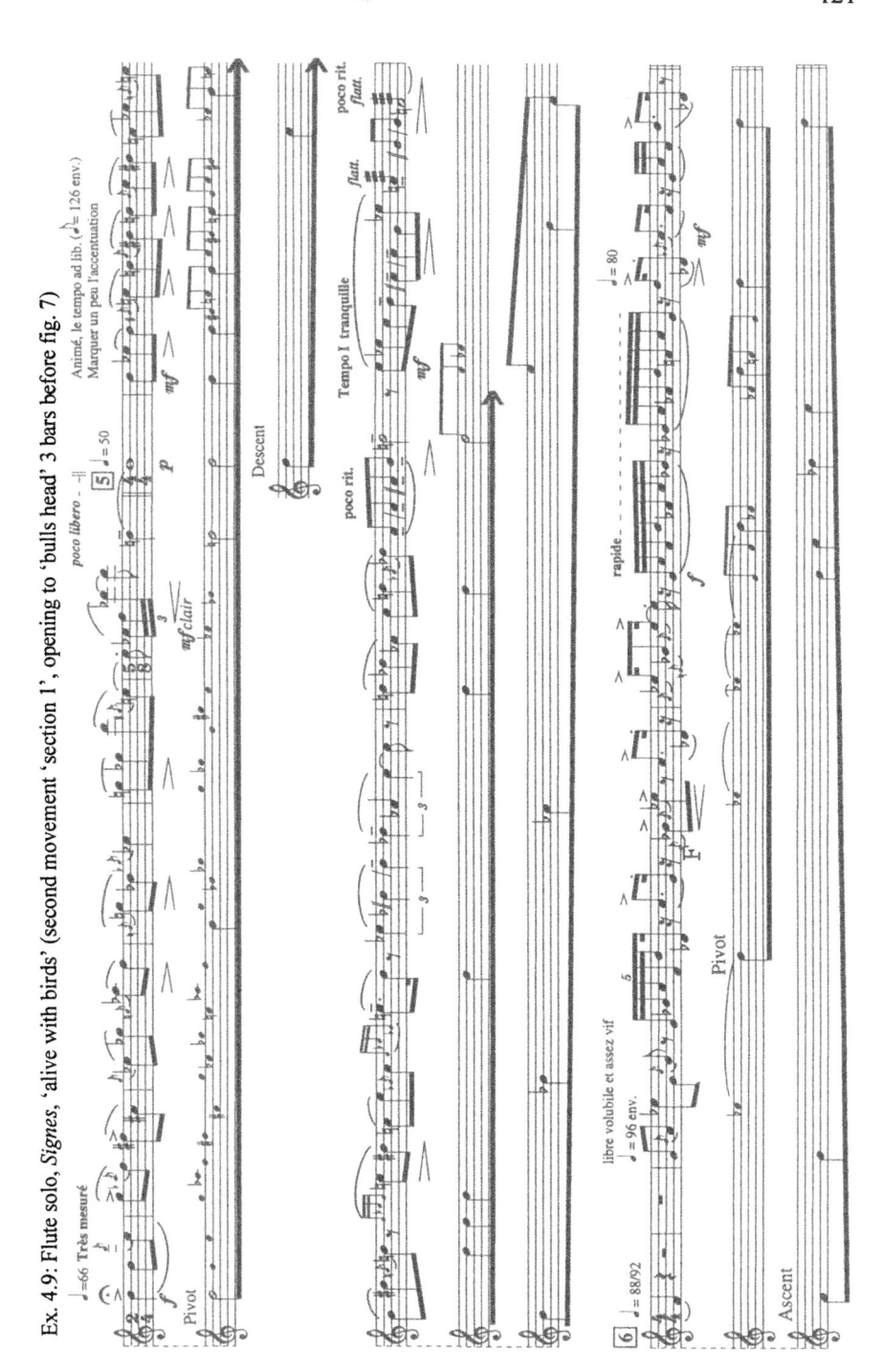

Ex. 4.9: Flute solo, *Signes*, 'alive with birds' (second movement 'section 1', opening to 'bulls head' 3 bars before fig. 7)

three adjacent semitones, (including the interlocking semitone and tone, already mentioned), and those containing permutations of minor third and semitone (cf. Ex. 4.7). The incorporation of third-tone microintervals merely serves to decorate individual cells, enhancing their expressive quality through an extension of the tone into three step-wise movements rather than two. As the third-tones appear only in adjacent motion, their effect is colouristic.

While the majority of solo flute monodies in *Signes* illustrate these characteristics, section '7' of the second movement presents the very specific oriental allusion to the Chinese clay-whistle, or 'xuan' already mentioned (Ex. 4.4a). The piccolo substitutes the flute and is combined with repetitive rhythmic patterns on Chinese cymbals, temple blocks and toms to complete the association. (Although African toms are used in this section, their restriction to a single repeated note paraphrases the sound and function of the oriental drum and does not therefore suggest the African and Afro-Cuban associations of its origins.)

Section '7' (like the one which precedes it) makes use of Ohana's layering technique in which different strands of musical ideas are superimposed without precise vertical co-ordination between the parts. Although this process is a type of aleatory counterpoint, Ohana described the process as 'more combinatoire than aléatoire' as there is no freedom or chance involved in the material itself.[10] The expression 'combinatoire' counterpoint may therefore be a more appropriate description. The technique may involve the superimposition of material in different ways; the material may be of similar type and all unmetred (sometimes to be repeated ad libitum in which case the duration of the section is decided by the conductor); the material may be of different types, some of which is metred and some of which is not. The duration of the section in the latter case is determined by the metred material. In section '7' (Ex. 4.4a), the 'combinatoire counterpoint' is of the latter type; while the 'oriental' material on percussion and piccolo is metred, the more melodic material on third-tone zither is unmetred and is to be repeated ad libitum until the end of the section. The more complex polyphonic texture of Section '6' also makes use of similar 'combinatoire counterpoint' but does not require the unmetred material to be repeated ad libitum; while the cluster-chords on the piano (providing harmonic density) aremetred, all of the material in the remaining instruments is unmetred. The piano (marked 'très mesuré') provides the orientation-point for the flute, third-tone zither, xylorimba and skin percussion which are to co-ordinate their respective and varied material only approximately. While the section begins at the tempo $\downarrow . = c. 112$ for all instruments except the xylorimba (which is $\downarrow = c. 69$), the flute and xylorimba (and bongos) are changed during the section to $\downarrow . = 72$ and $\downarrow = 108$, respectively, to ensure that no unintended vertical co-ordination takes place. The effect is of a polyphony which although complex, appears to be produced with the spontaneity of improvisation. The zither, piano and percussion create a textural sound-carpet against which the incantatory melody of the flute is superimposed.

The final section of the second movement concludes with a stately, chant-like melody that is distilled from the incantatory material of the flute. Moving homophonically with piano and xylorimba, the individual features of the slowed-down incantation blends both Bartókian and oriental characteristics in an essentially Ohanian guise (see Ex. 4.10).

Ex. 4.10: Chant-like melody, *Signes* (second movement, concluding bars)

Reproduced by kind permission of Editions Amphion, Paris / United Music Publishers Ltd.

If compressed within an octave, the individual units of the melodic line reveal Bartókian intervallic cells. The pentatonic features of the chant-like melody as a whole, combined with its performance style (non vibrato) and melodic parallelism in the piano and xylorimba, are evocative of traditional orientalism.

Although the xylorimba doubles the flute and piano at the lower octave, the 'false octave' parallelism (mainly in minor ninths in the lowest register of the piano), is intended to create a sense of acoustic blurring, paraphrasing the effect of microintervals. The contour of the final unit, with the falling perfect fourth containing a minor third, further alludes to both source-types. Ohana's instinctive blending of disparate musical influences to create his own distinctive but homogenous compositional language, is reflected in his views on Bartók expressed in an article written about the same time he completed work on *Signes*:

> Situated at the meeting point of East and the West, the music of Bartók represents one of the most beautiful syntheses possible of the different threads that weave through all art and spiritual dimensions of our modern civilisation.[11]

Many sections of *Signes* make use of similar note-for-note parallelism to thicken-out chant-like monodies and create harmonic density. While *Signes* does not parody the actual shape of plainchant in the manner of many later works (even allowing for distortion through octave displacement), sections of parallelism and thickened monody are chant-like due to their evenness of rhythmic motion and organum-like homophony, the calm and serenity of which contrasts with the more intense rhythmic activity of the incantatory melodic types.

The harmonic colour that is implicit either in a monody or in its harmonic shadowing, obeys the principles of alternation, juxtaposition and combination of contrasting interval types. This also applies to sections of 'combinatoire' counterpoint where individual pitch, but not vertical co-ordination, is determined. In sections devoted purely to rhythmic texture there is rarely an underlying harmonic scheme, unless a pitched instrument is present. While the extreme registers of the piano are often used without pedal to paraphrase the sound of percussion, the sostenuto pedal (third pedal) can allow a chosen harmonic colour to emerge from the texture as a background resonance. Ohana's harmonic procedures are examined in detail in Chapter 6; his processes of intervallic differentiation yield two main harmonic schemes which have been defined as Timbre I and Timbre II. *Signes* is the first work to involve these processes in the more systematic way characteristic of his mature music. Table 4.3 traces the harmonic schemes of *Signes*, relating them to the predominant texture of each sub-section according to the definitions of Table 4.2, although with further clarification of the melodic types.

While in some sections a particular harmonic scheme may predominate or involve the move between schemes, other sections are harmonically neutral. The absence of either harmonic scheme reflects the independence of rhythm, and sometimes melody, as a self-sufficient parameter which can exist without harmonic colouration. Monody can exist without either one of the contrasting schemes predominating, as in section '1' of the second movement, although here the isolated interpolations of bell-like chord-aggregates between each sentence of incantatory monody gradually effect the emergence of Timbre I by the end of the section. The intervallic properties of a monody can suggest either one of the harmonic Timbres, although monodies of the incantatory type tend to be associated more frequently with Timbre I. When thickened with the parallel movement of other parts, monodies tend to be associated with Timbre II. There are incidents where both harmonic Timbres are combined; in section '2' of the third movement, the intervallic properties of the melodic line are characteristic of Timbre I (tritonal), while the intervallic properties of the parallel movement reveals the harmonic colour of Timbre II. Other instances include the simultaneous superimposition of the Timbres to create denser chord-aggregates than either alone would permit, even with the use of added-notes, clusters or added-resonance. This occurs in the final chords of the last section of the sixth movement where chords belonging to Timbre I are sounded with chords of Timbre II, the predominating scheme of the section. The means in which the Timbres are here superimposed reveals Ohana's pianistic approach to harmony; the chord-aggregates of each Timbre are designated to the respective hands of the piano and celesta. Although essentially colouristic, the third-tones of the zither which provide added-resonance, are more closely associated with Timbre I (cf. Chapter 6). The fragmented melodic material in the flute which combines Bartókian intervallic cells with Stravinskian octave displacement and is supported by sustained chords of zither, piano, celesta (and added-resonance of metal percussion), initially emphasises Timbre I (via the tritone 'F' to 'B♮') but subsequently moves towards Timbre II (via reiteration of pitches from the underlying chord-aggregate). While all movements except the first involve the basic alternation and juxtaposition of the respective Timbres, the work as a whole can be heard to move from a harmonic colour that is predominantly Timbre I to one that is predominantly Timbre II. The sixth movement presents the harmonic structure of the whole work in microcosm, emphasised through the compression of timbral contrast in the fourth and fifth sections which begin and end in different harmonic colours.

Rhythmic procedures in *Signes* reveal the new refinement characteristic of the mature works. While Ohana first experimented with his quasi-aleatory, 'combinatoire' counterpoint in *Cinq séquences*, superimposition of different horizontal strands without precise vertical coordination is developed further in *Signes* which incorporates this technique more extensively. Closely aligned with the simple layering of material, 'combinatoire' counterpoint is derived from procedures common in African tribal music and also found in some Spanish folk music. In Ohana, either process may involve the superimposition of material which is similar (all melodic or all rhythmic) or dissimilar (melodic against rhythmic). Whereas 'combinatoire' counterpoint involves one or more parts being unmeasured, or subject to independent tempo indications, simple layered textures are measured, the coincidence between parts being defined. In section '3' of the second movement the flute and third-tone zither superimpose two melodies which are measured, while in section '3' of the sixth movement flute and xylorimba superimpose two melodies which bear different tempo indications, are unmeasured and to be played freely. The first illustrates simple layering, the second is 'combinatoire' counterpoint. More complex layering occurs in section '4' of the second movement where different melodic types are superimposed, while the opening section of the third movement involves more complex 'combinatoire' counterpoint in which rhythmic textures are superimposed (see Ex. 4.5). Examples of the superimposition of different material occur in the second movement: in section '6' melodic, rhythmic and harmonic textures are combined in an extended section of 'combinatoire counterpoint'; in sections '7' and '8' fragmented incantatory monodies are layered against repetitive rhythmic patterns.

Table 4.3: Harmonic schemes in *Signes*

Section & Figure		Harmonic Scheme: Timbre	Texture
\multicolumn{4}{c}{Movement I – night}
1	0–1	I	thickened monody
2	1–2	I	incantatory monody
3	2–3	I	homophony
4	3–4	I	thickened monody – chant-type
5	4–end	I	ostinato
\multicolumn{4}{c}{Movement II – birds}
1	to bull*	none – I	incantatory monody
2	bull–7	none	'combinatoire counterpoint'
3	7–8	I – none	layered monody
4	8–10	none – II	layered monody
5	10–11	I	incantatory monody
6	11–12	II	'combinatoire counterpoint'
7	12–13	none	'combinatoire counterpoint'
8	13–14	none	layered monody + rhythm
9	14–15	I – none	incantatory monody
10	15–end	Timbre II	heterophony & thickened monody – chant-type
\multicolumn{4}{c}{Movement III – rain}
1	16–17	none	'combinatoire counterpoint'
2	17–18	I + II	thickened monody – chant-type & heterophony
3	18–19	none	'combinatoire counterpoint'
4	19–end	II	melodic layering & heterophony
\multicolumn{4}{c}{Movement IV – spiders' webs}
1	to 20	II – I	monody
2	20–21	I	incantatory monody
3	21–22	II	heterophony
4	22–end	I	incantatory monody

Movement V – wind

1	to 23	none	rhythm
2	23–24	II	rhythm
3	24–25	I – II	rhythm
4	25–26	II	rhythm
5	26–27	I + II	thickened monody
6	27–29	none – II – none	rhythm (+ thickened monody)
7	29–end	II	thickened monody

Movement VI – sun

1	to 30	I	heterophony
2	30–31	I	'combinatoire counterpoint'
3	31–32	I	'combinatoire counterpoint'
4	32–33	I – I	thickened monody – chant-type
5	33–34	II – I	thickened monody – chant-type
6	34–35	II	incantatory monody
7	35–end	II (+I)	incantatory monody

Note: (*) Movement II: the second section substitutes a figure number for a drawing of a bull's head.

Some of the rhythmic innovations of *Signes*, as far as vocabulary is concerned, are concentrated in the fifth movement (cf. Ex. 7.9). This movement explores a range of rhythmic textures; rhythm appears both coloured by harmonic resonance and as an independent parameter free of harmonic colouration. As the movement progresses, melodic material is distilled from the rhythmic structures and appears in sections of rich, chordal parallelism. Although the movement as a whole makes use of the full range of the piano, its lowest registers are particularly exploited, 'détimbré' without sustaining pedal (and sometimes with 'una corda'), to suggest drums. The percussiveness of the movement is enhanced by the use of African toms, bass drum, maracas and tambourine, in addition to some unpitched metal percussion for resonance. For the occasional interpolations of the chromatic zither, wooden sticks are specified for their harsher, percussive sound. According to the composer, the rhythmic patterns of the fifth movement are of African and Afro-Cuban origin;[12] the quintuplet divisions common to much African music are prominent throughout (they also appear in other movements) as are the syncopations of the Cuban tango, contradanza and its related derivations.[13] Distilled from the percussive texture in the third section of the movement, a slower passage emerges with a seductive melody marked 'rythmé avec nonchalence', whose Afro-Cuban rhythms are coloured with chord-aggregates suggestive of jazz (see Ex. 4.11).

The use of all three pedals is specified in the piano writing of *Signes*, as in all his works for the instrument. The instruction to use the third pedal (sostenuto), which can sustain selectively, as distinct from the simple sustaining pedal, which sustains uniformly, permits the harmonic colouration to emerge from the rhythmic texture as a background resonance. In this way, the harmonically neutral rhythmic material of section '2' of the fifth movement is set against a background of chord-aggregates belonging to Timbre II. This also applies to the rhythmic episodes in sections '4' and '5', and the Bartókian monody of the final section.

Ex. 4.11: *Signes*, 'beaten by the wind' (piano, fig. 24–5)

Reproduced by kind permission of Editions Amphion, Paris / United Music Publishers Ltd.

The Sigma Series

The multi-cultural associations of *Signes* may represent an additional 'sign' indicative of the crystallisation of Ohana's mature musical language. Although his mature style may be regarded as eclectic, it is no longer derivative in the manner of his earlier works. His use of African, Afro-Cuban and Spanish rhythms is absorbed into a language that no longer draws exclusively on any one of these traditions but has become a unified whole. While his synthesis of Stravinskian and Bartókian characteristics into a language that combines Eastern and Western elements is both personal and original, his incorporation of Debussian textures into a quasi-oriental sound-world (which has parallels with other composers during the 1960s), is just as instinctive. The cross-fertilisation of textural relationships equating percussive properties of melodic instruments and melodic properties of percussion is not only a feature of *Signes* but a preoccupation of many works of the Sigma Series, and one which reflects his researches both into folk music and the electronic medium at Pierre Schaeffer's studio of the French radio (cf. Chapter 1). The discoveries of *Signes* paved the way for the stylistic proliferation that took place in the Sigma Series and beyond.

Following the completion of *Signes*, Ohana embarked on a series of works which, for him, represented a continuity of stylistic development into a range of other genres. These are the eleven works comprising what has here been called the Sigma Series (see Table 4.4). If *Signes* was the root of Ohana's compositional tree, the works of the Sigma Series symbolised the growth and proliferation of that tree. Ohana signalled the special, personal significance of these eleven works with a secret cipher; they all have poetic titles beginning with the letter 'S'. According to the composer, the reversed Greek sigma symbolises evolution,[14] hence the designation of this group of works as the Sigma Series. Being impractical to incorporate a reversed, non-latinate character, Ohana used instead the conventional, latinate equivalent. His fascination for esoteric devices and symbols, illustrated by the graphic signs used in *Signes*, may have been precipitated by his studies as an architect, as well as during his war service with British Intelligence. Composed over more than a decade from 1965 to 1976, much of the Sigma Series was completed sequentially, although non-Sigma works gradually interpolated the series, particularly during the 1970s. While the works of the Sigma Series reflect continuity of stylistic development, they also represent diversity in their range of genres. The progressive interpolation of other works into the series is testimony to Ohana's stylistic proliferation.

Table 4.4: The Sigma Series

Date	Title	Designation
1965	*Signes*	flute (piccolo), 2 zithers, piano, 4 percussion
1966	*Synaxis*	concerto for 2 pianos, percussion & orchestra
1967	*Syllabaire pour Phèdre*	chamber opera
1968	*Sibylle*	soprano, percussion, tape
1969	*Silenciaire*	concerto for percussion & strings
1970	*Stream*	bass & string trio
1970	*Syrtes*	cello and piano
1971	*Sorôn-Ngô*	two pianos
1972	*Sarc*	oboe
1975	*Sacral d'Ilx*	harpsichord, oboe & horn
1976	*Satyres*	2 flutes

Although the Sigma Series incorporates works for a range of instrumental and vocal forces, incorporating the dramatic and non-dramatic, the musical language is based on the techniques established in *Signes* : the exploration of texture and timbre; the combination of the organic and the sectional; the juxtaposition of the static versus the active within a framework that is inherently ritualistic; the desire to recreate the spontaneity of improvisation within a composed score. The

Sigma Series also bears witness to a further development of his 'combinatoire' principle; players (or singers) being required improvise on given pitches. First appearing in *Syllabaire pour Phèdre*, this more developed technique became an important feature of his music from 1967 onwards.

After completing *Signes*, Ohana immediately began work on *Synaxis*.[15] Commissioned by the Groupe instrumental de percussions de Strasbourg, to whom the work is dedicated, *Synaxis* explores further the textural relationships between piano and percussion, expanding these forces to two pianos, four percussion soloists and an additional large percussion group in the body of the orchestra. (He returned to the combination of piano and percussion during the 1980s in the second book of *Etudes d'interprétation* (nos. XI and XII) and explored the relationship between harpsichord and percussion in *Miroir de Célestine* (arranged from the opera) completed in 1990.) The relationship between melodic properties of percussion and percussive properties of melodic instruments (including the voice) is investigated in *Syllabaire pour Phèdre, Sibylle* and *Silenciaire,* while *Syrtes, Sorôn-Ngô* and *Satyres* translate the interplay of the percussive versus the lyrical into more limited instrumental forces. The designation of solo percussion in *Synaxis* and *Silenciaire* is similar to that of *Signes*, although far larger in the two concertos. Both *Synaxis* and *Silenciaire* subdivide the percussion into different combinations of pitched and unpitched instruments; *Synaxis* into four solo groups (additional to the orchestral percussion), *Silenciaire* into six groups. The pitched percussion for *Synaxis* includes xylophone, vibraphone, Chinese cymbals, crotales, glockenspiel, xylorimba and seven African toms, while that for *Silenciaire* includes marimba, 2 xylomarimbas, 2 vibraphones, glockenspiel, twelve gongs, tubular bells and eight African toms in addition to some approximate-pitched percussion (Berber crotales, cow-bells and bottles). The unpitched solo percussion in *Synaxis* includes side-drums (with and without snare), tambourines, M'tumbas, bongos, Saharan drums (unpitched), bass-drums, tam-tams, gongs, suspended cymbals, cymbals, triangle, maracas, wood-blocks, temple-blocks. The orchestral percussion for *Synaxis* is also unpitched (except for one African tom and timpani) and includes bass drums, side-drums (with and without snare), two tam-tams and a selection of cymbals (suspended and non-suspended). The unpitched percussion in *Silenciaire* is similar (except for side-drums) although much larger, incorporating a selection of stones and sea-shells in addition to various unpitched gongs and five tam-tams. The vibraphone part in *Synaxis* requires metal rulers of specified length to sound non-chromatic chord-clusters equivalent to the black or white notes of the piano. Both solo piano parts also involve extensive use of chord-clusters and require a selection of felt-covered rulers to depress either all black or all white notes. Clusters spanning smaller outer intervals, or which are chromatic, can be played with combinations of the fingers, side of the hand or forearms. (*Sorôn-Ngô* also requires the use of similar felt-covered rulers.) Third-tone microintervals are used melodically and harmonically in both *Synaxis* (which also includes a third-tone zither) and

Silenciaire. Although *Synaxis* adapts many of Ohana's mature techniques to his writing for strings, this is given greater focus in *Silenciaire, Stream* and *Syrtes*.

Like *Signes*, the individual movements of *Synaxis* are to be played without a break and involve the juxtaposition of contrasting material which, within sections, is evolved through processes of organic variation. *Synaxis* also involves Debussian parallelism, Stravinskian incantatory melodies and pseudo-oriental heterophony. Although the work is an essay in instrumental texture, the titles of the individual movements, many of which allude to Medieval and Renaissance forms as well as more ancient traditions, reveal the influence of vocal music. Drawing on his experience in Schaeffer's electronic studio, much of *Synaxis* translates his researches on the electronic manipulation of the voice into an instrumental medium. In the preface to the score, Ohana described his objective for the work as a study of 'the essential aspects of sound-material – tessitura, timbre, rhythm, duration, density and harmonic synthesis', which are organised to proceed in 'the form of a ritual'. According to the composer, the word 'synaxis' is borrowed from primitive liturgy of the second century, the eight movements symbolising the unfolding of individual events in an imagined, ritual celebration. Due to the large forces involved in *Synaxis* and *Silenciaire*, layering techniques and 'combinatoire' counterpoint are used more extensively and appear not only as self-contained textures but also as sound-masses against which other material is juxtaposed. (Ex. 7.5 illustrates a rhythmic sound-mass incorporating African and Afro-Cuban rhythms.) While the sectionalism of *Signes* and *Synaxis* remains the basis of Ohana's approach to internal structure, in *Silenciaire* he abandoned subdivisions into designated movements, conceiving structure as an uninterrupted whole. Similarly, *Sorôn-Ngô* is a single movement work; despite a natural break at fig. 12, the revised version indicates that there should be no interruption to the overall continuity at this point.[16] *Stream, Syrtes, Sarc, Sacral d'Ilx* and *Satyres* are also single movement forms.

Ohana's fascination for percussion and experimentations in the electronic studio spawned the most dramatic innovation of the Sigma Series; a new approach to writing for the voice. Both *Syllabaire pour Phèdre* and *Sibylle* not only introduced his new vocal techniques but were the first of several works to incorporate pre-recorded tape using electronically manipulated sounds based on vocal sampling and involving the montage processes of 'musique concrète'. Amplification of the tape is limited to two loudspeakers which are to be positioned on either side of the stage or platform. While many of the vocal techniques in *Syllabaire* parody the effect of electronic manipulation, the most dramatic interaction of voice, percussion and tape occurs in *Sibylle* (discussed more extensively in Chapters 5 and 7):

> The vocal range from tenderness to sarcasm, from the cry or murmur to the fury of song, unravels itself in a structure of textural counterpoint. The percussion merges with the voice and the voice with the percussion, swapping their respective sound-colours until melting into a flood of sound in the magnetic tape.[17]

While neither work involves live interaction between the performers and tape, the sounds are sampled from vocal material in the respective scores. (*Sibylle* also includes material sampled from the percussion.) Thus the electronically manipulated material is heard, sometimes simultaneously, not only on tape but in its original form. Like many of the vocal innovations in the music of Berio and Ligeti of the 1960s, which also owed much to the electronic studio, Ohana's techniques stemmed from his perception of the voice as a sound-object. The wordless vocalisations in *Tombeau de Claude Debussy* reveal the beginnings of this approach. Ohana developed his techniques from a combination of his electronic researches and his experience of the many quite different means of vocal production characteristic of Spanish and African folk singing, as well as traditional Japanese music. Although *Syllabaire pour Phèdre* and *Sibylle* postdate *Circles, Visage* and *Sequenza III* of Berio, as well as *Aventures* and *Lux Aeterna* of Ligeti, Ohana's treatment of the voice reflects the logical outcome of his own researches more than the influence of others. As he chose to distance himself from his contemporaries involved both at Darmstadt and at the Concerts du Domaine musical, it is unlikely that he sought to imitate the music of composers associated with those groups. Even in the 1980s Ohana explained that he knew only a few of Berio's works, having discovered them in the 1970s; those works he knew he said he admired.[18] In a period when electronic composition was rapidly advancing, it is more likely that the desire to extend the range of vocal expression was instinctive for many composers. The vocal discoveries of the Sigma Series proliferated into non-Sigma vocal works of the late 1960s and 1970s, both dramatic (*Autodafé, Office des oracles, Trois contes de l'Honorable Fleur*) and non-dramatic (*Cris, Lys de madrigaux*, the Mass). Like Berio and Ligeti, Ohana considered the voice as a sound-object capable of producing a range of timbres of which song is only a part:

> Three quarters of vocal quality is lost in the pursuit of a certain idea of 'bel canto' and an entire musical territory is permanently excluded from the repertoire. This gag must be torn away and the true properties of the voice revealed. This has already long flourished in much well-known folk music, including Andalusian song, African choral songs and Japanese music. Europeans should feel inspired by this but without suppressing their own classical singing.[19]

Using the voice as an instrument capable of percussive as well as lyrical sound-textures, Ohana found a means of vocal expression which need not always be strictly melodic in the conventional sense. The vocal works of the Sigma Series engendered the innovations of *Cris*, the first vocal work to interpolate the series and the first to develop further the techniques explored in *Syllabaire* and *Sibylle*. These works involve many unorthodox techniques in addition to expressive singing: guttural modes of attack; voiced and unvoiced breathing; humming, screaming, shouting and whistling; rapid glissandi; extremes of tessitura; progressive closing of the mouth in controlled diminuendi; oscillations around a notated pitch; beating of the lips with the hand; singing through cardboard; singing through the nose or with the mouth closed; senza vibrato and

GROWTH AND PROLIFERATION 133

other non-espressivo indications. The use of third-tone microintervals and periodic designation of approximate intonation, further distances Ohana's use of the voice from normal conventions. Combinations of unorthodox techniques in vocal ensembles often parody the effect of electronic manipulations. They are also sometimes superimposed in sections of 'combinatoire' counterpoint. Ex. 4.12a and Ex. 4.12b illustrate some of the techniques introduced in *Syllabaire*.

Ex. 4.12a: *Syllabaire pour Phèdre*, 'Prologue' (fig. 9–10)

Ex. 4.12a: *(concluded)*

(*) les petites notes de la B.1 très gutterales

Reproduced by kind permission of Société des Editions Jobert, Paris / United Music Publishers Ltd.

As the first work to raise the curtain on Ohana's new vocal techniques, *Syllabaire pour Phèdre* initiated a new relationship between language and sound. Text is treated as an additional sound-material which may either be recognisable or disintegrated into onomatopoeic phonemes and morphemes. The 'syllabaire' of the work's title has often been mistranslated into English as 'spelling-book', although it in fact refers to the syllabisation of the text.

For me the recourse to text tends to be isolated in so far as I use it at all. In my recent works, music and text is merged together through the use of phonemes and syllables in order to create an imaginary language in which music provides the meaning by a blend that is half-way between pure sound and words.[20]

Avoiding the international phonetic alphabet, Ohana's onomatopoeic phonemes and morphemes reflect his instinctive approach to timbral contrast and largely follow the rules of French pronunciation. Certain consonants are required to approximate the characteristic of another language; the rolling 'r' of Italian or the 'th' of English. In some instances Ohana specifies a ventral or guttural voiced attack associated with the Japanese Kabuki. Plosive consonants produced in different parts of the mouth, such as 'te-ke-te-ke', 'tch-k-tch', 'ka-ta', 'ké-té', 'ts', 'tssss', paraphrase the sound of percussion and are often associated with rhythmically active textures where pitch is sometimes approximate.

Very often I prefer and desire approximate intonation. What interests me is the quality of the voice and not its accuracy .... When one listens to the great singers of the Flamenco, the African choruses and the traditional Japanese singers, one realises that music is very beautiful without the notes having established any strict harmonic implications relating to our pitch sense or diatonic system.[21]

The phoneme-types 'tom', 'toung', 'ttinngg', 'téounngg', 'tann-go', 'tanng' tend to occur in rhythmically active sections incorporating African or Afro-Cuban patterns and, suggesting the sound of drums, are particularly associated with male voices. More expressive, legato lines are articulated by the alternation of open and closed vowels, 'a-o-a-o-a', 'é-o-a', 'é-o-é-o', with careful attention being accorded the subtle distinctions of pronunciation for accented vowels (é, è, ô, â). Although 'h' is not aspirate in French, vowels are sometimes combined with this soft consonant: 'hé', 'ha', 'ho', thus approximating the pronunciation of non-allied words such as 'les halles' or les haricots', as opposed to 'les harmonies'. The phonetic properties of Ohana's name allowed the composer to make cryptic reference to his own authorship, embedding a quasi-musical signature into certain phonemes, 'O-Ha-Na', 'O-A-Ha'. While this does appear in the vocal works of the Sigma Series, it is particularly exploited in *Trois contes de l'Honorable Fleur*. (The title of the work is a pun on his own name, 'Ohana' meaning 'Honorable Flower' in Japanese, cf. Chapter 2). The principle of phonetic text-shadowing is developed further in *Cris,* the first non-Sigma vocal work to interpolate the series. Ohana's careful use of upper and lower case letters in his phonetic notation suggests the particular emphasis to be given to the articulation. If text occurs at all it is reserved for particular effect; a single word or phrase may emerge from the phonetic articulation as in *Sibylle,* where isolated French, Greek and Latin words appear, including not insignificantly the word 'Sigma'. *Stream* incorporates English, Spanish and Russian text fragments, in addition to French. In such cases the spelling of the original word is often altered to emphasise is phonetic character; in *Sibylle,* 'Sigma soles sed' becomes 'Ssigma ssoless Sed'). Polyglot textual allusions are a feature of vocal works which interpolate the Sigma series, *Cris, Autodafé* and

Office des oracles, as well as many later vocal works, up to and including *Avoaha*. The dramatic necessities of *Syllabaire pour Phèdre* result in larger sections of text being presented as spoken narration or declamatory speech-song. *Syllabaire* also involves the superimposition of wordless vocalisations against declaimed text, a device particularly associated with the main protagonist; the vocalisations of the coloratura soprano suggest the psychological state of Phèdre, while the speech-song of the mezzo-soprano accounts for her actions. (Similar techniques are also used in the opera *La Célestine*.) The intensely expressive, quasi-improvisatory vocalisations of the coloratura soprano exploit the highest tessitura and even surpass top 'E♭' (see Ex. 4.13). Ohana refined and developed his new approach to vocal writing further in *Cris*, composed immediately following *Syllabaire* and *Sibylle*.

Ex. 4.12b: *Syllabaire pour Phédre*, 'Episode I' (fig. 27)

Reproduced by kind permission of Société des Editions Jobert, Paris / United Music Publishers Ltd.

Resulting from the series of radiophonic scores of 1963 to 1966, *Syllabaire pour Phèdre* represents the culmination of Ohana's immersion in classical subjects based on Euripides. It conforms to the structural architecture of Greek tragedy (as does *Autodafé*) and includes a chorus and choryphée who comment upon the action, rather than participate in it. Although a chamber opera, *Syllabaire* may be better categorised as music-theatre; the roles of Thésée and Hippolyte are enunciated largely in speech-song. The character of Phèdre is enacted by two soloists; a mezzo-soprano portrays the public persona (the part includes as much declaimed text as actual singing) while the coloratura soprano represents her alter ego. The recounting of the tragedy is static rather than conventionally dramatic and presumes an audience's familiarity with the subject (not unreasonable in France where Racine's version is one of the classics of great literature). As in Racine the action takes place off-stage, the main substance of the drama being concerned with the state of mind of the protagonists. The ritualistic stasis is further emphasised by the lack of dialogue between characters which are also intended to be entirely motionless, after the manner of the

Ex. 4.13: *Syllabaire pour Phèdre*, 'Epilogue' (fig. 61–64)

Reproduced by kind permission of Société des Editions Jobert, Paris / United Music Publishers Ltd.

Japanese Noh plays. Equating the archetypes of Greek tragedy with those of Japanese theatre, Ohana required, in the original production, that the instrumental ensemble should form part of the visual dimension of the performance; according to traditional practice in many Japanese theatrical forms, he positioned the players on the stage around a circular wooden platform on which the actors and singers were to stand. Ohana was by no means alone in his attraction to the formality and ritualism of Japanese theatre. While the composer himself accounted for his eclecticism by referring to the long history of orientalism in France, his attraction to Japanese traditions forms part of the wider, aesthetic trend of the 1960s which includes Messiaen's *Sept Haïkaï*, as well as his own *Signes*. Britten's *Curlew River* and *Burning Fiery Furnace* also have much in common with the sense of tragic inevitability purveying *Syllabaire pour Phèdre*. Both composers also make use of techniques of melodic layering, some degree of controlled aleatorism and share a common interest in plainsong. The 'curlew' sign used by Britten as a replacement for the fermata in *Curlew River* is, in some respects, not unlike Ohana's drawing of 'bulls' to denote sections of special significance. Ohana declared his admiration for the music of Britten in his last published interview and cited *Curlew River* among his particularly favourite works.[22]

The Japanese themes welded into *Syllabaire pour Phèdre* represent a continuation of the 'oriental landscape' first explored in *Signes*. These were developed further eleven years later in a non-Sigma work also of the music-theatre genre, *Trois contes de l'Honorable Fleur*. This later work borrows from Japanese Noh, Kabuki and Bunraku traditions in its subject matter and production, as well as in its instrumentation.[23] The classical, hellenic aspects of *Syllabaire* proved a more enduring preoccupation of the Sigma Series and re-emerged in *Sibylle, Syrtes, Sarc, Sacral d'Ilx* and *Satyres* (cf. Chapter 2), as well as many subsequent non-Sigma works. While the vocal techniques of *Syllabaire* were explored further in *Sibylle* and *Stream*, the theatrical dimension stimulated the remaining vocal works of the Sigma Series; both *Sibylle* and *Stream* were conceived as short, monodramas to be enhanced with theatrical lighting, mime and shadow theatre. *Sibylle*, featuring soprano, is a portrait of the soothsayer of Greek mythology and has much in common with Berio's *Visage* in its treatment of the voice, use of the tape and contemplation of the female condition. *Stream*, featuring bass, presents a succession of male characters which are suggested through contrasting vocal and instrumental material, the periodic emergence of polyglot text and its section subtitles (Machinaire, Colloque, Conspiration, Soliloque).

The sequential composition of the Sigma Series was first interrupted by the interpolation of the harpsichord concerto *Chiffres de clavecin*, completed the same year as *Sibylle* in 1968. The 'Chiffres' of the title once again reflects Ohana's fascination for secret signs or ciphers; the notation of music on the page can be understood as a form of code known only to the initiated. Resulting from a commission by the Polish harpsichordist Elisabeth Chojnacka, it adapts techniques derived from early polyphony. Whereas these preoccupations are implicit in *Synaxis* which makes reference to diaphony, organum, antiphony and trope, the technique of cantus firmus is particularly developed in *Chiffres* (cf. Chapter 5). The proliferation of Ohana's mature style is exemplified by the successive interpolations of other works into the Sigma Series. The interpolations represent the more extended branches of the compositional tree which took root with *Signes* and subsequently grew and evolved with the Sigma Series. By the middle 1970s, there were so many interpolations, or extended branches, that continuation of the series after *Sacral d'Ilx* and *Satyres* would no longer be meaningful. There was nevertheless a sense of continuity between works which interpolated the series, as between the works of the series itself. Although entirely continuous, the five movement structure of *Chiffres de clavecin* is developed further in *Cris*, the second work to interpolate the series in 1968–9. Like earlier works of the Sigma Series, including *Signes, Synaxis* and *Syllabaire pour Phèdre, Cris* conforms to a symmetrical movement plan (cf. Chapter 8). *Chiffres* does not. The return to symmetrical forms may reflect Ohana's fascination for certain aspects of the architecture of Greek tragedy which he used as the framework for *Syllabaire pour Phèdre*, but also has an important parallel in Dutilleux's quinpartite forms of the same period. *Cris* reveals another continuity with the Sigma Series through its further expansion of Ohana's new approach to vocal writing. It is untypical of his work as a whole in its recourse to contemporary political themes. (The political themes in *Autodafé* are historical.) Profoundly moved by the events of Spring 1968, in Prague as well as in Paris, Ohana interrupted the Sigma Series to write a work which could stand as a memorial to victims of oppression;[24] the cries of the title refer to the most intense outpourings of human expression which are presented in various contexts in each of the five movements. The work includes a memorial to the victims of the concentration camps in the fourth movement, 'Mémorial 44' (cf. Chapter 8, see Ex. 8.1).

Resuming the Sigma series in 1969, less than a year after completing *Sibylle*, four Sigma works were completed in rapid succession: *Silenciaire*, *Stream*, *Syrtes* and *Sorôn-Ngô*. Another work composed for Les Percussions de Strasbourg, this time in collaboration with the Lucerne Festival Strings, who initiated the commission, *Silenciaire* was described by Ohana as a sort of breviary for the celebration of the ritual of silence.[25] Seams of rests, like the patterns of veins in wood or marble, are woven into the pointillist textures of the sound-masses in aleatory counterpoint. The rests, even if very short, are considered as important as the notes themselves and thus enhance contemplation of silence. The concept has parallels in Messiaen's explanation of rhythm being defined as much by the silence which follows a note, as by the note itself.[26] In Ohana's programme note for *Silenciaire*, he described awareness of silence as the source of creation and life.[27] Like *Synaxis*, his earlier percussion concerto, *Silenciaire* explores not only the rhythmic dynamism of percussion but also its textural and pseudo-melodic capabilities. The strings are largely metamorphosed into an additional arm of the percussion ensemble, but also provide harmonic resonance and are exploited for their ability to produce more sustained melodic sound-masses. In the aleatory section of the work where four sections entitled 'Aventures' may be played in any order ad libitum (cf. Chapter 8), Ohana described the strings and percussion as 'opposing armies' which become accomplices in the adventure of form.[28]

Although Ohana began work on *Sorôn-Ngô* in 1969, as a result of a commission from Geneviève Joy and Jacquéline Robin to celebrate the twenty-fifth anniversary of their celebrated two-piano duo, it was not completed in its final version until 1971. Like *Signes* (the fifth movement) and *Synaxis*, *Sorôn-Ngô* focuses on the rhythmic and percussive capabilities of the piano (see Ex. 4.14), the suffix 'ngo' signalling the work as an evocation of African and Afro-Cuban ancient, tribal dances (cf. Chapter 2). *Stream,* for bass and string trio, is relatively speaking more melodic but, described by Ohana as a 'sort of liturgy of sound',[29] parallels some of the ritualistic aspects of earlier works of the Sigma Series. Exploring the sonorities of the male voice in a dramatic monodrama, it takes its title from the stream-of-consciousness-like utterings of the bass and is in many ways a sibling work to *Sibylle*. In terms of string writing, *Stream* illustrates a compositional continuity from *Silenciaire*.

Ex. 4.14: Sorôn-Ngô (fig. 32–33)

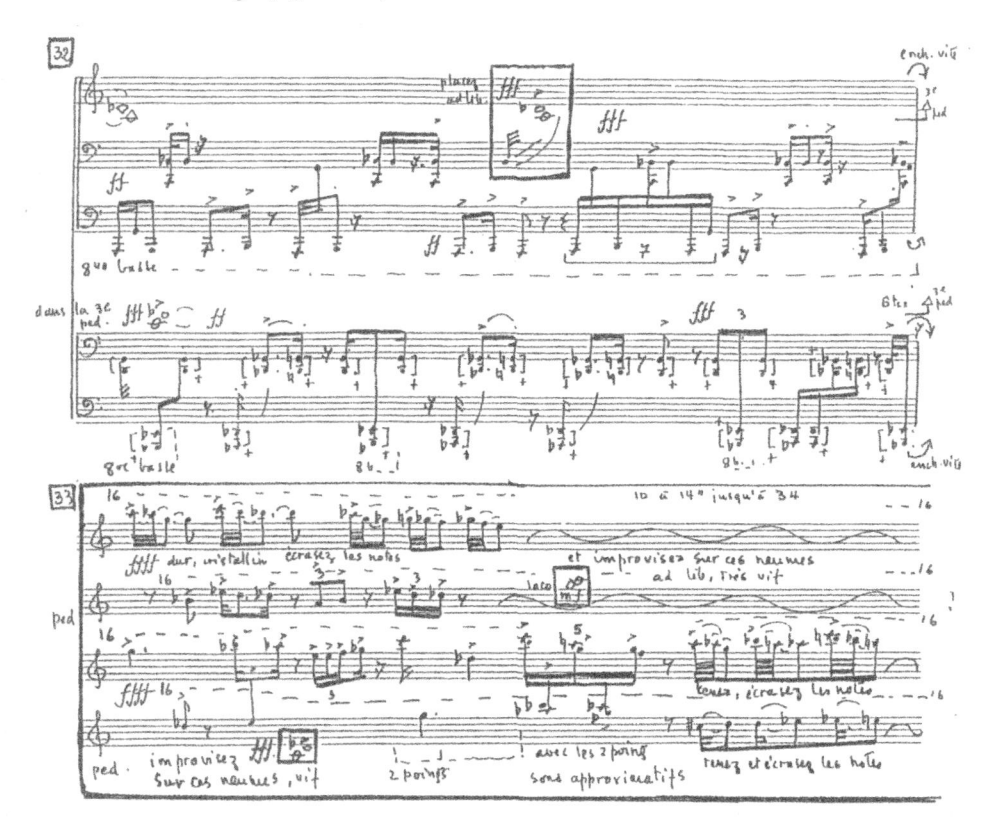

Reproduced by kind permission of Société des Editions Jobert, Paris / United Music Publishers Ltd.

Syrtes, for cello and piano, was the result of a personal commission from Rostropovich, with whom it is likely Ohana first came into contact through Dutilleux.[30] (Dutilleux also gave some of Ohana's scores to the Russian composer Edison Denisov during his first visit to the Soviet Union in 1970.[31]) Like the first Paris performance of Dutilleux's cello concerto *Tout un monde lointain*, the première of *Syrtes* was delayed as a result of the travelling restrictions placed upon Rostropovich by the Soviet authorities.[32] The most substantial and demanding of Ohana's works for cello and piano, *Syrtes* incorporates all the main features of Ohana's mature style. Borrowing its title from the ancient names for the gulfs of Sirte and Gabès on the north African coast, there are many effects which suggest percussion: rhythmic patterns (often including quintuplets) fragmented between the parts; the rapid alternation of two or three pitches in idiomatic patterns to parody the sound of drums; emphasis of low tessitura; martellato and glissando double-stopping; fortissimo glissando pizzicati, often near the bridge; snap-pizzicati; rapid alternation of bowed and pizzicato double-stopping; playing with the bow on the bridge, as well as col legno; ponticelli on the wrong side of the bridge; the playing on the strings of the piano with hard- or soft-headed sticks. Sections which are primarily melodic, as opposed to rhythmic, alternate between the incantatory and the chant-like and make systematic use of third-tone microintervals. Although there is almost no recourse to ad libitum techniques, the work being entirely composed, the overall effect is one of spontaneous improvisation. If *Syrtes* explores the percussive and at times angular capabilities of the cello, a far more lyrical and expressive character is revealed in Rostropovich's second and much later commission of the 1980s for a cello concerto. Like Dutilleux's concerto *Tout un monde lointain*, *In Dark and Blue* exploits sheer beauty of tone and melodic expression, and regularly gives prominence to the high registers of the cello. The intervening cello works of the middle 1970s also exploit the expressive capabilities of the instrument; the short Conservatoire test-piece *Noctuaire* and the first concerto *Anneau du Tamarit*.

During the early 1970s, the Sigma series was increasingly interrupted by commissions for large-scale works: *Autodafé*, *T'Harân-Ngô* and *Office des oracles*. The chamber works which represent the last three of the Sigma Series, *Sarc*, *Sacral d'Ilx* and *Satyres* serve almost as postscripts to his main compositional thrust, the purpose of the series to effect the growth and proliferation of his mature style having been fulfilled. *Sarc*, for solo oboe, is a virtuoso show-piece. An incantatory monody, incorporating a range of experimental techniques including multiphonics, harmonics, percussive use of the keys and microintervals, it exploits the full, expressive range and tessitura of the instrument. Almost entirely unmeasured, the effect is of spontaneous improvisation. Reflecting the experimental aspects of the piece, the title has no literal meaning, the word having been invented by the composer for its phonetic value. *Satyres*, for two flutes and the last work of the Sigma Series, is similarly incantatory and ritualistic, incorporating a wide range of experimental techniques. With the greater possibilities inherent in the use of two instruments, 'combinatoire counterpoint' and other layering techniques, enhance the effect of spontaneous improvisation although the material itself is composed.

Like *Sarc* and *Satyres*, *Sacral d'Ilx* was conceived as a single-movement work, but its greater length allows for a more complex internal structure which is descended from Debussy's piano *Etudes*. In *Sacral'd'Ilx* Ohana reasserted the importance of Debussy as his spiritual father, rediscovered in the impressionistic pianism of the *24 Préludes*, another large work interpolating the Sigma Series during the early 1970s. In this way *Sacral d'Ilx* harks back to the discoveries not only of *Signes* but also of *Tombeau de Claude Debussy*.[33] Borrowing its scoring for harpsichord, oboe and horn from the fourth of Debussy's *Sonates pour divers instruments*, *Sacral d'Ilx* pays homage to Ohana's closest musical ancestor, although there are no thematic quotations or paraphrases. The many descriptive indications, with their evocations of atmosphere and flexible rubato, are also more suggestive of Debussy than some of Ohana's immediately preceding works: 'calme', 'libre', 'animé un peu', 'clair', 'mystérieux', 'un peu plus large', 'libre carillonant', 'sonore', 'lumineux', 'brillant', 'rude'. The poetic evocation is of some ancient tribal ceremonial taking place in an imagined Arcadian landscape. Although less overtly percussive than some earlier Sigma works, *Sacral d'Ilx*, as its title suggests, is incantatory and ritualistic. Many of Ohana's characteristic techniques are employed: 'combinatoire counterpoint', some of which involves purely rhythmic material; multiphonics, unusual effects of breathing, flutter-tonguing, glissandi and microintervals (oboe and horn); and on the harpsichord, percussive attacks, glissandi, the playing of rhythms on the wood of the instrument, the use of clusters and rapid arpeggiations. The esoteric title makes a two-fold reference; while 'sacral' is suggestive of primitive ritual, 'Ilx' is the ancient name of the town of Elche on the Mediterranean coast of southern Spain, famous for its pre-Roman statue known as the 'Lady of Elche'. Ohana's use of the ancient place-name enhances his suggestion of an Arcadian landscape, the ancient world described in his original programme notes 'cut from the rock, fashioned in bronze or gold, at the edge of the land, and populated by pagans and fantastic, mythological animals ...'.[34]

The works of the Sigma Series bear witness to an important compositional journey which reflected not only Ohana's stylistic growth and proliferation but continual evolution. With *Signes* and the Sigma Series Ohana found his true compositional identity, solved the problem of his instinctive eclecticism and established a unified language that was no longer derivative in the manner of his early works. Each work of the Sigma Series, particularly up to 1971, contained the compositional seeds which generated its successor and thus projected the discoveries of his music forwards. This process gradually extended itself into the non-Sigma works until, by the early 1970s, those works which interpolated the series had seized the compositional initiative, the purpose of the series having been fulfilled. The works of the Sigma Series established Ohana not only as one of the leading innovators of the contemporary avant-garde but as a distinctive and original creative voice.

Notes to Chapter Four.

1   The present author in conversations with the composer in Paris, February 1983 and March 1984.
2   The present author in conversation with the composer in Paris, March 1984.
3   Ibid.
4   E. Markham, 'Japanese Music', *The New Oxford Companion to Music* Vol. i, ed. D. Arnold (Oxford, 1983) pp. 968–85.
5   R. Wolpert, 'Chinese Music', *The New Oxford Companion to Music* Vol. i, ed. D. Arnold (Oxford, 1983) p. 371.
6   M. Ohana, 'Béla Bartók', *Le nouvel observateur* (18 August 1965). Cited from the composer's MS version (p.3) a copy of which is in the possession of the present author.
7   C. Bodman Rae, *The Music of Lutosławski*, 3rd edn (London, 1999) p. 35.
8   The present author in conversation with the composer in Paris, April, 1992.

9 E. Harich-Schneider, *A History of Japanese Music* (Oxford, 1973) pp. 82 and 110.
10 The present author in conversation with the composer in Paris, June 1988.
11 M. Ohana, 'Béla Bartók', *Le nouvel observateur* (18 August, 1965). Cited from the composer's MS version (p.1) a copy of which is in the possession of the present author.
12 The present author in conversation with the composer in Paris, April 1984.
13 Alejo Carpentier, 'Les noirs', 'Afro-cubanisme' in *La musique à Cuba* trans. R.L.F. Durand (Paris, 1986) pp. 123–36 and pp. 251–66.
14 In mathematical terms, the sigma 'Σ' also represents, more conventionally, the concept of 'summation'.
15 Although the score of *Synaxis* indicates that it was composed between September 1965 and January 1966, the preliminary sketches were made immediately after completing *Signes*.
16 Fig. 12 represented the end of the piece in its first version, premièred on 17 December 1970. The work was revised in 1971 and premièred in its final version on 22 June 1971.
17 M. Ohana, programme note for *Sibylle*. Reproduced by C. Prost in 'Catalogue raisonné' *La Revue musicale* (1986) p. 205.
18 The present author in conversation with the composer in Paris, June 1988.
19 M. Ohana, interview (in French), R. Lyon (1978) p. 43.
20 M. Ohana, interview (in French), A. Grunenwald (1975) p. 61.
21 M. Ohana, interview (in French), R. Lyon (1978) p. 43.
22 M. Ohana, interview (in French), J.C. Marti (1991) p. 10.
23 C. Rae, 'Music-Theatre and the Japanese Noh', 'The Music of Maurice Ohana' Vol. 1 (diss. U.of Oxford (1989) pp. 270–88.
24 P.A. Castanet, '1968: A Cultural and Social Survey of its Influences on French Music', *Contemporary Music Review* Vol. 8, 1, (1993) pp. 25–30.
25 M. Ohana, programme note for a performance of *Silenciaire* at the Fêtes du Solstice du Château de Ratilly, June 1970, reproduced by C. Prost in 'Catalogue raisonné', *La Revue musicale* (1986) pp. 206–7.
26 R. Sherlaw Johnson, *Messiaen* (London, 1989) p. 32.
27 In C. Prost (1986) op.cit. p. 206–7.
28 Ibid.
29 M. Ohana, programme note for a performance at the Espace Cardin in Paris on 15 March 1972 (also the première of *Syrtes*) reproduced by C. Prost (1986) op. cit. p. 208.
30 Rostropovich's commission of Dutilleux's cello concerto *Tout un monde lointain* dates from the early 1960s.
31 H. Dutilleux, *Mystère et mémoire des sons - entretiens avec Claude Glaymann* (Paris, 1977) p. 93.
32 Like the première of the Lutosławski's Cello Concerto on 14 October 1970, the première of *Tout un monde lointain* took place at the Festival d'Aix-en-Provence on 25 July 1970, before the Soviet restrictions affecting Rostropovich took effect.
33 C. Rae, 'Debussy et Ohana: allusions et références', *Cahiers Debussy* Nos 17–18 (1993–94) pp. 103–20.
34 Reproduced by C. Prost (1986) op.cit. p.21.

1. The composer's family home on Boulevard d'Anfa, Casablanca.

2. The composer at the time of his first public recital aged 11.

3. The composer aged about 23 at the time of his Paris début recital.

4. The composer c. 1941 (standing centre back row) shortly after joining the British Army.

5. The composer (seated at the piano) with Ataulfo Argenta during rehearsals for the first recording of *Llanto for Ignacio Sánchez Méjías* (*c*. early 1950s)

6. 'Paso'. Drawing by the composer (*c.* 1955) of the Spanish procession of Holy Week

7. The composer (front third from the left) with members of his family in Casablanca.

8. The composer playing tennis at the Bois de Boulogne.

9. The composer (*c*. 1985) at his Paris flat, rue Général Delestraint.

10. The composer (right) with Roland Hayrabedian, c. 1990.

CHAPTER FIVE

The Role of Monody

> My music is monodic and that which is added to it is just a trail or shadow. The soul of it is fundamentally monodic and whether it is a sequence of chords or masses of sound, it is fundamentally monodic.[1]

Musical density in Ohana's mature music results from a predominantly linear approach in which horizontal motion is thickened to create vertical texture. Not unlike numerous instances in the music of Debussy, Messiaen and Dutilleux, the horizontal, rather than the vertical, becomes the primary, generative element. In Ohana, monody is the source from which the main driving-force of his music springs and is therefore the first element to be discussed in relation to his mature musical language.

Ohana's view of his music as primarily monodic should be understood against the background of musical influences described in his writings and interviews as having shaped his compositional development (cf. Chapters 1 and 2). Despite their individual differences, Ohana considered all the traditions which fed his music to be united not only through the importance each accords to the voice, but through their essentially monodic and in some cases, improvisatory roots. Thus, he had no qualms in drawing as much from Spanish folk and African tribal music, as from plainsong, the Medieval and Renaissance vocal repertoire and the Chinese and Japanese theatre music he discovered in the 1950s and 60s. Although appearing superficially as mere rampant eclecticism, many of the sources on which he drew are themselves related, culturally and historically. For this reason the Spanish folk and African tribal music experienced in his youth led him naturally to Afro-Cuban music, jazz and Negro spirituals. His intensive study of plainsong and much of the repertoire of the Medieval and Renaissance at the Schola Cantorum, encouraged him to consider the compositional implications of the vocal, as well as rhythmic, traditions of his inherited folk music. Fully understanding the complex roots and regional diversity of Spanish folk music, as is witnessed in his writings,[2] he did not consider it out of place to draw on a wide range of sources. Indeed, Ohana's eclecticism could be considered traditional not only in terms of twentieth century music as a whole but, more specifically, in a French compositional context; France has long enjoyed a fascination of what to the Anglo-Saxon may appear exotic cultures, while the acceptance of the eclectic approaches tradition itself.

Vocal music represents the largest proportion of Ohana's work from *Llanto pour Ignacio Sánchez Mejías* to his last work *Avoaha* and contains some of his most personal statements. Despite the intimacy Ohana felt with the piano, his own instrument and the tool with which he composed, he wrote his epitaph in *Swan Song* for unaccompanied voices (cf. Chapter 9, and Ex. 9.1). His last years represented an Indian summer of composition for the voice, from the gargantuan opera *La Célestine* to the choral miniatures *Nuit de Pouchkine* and *Tombeau de Louize Labé*. Taking the natural expressiveness of the human voice as his compositional starting-point, a preoccupation with monody and the emphasis of the horizontal was a natural consequence, influencing his orchestral and instrumental writing just as profoundly. Considering all the traditions on which he drew to be based on different types of chant, and therefore music primarily to be sung, all Ohana's music stems from vocal origins.

> The most fundamental aspect of my music is that it should be able to be sung. It must be accessible to the human being in the simplest form in which he can apprehend music.[3]

Dutilleux has praised Ohana's vocal works most of all. Sharing a similar admiration for the timbral beauty of female voices, he has cited in particular the expressive incantations of *Office des oracles* and the two Avignon Festival commissions of the 1970s, the Mass and *Trois contes de l'Honorable Fleur*, as being among his favourite works.[4] Incantatory, monodic vocalisations are as characteristic of these works as the early *Cantigas* which opened the path to subsequent vocal development. The incantatory monodies can be contemplative and expressive, as in 'Pythié' of *Office* (cf. Ex. 8.2) or more extrovert, as in *Trois contes*. The contemplative type belong to the special category of 'Sibylline' monodies (cf. Chapter 2). Particularly associated with the female voice, they are characterised by a static quality, any sense of metrical time being suspended (they are usually unmetred), their sheer beauty of sound and lyrical eloquence. They may be reserved to a solo voice, as in *Sibylle*, successive solo voices, as in 'Cantiga del azahar' of *Cantigas*, or divided simultaneously between two or more solo voices as in the 'Kyrie' and 'Trope' of the Mass, 'Debla' of *Cris*, 'Calypso' and 'Miroir de Sapho' of *Lys de madrigaux* and, most dramatically, as in the three prophecies of the Sibyl in the opera *La Célestine* (see Ex. 5.1).[5]

More wide-ranging in mood and expression are the vocalisations of *Sibylle* which illustrate well Ohana's process of continuous extension by variation and addition, characteristic both of his extended monodies and much of his linear construction. This process is the essence of what Ohana described as 'coral-reef' form (cf. Chapter 8). Although Ohana used his analogy of organic growth in relation to the organisation of large-scale structure, the process can be seen operating in microcosm in *Sibylle*. Ohana's approach has parallels with Dutilleux's concept of progressive growth but the overall effect is different, creating the impression of spontaneous improvisation while the material is entirely composed. (Ohana's aleatory techniques affect the way material is put together rather than the way it is invented.) The first sub-section of *Sibylle* presents such an incantatory, monodic vocalisation (see Ex. 5.2).[6] Like any succession of pitches intended to be sung and therefore articulated through breathing, the monody is constructed from a hierarchy of sentences and phrases of varying lengths, the building blocks of which are small cells characterised by melodic shape or gesture. The cells combine to form phrases which in turn form sentences and eventually sections which articulate the larger structure, although

Ex. 5.1: *Les trois prophéties de la Sibylle*, 'Première prophétie' (fig. 4–5)

© 1995 Gérard Billaudot Editeur S.A. Paris successeur. Reproduced by kind permission.

the character of the material may be contrasted between sections. These monodic vocalisations are typically unmetred.

The first sentence of the monody comprises three long phrases each of which begins with a sustained note (F, F–1/3-tone, F♯), two of which are decorated by third-tone oscillations. The phrases contain six, four and three cells, respectively, which are variants of previous cells. The third-tone oscillation is a commonly used opening or closing gesture and appears extensively throughout Ohana's vocal as well as instrumental music. Here opening a phrase, it is derived from the expressive, declamatory mordent-appoggiature on descending semitones characteristic of the 'ay' exclamations of the Cante Jondo. Ohana prolongs the mordent into an oscillation which is transmuted to sound after the initial note, instead of before. The semitone is contracted into third-tone microintervals which, according to Ohana, occur naturally in Spanish folk song. The third phrase opens with a variant form of the oscillation; slowed down, each pitch is exactly notated, the effect being consequently more melodic. The phrases and cells of the first sentence are of a particular melodic shape which is widespread in Ohana's mature works; they move around a referential note and are here defined as 'pivotal'.[7] There is one example of a cell incorporating a 'double-pivot'; in the second phrase, the second cell begins and ends on E but emphasises F in a melodic line which curls about this pitch in a circling motion, F, F–1/3-tone, and F–2/3-tone being central in frequency and position. As the cells of the first sentence are united by their pivotal character they can be seen to represent a block of material of one basic melodic type which has here been called 'Melodic A'. New and contrasting melodic material is introduced in a cell which acts as a postscript to the first sentence; marked 'clair', it is characterised by more overtly expressive movement in disjunct intervals and has been called 'Melodic B'. An interpolated phrase, it anticipates the more extended appearance of 'Melodic B' at fig. 1 (see Ex. 5.2).

Ex. 5.2: *Sibylle* (opening to fig. 2)

THE ROLE OF MONODY 149

Reproduced by kind permission of Société des Editions Jobert, Paris / United Music Publishers Ltd.

The structure of the second sentence is more complex. Instigated by the entry of percussion and marked 'animé', it juxtaposes two phrases of contrasting material; the first phrase introduces more rhythmically active material characterised by repetitive, Stravinskian *acciaccature*, here called 'Texture A', while the second presents four cells developed from 'Melodic B'. The rhythmic incisiveness of 'Texture A' anticipates the material of the new sub-section beginning at fig. 2. Dove-tailing material this way, Ohana manages to blur the seams between sentences and the impetus of the organic variation process is maintained. Although the material of the first sub-section presents variety and contrast, there is an underlying unity; the larger structure of both sentences outlines a melodic shape that determines the length of the section and unifies fragmentary material. The first sentence rises an augmented second from F to

G♯. The interpolated phrase continues the ascent to the upper G at an intermediate climax, although it concludes on an A♭ (enharmonically equivalent to the G♯), The first phrase of the second sentence outlines a chromatically ascending shape (G-A♭-A-B♭-B-C) and the second phrase effects an ascent to the main climax on the high A at the end of the section. The ascending glissandi and conjunct movement of some individual cells supports the upward drive. There is a further unifying feature linking the pivotal, conjunct material of 'Melodic A' and 'Texture A' with the contrasting material of 'Melodic B'; while the cells of the second phrase of the second sentence are characterised by the predominance of the major seventh and disjunct motion, the gravitation towards the E♭ is pivotal. In this way, potentially disjointed material maintains a sense of impulsion and expressive drive, while the creating the effect of free improvisation.

The opening section of *Sibylle* is a relatively simple example of the organic process involved in generating a horizontal line by adding successive cells through continuous extension. The length of phrase or sentence depends on the character of the cells involved and the extent to which they are varied. This in turn depends on the individual requirements of each work. In subsequent sections of *Sibylle* the process of organic extension becomes progressively more complex, intensified by the additional exploration of textural interplay between the voice and percussion. The relationships between Ohana's cells are indeed analogous to the continuous life-cycles of colonies of microscopic polyps which form a coral-reef; in the same way that no two sections of coral can be identical (although similar), Ohana's horizontal lines are extended in their own unique way, depending on the character and shape of the melodic cells involved. There is no uniform system applied either to the choice of melodic cells, with respect to their character, or the process of variation and ornamentation, this being the result of the composer's musical instinct. This is in keeping with Ohana's desire to recreate an atmosphere of improvisation within the confines of a composed score. As he often indicated, Ohana's approach to horizontal extension descended from formal procedures in the Debussy piano *Etudes*, in particular 'Pour les quartes' and 'Pour les sixtes'.[8] Many aspects of large-scale form are thus generated from the inside out, rather than the reverse:

> Form is determined by the germ of the sound-material and as a result is very different from one work to another ... we are in an epoque where form must establish itself on its own, born from the vegetal or biological growth of a work ... . Debussy has already said this.[9]

The linear process of horizontal extension can be seen translated into an instrumental medium in 'Quintes', from the *Etudes d'interprétation* for piano (see Ex. 5.3). The parallelism in fifths thickens the monodic line to provide the 'trail or shadow' of harmonic resonance. In the example, drawn from the middle of the first main section of the piece, the individual cells of the first phrase of the first sentence yield a descending melodic line, while overall they combine to form an ascending phrase. This leads to the climax of the sentence at the opening of the second phrase where cells are more gestural than melodic.

Ex. 5.3: *Etudes d'interprétation* (I), 'Quintes' (p. 22 of the score)

Following the climax, the cells of the second phrase descend, thus balancing the underlying, ascending motion of the first phrase. In contrast, the second sentence of the example is more reposeful and the melodic units are pivotal.

Composed for piano, the example from 'Quintes' is unable to transliterate one of the most characteristic features of Ohana's incantatory monodies; the use of third-tone microintervals to enhance expressive intensity. The expansion of the conventional semitone scale with microintervals was an instinctive response to the various folk musics. As Ohana explained in his 1968 article, micro-intervals occur naturally in the songs of certain types of folk music.[10] Eschewing the quarter-tone from his transitional period onwards, Ohana incorporated the less common third-tone microinterval which he heard as having 'a sharper and more crystalline quality'.[11]

> That which is called the quarter-tone is an ambiguity ... in reality it does not exist. In fact it is a mode of attack either above or below a note, with guttural, labial or dental interferences which affect the pitch. The third-tone, on the other hand, does exist, although in a passive sense. The whole-tone scale of Debussy contains the scale in third-tones, like something imagined that has become real with the passage of time.[12]

The quarter-tone does, of course, exist and has been widely explored by many composers including Carrillo, Cage, Hába, Ives, Ligeti and Vïshnegradsky, to mention only a few. Ohana considered the quarter-tone an artificial invention, while the third-tone is a more spontaneous phenomenon found naturally not only in the Cante Jondo but also Sephardic and Arabic eastern Mediterranean as well as north African traditions. As the third-tone interval is larger than the quarter-tone, singers and instrumentalists have less difficulty in recognising and reproducing this microinterval. Ohana frequently incorporated the zither tuned to third-tones in vocal ensembles as a means of training singers to pitch the microintervals and supporting them in performance. While continuing to make use of the conventional division of the octave into twelve semitones, Ohana developed a separate system of tuning in micro intervals. Although not a new invention in the history of music, he worked out a subdivision of the octave into eighteen third-tones based on the two whole-tone scales of conventional equal temperament (see Ex. 5.4).

Unlike quarter-tone scales, Ohana's third-tone scales preclude the appearance of semitones, this distinguishing his own system from that of Busoni. In melodic context, however, Ohana's third-tones are freely juxtaposed with semitones to provide melodic colouring and an expanded range of expression. In considering Ohana's derivation of third-tones from the whole-tone scale, it is interesting to note that Debussy, in his conversations with Ernest Guiraud, referred to a division of the octave into eighteen degrees, proposing that the tonal scale should be enriched by other scales.[13] Debussy also, rather curiously, referred to 24 semitones and 36 whole-tones in the octave. Whether Debussy was thinking of microintervals or not, the third-tone scale is implicit in the whole-tone scale, as Ohana said, 'something imagined made real with the passage of time.'[14]

Ex. 5.4: Ohana's two scales of third-tone mictrointervals
(notation can be its enharmonic equivalent)

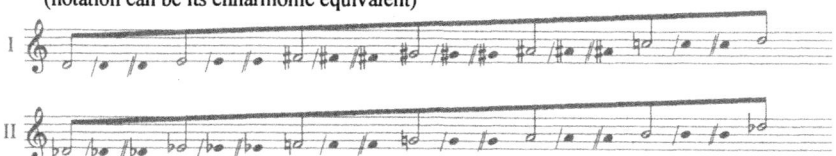

Having outlined the basis of Ohana's process of melodic extension, some of the chief features which characterise other aspects of his melodic writing should be considered. Certain distinctive melodic shapes recur throughout his mature music with such regularity that they approach an instinctive process of self-quotation, like personal, musical signatures. Ex. 5.5 illustrates a melody from *Kypris* which emerges from the texture like a fragment of half-remembered song.

Ex. 5.5: *Kypris* (piano, fig. 6)

Reproduced by kind permission of Société des Editions Jobert, Paris / United Music Publishers Ltd.

The melodic shape overall is of the pivotal type, the minor second and third both emphasising the referential note F. Ascending chromatically in the upper pitches, the climax is reached at the tritone (F♮-B♮) before returning to the referential note via a minor second. These features are all characteristic of many Spanish folk song-types but are strikingly similar to the Moorish, saeta-like melodies used by Albéniz in 'El Albaicin' (notably the theme at bar 67). Without citing actual folk melodies Ohana, like Albéniz, has them in his blood and imbues his music with richly evocative, melancholic reference. Another Spanish song-type melody appears in the second section of 'Cadences libres' from *Etudes d'interprétation* (I) (see Ex. 5.6a).

154 THE MUSIC OF MAURICE OHANA

Ex. 5.6a: *Etudes d'interprétation* (I), 'Cadences libres' (Lent, souplement rythmé)

Reproduced by kind permission of Société des Editions Jobert, Paris / United Music Publishers Ltd.

Like the example from *Kypris,* the melodic line is thickened with parallel movement to create harmonic resonance, is pivotal, ascends in the second phrase, emphasises the minor third and incorporates linear chromaticism to enhance expressiveness. Particular prominence is given to the oscillation about the major second which gradually transmutes into the ascending major second cell, commonly used throughout Ohana's melodic writing. Although these features are also characteristic of the Moorish melodies in 'El Albaicin', Ohana intended the melody to allude to the Andantino tranquillo 'Pantomima' of Falla's *El Amor brujo*.[15] Also in 7/8, Ohana described both his own melody and the Falla model as examples of the flamenco Tango (a much older form than the modern Argentinean dance), in which, according to Ohana, the 3+2+2 pattern is an example of the Greek epitrite rhythm on which so much Spanish music is based (cf. Chapter 7).[16] The first section of 'Cadences libres' is built around another allusive, Spanish melody in which the epitrite rhythm is implicit (see Ex. 5.6b).

Ex. 5.6b: *Etudes d'interprétation* (I), 'Cadences libres' (Souple sans rigueur)

Reproduced by kind permission of Société des Editions Jobert, Paris / United Music Publishers Ltd.

Again, the melodic line is essentially vocal and thickened with harmonic shadowing, although there is greater variety of cell type; linear chromatic, ascending and descending, as well as pivotal, while the minor second is emphasised as much as the minor third. The distinctive ascending major second cell, which originates from the flattened seventh of modal folk songs, prepares for the melody of the second section which is also set in relief from its surrounding texture by its pseudo-tonality. Both melodies illustrate similar quasi-cadential features; both conclude with pivotal cells containing the ascending major seconds separated by a major third. This cell suggests the quasi-cadential melodic shape found not only in plainchant but in folk song, jazz-blues and Negro spirituals. Ex. 5.7 from the second of the *Trois contes de l'Honorable Fleur* illustrates the basic shape of a falling major second, while the intervals of the individual cells expand from a minor third to a tritone to reveal the underlying linear chromaticism.

Ex. 5.7: *Trois contes de l'Honorable Fleur*, 'Le vent d'Est enfermé dans un sac' (soprano, flute, clarinet, piano, cello, fig. 59–60)

Reproduced by kind permission of Société des Editions Jobert, Paris / United Music Publishers Ltd.

Another important cell-type is often reserved for the end of a phrase or sentence. As in some plainchant melodies, a step-wise descending line has a quasi-cadential function, although in Ohana these melodic formations are transformed to incorporate a tritone and a concluding descending third. Ex. 5.8 from 'Calypso' of *Lys de madrigaux* illustrates three chromatic cells, each of which is successively extended by an additional note.

Ex. 5.8: *Lys de madrigaux*, 'Calypso' (reduction, fig. 6–7)

Although the overall shape outlines a descending major third, the most audible patterns are the ascending chromatic line, which increases tension, and the concluding tritone which incorporates the chromatic descent and minor third as the release of tension. The appearance of the minor third at the end of the phrase originates from vocal gesture typical of many types of folk song and is another frequently appearing cell. There are other instances of the cadential tritone without step-wise movement. Ohana's quasi-cadential tritone has an intriguing parallel with Messiaen who argues in his *Technique de mon langage musical* how an F♯ can 'resolve downwards' to C. Although Ohana did not develop a regulated harmonic system such as that of Messiaen, the tritone does play an important role in his harmonic vocabulary, as shall be shown in the following chapter.

Ohana's song-like fragments often have a special significance for the composer and occur at the emotional heart of a work (or movement). Characterised by a sense of calm and repose they evoke an atmosphere of intimate spirituality and are always played quietly:

> I think very important things are said mezza voce. Chopin has shown us the path beautifully in that, and so has all that Medieval music of which I am so fond.[17]

Many are pseudo-tonal or pentatonic and suggest folk-song melodies or Negro spirituals. Unlike Ohana's incantatory monodies, third-tones rarely appear melodically. 'Septièmes' from *Etudes d'interprétation* (II) was composed in memoriam Béla Bartók; the concluding section, entitled 'Deep Night', includes a haunting melody suggestive of central European folksong (see Ex. 5.9).[18] Based on the pseudo-tonality of a modal F♯ minor, although obscured by the harmonic shadowing, the melody incorporates melodic cells which emphasise descending fourths and thirds, characteristic of much central European folk song. Despite Ohana's specific reference to Bartók and the very Magyar allusion in the fourth phrase, 'Deep night' shares a number of features with both the Passacaille theme of Ravel's A minor Piano Trio and 'Jimbo's Lullaby' from Debussy's

THE ROLE OF MONODY

Ex. 5.9: *Etudes d'interprétation* (II), 'Septièmes' (closing section 'Deep Night')

Reproduced by kind permission of Société des Editions Jobert, Paris / United Music Publishers Ltd.

Children's Corner; not only is 'Deep Night' modal and pivotal, but the essentially vocal melody is not unlike the Ravel and Debussy themes in character as well as spirit. The third movement of *Lys de madrigaux* is based on a similar pivotal melody which, according to the composer, is a traditional Negro spiritual (see Ex. 5.10). Entitled 'Star Mad Blues' the melody sets an

Ex. 5.10: Negro spiritual melody in *Lys de madrigaux*, 'Star Mad Blues'

Reproduced by kind permission of Société des Editions Jobert, Paris / United Music Publishers Ltd.

enigmatic English text by the composer: 'O Orion! O Moon! Waning moon, O sweet Milky-Way! Am I star mad because I'd rather watch you than live in this wild world?'. Like 'Deep night', the melody is intimate and contemplative but accords greater emphasis to the cell of the modal, ascending major second and includes more chromatic colouration, in particular the so-called blue-notes of jazz (the flattened third, fifth and seventh). Ohana indicated other examples of actual or paraphrased Negro spiritual melodies in the *24 Préludes*, *Anneau du Tamarit*, 'Gloria' of the Mass, Piano Concerto, Second String Quartet, *Kypris*, the *Etudes d'interprétation*, *Swan Song* and *Avoaha*. In addition, many of these works, particularly the *24 Préludes*, *Anneau du Tamarit* and the Piano Concerto, incorporate rhythmic and harmonic allusions to jazz and blues.

While similar song-like melodies or melodic fragments appear in a wide range of Ohana's mature works, there are many instances of allusion to distinctive melodic fragments of other composers, not only Albéniz, Falla and Debussy but also Stravinsky. Emerging only briefly, these melodic parodies are never indicated in the score, their recognition depending on the listener's familiarity with the work from which the fragment is drawn. A technique first explored in the transitional period in *Tombeau de Claude Debussy*, where the majority of paraphrases and allusions were quite conscious, many of Ohana's later allusions may have been instinctive, being triggered by a basic similarity of melodic shape between his original melodic designs and the particular shapes of the given parody. Conspicuous in Ohana's mature and late music are references to *The Rite of Spring*, one of the Stravinsky scores permanently shelved by Ohana's piano in his Paris flat. A striking example of Stravinskian reference occurs in the first tale of *Trois contes de l'Honorable Fleur*. A fragment paraphrasing the famous bassoon solo which opens Stravinsky's 'Adoration of the Earth' is heard as the culminating phrase of an extended monody, also for solo bassoon (see Ex. 5.11). Due to the timbral associations of the upper register of the bassoon, the effect is intentionally humorous, the reference being long anticipated by most listeners.

Ex. 5.11: *Trois contes de l'Honorable Fleur*, 'Ogre mangeant des jeunes femmes sous la lune' (fig. 37)

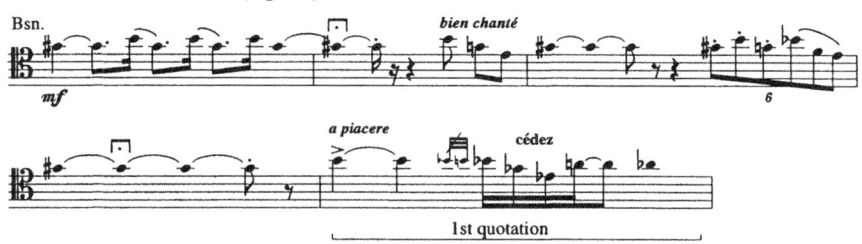

Reproduced by kind permission of Société des Editions Jobert, Paris / United Music Publishers Ltd.

This quotation opens a sequence of witty allusions to *The Rite*. An evocation of a primitive percussive dance, 'Danse de Mort', immediately follows Ohana's first quotation, just as the Introduction to 'Adoration of the Earth' is followed by 'Dances of the Young Girls' in *The Rite*. This is followed by a parody of melodic and rhythmic fragments from the 'Ritual of Abduction' and 'Sacrificial Dance' (Ohana's instrumentation gives similar prominence to the brass and woodwind), which maintains the references to the Stravinsky model ('Ogre mangeant des jeunes femmes sous la lune' figs. 40, 41 and 44). A second appearance of the bassoon solo from the 'Adoration' occurs towards the end of Ohana's first tale, together with a parody of the oscillating quavers (Ohana fig. 48) which also appear in the introduction to the second part of *The Rite*, 'The Sacrifice'. The purpose of this complex sequence of quotation and allusion is to provide a witty contrast between the sombre, sacrificial symbolism of Stravinsky and Ohana's intentionally humorous story of the not-so-innocent young girl who, far from being the victim herself, succeeds in murdering the ogre and becomes one in her turn (cf. Chapter 2).

Not all Stravinskian references in Ohana are as intricate as in *Trois contes*. Far more common in Ohana's mature music are his allusions to another melodic fragment from *The Rite* ; the theme which opens 'Mystic Circles of the Young Girls' (fig. 91) and emerges in the preceding introduction (see Ex. 5.12a).

Ex. 5.12a: Stravinsky, *The Rite of Spring*, 'Mystic Circles of the Young Girls' (fig. 91)

© Copyright 1912, 1921 by Hawkes & Son (London) Ltd.

Ohana's attraction to this melodic fragment could well result from its folk song origins and modal character. When considered as a melodic cell, it also contains both the oscillating major second, the falling third and emphasises perfect intervals (cf. Chapter 7). In *Kypris*, for oboe, viola, double bass and piano, a nocturne in praise of the Cretan Goddess of Love, the quotation appears at the climax of a piano cadenza which concludes an animated, contrapuntal episode (see Ex. 5.12b). It is alluded to again in the rhythmic ostinato (significantly

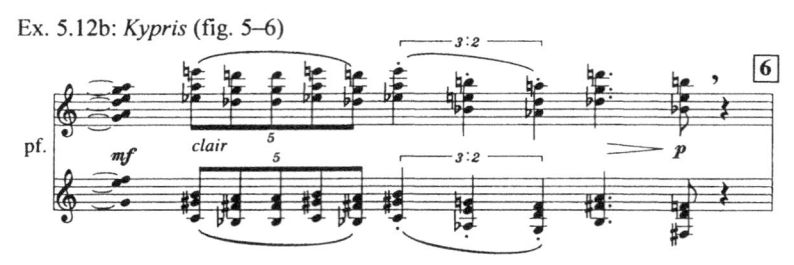

Ex. 5.12b: *Kypris* (fig. 5–6)

Reproduced by kind permission of Société des Editions Jobert, Paris / United Music Publishers Ltd.

marked 'mystérieux') on piano and double bass which underpins the final section; the chordal repetition, resonance and use of pizzicato in the double bass also evoke the effect of a ghostly, guitar 'tambora' (see Ex. 5.12c). The same melodic fragment provides the germ for one of the main melodic ideas in *Livre des prodiges*. First suggested in the short introductory 'Clair de terre', it is subjected to a range of transformations before appearing near the end of the work, in the penultimate section also entitled 'Clair de terre' (see Ex. 5.12d). While Stravinsky's fragment is here alluded to, rather than actually quoted, the emphasis of the oscillating major second followed by the falling minor third distils the basic elements of the melody, despite the absence of perfect intervals in Ohana's transformation. That the first element in Stravinsky's fragment, the oscillating major second, provides the main focus for Ohana's transformations of this melodic idea, including several allusions to the oscillating quavers of the Introduction to 'The Sacrifice', also results in considerable use of referential notes. This is an important feature of the melodic material throughout the work and one which recalls the melodic language of Dutilleux.

Ex. 5.12c: *Kypris* (fig. 17)

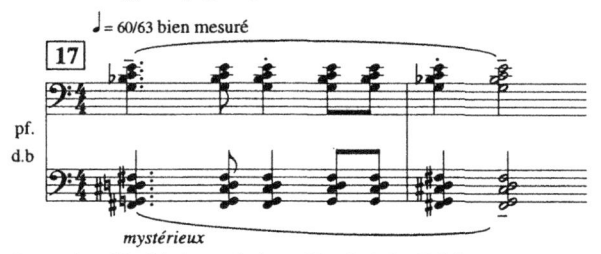

mystérieux

Reproduced by kind permission of Société des Editions Jobert, Paris / United Music Publishers Ltd.

Ex. 5.12d: *Livre des prodiges*, 'Clair de Terre' (reduction, fig. 73)

blanc, sans vibr.

Reproduced by kind permission of Société des Editions Jobert, Paris / United Music Publishers Ltd.

Intended as a commentary on *The Rite of Spring* and inhabiting the same world of pagan ritualism, *Livre des prodiges* is not only a concerto for orchestra but virtually a catalogue of Stravinskian allusion. The scoring, as well as Ohana's orchestration is very like that of Stravinsky (although Ohana uses a larger percussion section); similar effects include the use of *fortissimo* muted trumpets and horns 'pavillon en l'air' in sections evoking frenzied tribal dances, as well as *pianissimo* flutes and bassoon accompanied with sustained string harmonics to suggest vast plains of emptiness. The powerful rhythmic drive of Ohana's score, his use of ostinati and modal melodies, many of which incorporate Stravinskian *acciaccature*, particularly in the woodwind writing, further enhance the many textual allusions. In 'Cortège des taureaux ailés' (one of the magical prodigies of the title) Ohana alludes to the 'pesante' section of 'Spring Rounds' (*The Rite,* fig. 49) with similar incantatory, woodwind interpolations (fig. 10). The sub-divided, bipartite structure of *Livre* is also derived from *The Rite*. Allusion is taken a step further in 'Soleil renversé' (the inverted sun suggests impending apocalypse) which includes a fleeting reference to the work of another composer; strident tritones in the lower orchestra combined with a tremolando in strings and percussion paraphrase, Mussorgsky's 'Baba Yaga' from *Pictures at an Exhibition*.

Reference to the music of other composers is not the only type of melodic allusion in Ohana. Having been attracted to traditional Chinese and Japanese theatre since the 1950s and 1960s, certain works incorporate pseudo-oriental melodies and ornamental figurations. Such allusions occur chiefly, although not exclusively, in works he considered Japanese in character and influence, notably *Signes* and *Trois contes de l'Honorable Fleur*. (While Ohana considered the tragic architecture of *Syllabaire pour Phèdre* similar to the static dramas of the Japanese Noh and indicated that the work should be produced in the same manner, the musical style is not Japanese in the same way as *Signes* or *Trois contes*.) Although Ohana's designation of these parodies was personal and subjective, the allusions are characterised by their adaptation of well-known features of Japanese music: microtonal alterations of pitch through wavering, sliding and pinching of notes; florid embellishments and ornamentation; heterophony; the use of similar percussion instruments which traditionally articulate Japanese theatrical ritual. Many of these features enhance a sense of stately ceremonial, particularly in *Trois contes* and create a predominantly static effect. Ohana's choice of instrumentation in his 'Japanese' works is designed to paraphrase the sound of traditional Japanese instruments, including the Koto, bamboo flute, Shô and ceremonial percussion.[19] There is also an interesting parallel between Ohana's linear process of continuous extension in his incantatory melodic writing and the chains of standardised melodic formulae which generate the florid, vocal melodies in much Japanese Court music and Buddhist chant.[20]

Central to Ohana's wider vocabulary of allusive melodic writing are his parodies of the shape or pattern of plainchant. Together with the folk music Ohana knew from his youth, plainchant was one of his most important early influences:

> My writing was built entirely upon plainchant in Paris, where I studied at the Schola Cantorum, and by meditating on my own folk music; that is the Andalusian chant, the Flamenco so-called, the Cante Jondo, the rhythms and melody, then its prolonged roots in the past ... the Greek roots, the Jewish roots, the Arab roots ...[21]

This statement (as well as others found in Ohana's writings) illustrates Ohana's view of the relationship between sacred and popular vocal traditions fundamentally as types of chant. A similar view is expressed by Willi Apel who drew attention to the parallels between the many differing repertories of plainchant and folk song.[22] Apart from two isolated examples of actual plainchant melodies in the opera *La Célestine*, where, for specific dramatic purposes Ohana incorporated settings of the Te Deum ('Le camp des Rois Catholiques à Sante Fé') and Dies Irae ('La mort de Célestine' and 'Eloge de la Célestine'), Ohana preferred to paraphrase the contour of plainchant rather than cite specific melodies. These parodies are characterised by predominantly stepwise motion in adjacent intervals, a phrase structure reflecting the patterns of vocal respiration and overall flexibility of rhythmic movement. Some of Ohana's plainchant parodies, particularly those in instrumental works, distort the intervallic structure to allow a larger registral compass than would normally occur. This appears most dramatically in the first of the *24 Préludes* where the melodic line ascends from the sonorous depths of the piano to its highest register in a single phrase. Typically Ohana's plainchant parodies are unmetred.

The principles of antiphonal and responsorial singing associated with plainchant and the vocal repertories of the Medieval and Renaissance, are also adapted being particularly suited to Ohana's sectional approach to form (cf. Chapter 8). The opening solo of the Piano Concerto is typical of Ohana's approach to plainchant parody; thickened with harmonic shadowing to provide resonance, the uppermost note is emphasised through the indication 'timbrez la note supérieure'. A further instruction in the score explaining that the rests should be 'like breathing' enforces the vocal origins of Ohana's melody. A simplification of the solo part is reproduced in Ex. 5.13a to reveal the basic melodic outline. While according to the conventions of psalmody repetitions of each note are articulated according to the requirements of text, here Ohana joins many of the repeated notes with slurs. Ex. 5.13b illustrates another plainchant parody, also from the Piano Concerto, which incorporates an allusion to 'Mystic Circles of the Young Girls' from *The Rite of Spring*.

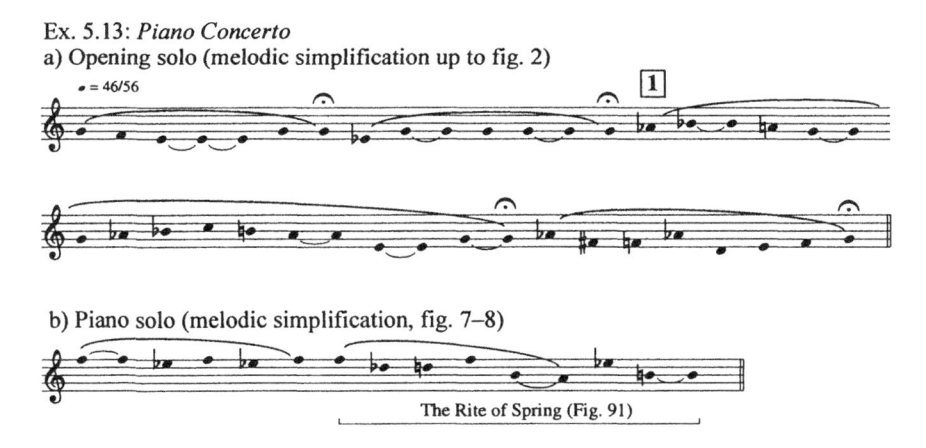

Ex. 5.13: *Piano Concerto*
a) Opening solo (melodic simplification up to fig. 2)

b) Piano solo (melodic simplification, fig. 7–8)

The Rite of Spring (Fig. 91)

Characteristic of Ohana's plainchant parodies is the notation as note-heads without stems, described by Ohana as 'neumes'. Designed to enhance rhythmic flexibility, the neumes are intended to preserve their relative values, Ohana invariably providing a metronome marking to suggest movement equivalent to crotchets. (At phrase-endings, the neumes are usually tied to stemmed notes in order that a rest may be inserted to indicate the pattern of vocal respiration.) While this by no means a system peculiar to Ohana (having been used by many composers since 1945), this notation lends the melodic line a greater flexibility in a manner reflecting plainchant itself. In the preface to the score of the *Etudes d'interprétation* Ohana explained: 'The notes written without tails represent values that according to the taste of the performer, are lightly variable (from 10% to 15%) in relation to the basic indicated tempo.' Ohana frequently used his neumes as a neutral rhythmic value suitable for combining with other, similar melodic lines to create purely melodic sound-masses of like material in aleatory counterpoint. In such cases each melodic pattern is repeated ad libitum and there

164   THE MUSIC OF MAURICE OHANA

is no fixed vertical coordination. In Ex. 5.14 from the 'Gloria' of the Mass (such a sound-mass provides a background texture for additional plainchant parodies

Ex. 5.14: Messe, 'Gloria', (fig. 35)

Reproduced by kind permission of Société des Editions Jobert, Paris / United Music Publishers Ltd.

(soprano and mezzo soloists, oboe, trumpet and vibraphone) in which the coordination between the parts is prescribed. Without the entry of the rhythmically fixed material the sound-mass could have continued indefinitely; the entry of the soloists and instrumental ensemble defines the duration of the section and brings the 'Gloria' to a close. In other contexts where there is no entry of a rhythmically fixed part, the duration of the sound-mass is determined by the conductor.

The combination of plainchant-like melodic fragments in aleatory counterpoint to create background texture, contrasts with the synchronized, note-for-note organum-like parallelism of other melodies which function as melodic foreground. This latter technique belongs to a group of procedures descended from early polyphony that is common throughout Ohana's mature music. While examples can be found in nearly every work, 'Sylva' from *Cadran lunaire* and 'Quintes' from the *Etudes d'interprétation* are essays in this process alone (cf. Ex. 6.1b and Ex. 6.2b). In movements such as these, characterised by an atmosphere of peace and contemplation, duplication occurs primarily at the fourth, fifth and major seventh. More agitated, rhythmically active melodies involve a parallelism which tends to duplicate in ninths, seconds, or occasionally tritones. Although this is not an inflexible rule, it does appear as a general trend. Marked 'très vif, agité', the twenty-second of the *24 Préludes* is more extrovert than either 'Sylva' or 'Quintes' and involves a two-fold parallelism (see Ex. 5.15).

Two independent monodies are combined without precise vertical co-ordination; conveniently pianistic, the upper (right-hand) monody is duplicated in major ninths, while the lower (left-hand) monody is duplicated in major seconds and thirds. These timbrally more dissonant intervals are more akin to the harmonic thickening found in the 'Organum' movement of *Synaxis*, at the opening of the Piano Concerto, and in the 'Déchant' movement of *Cinq séquences*, which is entirely concerned with discant counterpoint. (This is also explored in the first and last movements 'Polyphonie' and Hymne'.) Another form of Ohana's parallelism is suggestive of more florid styles; a chant-like melody is sometimes reproduced against the same melody moving in shorter durations. This type of parallelism occurs predominantly in sections of motoric rhythmic impulsion characterised by a-symmetrical quintuplet divisions, such as 'Circé' in *Lys de madrigaux*, 'Cortège des taureaux ailés' in *Livre des prodiges*, or the 'Triomphe de Christophe Colomb à Seville' in *La Célestine*.

With Ohana's many allusions to plainchant and organum, it is not surprising that in several works he includes material which parodies the role of a cantus firmus. Paraphrasing its original function, a cantus firmus in Ohana is a fixed part (or groups of parts) which provides the basis for a polyphonic texture against which other parts are set in counterpoint. As the other parts often comprise layers of aleatory counterpoint, Ohana's canti firmi provide a point of orientation for the texture as a whole and define the overall duration of the aleatory section. Canti firmi are found in *Chiffres de clavecin, Cris, Silenciaire, Office des oracles, Sacral d'Ilx* and *Trois contes de l'Honorable Fleur*. First

Ex. 5.15: *24 Préludes*, no.22 (opening section)

Reproduced by kind permission of Société des Editions Jobert, Paris / United Music Publishers Ltd.

appearing in *Chiffres de clavecin*, Ohana explains the cantus firmus in the preface to the score: 'The designation cantus firmus indicates that the instrument to which it applies must play the complete material through once (although the tempo may be ad libitum). The other instruments align themselves with the duration of this material either by repeating their own fragments or modifying their tempo (or placing of the neumes).' A cantus firmus is first used in the 'Contrepoints' section of the first movement of *Chiffres de clavecin* (fig. 3) where metred material on two horns provides a point of 'fixed' orientation around which a complex web of 'combinatoire' counterpoint is woven. Another cantus firmus controls the 'Passacaille' section (sub-titled 'contrepoint doubles') of the second movement (fig. 24) and is placed against the solo harpsichord. Here the soloist provides rhythmically 'fixed' material against which three blocks of contrasting material (on percussion, wind and strings respectively) are freely juxtaposed in aleatory counterpoint. Representing the 'contrepoints doubles' of the sub-title, the cantus firmus in the harpsichord provides the point of orientation for the ensemble, although it parodies neither pre-existent material nor plainchant. Percussive and rhythmically disjointed, the harpsichord cantus firmus is not melodic, nor does it relate to the material of the juxtaposed blocks, but simply represents the leading part within the section. Many of Ohana's canti firmi, function in this way. The solo harpsichord is also designated as a cantus firmus in the following section entitled 'Chaos d'accords' (fig. 36); here the more melodic material of the cantus firmus is related to the strident interpolations of the orchestra. The third movement of the concerto, 'Etoiles, nuées' (fig. 39), also incorporates a cantus firmus but as a series of unmeasured (although precisely notated) repeated chords which provide the foreground for a sound-mass of melodic fragments in aleatory counterpoint. Thus the function of the cantus firmus is the same as in earlier sections, although its musical context entirely different.

Such structural localisation is characteristic of most of Ohana's canti firmi with the exception of that in the second tale of *Trois contes de l'Honorable Fleur* (first heard on flutes and clarinets at fig. 53). Subject to more conventional treatment, this cantus firmus migrates into the other parts, is audibly distinct as a melody, and is set in relief both in terms of its rhythmic values, tempo and timbral associations. It is paraphrased and elaborated and appears, in various guises, in two out of three movements of the work. Like the cantus firmus in *Office des oracles,* where melodic material on a trio of trombones is used to symbolise the appearance of the minotaur in 'Minotaure aux miroirs', the cantus firmus in *Trois contes* is used to signal action in the music-theatre production; in the second tale it is associated with appearances of the 'East Wind' and a 'winged dragon', while in the third it symbolises the 'naughty monkeys' (cf. Chapter 2). While the cantus firmus appearing in *Silenciaire* is more abstract being chiefly rhythmic, in *Cris* and *Sacral d'Ilx* the canti firmi parody the melodic shape of plainchant. Appearing in the first movement of *Cris*, 'Générique' (figs. 6–7), the cantus firmus is represented by the tenor parts, against which mezzo-sopranos present a melodic and rhythmic transformation while sopranos provide percussive, background texture in a web of aleatory counterpoint. Emerging only in the final section of *Sacral d'Ilx*, the cantus firmus is distilled from material that has gone before (fig. 32). Represented by oboe and horn in two-part, organum-like parallelism, the freely juxtaposed material in the harpsichord provides contrapuntal variants (see Ex. 5.16).

The Mass, perhaps surprisingly, does not designate any parts as canti firmi, although much of the material parodies plainchant. The work does, however, refer to the technique of conductus, this appearing in the second of the three subsections of the 'Agnus Dei' (fig. 51). The conductus section comprises a setting of the Agnus Dei text for mezzo-soprano in a declamatory, syllabic style in a monody of sustained neumes that parodies the shape of plainchant. This is accompanied by the choir and instrumental ensemble who present rhythmically

Ex. 5.16: *Sacral d'Ilx* (fig. 32)

Reproduced by kind permission of Société des Editions Jobert, Paris / United Music Publishers Ltd.

disjointed, homophonic material; a thickened monody, set in an internally synchronized note-for-note manner suggesting discant. Another example of conductus appears in the seventh movement of *Avoaha*, entitled 'Conductus'; setting Latin text by Seneca, a melody paraphrasing plainchant sung by tenors and basses in organum-like parallel fifths, is described in the score as 'in the colour of Gregorian chant'. The Mass also includes an extended, monodic vocalisation designated as a Trope, which can be performed either after the Alleluia, or following the Agnus Dei. Although textless, the phonemes which articulate the monody allude to certain words in a manner suggestive of text troping: 'virgin' appears as 'vi-hi-hir-henn' and '(v)Ir-h-en'; 'Mary' as 'Ma-ré'; 'santa' as 'Sa-haann-nta' and 'sa-oa-han-taa'; and in a concluding quasi-cadence Ohana's own name appears hidden as 'o-ha-ha'.[23] An earlier example of a movement entitled 'Trope' appears in *Synaxis* ; written entirely in third-tone microintervals, the tropes comprise successions of phrases in note-for-note melodic parallelism and provide a contemplative interlude to the work as a whole. Ohana's early and transitional works also allude to the techniques of early polyphony: *Cantigas* was his first work to explore antiphonal and responsorial structures, while *Cinq séquences* suggests a variety of techniques in its movement titles. *Si le jour paraît...* makes reference to the secular Medieval repertoire in borrowing the titles of Troubadour song-types (cf. Chapter 3) while the much later Second String Quartet contains an Alborada which, although Spanish, is a distant cousin of the Provençale Alba.

While features of many musical traditions are drawn together from a broad spectrum of both geography and epoch, Ohana's melodic language successfully incorporates a wide-ranging vocabulary. Based on the common-denominator of the human voice, he synthesised disparate sources into a unified style that is not only dynamic but lyrical and expressive. With the horizontal dimension of monody as the inspirational source of Ohana's music, the vertical dimention is created through processes of linear thickening. The means through which the resultant harmonic 'trail or shadow' is constructed remains to be discussed in the following chapter.

Notes to Chapter Five.

1   M. Ohana, interview (in English), M. Oliver (1984).
2   In particular 'La géographie musicale de l'Espagne', *Journal musical français* Nos 47–8 (Paris, March–April 1956) pp. 1–8 and 'Horizons espagnols', Festival de Montauban, Cahier no. 6 (1962).
3   M. Ohana, interview (in English), M. Oliver (1984).
4   H. Dutilleux, *Mystère et mémoire des sons: entretiens avec Claude Glaymann* (Paris, 1997) pp. 159–60 and p. 200.
5   Extracted as a concert work for 2 sopranos, piano and percussion, *Trois prophéties de la Sibylle*.
6   Guy Reibel does not identify Ohana's compositional process in his survey article 'La musique vocale et chorale de Maurice Ohana', *La Revue musicale* (1986) pp. 71–87.
7   C. Prost describes a similar phenomenon in 'Poétique musicale de Maurice Ohana', *La Revue musicale* (1986) pp.107–28, but refers to them as 'archetypal circular schemes'.
8   The present author in conversation with the composer in Paris, June 1988.
9   M. Ohana, interview (in French), P. Ancelin (1964).
10 M. Ohana, 'Microintervals: Experimental Media II', *Twentieth Century Music* ed. R. Myers (London, 1968) pp. 147–50.
11 Ibid. p. 150.
12 M. Ohana, interview (in French), R. Lyon (1978) p. 42.
13 'Conversations with Ernest Guiraud', recorded by Maurice Emmanuel, reproduced in E. Lockspeiser *Debussy his Life and Mind*, Vol. I (London, 1962) pp. 173–4. Also presented by A. Hoérée in *L'Avant-Scène Opéra* No. 11, (Sept–Oct, 1977) p. 144 .
14 M. Ohana, interview (in French), R. Lyon (1978) p. 41.
15 The present author in conversation with the composer in Paris, March 1983.
16 Ibid.
17 M. Ohana, interview (in English), M. Oliver (1984).

18 The emphasis of perfect fourths and major seconds is also reminiscent of the opening of Bartók's *Concerto for Orchestra* and, perhaps, the beginning of *Duke Blubeard's Castle*.
19 See C. Rae, 'Music Theatre and the Japanese Noh', 'The Music of Maurice Ohana' (diss. U. of Oxford, 1989) pp. 270–88.
20 E. Harich-Schneider, *A History of Japanese Music* (Oxford, 1973).
21 M. Ohana, interview (in English), M. Oliver (1984).
22 W. Apel, *Gregorian Chant* (London, 1956) p. 4.
23 The repetition of 'ha' rather than 'na' prevents Ohana's allusion to his own name from being too obtrusive.

CHAPTER SIX

Harmony as Colour and Timbre

Ohana considered vertical texture to result from the horizontal process of harmonic shadowing, ranging from simple parallelism to more complex sound-masses. He evolved his harmonic language through exploring relationships between sound-colour and intervallic timbre. Like many composers of his generation, Ohana's concept of harmony is neither functional nor form-generating but is best understood in terms of density and timbral contrast. In the middle 1960s, when his musical language as a whole crystallised into maturity, Ohana described what he considered to be the primary elements of music:

> Music is made first and foremost from melody, rhythmic motion and a sound-mass that gives music its density. Let us say sound-mass as now harmony no longer exists.[1]

If the conventional role of harmony involves not only vertical co-ordination but the functional and structural considerations inherent in the tonal system, then many composers writing in the twentieth century, particularly the second half, might indeed conclude that this kind of harmonic concept could no longer exist. The separation of harmony from any traditional meaning and its redefinition as density and sound-mass is by no means peculiar to Ohana but may even be considered a conceptual phenomenon at its most fashionable in the 1960s. Similar preoccupations can be found in Lutoslawski's music of this time, notably in *Jeux vénitiens* (1961), *Trois poèmes d'Henri Michaux* (1963) and the Second Symphony (1967).[2] Ligeti, too, explored chromatic complexes of different density and timbre in *Atmosphères* (1961) and *Volumina* (1962) while the 'clouds' and 'galaxies' of Xenakis relate to the behaviour and interrelationships of sound-masses. Although Ohana was certainly aware of the music of these composers at the time, he was aesthetically closer to his friend Dutilleux (who was beginning to experiment with sound-mass densities in *Métaboles* of 1959–64), whose music he admired.[3] It is significant that Ohana had also long admired the music of Varèse whose shifting plaines represent earlier examples of techniques associated with the interaction and juxtaposition of textural and harmonic densities.[4] The notion of what is meant by a sound-mass is not always clear, and although this expression has come into common use, it is by no means an exact term. While it is sometimes associated with a texture where individual pitches are no longer distinguishable as separate entities, and can therefore be applied to sound-blocks of indeterminate pitch, or clusters, it can also be applied to describe a body of distinct, or defined pitches. Ohana used the term 'masse sonore' to describe all his harmonic densities, whether resulting from relatively simple processes of melodic parallelism, or from his more complex techniques of aleatory counterpoint, as in the 'Gloria' of the Mass (Ex. 5.14) where the material but not its vertical coincidence, is defined. As the choice of pitch in Ohana's music is not a free parameter, even in ad libitum sections where pitch-order or rhythm may be undefined, the harmonic colour of his 'masse sonore' is thus always determined. The means by which Ohana varied the harmonic colour was through a process of intervallic differentiation in which contrasting intervals and interval combinations could be exploited to create a language of timbre.

Evolving through the horizontal process of harmonic shadowing, the essence of Ohana's 'masse sonore' in his mature music can be described in terms of two main harmonic colour schemes, or timbral groups, which result from the differentiation and juxtaposition of contrasting interval types. One group is relatively dissonant and emphasises minor seconds (or inversionally related intervals) and tritones, while the other is more consonant and is characterised by the predominance of major seconds (and inversionally related intervals) and the perfect intervals of fourths and fifths. While the more dissonant timbral group occurs in a variety of musical contexts, it is often associated with the indications 'froid', 'âcre' or 'métallique'. The more consonant timbral group is most characteristically associated with an atmosphere of calm repose and typically appears with designations such as 'doux', 'cristallin', 'sonore', 'sans dureté' and 'clair'. It is this latter group which presents some of the composer's most expressive and personal musical statements. To reflect Ohana's colouristic approach to harmony, these contrasting schemes have here been defined as 'Timbre I' and 'Timbre II'.[5]

While there is some intervallic overlap between Ohana's timbral groups which facilitates ease of 'colour mixing' or blending (interval classes 2, 4 and 5 are common to both groups), Timbre I is defined by the emphasis of the tritone and minor second both of which are exclusive to the group. The minor third is exclusive to Timbre II. Both timbral groups exhibit primary and secondary characteristics. While chord structures in Timbre I emphasise the minor second and tritone at primary level, perfect intervals may appear embedded within larger chord-aggregates or be interpolated between successions of tritones (hence inclusion at primary level), although such intervals do not dominate the audible harmonic colour.[6] At secondary level, the tritone colouring results in the association of Timbre I with the whole-tone scale (interval classes 2, 4 and 6). Timbre II, at the primary level, gives aural emphasis to interval combinations based on major seconds and the perfect intervals (interval classes 2 and 5) and at the secondary level interval characteristics associated with the pentatonic scale (interval classes 2, 3, 4 and 5). The more complex the chord-aggregate combinations, the more likely is it for secondary characteristics to be present. The divisions are summarised in Table 6.1.

What can not be illustrated in Table 6.1 is the emphasis given to certain interval combinations through the actual layout of chords. Combined with a careful use of register, aural predominance is given the interval combinations characteristic of the particular harmonic scheme in effect, even though other 'foreign' intervals may sometimes be present. It is this aural predominance which governs the harmonic Timbre at any particular moment at either primary or secondary level. While the conventions of set-theoretical terminology provide a useful shorthand for codifying the main intervallic features of Ohana's timbral groups, the method is not able to distinguish between inversionally related intervals or reflect the aural predominance given to any particular interval class through the use of register or layout. In order to achieve timbral variation, as well as ease of colour mixing between the timbral groups, Ohana makes use of certain colouristic devices, including clusters, added-notes, resonance and third-tone microintervals, to disguise or to enhance the timbral density.

Table 6.1: The timbral divisions of Ohana's 'Masse Sonore'

		Interval classes* (adjacent and non-adjacent)
Timbre I — primary level	1 5 6
Timbre I — secondary level (whole tone scale)	2 4 6
Timbre II — primary level	2 5
Timbre II — secondary level (pentatonic scale)	2 3 4 5

Note: (*) the figures represent interval classes, they are *not* interval vectors.

Although Ohana's process of harmonic shadowing can be defined in this way (and he did express verbal agreement),[7] he never clarified his processes of intervallic differentiation in any writings or published interviews, rather eschewing all discussion of the more intimate aspects of his compositional process.

> Well that's a sort of secret I'm not too keen on revealing. I mean I am a very superstitious man and one of my main beliefs, my creeds, very deeply rooted, is that enormous work of introspection and of research within my own self may be misinterpreted if I talk about it: it doesn't go into words, it goes into music ... . So much so that I believe it would bring me ill luck if I reveal those things, so I'd rather deliver the result but not talk about the kitchen secrets as one might call them, vulgarly.[8]

Ohana's rejection of formalised, pre-compositional systems would suggest that his own procedures resulted more from instinct, rather than from any premeditated process. Consequently, his use of the contrasting timbral groups is not wholly systematic. Debussy's remark: '... There is no theory. You have merely to listen. Pleasure is the law ...',[9] is entirely appropriate to Ohana who emphasised the importance of the nature of sound itself as his compositional point of departure: 'For me it is physical sound which remains the essential basis of music and this will be so until the end of time, or just as long as mankind exists.'[10] Ohana never made any secret of his preference to compose, or at least begin the compositional process, at the piano (on his American model D Steinway[11]): 'I search much at the piano – mine is very rich – like composers used to.'[12] As a consequence, many of Ohana's chord formations and interval combinations are essentially pianistic in origin; the conspicuous use of keyboard instruments, piano, harpsichord or small organ, as auxiliaries in so many of his orchestral and vocal works may also reflect the pianistic origins of his compositional process. Ohana underlined the importance of tactile discovery: 'Being a pianist, and passionately so at that, I also learned music through my fingers just as much as with my ears, or through the study of scores.'[13]

One of the most simple of Ohana's harmonic shadowing processes, characteristic of vocal as well as instrumental music, is his note-for-note, organum-like parallelism which is not only an essential feature of his mature style but indicative of his aesthetic alignment. Such parallelism occurs in either timbral group, and even though the musical textures themselves may sometimes be quite thin, the particular harmonic scheme in effect at any time can be identified from the aural emphasis given to certain intervals or interval combinations. In this way the opening of 'Mouvements parallèles' from *Etudes d'interprétation* (see Ex. 6.1a) represents Timbre I through monodic duplication at interval class 1 (minor ninths and major sevenths) and the opening of 'Sylva' from *Cadran lunaire* (see Ex. 6.1b) represents Timbre II through duplication chiefly at the fifth (and occasionally fourth), interval class 5.

Ex. 6.1a: *Etudes d'interprétation* (I), 'Mouvements parallèles' (bars 1–9)

Reproduced by kind permission of Société des Editions Jobert, Paris / United Music Publishers Ltd.

Ex. 6.1b: *Cadran lunaire*, ' Sylva' (opening statement)

© 1983 Gérard Billaudot Editeur S.A. Paris. Reproduced by kind permission.

Although the examples here are drawn from works for solo piano and for solo guitar, respectively, the process is applied in the same way in larger instrumental ensembles, as well as in the vocal music. While both examples are marked 'lent' and 'nocturne', Timbre II is given the additional instruction 'doux'. In Ex. 6.1a the melodic line emphasises intervals of classes 1 and 6 in its basic outline, the harmonic colour of Timbre I being implicit therefore horizontally, as well as vertically. In what is effectively a thickened monody, the lower line being required to have less dynamic nuance than that of the upper which it shadows, it is the monody which generates the harmonic colour. Another important feature characteristic of sparse textures in Timbre I, is illustrated in this example which involves extremes of register to create an effect of aural blurring (a phenomenon found not just in the piano music); instead of distinct pitches, the effect, harmonically speaking, is one of octaves which sound false or out of tune. The effect paraphrases the sound of microintervals, equal-temperament being blurred not only by interval combination but by octave position. (A similar paraphrasing of microintervals is found in Messiaen's transcriptions of bird-song, although his use of register is different.) It is significant that Ohana rarely uses the minor second in sections of exposed note-for-note parallelism as the effect would be one of a single sound phenomenon as opposed to that of separate melodic lines, one shadowing the other. In Ex. 6.1b, the contour of the melodic line emphasises interval classes 3, 4, and 5, Timbre II being thus present horizontally, as well as vertically. While there are two examples of the tritone appearing melodically, as well as another of major sevenths appearing vertically, they are not sufficiently conspicuous to alter the overall colour of the harmonic shadow, the effect of these 'foreign' intervals being analogous to chromatic notes in conventional, diatonic harmony. This example also involves third-tone microintervals to enhance the melodic expressiveness of the ascending major second which ends the phrase.

Ohana's harmonic shadowing may occur in simple, two-part parallelism or in denser textures where parallel chords are made up of superimposed combinations of intervals associated with either timbral group. The opening of the eleventh of the *24 Préludes* (see Ex. 6.2a) again exploits the timbral coldness of registral extremes but incorporates features of Timbre I at both primary and secondary levels. The parallelism of the outer intervals involves interval class 1, while the

Ex. 6.2a: *24 Préludes*, no.11 (bar 1)

Reproduced by kind permission of Société des Editions Jobert, Paris / United Music Publishers Ltd.

internal interval combinations make use of interval classes 2 and 4 from the secondary level. Although the tritone is not present, the harmonic colour is still that of Timbre I due to the aural predominance of interval class 1, achieved externally and internally. Any possible timbral warmth that may be inherent in the upper major third is countered by the harshness of the sevenths and ninths. Each chord in this note-for-note parallelism is the same (p.c.set 4–3; 0,1,3,4) with the exception of the second chord which contains a colouristic added-note 'C'. It should be noted that the added-note does not alter the essential character of the chord; resulting from simple pianistic convenience, it is to be played by the right-hand thumb together with the B♮. Parallelism in thicker textures is also found in Timbre II. The concluding section of 'Quintes' from the *Etudes d'interprétation* intensifies and enriches the harmonic density with more complex chord-aggregates made up of superimposed fifths (see Ex. 6.2b).

Ex. 6.2b: *Etudes d'inteprétation* (I), 'Quintes' (closing section)

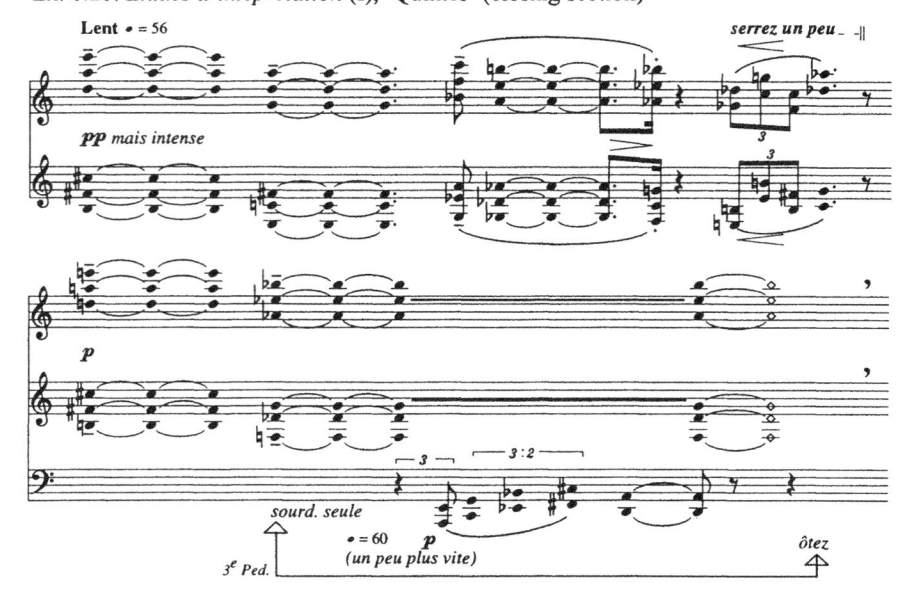

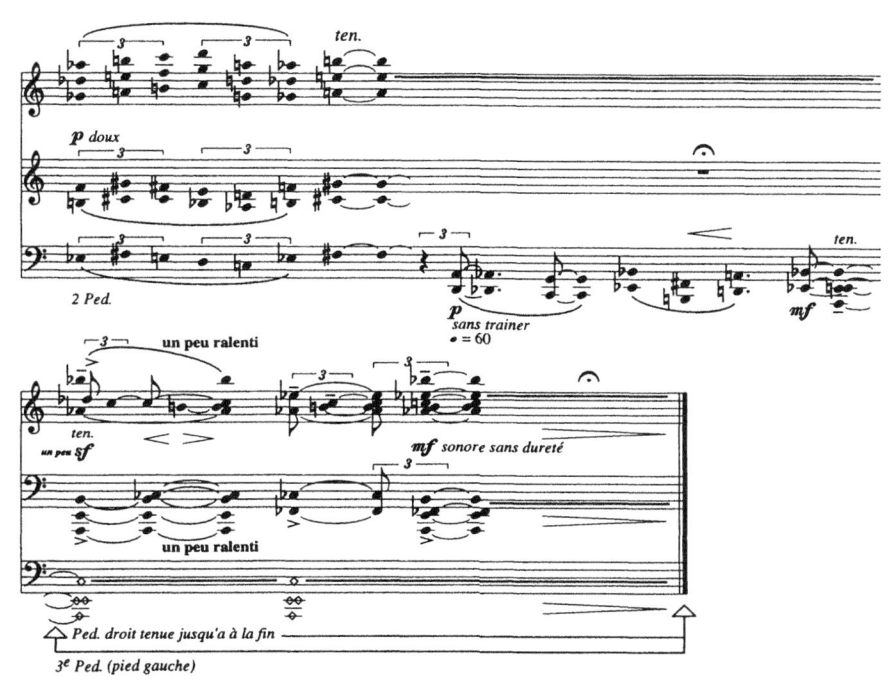

Reproduced by kind permission of Société des Editions Jobert, Paris / United Music Publishers Ltd.

Similar parallelism in perfect intervals supports the prayer-like melody in 'Eléis' of *Swan Song* which is also contemplative. (Although other 'foreign' intervals are present they are aurally subordinate.) As its title suggests, 'Quintes' is a study about the interval of a fifth and has much in common with Debussy's *Etude pour les quartes* not least through the monodic inspiration and atmosphere of contemplation.[14] While Ligeti's eighth and eleventh piano studies 'Fém' (1989) and 'En suspens' (1994) share many of the compositional preoccupations of 'Quintes' (the contemplative spirit of the closing 'semplice, da lontano' section of 'Fém' is particularly close) his approach to pianism as a whole in the *Etudes* has many parallels with Ohana's innovations in both the *Etudes d'interprétation* and *24 Préludes*.

Parallelism about the fifth or fourth, characteristic of Timbre II and found throughout the mature and late music, bore a special, personal significance for the composer. According to Ohana, these intervals and the melodic lines which they enhance, create an atmosphere of serene calm which, while essentially static, was for him spiritual and eternal. (The Mass includes much parallelism at the fourth, notably in the 'Gloria'.) The movements, or sections, in which such parallelism occurs represent some of his most personal expressions and, according to Ohana, evoked what is described by flamenco musicians as 'sonido negro' (black sound).[15] After performing and discussing some of the *Etudes d'interprétation* with Ohana at his Parisian flat, he wrote the words 'sonido negro' on the facsimile copy of the manuscript score of 'Quintes' and explained how both this piece and 'Agrégats sonores' (No. 3 of the same set) captured the mysterious and illusive magic of the 'duende'.[16]

> Black sound provoke the appearance of the 'duende' – this magic enclosed in sound which strikes us down when it appears, but that can be defined by no-one.[17]

This phenomenon is known to be a preoccupation of performers of the Spanish flamenco.[18] The poet Federico García Lorca devoted entire lectures to the subject:

> All that has dark sounds has 'duende' ... these dark sounds are the mystery, the roots thrusting into the fertile loam known to all of us, ignored by all of us, but from which we get real art ... a mysterious power that everyone feels but which no philosopher has explained...Dark sounds behind which we discover in tender intimacy volcanoes, ants, gentle breezes, and the Milky Way clasping the great night to her waist.[19]

Ohana's concept of harmonic shadowing has many precedents, most notable among them being Debussy to whom Ohana was closest both aesthetically and technically: 'Debussy was another of my ancestors and I pay great attention to the ways he has opened.'[20] It is not insignificant that Debussian parallelism first emerged as a characteristic feature of Ohana's musical language in *Tombeau de Claude Debussy* where the opening of the first movement 'Hommage' paraphrases the opening of Debussy's Prélude 'La terrasse des audiences du clair de lune'.[21] While the Debussy *Préludes* represent an important influence on much of Ohana's mature music, notably *Si le jour paraît...*, *Signes*, the *24 Préludes* and *Sacral d'Ilx*, he also cited the Debussy *Etudes* as having been of profound compositional significance to him not only for their sectional approach to form and often quasi-improvisatory character but also their treatment of harmony.[22] Debussy's use of the whole-tone scale represented another of the 'ways opened' to Ohana who based much of his harmonic colouring on an extension and development of the intervallic properties of the two possible scales of six whole tones. Messiaen, too, implicitly acknowledged the importance of Debussy's harmonic discoveries when he listed the whole-tone scale as the first of his Modes of Limited Transposition.[23] Debussy's use of chains of similar (sometimes identical) chords to colour and thicken the melodic line without actually harmonising it is well known and well documented, as is that of Satie, another composer to whom Ohana felt aesthetically close. Such parallelism, especially when combined with whole-tone harmonies, often creates a sense of motionlessness, making the music seem suspended in time, the tensions and polarity of functional harmony having been dissolved. Similar textures are not uncommon in Messiaen and can be found in many of his early piano *Préludes* (notably 'Cloches d'angoisse et larmes d'adieu') which themselves owe much to Debussy, as well as in the later piano works of the 1940s and 1950s; the supremely expressive 'Amen du Désir' from *Visions de l'Amen* displays a similar melodic thickening, although here it is set against the background of a clear, tonal environment (G major). The process is also a familiar feature of jazz harmony and an important aspect of Ligeti's treatment of harmonic density in the *Etudes pour piano*.

The individual features of Ohana's contrasting timbral groups can be defined in more detail. As shown in Table 6.1, the tritone is exclusive to Timbre I and represents what may be called the 'primary' harmonic characteristic of the group. Ohana's preoccupation with the tritone dates from the period of his early works, the seeds of his later harmonic thinking being evident in *Llanto por Ignacio Sánchez Mejías* which makes extensive use of chords constructed from superimposed tritones. While such structures appear throughout the work they are a particular feature of the choral refrains in the first movement 'La cogida y la muerte' (see Ex. 6.3). Here the sound-colour of the fully formed four-note chord (p.c.set 4–9; 0,1,6,7) is uncompromisingly austere, the other resultant and non-adjacent intervals (the minor ninth, minor second, interval class 1 and perfect fifth, interval class 5), adding to the overall harshness of the chord.

Ex. 6.3: *Llanto por Ignacio Sánchez Mejías*, 'La cogida y la muerte' (reduction, bars 191–9)

© 1966 M.R. Braun, Gérard Billaudot Editeur S.A. Paris successeur. Reproduced by kind permission.

Ohana's tritonal chord-structures are more subtly constructed in his mature works. Ohana evolved two main tritonal chord-types, peculiar to Timbre I, which have here been designated as Chords T–Ia and T–Ib (see Ex. 6.4). Both chords contain interlocking tritones and are vertically symmetrical about their central interval, although the intervallic properties inherent in each chord are otherwise contrasted.

Ex. 6.4: Timbre I - Chords T–Ia and T–Ib

The tritones in both chords are interlocking, appearing in collapsed form rather than superimposed. Both are closely related and reveal internal and external manifestations of particular interval classes. Chord T–Ia is symmetrical about a minor second and spans a major seventh (interval class 1), while Chord T–Ib is symmetrical about a major second and spans a minor seventh (interval class 2). The internal symmetry created through the use of two tritones, as opposed to the single tritone chord (e.g. C–F♯–C), already extensively used by other composers, yields chord-aggregates of greater intervallic complexity which not only succeed in excluding the octave but also permit subtle variations of what may be called colour shading, while still belonging to the same timbral group. This is another feature that has most probably been derived by the composer through instinct, the particular layout of both chord-types, in closed form, being clearly pianistic in origin. The complete intervallic properties of each chord can be seen in Table 6.2, although it should be emphasised that the layout of each chord, even in open formation, reflects their primary, aural characteristics (intervals classes 1 and 6 for Chord T–Ia; interval classes 2 and 6 for Chord T–Ib), which may otherwise be obscured in conventional set-theoretical terminology. The interval vector does, however, show that each chord contains three pairs of intervals, the only pair they have in common being that of the tritone.

Table 6.2: Timbre I – Chords T–Ia and T–Ib

	pitch classes	interval class (adjacent)	p.c.set	interval vector
T–Ia			4–9 (0,1,6,7)	[2 0 0 0 2 2] Timbre I – primary level
	B	} 5 – perfect 4th		
	F♯/G♭	} 1 – minor 2nd		
	F	} 5 – perfect 4th		
	C	} 1 – minor 2nd		
	(B)			
T–Ib			4–25 (0,2,6,8)	[0 2 0 2 0 2] Timbre I – Secondary level
	D	} 4 – major 3rd		
	B♭	} 2 – major 2nd		
	A♭	} 4 – major 3rd		
	E	} 2 – major 2nd		
	(D)			

NB: Chords T–Ia and T–Ib do not always consist of these pitch classes.

Chord T–Ia represents Timbre I at its primary level (adjacent and non-adjacent interval classes 1, 5 and 6). The predominant intervallic colour is that of the tritone (interval class 6) and the minor second, together with its inversionally equivalent intervals, the major seventh and minor ninth (interval class 1). As these intervals combine to outnumber the adjacent perfect fourths (interval class 5), it is these which lend the chord its characteristic harshness. Few composers would disagree that the minor second and tritone complement each other, as both are dissonant. Certainly, the harmonic ambiguity of Chord T–Ia (tritones and perfect fourths) gives Ohana scope for additional timbral contrast while remaining within the overall harmonic colour scheme of Timbre I. The opening of *Signes* (see Ex. 6.5) subdivides Chord T–Ia into its component fourths, while the particular instrumental colour, here the zither, ensures that the first interval pair continues resonating while the second pair is sounded. The tritone is further enhanced through its appearance in the melodic line. Here, the emphasis of the fourths softens the dissonance and implicit harshness of Timbre I, the overall effect being more subtle than in the tritone chord of the *Llanto* above.

Ex. 6.5: *Signes,* (first movement, reduction bars 1–5)

Reproduced by kind permission of Editions Amphion, Paris / United Music Publishers Ltd.

Timbre I is characterised at its secondary level by Chord T–Ib (adjacent and non-adjacent interval classes 2, 4 and 6). This chord shares many of the intervallic properties of the whole-tone scale with which the secondary level of Timbre I is often associated; the chord is symmetrical about the major second and spans the inversionally equivalent minor seventh. While the whole-tone scale can be defined in terms of two possible sequences of six notes each proceeding in adjacent steps of a major second (interval class 2), it can also be considered as a chain of interlocking tritones (interval class 6) or as a chain of interlocking major thirds (interval class 4). The interval span of the scale encompasses an augmented sixth (enharmonically, a minor seventh, interval class 2). Due to the presence of the major second, Chord T–Ib often appears in positions other than its basic form. In another example, also from the opening section of *Signes* (see Ex. 6.6), Chord T–Ib appears in a closer formation, emphasising the major seconds through layout and instrumentation.

Here Chord T–Ib (p.c.set 4–25, [020202]) is enhanced with the added-colour device of clusters in semitones and third-tone microintervals on piano and zither respectively (indicated by the asterisked brackets). The melodic line draws its pitches from the same whole-tone scale from which each manifestation of

Ex. 6.6: *Signes*, (first movement, reduction bars 8–10)

Chord T–Ib is created. The melodic line taken as a whole does not, however, yield Chord T–Ib, but a similar chord (p.c.set 4–24, [020301]) sharing similar intervallic properties. The vectors of both chords reveal the same essential characteristics as that of the whole-tone scale ([060603]) from which they are distilled. It should be noted that the piano does not double the zither exactly throughout this passage; the pitches 'C' and 'F♯', being added in the last two chords of the second bar of the example. While it could be argued that these pitch classes are already present in the prime form of 6–35 (and 4–25), they are not actually present in the specific whole-tone scale in use but represent the introduction of a subtle change of harmonic colour (according to the conventions of set theoretical analysis both whole-tone scales are defined in terms of the same p.c.set name 6–35). The addition of a new tritone from the other whole-tone scale does not alter the overall scheme, Timbre I. When defined in terms of p.c. set analysis, these additional notes combine to form p.c. sets which reveal further relationships: the set complements 5–28 and 7–28; and their respective subsets 4–25 and 6–30. (Although not actually present, Chord T–Ia (4–9) is also subset of 7–28.) Although parallel movement in major seconds could, in another context, suggest Timbre II, the presence of the tritone and involvement of the whole-tone scale indicate that the harmonic colour in effect is that of Timbre I, at its secondary level. The presence of semitones and third-tones in the clusters further supports Timbre I; semitones are characteristic at primary level, while third-tones, (being derived from the whole-tone scale) are characteristic at secondary level.

Chords T–Ia and T–Ib are sometimes combined to create greater harmonic density, although they tend to remain identifiable as separate entities even if sounding together in complex chord-aggregates. Their individual identities are preserved either through the particular instrumental (or vocal) grouping or, in keyboard works, through the designation of the hands. In the fifteenth of the *24 Préludes*, Chord T–Ib appears in the right-hand while Chord T–Ia appears in the left (see Ex. 6.7).

Ex. 6.7: *24 Préludes*, no.15 (bars 22–3)

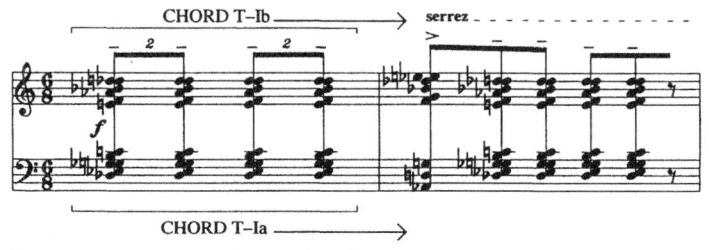

Reproduced by kind permission of Société des Editions Jobert, Paris / United Music Publishers Ltd.

Both chords are in closed position and incorporate added-notes (Chord T–Ib – D♭ and F; Chord T–Ia – B and E♭) which are designed to intensify the overall harshness of one of the most acrid of Ohana's chord-aggregates, the aural violence of which is further emphasised by the dynamic marking. Again, this texture is the result of pianistic convenience, the added-notes being situated neatly under the hand in each case, although they are carefully chosen to enhance the aural predominance of interval class 1, the whole chord-aggregate embracing a minor ninth. This particular prelude is intended as an evocation of Spanish flamenco guitar playing and bears the indication 'fouetté comme un rasgueado,[24] acéré, violent'. The semitonal clash is a well-known harmonic characteristic of the flamenco; the prelude alternates short sections suggesting the percussive texture of the guitar rasgueado with brief monodies in the manner of the Cante Jondo lament. The rhythmic patterning further supports the Spanish allusion. Containing a total of eleven notes (the 'D♭' here being duplicated in bar 22 of the example above), it should be noted that Ohana is generally careful to avoid twelve-note chords, their intervallic density being in danger of neutralising his harmonic language of timbral contrast. A rare example of a 12-note chord occurs at the end of the last movement of *Lys de madrigaux* where, as a result of successive vocal entries, it appears as a semitone cluster thickening out the outer interval of a major seventh (see Ex. 6.8). Despite the use of all 12-notes, the harmonic colour is that of Timbre I due to the aural emphasis of the major seventh and the E♭–A tritone in the melodic line of the soprano soloist which emerges from the chord.

Unlike Timbre I, the harmonic scheme of Ohana's Timbre II does not yield specific chord-types, although certain interval combinations form chord-aggregates characteristic of this timbral group. As illustrated in Table 6.1, the main feature of intervallic differentiation distinguishing Timbre II is the exclusion of the minor second and tritone. This results in a predominance of chords constructed from combinations of major seconds and perfect fourths (as in the 'lent, souplement rythmé' melody from 'Cadences libres' Ex. 5.6a), or combinations of superimposed fifths (as in 'Quintes', Ex. 6.2b) these representing Timbre II on its primary level. An important feature of both perfect intervals when superimposed (sharing a common note), and one frequently exploited by Ohana, is that the resultant interval spanned in each case belongs to interval class 2. (Evident in each of the two superimposed chords in Ex. 6.2b, although the interval separating them is a colouristic minor second.) As a result of the particular emphasis given to interval classes 2 and 5, Timbre II is often associated with pentatonicism. Interval classes 2 and 4 are thus common to both Timbres, although these interval classes appear in entirely different sound-contexts.

Ex. 6.8: *Lys de madrigaux*, 'Miroir de Sapho' (reduction, fig. 44 to the end)

Reproduced by kind permission of Société des Editions Jobert, Paris / United Music Publishers Ltd.

Indicative of Ohana's pianistic approach to harmony are the chord structures in Timbre II which either make use of only the black-notes of the piano keyboard, or exploit the timbral contrast between black and white-note combinations. This phenomenon is not only an important feature of Stravinsky's *Petrushka*, pre-empted by Ravel in *Gaspard de la nuit* although less stridently, but was widely explored by Debussy (notably in *En blanc et noir* and the *Etudes*). It can also be found in Lutosławski, another pianist-composer, as well as in Ligeti. While this feature is found throughout Ohana's instrumental and vocal music, it is central to the harmonic vocabulary of his piano music where black and white-note clusters are frequently juxtaposed. Such clusters are precisely notated and are to be distinguished from his chromatic clusters which are more commonly associated with Timbre I. (Ohana explained his notational system for distinguishing between cluster-types in the preface to his scores; a bracket against the outer pair of notes marked with and asterisk (Ex. 6.6) denotes a chromatic or microinterval cluster, while a cross above the bracket (see Ex. 6.9) denotes a black or white-note cluster.[25]) In the example from the Piano Concerto below, some of the clusters are intended to be played by the palms of the hand, although there are many examples throughout his keyboard writing (for harpsichord as well as for piano), where the forearm or felt covered rulers are required to depress cluster-chords spanning a larger compass.

Ex. 6.9: *Piano Concerto* (solo piano, fig. 9)

Reproduced by kind permission of Société des Editions Jobert, Paris / United Music Publishers Ltd.

Here the outer intervals of the black- and white-note correspond to the distinguishing characteristics of Timbre II. These types of clusters (where intervallic timbre is clearly defined) are often associated with strident dynamic markings and sometimes the description 'brillant'. A more extended juxtaposition of black versus white notes occurs in the thirteenth of the *24 Préludes* (see Ex. 6.10). Also in Timbre II, but marked '*ppp* léger, confus', the overall effect illustrates the close relationship of Ohana's music to his French, pianistic ancestors and recalls similar textures found in the Debussy *Préludes* and *Etudes*. While such textures can also be found in the piano music of Ravel, what Ohana considered to be effect for mere pianistic virtuosity attracted him less to the solo piano music of Ravel than to that of Debussy in the search for his own compositional guidance. Ohana was also of the opinion that the necessity of performing the piano music of Ravel in conservatoires and international competitions has led to the comparative neglect of the piano works of Debussy by many young virtuosi.[26]

The two independent horizontal lines in Ex. 6.10 represent two shades of harmonic colour. The whole section is set in motion without precise vertical coordination. Ohana's instruction (in the lower part) to 'improvise on these notes' allows the designated pitches to be performed in any order and in any rhythmic pattern; it is not intended to suggest the introduction of different or additional pitch-material.[27] The lower part presents a succession of melodic units outlining intervallic shapes associated with the pentatonic scale (perfect fourth, major second and minor third), uses only black keys, and is representative of Timbre II. The upper part uses white notes almost exclusively but while it outlines many interval classes belonging to Timbre II it also has some features of Timbre I, notably the minor second and tritone which occur within the figurations without being given particular prominence. Again these interpolations, and the separation of the parts by a semitone, may be seen as decorative colourations (chromaticisms in conventional terminology), the overall scheme being that of Timbre II.

Ex. 6.10: *24 Préludes*, no.13 (central section)

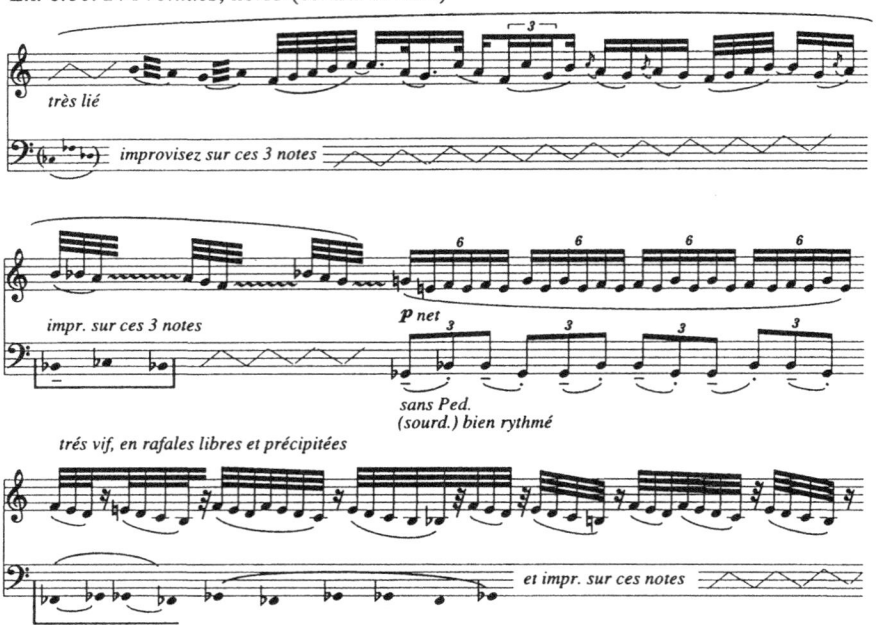

[musical notation with markings: *très lié*, *improvisez sur ces 3 notes*, *impr. sur ces 3 notes*, *p net*, *sans Ped. (sourd.) bien rythmé*, *très vif, en rafales libres et précipitées*, *et impr. sur ces notes*]

Reproduced by kind permission of Société des Editions Jobert, Paris / United Music Publishers Ltd.

The interval properties of Timbre II, particularly those of the pentatonic scale, approach, in some contexts, a quasi-tonality. The added-sixth chord is embedded within the pentatonic chord. Often considered particularly French, this luxuriant chord is not only found in Debussy but is a distinctive feature of Messiaen's harmonic vocabulary, particularly of the 1940s. An important aspect of Ohana's Timbre II which may be considered a special nuance of this timbral group, is the quasi-tonal reference developed from his use of pentatonic colouring. His tonal references always suggest major keys and tend to be reserved for music bearing a special, spiritual meaning, often occurring in the emotional heart of a work. (It is not insignificant that tonal reference is also an important aspect of the harmonic technique of Dutilleux.) According to Ohana, the third movement of *Lys de madrigaux* is a setting of a Negro-spiritual melody, 'Star Mad Blues' (see Ex. 6.11 and Ex. 5.10). Although the original notation of the score is designed visually to obscure the tonal reference (through the use of enharmonic equivalents and added-notes), the actual sound of the harmonic trail which shadows the melody orients around F♯ major as is shown in the renotated example below.

Ex. 6.11: *Lys de madrigaux*, 'Star Mad Blues' (harmonic reduction, fig. 22)

'Miroir de Sapho' [sic], the sixth movement of *Lys de madrigaux*, includes another quasi-tonal section, this time in F major. Once again the tonal reference is obscured, not only visually through the notation, but also texturally, as the organ part which provides the tonal focus is ornamented by nine layers of independently moving melodic cells repeated, ad libitum, in aleatory counterpoint (figs. 41–42). This tonal reference, like many others, contains added-notes which both enhance Timbre II as well as borrow colour nuance from Timbre I. Another tonal reference in the *24 Préludes* may indicate the source of some of Ohana's added-note colouring. Dedicated to the memory of Fats Waller and Count Basie, the ninth prelude is orientated towards a tonal environment of E♭ major and, in addition to clusters and effect of resonance, includes many of the chromatic colourings normally associated with blues harmony. Like 'Star Mad Blues', the ninth prelude represents a point of repose in the work as a whole. The C major tonal reference which concludes 'Contrepoints libres' of *Etudes d'interprétation* (lent, sans traîner) is more triadic and less overtly blues-inspired although it still makes use of flattened sixths and sevenths.

Ohana's subtle blending and mixing of the colour palette of his timbral schemes through the use of colouristic devices (added-notes and clusters) is largely the result of compositional instinct and is not systematic. While added-notes may introduce a localised variation of nuance, they may also serve to evoke a specific musical allusion, as in the fifteenth of the *24 Préludes* where added-notes are intended to suggest a harmonic characteristics of the Spanish flamenco (see Ex. 6.7). Many added-notes which emphasise interval class 1, characteristic of Timbre I, may owe their origins to Ohana's intimate knowledge of Spanish folk music. In his early compositional period, Ohana consciously sought to adopt certain harmonic characteristics of Spanish music, not only the simultaneous sounding of major and minor thirds, but most notably, the accented descending semitone appoggiatura, also exploited by Falla and Albéniz and a well-known cliché of the flamenco style. Rather than preserving these features in their original and well-used harmonic and rhythmic context, Ohana combined the dissonance to form chords where the concept of resolution ceases to have any meaning.

Another of Ohana's colouristic devices is that of added-resonance which is not unlike that described by Messiaen in *Technique de mon langage musical*, although the similarity is more likely the result of common musical ancestry than any direct musical influence. In Ohana, added resonance is most characteristic of his piano music, although the principle can be translated into other genres. It can occur as a note, glissando, chord or cluster played quietly to enhance the resonance of a chord already sounding in another register, or may be a note, glissando or chord played more loudly, often in an upper register, also to enhance existing resonance in another register. In the piano music, added resonance is sometimes achieved through silently depressing a chord, or cluster to provide a silent but resonating chord, or cluster against which a variety of harmonic colour can be juxtaposed (see Ex. 6.12a and Ex. 6.12b). This effect is

Ex. 6.12a: *24 Préludes*, no.12 (opening)

Reproduced by kind permission of Société des Editions Jobert, Paris / United Music Publishers Ltd.

only possible through the use of the sostenuto pedal and is exploited systematically in 'Troisième pédale' of the *Etudes d'interprétation*. Dutilleux also exploits this effect in his piano music, perhaps most dramatically in the first of his *Figures de résonances* for two pianos. The result of added-resonance is to bring the concepts of harmony and timbre closer together, enabling harmony to function entirely as timbre.

Ex. 6.12b: *Etudes d'interprétation* (I), 'Troisième pédale' (opening)

[musical score excerpt]

f animé, vif
sans Ped.
3ᵉ Ped   *laissez entendre les résonances sur 3ᵉ Ped.*

* *appuyez 2 règles sur les touches (sans jouer) tenez avec la 3ᵉ Ped.*

ten.   retenu
sf   ten.   *mf doux, sonore*

Reproduced by kind permission of Société des Editions Jobert, Paris / United Music Publishers Ltd.

One of the most distinctive features of Ohana's harmonic vocabulary is his use of third-tone microintervals. While his use of third-tones developed initially from a desire to enhance the intensity and expression of a melodic line, they also appear in a harmonic context. Distinct from quarter-tones (cf. Chapter 5), these intervals are created from the whole-tone scale and are thus primarily associated with Timbre I, although are not exclusive to this scheme. Unlike other composers whose harmonic use of microintervals is largely reserved for occasional glissandos, Ohana uses third-tones to fill out interval combinations belonging to either Timbre I, or Timbre II. In the example from *Lys de madrigaux* (see Ex. 6.13a), third-tone clusters (zither and voices) are sounded against semitone clusters to provide a harmonic shadowing emphasising interval features of Timbre I. Ex. 6.13b from the final movement of *Signes* shows third-tone clusters against black- and white-note clusters associated with Timbre II.

The only instrument so far able to play third-tone clusters is the concert zither which appealed to Ohana for its 'sharp and crystalline sound quality'.[28] It is for this reason that the instrument is conspicuous in so many of his scores. Ohana has suggested the use of third-tone microintervals to be a logical extension of the harmonic vocabulary of both Debussy and Ravel:

> The use of these new intervals seems to me to be a natural step towards the conquest of one more of the harmonics coming next after Debussy's ninths and Ravel's elevenths and thirteenths.[29]

190 THE MUSIC OF MAURICE OHANA

Ex. 6.13a: *Lys de madrigaux*, 'Calypso' (fig. 3)

Reproduced by kind permission of Société des Editions Jobert, Paris / United Music Publishers Ltd.

Ex. 6.13b: *Signes*, (sixth movement, fig. 33–4)

Reproduced by kind permission of Editions Amphion, Paris / United Music Publishers Ltd.

Ohana was not alone as a composer of the second half of the twentieth century having evolved a harmonic vocabulary concerned with intervallic contrast. Lutosławski also adopted a principle of intervallic differentiation to achieve contrasting effects of harmonic timbre from particular intervallic sound qualities. He sometimes used the Italian descriptions 'soave' and 'rude' ('sweet' and 'coarse'), which first appear in the last of his *Five Songs* (1957), to represent two distinct and contrasting harmonic effects comprising different intervals. The principle is also used in *Chain 2*, 'Dialogue for Violin and Orchestra' (1985), where the same two terms are used in the second movement to denote intervallic differentiation between 'soave' (major second, perfect fourths and fifths) and 'rude' (minor seconds and tritones).[30] This is essentially the same differentiation as between Ohana's Timbre I and Timbre II. While Ohana and Lutosławski were quite different in cultural origin, they shared a common musical parentage which is indifferent to the functions and conventions of Austro-German harmonic thinking and traditions. During the last years of his life, Ohana spoke of his admiration for Lutosławski's music.[31]

Despite Ohana's ironic statement that 'harmony no longer exists', it may be seen how, on the contrary, music cannot exist without harmony, although the role of harmony itself may have changed. With a concept of harmony that is chiefly one of timbre, the result is a harmonic language that is fundamentally static. Precisely this type of harmonic thinking has led many composers, including Debussy and Messiaen, to develop an approach to form that is sectional rather than developmental. Lockspeiser stated that Debussy's greatest achievement was not just the development of a new harmony, but the creation of a new concept in formal thinking that was liberated from the diatonic relationship between chords as the motivating force behind the generation of the music.[32] Clearly belonging to this anti-symphonic tradition, Ohana can be seen as a French composer by taste, education and habit, if not by birth. The more dynamic force of Ohana's music is created through his approach to rhythmic activity and motion.

Notes to Chapter Six.

1. M. Ohana, interview (in French), P. Ancelin (1964).
2. In his later works of the 1970s and 1980s. Lutosławski moved away from this position. C. Bodman Rae, *The Music of Lutosławski* (London, 1994).
3. Dutilleux admired the music of both Ligeti and Lutosławski; see C. Potter, *Henri Dutilleux his Life and Works* (Ashgate, 1997) p. 132.
4. The present author in conversation with Ohana in Paris. It should also be pointed out that Ohana's acquaintance with Jolivet may have brought him into direct contact with Varèse in the 1950s.
5. C. Rae, 'The Music of Maurice Ohana', Vol. I, (diss. U. of Oxford (1989) pp. 139-63.
6. The term 'chord-aggregate' refers to two or more superimposed chords.
7. The present author in conversation with the composer in Paris, June 1988.
8. M. Ohana, interview (in English), R. Langham Smith (1993) p. 128.
9. Debussy-Guiraud Conversations, collected by Maurice Emmanuel, reproduced in E. Lockspeiser, *Debussy his Life and Mind*, Vol. I (London, 1962) p. 207.
10. M.Ohana, interview (in French), P. Ancelin (1964).
11. Ohana considered American Steinways to have a softer, more singing tone than their German counterparts.
12. M. Ohana, interview (in French), M. Cadieu (1980) p. 42.
13. M. Ohana, interview (in French), A. Grunenwald (1975) p. 60.
14. C. Rae, 'Debussy et Ohana: allusions et références', *Cahiers Debussy* Nos 17-18 (Paris, 1993-4) pp. 117-20.
15. The present author in conversation with the composer in Paris, Spring 1982. The *Etudes d'interprétation*, like all his mature solo piano music, were composed on his American Model 'D' Steinway.
16. Ohana wrote 'sonido negro' on the manuscript facsimile belonging to the present author. Conversations with the composer in Paris, November 1982.
17. M. Ohana, 'La Géographie musicale de l'Espagne', *Journal musical français* (April, 1956) p. 1.
18. For further discussion of the 'duende' see C. Schreiner, ed., *Flamenco, Gypsy Dance and Music from Andalusia* Eng. trans. M.C. Peters (Amadeus Press, Portland, Oregon, 1998).
19. F. García Lorca, 'Theory and Function of the Duende', reproduced in *Selected Poems* trans. J.L. Gill (London, 1984) pp. 127-39.
20. M. Ohana, interview (in English), M. Oliver (1984).
21. C. Rae, (1993-4) op. cit. pp. 117-20.
22. The present author in conversation with the composer in Paris, February and March 1982.
23. O. Messiaen, *Technique de mon langage musical* (Paris, 1942).
24. 'Rasgueado' from the Spanish 'rasguear' meaning 'to stroke' is the name given to the technique of flamenco guitar playing in which five or six strings are struck rapidly and percussively in either upward or downward motion.
25. For example, the performing notes for the *24 Préludes*.
26. The present author in conversation with the composer in Paris, March, 1984.
27. The present author in conversation with the composer in Paris, March 1983.
28. Ohana, 'Microintervals, Experimental Media II ', *Twentieth Century Music* ed., R. Myers (London, 1968) p. 150. (Original in English).
29. Ibid.
30. C. Bodman Rae, *The Music of Lutosławski* (London, 1994) pp. 61-2 and 203.
31. The present author in conversations with the composer in London, April 1990 and Paris, April 1992.
32. Lockspeiser, *Debussy His Life and Mind,* Vol. ii (London, 1965) p. 230.

CHAPTER SEVEN

Rhythm and Aleatorism

Since Stravinsky's discoveries in *The Rite of Spring*, many composers of the post-war years have considered rhythm independently from other musical parameters, Messiaen being one of the most notable. The traditional role of rhythm has been subjected to profound and wide-spread reassessment, engendered not only by Stravinsky and Messiaen, but by the rediscovery of techniques derived from the Medieval and Renaissance periods, as well as from different folk musics and non-Western traditions. Ohana's instinctive desire to address the problem of rhythm was both the result of his own investigations into the folk music he had known since his youth and part of a wider continuity. He, too, drew lessons from Stravinsky, specifically *The Rite*, in the search for solutions to many compositional problems including those of rhythm, metre and texture. It is also interesting to note that the phrase from 'Mystic Circles of the Young Girls' and the Introduction to 'The Sacrifice' which is so conspicuous in Ohana's mature melodic vocabulary (cf. Chapter 5) is the first example from *The Rite* to be discussed in Boulez' influential analysis, although it is unlikely that Ohana was familiar with the article at the time of its first publication.[1]

Ohana conceived his approach to rhythmic structure in terms of the juxtaposition of texture and timbre. While preserving its more traditional role as the localised articulation of melody and harmony within a framework of metred divisions, Ohana evolved a treatment of rhythm as an entity which could exist independently from other musical parameters. Ohana used rhythm as a means of extending his concept of the sound-mass:

> I find that the contribution of both the harmonic and rhythmic sound-mass is enormous and until now has largely been ignored. It plays an immense role in rhythmical structure.[2]

Ohana's 'masse sonore' applied not only to the harmonic 'trail or shadow' but also to the creation of rhythmic sound-texture, a concept which has parallels with the radical innovations of Varèse, whose music Ohana knew and admired.[3] Although an important and characteristic aspect of Ohana's music, it is one facet of a multi-faceted approach to rhythm which concerns the juxtaposition of different rhythmic types in a mosaic of sectionalism. When layers of rhythmic cells are superimposed in unmetred sections of aleatory counterpoint, to create rhythmic sound-texture, the effect is often static. Such manipulation creates a sensation of activity without impulsion, and rhythm becomes a sound-object where individual patterns are blurred into a single, sound-phenomenon (cf. Ex. 4.5). The danger of overall stasis is avoided by the juxtaposition of this type of textural rhythm with other work or movement sections in which rhythms are generated in a manner not unlike his horizontal process of monodic extension, individual patterns being audible and recognisable. This more conventional type of linear rhythm may be unmetred or metred. The unmetred type often occurs with incantatory and monodic vocalisations (cf. Ex. 4.6a and Ex. 5.1), while the metred is more dynamic and extrovert, being associated with evocations of ritual frenzy, as in the fifth movement of *Signes* (Ex. 7.9) the 'Cortège des taureaux ailés' movement of *Livre des prodiges* (see Ex. 7.1a), and 'Eros noir' of *Avoaha* (see Ex. 7.1b). These types are contrasted with repetitive motor rhythms which are also metred and often characterised by asymmetrical accentuation, as

Ex. 7.1a: *Livre des prodiges*, 'Cortège des taureaux ailés' (reduction fig. 2–4)

Reproduced by kind permission of Société des Editions Jobert, Paris / United Music Publishers Ltd.

Ex. 7.1b: *Avoaha*, 'Eros noir (Rumba-Alleluya)' (reduction fig. 28–9)

© 1993 Gérard Billaudot Editeur S.A. Paris. Reproduced by kind permission.

in 'Triomphe de Christophe Colombe à Seville' in the final tableau of *La Célestine*, and 'Circé' of *Lys de madrigaux* (see Ex. 7.1c). There is a fourth rhythmic type which could be described as 'neutral rhythm'; notated in 'neumes'

Ex. 7.1c: *Lys de madrigaux*, 'Circé' (reduction bars 3–10)

Reproduced by kind permission of Société des Editions Jobert, Paris / United Music Publishers Ltd.

(stemless note-heads) this is chiefly associated with Ohana's evenly moving, plainchant parodies (cf. Chapter 5) and thickened monodies (cf. Ex. 6.1b). Thus, Ohana's overall approach to rhythm is one of contrast: impulsion and activity versus texture and stasis; the motoric and repetitive versus the varied and fragmented; the lyrical versus the percussive.

The most decisive influence on Ohana's rhythmic vocabulary came from his knowledge of Spanish folk and African tribal music (cf. Chapter 1). Many rhythmic patterns, as well as his means of combining them, were essentially derived from these traditions. Although the forms and performance style of Spanish folk music, in particular the flamenco, provided the compositional catalyst for the majority of his early works, he also explored the use of African and Afro-Cuban rhythms and rhythmic procedures in one work of the early period, the *Etudes chorégraphiques* for solo percussion. While the compositional possibilities inherent in African and African related traditions were first investigated in this work, they are otherwise uncharacteristic of his early period. Ohana's real quarrying of these rhythms and procedures as a source for many of his own compositional processes took place in his mature music. They also provided a model for the aleatory counterpoint, not found in his early works, which subsequently became a distinctive feature of his mature music.

> Primitive peoples, Africans in particular, have always practised so-called aleatory music and with various success, obtaining sometimes astounding results and other times nothing at all.[4]

Through his practical experience of Spanish folk and African tribal music, Ohana observed significant features in common: similarity of specific rhythms; the superimposition of repetitive patterns to create complex, resultant cross-rhythms; the use of percussion, percussive effects and hand-clapping techniques (called 'palmas' in Spain).[5] These traditions also share similar preoccupations with the use of rhythm as an independent musical parameter, as well as a vehicle for expressive performance in its own right. Hemiola and syncopation are important features of the rhythmic vocabulary of both traditions and both also have a distinct repertoire of specific rhythms (although these may vary from region to region) which provide the basis for extemporisation. In both traditions the rhythms produced by the movement of dancers' feet (part of a large repertoire of 'body' percussion) are considered an integral part of the performance, although this is particularly developed in the Spanish 'zapateado' (heel and foot stamping) and 'taconeo' (heel tapping) techniques of the flamenco.[6] Both traditions exploit differentiation of relative pitch to articulate rhythmic patterns. This is achieved in African music on a wide range of skin (as well as metal, wood and stone) percussion, and in the Spanish flamenco through the playing of rhythmic accentuations (golpe) on the wood and tapping plate, as opposed to the strings, of the guitar (sometimes with both hands), and also through the use of castanets which have two distinct tones (high 'hembra' and low 'macho').[7] Flamenco hand-clapping techniques also involve a hierarchy of rhythmic accentuation through distinguishing strident claps with the use of flat palms (palmas fuertes) and more muffled, less accentuated claps with the use of cupped palms (palmas sordas).[8] Both traditions make use of plucked string instruments which are able to articulate intricate rhythms, or rhythmic accentuations, in a melodic or harmonic context. While the guitar is both an accompanimental and solo instrument for the flamenco, various types of lyres, lutes and harps are also used in traditional African music.[9] Ohana became particularly interested in the musical cross-fertilisation which took place between these traditions as a result of the population migrations between Spain, Africa, South America and Cuba.[10] For this reason, Ohana not only incorporated Afro-Cuban rhythms into his music but considered Negro spirituals and jazz a modern refinement of African music and therefore part of his own musical and cultural heritage. His investigation of these themes culminated in the opera *La Célestine* and his last work *Avoaha*.

However complex the relationships between Spanish and African musical traditions, one of the most crucial factors in respect of their influence on Ohana's music, is that they are improvisatory. As with monody, Ohana's realisation of rhythm is based on recreating the spontaneity of improvisation within the confines of a composed score, this applying as much to rhythmic textures in aleatory counterpoint as to his incantatory monodies and driving, repetitive, motor rhythms. Fundamental to his rhythmic manipulation and to the creation of the effect of improvisation is the treatment of rhythm in self-contained cells which can be either extended in a process of addition and variation, superimposed, or simply repeated. The patterns of many of these cells are derived, consciously as well as intuitively, from Spanish and African sources, and tend to be made-up from multiplications of the smallest duration (as opposed to subdivisions of larger beats), the concept of collective pulse often being abandoned in unmetred structures. (As in many of Messiaen's rhythms, however, such an approach need not always preclude the presence of pulse.) The rhythmic fragmentation resulting from a lack of collective pulse is magnified by the separation of rhythmic cells by rests which do not correspond with the values of the preceding cell but represent free, quasi-respiratory articulations. *Sibylle* illustrates this linear approach with successive rhythmic cells being extended in a process of continuous variation, imitation and addition (see Ex. 7.2a).

In the soprano line a cell of a single staccato quaver is gradually expanded, engendering new cells of increasing length and rhythmic variety. The cells are separated by rests. The process is echoed in the percussion which provides additional variants until a climax is reached. As with the monodic version of this process, the cells combine to form phrases which can in turn form sentences and sections. The second phrase of this section introduces melodic material (cf. Chapter 5) which provides further contrast to the activity of the rhythmic cells which have been defined here as 'Texture B'.[11] The third phrase returns to the process of alternation, extension and free variation of the rhythmic cells. This process does not always involve strict, vertical co-ordination between parts; cells may be extended independently, the respective parts being superimposed in a form of aleatory counterpoint where the material, but not its co-ordination, is defined (see Ex. 7.2b). The soprano and percussion are freely combined until the instruction to follow the voice 'note for note'. (The rhythmic cells are defined through the notation of the beaming.) The soprano is also required to play crotales 'ad libitum', further intensifying the sense of rhythmic activity, the section being marked 'rapide, désordonné'.

Ex. 7.2a: *Sibylle* (fig. 2–3)

[Musical notation excerpt]

Reproduced by kind permission of Société des Editions Jobert, Paris / United Music Publishers Ltd.

A later section of *Sibylle* (figs. 9–10) introduces a rhythmic canon between soprano and percussion where the vertical co-ordination is approximate. Defining the beginning of the section with the entry of cymbals, the ensuing imitation of the soprano by the percussion is set in motion after five quavers, the resultant rhythms of the combined parts being undefined. The relative freedom of vertical co-ordination is further enhanced by the instruction to play 'freely'. Only the slight alteration of three cells in the percussion prevents the episode from being an exact canon; the inexact imitation takes the form of augmentation and free transformation, although the shape of the original rhythm remains clear. The effect of this process is quasi-improvisatory; a leading part is shadowed by a subsidiary part which must have time to hear the rhythm of the first and thus remains always at least a cell behind. In this way a single, improvisatory line is given a contrapuntal dimension. As in Ex. 3.11, Ex. 4.5, Ex. 5.6b and Ex. 6.10, this type of counterpoint is another example of what Ohana described as the 'combining' of parts. Acknowledging that the process is essentially linear and does not involve freedom or chance in the material itself, he described the technique as 'more combinatoire' than 'aléatoire'.[12] The only free parameter is that of the precise moment of vertical coincidence between parts, the harmonic colour, texture and individual rhythmic shape being defined. Each part is thus conceived individually and horizontally, rather than simultaneously and vertically.

Ex. 7.2b : *Sibylle* (fig. 5)

Reproduced by kind permission of Société des Editions Jobert, Paris / United Music Publishers Ltd.

What may be called Ohana's 'combinatoire' counterpoint can also involve the superimposition of unmetred material in different tempi, as in the 'Tympanum' movement of his First String Quartet, *Cinq séquences* (cf. Ex. 3.11), the first work to incorporate this aleatory technique. Belonging to Ohana's transitional period and therefore composed at the time when his mature style was emerging, this quartet does not explore the technique extensively, its appearance being isolated to only one movement. 'Tympanum' also incorporates many percussive effects (including col legno and a range of pizzicato techniques elsewhere in the movement) to emphasise rhythm and texture, as distinct from melody or harmony. Where differentiations of pitch occur, they serve to articulate the rhythmic outline in the manner of skin percussion, rather than provide any sense of melody. Unlike the examples in *Sibylle,* each of the four parts in the 'combinatoire' sections of 'Tympanum' is self-contained and for this reason the technique is not unduly difficult to realise in performance. In this way Ohana creates a sound-mass of aleatory counterpoint which treats rhythmic texture independently from other musical parameters. As there is no coincidence between the layers, the effect is of a single texture which is fundamentally static, although rhythmically active. A similar effect can be achieved in rhythmic sound-masses in which the constituent parts follow the same or only slightly differentiated tempi.

There are many more extended examples of this technique in Ohana's mature music, some of the most notable occurring in the percussion concertos *Synaxis* and *Silenciaire.* In some later works, including *Sorôn-Ngô,* the First Cello Concerto *Anneau du Tamarit* and the Piano Concerto, rhythmic material in different tempi is superimposed in much longer sections. In *Anneau du Tamarit* (see Ex. 7.3) three distinct rhythmic strands moving in three separate and flexible tempi are superimposed according to Ohana's 'combinatoire' principle; toms and m'tumbas at $\bullet = c.$ 56, piano (and later brass) at $\rfloor = 132-136$, strings (and later woodwind) at $\rfloor = 120/126$. The solo cello adds a fourth strand which weaves freely between the rhythmic parts to provide the main melodic interest. Although the orchestral parts combine to create a rhythmic sound-mass, the presence of a contrasted melodic idea in the solo part prevents the effect from being mere static texture.

In another example of a rhythmic sound-mass, in which the parts operate in the same tempo, the constituent rhythmic cells are derived from the text (see Ex. 7.4). In the chamber opera *Syllabaire pour Phèdre,* the name of Hippolyte, the object of Phèdre's desire, is repeated to provide a background texture against which the declamatory speech-song of Phèdre herself is superimposed. The variations of rhythmic shape result from the different articulations of French pronunciation. The chorus is instructed to declaim in the manner of speech, thus preserving purity of rhythmic texture.

Ohana's linear concept of rhythmic layering has a direct parallel with certain aspects of the rhythmic organisation of African tribal music in which layers of repetitive patterns, usually played on drums or by the clapping of hands, are superimposed.[13] Similar, although less complex, rhythmic layering occurs in

Spanish flamenco, and is also performed in hand-clapping ensembles ('palmas'). The greater complexity of the African music results in part from the additive nature of the constituent rhythms which are then superimposed. In African music, each rhythmic layer considered individually may be relatively simple but, when combined, may produce far more complex resultant cross-rhythms.[14] The individual rhythms typically involve asymmetrical patterns and accentuations. If observed from a European point of view, that is vertically with pulsation and metre common to all layers, these rhythms seem highly complex with syncopation, hemiola and many other types of cross-rhythms barely comprehensible with the ear alone. If approached from an African point of view,

Ex. 7.3: *Anneau du Tamarit* (fig. 15–16)

RHYTHM AND ALEATORISM 203

that is horizontally, with pulsation and metre individual to each layer, the rhythms in each part are relatively simple and easily copied or imitated. In simple terms, much African music is based on a clash of rhythms where even a song which appears to be mono-rhythmic will, on investigation, turn out to be constructed of two independent but related rhythmic patterns, one inherent in the melody and one belonging to the accompaniment.[15] Rhythmic patterns created both through clapping and combinations of drums, are designed to provide a

Ex. 7.4: *Syllabaire pour Phèdre*, 'Episode I' (fig. 15)

Reproduced by kind permission of Editions Amphion, Paris / United Music Publishers Ltd.

solid, metrical basis for songs in free rhythm which are superimposed over them. There is neither a regular coincidence of beat in the European sense (although there may be a regularity or continuity of pulse), nor any hierarchy of accent as each clap or drum-beat is considered to be of equal importance. The monody which these patterns are designed to accompany may be sung at a different tempo to that of the drums and the clapping.[16] This process is adapted by Ohana who frequently uses his sound-mass as a background texture against which independent foreground material is superimposed (as in Ex. 7.3). Ohana's technique is both effective and performable, once players realise they are to focus on their individual part rather than the coordination of parts.

In African music, superimposed rhythmic patterns are differentiated by another important principle which is also adapted by Ohana. Whereas in hand-clapping, the various rhythmic patterns have a simultaneous starting-point, and so always contain one recurrent beat where they coincide (also true in the flamenco), in drumming the main beats rarely coincide.[17] A basic feature of African drumming in general is that the ensemble never starts together, the entries of each pattern being staggered. In drumming patterns, a minimum of two drums are required; a 'master' drum and a 'subordinate' drum (or drums). The 'master' drum sets the process in motion and then improvises on constantly changing rhythmic patterns. The 'subordinate' drum plays repetitive patterns to provide a foundation for the improvisations of the 'master'. The greater the number of subordinate drums, the more complex is the rhythmic texture supporting the improvisations. The 'master' is thus the commentator, while the others simply repeat single patterns, or two closely related patterns, with little or no variation.[18] Ohana drew freely on these principles both in his rhythmic sound-masses and in his 'combinatoire' counterpoint. Although not African in sound, the polyphonic texture which opens the third movement of *Signes* (cf. Ex. 4.5) illustrates his adaptation of the approach, the bongos approximating the role of the master drum. The two concertos for percussion, *Synaxis* and *Silenciaire*, were among the earliest of Ohana's works to exploit the process extensively.

While Ohana's approach to rhythmic layering was derived from African models, as were many of the individual rhythms, he did not necessarily adhere strictly to the concept of the 'master' drum. The 'Tympanum' movement of *Synaxis* also includes sections where individual rhythmic layers are equal and evolve independently (see Ex. 7.5). ('Tympanum' is a title always indicative of particular rhythmic intensity.) The specific instruction here is for equality between the four percussion soloists, 'aucune des quatre percussions solistes ne doit dominer'. Their mutual independence is enhanced by the separate tempo indications for each of the four rhythmic strands, ranging from ♩= 66, 92, 112 to 132. While none of the parts paraphrases the role of the 'master' drum, the African principle of layering to create resultant rhythms of considerable complexity is preserved. In this way, Ohana absorbed the processes he discovered in tribal music without becoming a slave to them. His aim was not

206   THE MUSIC OF MAURICE OHANA

to transcribe African rhythmic procedures but to apply basic principles in such a way as suited the context of his own work.

Ex. 7.5: *Synaxis*, 'Tympanum' (fig. 7–8)

Reproduced by kind permission of Editions Amphion, Paris / United Music Publishers Ltd.

Ohana began to consider the compositional possibilities of adapting African drumming techniques in his early period. Although he started working on the *Etudes chorégraphiques* in 1955, his revision of 1961–63 (cf. Chapter 3) may have stimulated his interest to develop the techniques further, precipitating the innovations of *Cinq séquences,* as well as the ensuing works of the Sigma Series and beyond. It is for this reason that the rhythmic aspects of the *Etudes chorégraphiques* are to be discussed here, despite the work belonging to Ohana's early period. Although Ohana's approach to percussive texture in some ways recalls *Ionisation* of Varèse, the resemblance is merely superficial; the real compositional stimulus came from Ohana's contemplation of African principles.

A range of pitched and unpitched percussion is required, reflecting all the main groups, with the skins playing the rhythmically generative role. The earliest of his works to draw on African techniques, many processes are less developed than in his more mature works. Apart from two short sections in the second movement (one of which is a cadenza), the score is notated in vertically coordinated, metred rhythm throughout. The first of the four movements establishes a 2+2+3 and 3+2+2 cross-rhythm in equal quavers, over which various contrasting rhythms are superimposed. During the course of the movement, the 2+2+3 ostinato incorporated in a 2/4+3/8 measured 7/8 bar is transformed into a 3+1+2 in a 6/8 bar. This alters the accentuation and articulation while preserving a continuity of rhythmic character. The rhythmic accentuations are emphasised by pitch and certain combinations of drums which articulate the rhythm (often African toms). Ex. 7.6 lists the transformations of rhythmic ostinati throughout the first movement.

Ex. 7.6: *Etudes chorégraphiques.*
Transformation of rhythmic ostinati in the first movement

The second movement is more concerned with instrumental timbre and resonance than the first, but one section briefly experiments with the superimposition of metred and unmetred rhythmic layers. This texture is suggestive of the 'master' drum principle; the unmetred layer (played by two instruments) is free and improvisatory in character, while the metred layer (played on toms) is strictly repetitive in the manner of the 'subordinate' drums (see Ex. 7.7).

Ex. 7.7: *Etudes chorégraphiques* (second movement, fig. 56–7)

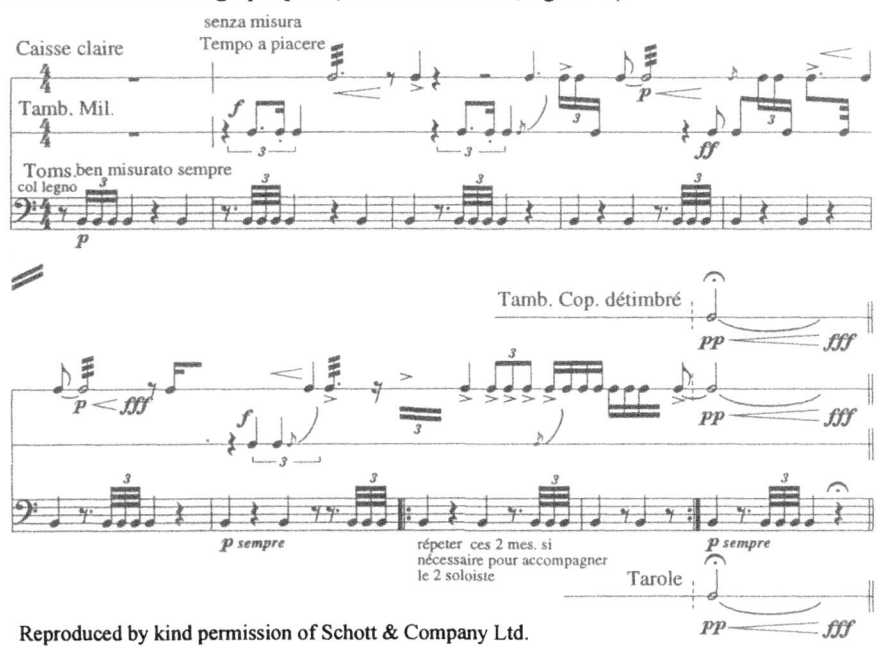

Reproduced by kind permission of Schott & Company Ltd.

The *Etudes chorégraphiques*, less developed technically than Ohana's later works, explore primarily the superimposition of metred ostinati. Ohana's 'combinatoire' counterpoint is more subtly developed in later works, *Signes* being the first to illustrate this technique more extensively and in a range of contexts (cf. Chapter 4). Although the technique was conceived in terms of a combination of instruments, or voices, Ohana gradually found a means of adapting his layering processes to works for a solo (but contrapuntal) instrument: the *24 Préludes* and *Etudes d'interprétation* for piano, *Deux pièces* for harpsichord and *Cadran lunaire* for guitar. That he composed only two works for an unaccompanied monodic instrument, *Quatre improvisations* for flute and *Sarc* for oboe, reflects the importance of this technique in Ohana's music. The eighth of the *24 Préludes* illustrates a particularly extended example of this process. Unmetred throughout, the opening section contains three episodes which not only involve the free combination of two independent layers of material, some with differing rhythmic patterns, others with similar, but bears the additional instruction that the pianist should 'improvise on the neumes', varying the given material 'ad libitum' with inversions, retrogrades and rhythmic alterations. In this context, Ohana uses the designation 'neume' to refer to the notation of his original material, an extension of his more wide-spread description of stemless note-heads. Aleatory counterpoint and free variation are thus closely related in Ohana's mature music, both reflecting Ohana's desire to restore the spontaneity of improvisation to composed music.

> So-called aleatory techniques require the same fundamental rigour and conventions as did the older techniques of figured bass and soloists' cadenza ... . The neume must be assigned first. Then follows the general outline and duration of the sequence to be improvised. It is up to the performer, according to their awareness, physical capability at that moment and in that place, to induce variations of co-ordination and density.[19]

Other means by which Ohana adapted his layering techniques for a solo instrument are more straight-forward and include the combining of independent parts with different tempo indications. In 'Cadences libres', from the *Etudes d'interprétation* a repetitive quintuplet pattern in two units of five semiquaver groups (♪ = 88) creates a background texture against which a melody, notated in rhythmically flexible neumes (tempo indication ♪ = c. 69), is juxtaposed. The whole section is marked 'souple, sans rigueur'. The superimposition of the two tempi combined with the contrasted musical texture ensures the lack of co-ordination of parts (Ex. 5.6b). Similar textures occur in *Cadran lunaire,* notably 'Candil', composed at the same time as the first book of *Etudes d'interprétation*. This type of layering illustrates the use of the background rhythm as texture rather than melodic articulation; rhythm and melody become separate elements, existing independently. In the example from 'Cadences libres', the presence of hemiola is indicative of the Spanish character of the melody; in this context rhythm is not texture but articulation. Thus rhythm here fulfils a two-fold function. A more complex example of the same procedure appears in the second book of the *Etudes d'interprétation,* 'Contrepoints libres', where the pianist is required to play four different tempi in four separate and unmetred parts, simultaneously (see Ex. 7.8). With tempo indications ranging between ♪ = 80–84 and ♪ = 120 in the right-hand, against ♪ = 100 and ♪ = 66 in the left-hand, it is questionable whether such a feat is really possible by a single player. It may well be that, in practice, the pianist must establish an underlying pulse common to each layer. The effect would then not be unlike the separation of parts required by Beethoven in the sixth variation of the last movement of the Op.109 piano sonata, particularly as in Ohana also, one of the parts is a trill. This too, is a pianistic feat of some difficulty.

Ohana's process of rhythmic layering occurs in different textural densities; for solo instruments, as in the *24 Préludes, Etudes d'interprétation, Deux pièces* and *Cadran lunaire,* or for large combinations, as in *Synaxis, T'Harân-Ngô* and *Livre des prodiges*. It can also involve the superimposition of contrasting metred material, as well as combinations of metred and unmetred. In large-scale works, such as *Office des oracles,* players and singers may be divided into

RHYTHM AND ALEATORISM 211

separate groups, the material associated with each group distinguished in the score by boxed-notation, not unlike that used by Berio in *Circles*. In *Office des oracles* this acts as an important aid for performance as three conductors are required to direct the three choral groups (and supporting ensemble) which are separated spatially.

Ex. 7.8: *Etudes d'interprétation (II)* 'Contrepoints libres' (p.21 of the score)

Reproduced by kind permission of Société des Editions Jobert, Paris / United Music Publishers Ltd.

Fundamental to all Ohana's rhythmic sound-masses is the horizontal approach which governs his musical textures. His view of monody as the main generating force of his music led him to evolve a musical language that is predominantly linear. This in turn resulted in a type of aleatory counterpoint which could combine melodic as well as rhythmic cells. While African tribal music was a major influence on the development of these techniques, Ohana's experience at the Schola Cantorum contributed to the evolution of a musical language that is more concerned with equality of parts in an emphasis of the horizontal, rather than the implicit hierarchy of the vertical:

> In my writing, most significant I think, are the discoveries concerning the Medieval concept of horizontal writing, especially as we are obsessed with vertical writing and the measured bar. The arm of the conductor falls on the beat and all sound-phenomena which are produced at that moment must coincide absolutely. Now in Medieval composition, the writing was horizontal with occasional vertical co-ordination seeming to happen by chance – a quite limited chance, but chance nevertheless.[20]

This rather contentious statement suggests another, parallel source of Ohana's horizontal approach to the creation of musical texture and indicates that his knowledge of these early vocal repertories may have contributed to the development of his layering techniques. It also suggests that Ohana was highly subjective in his view of other music. The complexities of mensuration are seemingly ignored purely because they were, for his purposes, not relevant. It is interesting to note that, during his last years, Ohana spent many hours studying the *Notre Dame Mass* of Machaut, explaining that the score was constantly beside him when he composed the vocal works of the late 1980s and early 1990s, in particular *Lux noctis*[21] and *Tombeau de Louize Labé*.[22] It is interesting to note, however, that his 'combinatoire' layering of rhythmic material occurs far less frequently in these late works. While *Swan Song* and *Tombeau de Louize Labé* are composed in vertically co-ordinated metred rhythm throughout, *Nuit de Pouchkine* and *Avoaha* include only one section of layered material, respectively; in each case, a sound-mass of melodic, plainsong-like fragments. In *Nuit de Pouchkine* this occurs between figs. 8–9 and, in *Avoaha*, towards the close of the final movement, 'El Dorado'. The movement away from rhythmic layering in his last years also extended to several instrumental works; while there is only limited use of 'combinatoire' counterpoint in *Anonyme XX siècle* for two guitars, the Third String Quartet *Sorgin-Ngo* and Second Cello Concerto *In Dark and Blue* are metred and strictly coordinated throughout. The ballet *Sundown Dances* is metred, with the exception of two episodes. The first occurs between figs. 27–32 and comprises three sub-sections: a sound-mass of layered melodic fragments repeated ad libitum (the duration to depend on the choreography), followed by two further sub-sections which superimpose two differently metred rhythmic ideas in different tempi. The second episode occurs at fig. 42 where African rhythms in strict tempo (but unmetred, on skin percussion) are set against metred and strictly coordinated homophonic material in the remaining ensemble. This provides a climactic conclusion to the preceding section. The string players, conductor and dancers are also required to 'yell' in tempo. That Ohana also used microintervals far less frequently in his late works may indicate a further refinement of compositional procedure, resulting in greater economy of means.

While Ohana's main rhythmic procedures have been examined, some consideration should be given to the components of his rhythmic vocabulary. Conspicuous among Ohana's rhythmic structures are frequent syncopations, asymmetrical patterns and quintuplet rhythms, as illustrated in the fifth movement of *Signes* (see Ex. 7.9), one of the first of Ohana's works to

Ex. 7.9: *Signes*, 'beaten by the wind' (piano solo, fifth movement, fig. 22–3)

Reproduced by kind permission of Editions Amphion, Paris / United Music Publishers Ltd.

incorporate them as a means of suggesting spontaneous improvisation. These patterns are a particular feature of African rhythm,[23] and are also to be found, albeit in entirely different contexts, in *The Rite of Spring*. In Ohana, these rhythms appear in many guises: as individual cells; as a series of cells forming ostinati; superimposed across metred rhythmic divisions; and combined with melody in unmetred phrases. They appear in asymmetrical divisions used either as five notes of equal attack, or subdivided into groups of 3+2, 2+3 or, more rarely, 4+1, 1+4. (They do not appear in symmetrical divisions, such as 2+1+2, or 1+3+1.) The second movement of *Lys de madrigaux*, 'Circé', uses a homorhythmic 3+2 and 2+3 five-grouping in alternation; superimposed on this is a subsidiary melody in 3:5 crotchet triplets (cf. Ex. 7.1c). This movement creates a strong, forward-driving, motor rhythm which has much in common with the asymmetrical quintuplets in Messiaen's *Cinq rechants*.

Other African rhythmic shapes used widely by Ohana were discovered directly as a result of his own experience in Africa, north and south of the Sahara, and indirectly via his knowledge of the music of South and Middle America and Spain. According to Alejo Carpentier, many of the rhythmic patterns in Ex. 7.10 originated in Africa, having been imported by the slaves and transformed by the local population.[24] This rhythm not only has many features in common with the dotted rhythms of the flamenco Tango (slower than the Argentinean), Habanera, Cuban Conga and Contradanza rhythms but also incorporates the Afro-Cuban syncopated cell used widely by Ohana.[25] According to Carpentier, the Conga and

Ex. 7.10: Rhythmic patterns of African origin
a) African rhythm

b) Afro-Cuban rhythm

c) Habanera

d) Tango   (slower than Habanera)   (very slow)

e) Conga

f) Contradanza

g) Most common rhythmic unit of Ohana

Contradanza represent the mixture of Spanish and African musics which resulted in the creation of new, exclusively Cuban rhythms. Migrations of population from Cuba back to Spain resulted in the re-introduction of these new rhythms to the Iberian peninsular. He also states that the syncopated rhythms of the Tango and Habanera were African in origin, as were many forms of syncopation and hemiola.[26]

Among Ohana's mature works there are certain movements or works which he specifically described as containing African or Afro-Cuban rhythmic patterns: the fifth movement of *Signes*; 'Délirante' in *Cris*; 'Son Changó' in *Office des oracles*; 'Mouvement parallèles' of the *Etudes d'interprétation* and many sections of *Sorôn-Ngô*, *T'Harân-Ngô*, *Livre des prodiges* and *Avoaha*.[27] Syncopated and quintuplet patterns are usually prominent in forward-driving motoric rhythms which are intended to generate the atmosphere of ritualistic, tribal dances. In some cases he sketched the imagined tribal ceremony in the manuscript scores of these works (cf. Chapter 2). Such movements tend to be in fast and accelerating tempi, building to a climactic frenzy of rhythmic delirium. Many are given titles incorporating the suffix 'ngo' which, according to Ohana, 'characterised incantatory dances from ancient tribal ceremonies.'[28]

The use of strict, metronomic metre in hand-clapping as a rhythmic basis for superimposed melody moving in a freer rhythm is not only found in African tribal music, but also in Spain, particularly in Andalusia. In the same way as the Africans superimpose layers of rhythmic ostinati in hand-clapping and drumming, the flamenco musicians of southern Spain combine patterns which produce complex resultant cross-rhythms. These polyphonies may appear as episodes in their own right or may be an accompaniment. One of many allusions to the flamenco in the opera *La Célestine* occurs in the ninth tableau where four of the leading characters (Célestine, Ruffian and the two prostitutes Aréis and Elys) paraphrase the flamenco hand-clapping technique (palmas). After establishing itself, this purely rhythmic texture provides the basis for another character, Sosie, to sing an erotic song in praise of the pleasures of Aphrodite. This is the purest evocation of the Spanish technique in any of Ohana's mature music. It stands out from the rest of the score through the absence of additional instrumental accompaniment.[29]

A Spanish rhythm used extensively throughout Ohana's music is, according to the composer, the Greek 'epitrite' rhythm from which the 6/8–3/4 hemiola of Spanish music originates.[30] From the Greek 'epi' (in addition) and 'tritos' (a third), the 3+2+2 rhythm is one which Ohana described not only as characteristic of Spanish music in general but common throughout the Iberian peninsula (see Ex. 7.11a). According to Ohana's writings on Spanish music, the rhythm was brought to Andalusia by the ancient Greeks during periods of trading between eastern and western Mediterranean ports. The rhythm is still widely known in Greece and appears in one of the oldest known Greek folksongs (see Ex. 7.11b). It is used extensively by Ohana and is a characteristic feature, appearing either in its original 3+2+2 format, as in 'Cadences libres' from *Etudes d'interprétation* (Ex. 5.6a), or in variant forms of diminution or augmentation. Ohana has drawn attention to Falla's use of this rhythm in the 'Pantomine' section from *El Amor brujo,* which he parodies in 'Cadences libres' (cf. Chapter 5).

Ex. 7.11

a) The Greek 'epitrite' rhythm

b) Kalamatianos (Greek folk song)

The epitrite rhythm is among the most well-known clichés of Spanish music, but was revitalised and given a new context in Ohana. He reworked the 3/4–6/8 hemiola, and its related 2/4–6/8, using them extensively throughout his music from his early period and into maturity. Whereas the metrical alternation might be used by Albéniz and Falla almost continually for the duration of a single work, Ohana uses it fleetingly as a single rhythmic cell without allowing it to dominate large-scale, rhythmic structure. 'Saturnal' from *Cadran lunaire* incorporates an extensive reworking of this pattern; the cell is subjected to various transformations some of which yield quintuplets as well as syncopations associated with the Tango, Conga and Habanera (cf. Ex. 7.10). Frequent changes of metre alternating with unmetred sections prevent the rhythm from being perceived in its conventional context. Repetition and alternation of these types of cell has the effect of mesmerising the ear into hearing the interplay of metre and cross-rhythm. The epitrite rhythm is also a source for other syncopations and cross-rhythms. In *Cadran lunaire* and elsewhere, Ohana makes use of cells which resemble the rhythmic pattern of the Sarabande. These are particularly conspicuous in the works of guitar due to the inevitably strong Spanish associations of the instrument. Another Spanish rhythmic feature which has become a basic cell of his rhythmic vocabulary, is the accented appoggiatura (on the beat), this being derived from a vocal attack common in the Cante Jondo and often accompanied by the expressive 'ay' declamation. This is, in turn, associated with a harmonic dissonance sounding with its own resolution, often used by Falla and Albéniz, and derived from the Phrygian descending cadential scale formula of Spanish flamenco (cf. Chapters 5 and 6). Ohana separated the rhythmic aspect of this feature from its harmonic context, although rarely from its melodic one. It most characteristically appears as an opening gesture at the beginning of a phrase.

Ohana's rhythmic vocabulary exists in a variety of contexts: in metred divisions and unmetred sections of free variation; as an articulation of melody and as a textural sound-mass. While the rhythmic cells can be traced back to their Spanish and African sources, the ways in which they are extended and combined, particularly in layers of aleatory counterpoint, owes much to the improvisatory procedures of folk music. Ohana's absorption of these popular traditions can perhaps be considered analogous to the absorption of the folk music which inspired Albéniz, Falla and Bartók. As with his treatment of melody and harmony, Ohana's approach to rhythm does not conform to any system or method. Rather his processes developed from the desire to recreate a sense of improvisatory spontaneity within the confines of composed music. His approach to aleatorism in form will be considered in the following chapter.

Notes to Chapter Seven.

1 P. Boulez, 'Stravinky demeure', originally published in *Musique russe*, Vol i, (Paris, 1953) pp. 151–224 and reproduced in *Relevés d'apprenti* (Paris, 1966) pp. 75–182, trans. S. Walsh, 'Stravinsky Remains', *Stocktakings of an Apprenticeship* (Oxford, 1991) pp. 55–110.
2 M. Ohana, interview (in French), P. Ancelin (1964).
3 Ohana's association with Jolivet may have brought him into contact with Varèse during the 1950s.
4 M. Ohana, interview (in French), P. Ancelin (1964).
5 M. Ohana, interview (in English), M. Oliver (1984).
6 C. Schreiner ed., *Flamenco Gypsy Dance and Music from Andalusia* Eng. trans. M.C. Peters (Amadeus Press, Portland Oregon, 1998).
7 Ibid. Although castanets were a 19th century innovation of the Andalusian gypsies, they have been incorporated into the current flamenco repertory.
8 Ibid.
9 H. Myers, 'African Music',*The New Oxford Companion to Music*, ed. D. Arnold (Oxford, 1983) pp.25–38.
10 Also investigated by the Magic-Realist novelist Alejo Carpentier in his historical study of Cuban music, *La música en Cuba* (Mexico, 1946).
11 The contrasting groups of melodic material in *Sibylle* were defined as 'Melodic A' and 'Melodic B', in Chapter 5. Sections of predominantly rhythmic activity have been defined as 'Texture A' and 'Texture B'.
12 The present author in conversation with the composer in Paris, Autumn 1984.
13 A.M. Jones, *Studies in African Music*, 2 vols (London, 1959).
14 A.M. Jones, 'African Rhythm', *International African Institute* Memorandum No. xxxvii (1970) p. 26.
15 Ibid. p. 27.
16 Ibid. p. 28.
17 Ibid. p. 39.
18 Ibid. pp.39–46.
19 M. Ohana, interview (in French), A. Grunenwald (1975) p. 63.
20 M. Ohana, interview (in French), R. Lyon (1978) p.43.
21 Although the first part of the choral diptych *Lux noctis - Dies solis*, *Lux noctis* was completed in 1988, five years after *Dies solis*.
22 The present author in conversation with the composer in Paris, June 1988, April, 1992, and London, April, 1990.
23 A.M. Jones, (1959) op. cit.
24 A. Carpentier, (1946) op. cit.
25 'Habanera' is often wrongly spelled as 'Habañera'. Instead of describing the popular dance from Havana, the incorrect spelling translates from Spanish as 'bathroom waste-pipe'!
26 A. Carpentier, (1946) op. cit.
27 The present author in conversation with the composer in Paris, June 1988.

28 M. Ohana, programme notes for *Sorôn-Ngô*, reproduced in *La Revue musicale* (1986) p. 207.
29 Other references to the flamenco in *La Célestine* are discussed in M.L. Martin, *La Célestine de Maurice Ohana* (Paris, 1999).
30 The present author in conversation with the composer in Paris, February 1983.

CHAPTER EIGHT

Symmetrical Structures and Approaches to Form

> I think one should be more like a bird-catcher than a bird-hunter: bring them alive by sheer power of magic, if possible, and rather fail than bring them back dead.[1]

Like many composers, Ohana was reluctant to make explicit the technical operations of his composition, the 'kitchen secrets' as he once called them. One reason for such reticence may stem from the instinctive nature of his creative process which owed much to his gift for improvisation (cf. Chapter 1). Considering himself as much a sorcerer with a book of spells as a musical craftsman,[2] he liked to equate the act of composing with the catching of birds by 'sheer power of magic', an analogy suggestive of spontaneity and instinct rather than a consciously intellectualised method. Far from suggesting any Messiaen-like preoccupation with bird-song, the mystical birds of Ohana's poetic metaphor represent the diverse musical ideas which provided the starting-point for each new work. Beginning with sound itself, Ohana made no secret of his predilection for composing at the piano, particularly at the very early stages, and began by assembling a range of individual even disjointed, musical ideas as sketches from which the final work would emerge.[3] In large-scale works, this process could take place even before the final details of instrumentation and orchestration had been established, although in works for smaller forces, the instrumentation or vocal grouping would have been known at the time of embarking on his sketches.[4] Only rarely envisaging a preconceived form into which his individual ideas could be moulded, he preferred to let the intrinsic properties of the material dictate the outer shape, from the inside out. As Ohana said: '... the main thing is to live through the work and then realise one day that it has been written and there it is, then it lives.'[5]

Ohana evolved a musical language based on linear processes. Vertical density resulted from conceiving texture in terms of superimposed layers, whether precisely co-ordinated, or subject to the relative freedom of his 'more combinatoire than aléatoire' counterpoint. While his colouristic approach to harmony could articulate structure, it was not designed to generate form, this being left to the more dynamic roles played by monody and rhythm. Although individual monodies or rhythms may be derived from processes of linear extension through variation and addition, his concept of textural and timbral contrast resulted in a sectional approach to structure. Ohana described his approach to form as that of a 'coral-reef' (cf. Chapter 5).[6] Just as the branch-like structures of a coral-reef are formed from the life-cycles of colonies of microscopic polyps, Ohana's music is made up of sections which result from the progressive extension, juxtaposition and superimposition of individual musical ideas. The metaphor reveals not only his closeness with nature but a type of structure that, like the coral-reef, is, paradoxically, both sectional and organic. The outer shape is a result of the behaviour of internal material and form is thus created from the inside, out. Ohana's sectionalism can therefore be understood as an extension of his linear processes; a spontaneous, quasi-improvisatory concept which, according to the composer, was derived from Debussy. Ohana described the piano *Etudes* as having influenced him the most in this respect, in particular 'Pour les agréments'.[7]

> I think he [Debussy] was perceiving form as the result of a development of the tone and the sound matter he was handling, much more than as a preconceived frame where he was going to put that material. So far as I am concerned, I never have a preconceived form but I wait for the things I find, that is the small bits of music that I want to put down when I'm trying to build a work and see what they absolutely want to be and how they want to be introduced and how they want to be followed and what relation they want to establish with the neighbouring periods, the neighbouring colours, the neighbouring instrumentation, which creates a sort of tension by contrast, or ... what they call in cinematic technique the 'enchainé' in French ... .[8]

In many articles and interviews Ohana repeatedly stated that he considered form an artificial problem which originated from the role of functional harmony in music of the Austro-German tradition. Once harmony had been liberated from its historical conventions, form ceased to have the same meaning. With his characteristically challenging iconoclasm Ohana stated: 'Form in our time no longer has any importance and we shall all be dead before it rediscovers any.'[9] As has already been shown (cf. Part One), Ohana belonged to a culture which was independent from, and indifferent to, Austro-German tradition. That he did not consider form an important issue reflected this independence:

> They [Austro-German composers] thought of form before writing the actual music, form being for them a preconception which it is not in me. Do not forget Debussy is another one of my ancestors and I pay great attention to the ways he has opened and it is obvious that his form comes out of his writing and not the contrary. I in fact believe form to be a very unimportant problem.[10]

Whether this statement is entirely accurate or not in its view of the compositional method of other composers, it reveals both Ohana's aesthetic alignment and his position on the issue of form; a consideration which has to be addressed by any composer, consciously or unconsciously. Ohana's view of the work of other composers, including Debussy, was selective, as well as subjective. While he may not have been aware of the various mathematical and proportional structures which it is now suggested were used by Debussy, it is interesting to note that those works which Ohana explained as having influenced his own approach to form most profoundly, notably the *Etudes*, are those in which mathematical and proportional structures appear the least.[11] Ohana's choice of the coral-reef metaphor to describe his approach to form underlines the importance of nature as an inspirational source (cf. Chapter 2):

> Rather than looking towards mathematics, I look towards biology, towards trees, their roots and the rocks....One composes in the hope of finding one day the ideal structures which correspond to the biological growth of music and the musical substance which we handle.[12]

Although Ohana drew on nature as a metaphor for musical structure, it was the image of growth and proliferation which fascinated him more than any wish to dissect actual structures to reveal mathematical schemes, such as fascinated Bartók in his discovery of the Golden Section in sunflowers and pine-cones. As it was the rigour of mathematics and what Ohana considered to be the limitations of rules and formulae which contributed to the abandonment of his architectural studies in the 1930s, it is not surprising that numerical schemes are not a preoccupation of his music.[13] Ohana's recourse to nature was in many ways pictorial and, in that sense, impressionist, as he emphasised the supremacy of musical colour over form and design.[14] The consequent danger of according musical colour such importance is the difficulty of avoiding weakness in overall structure. (This criticism was levied famously, if not infamously and inappropriately, at Debussy,[15] who considered the epithet impressionist merely a 'useful term of abuse'.[16]) Like Debussy, Ohana was aware of this danger. Although the proportional structures found in both Debussy and Bartók were not preoccupations shared by Ohana, he did experiment with another structural device embedded in their music; symmetry. In the early 1960s, significantly in *Tombeau de Claude Debussy*, Ohana began to explore symmetrical form as a means of imposing external shape on material that might otherwise appear meandering. In this way he countered any sense of formlessness that might arise from his predilection for linear processes and sectional contrast.

While proportional structures, notably those associated with the Golden Section are by definition organic, symmetrical structures are associated with inorganic nature. This is not as contradictory of Ohana's organic processes as may first appear; there are many precedents in Debussy for organic, proportional structures co-existing with inorganic, symmetrical structures, even within the same work.[17] Indeed the presence of symmetry, at whatever structural level, counters the effect of ever-growing organic forms to create a sense of structural stability. Whereas organic forms, whether proportional or not, are associated with growth, symmetry is associated with stasis. This may have been the structural example Ohana found in nature:

> ... The greatest example remains nature; in her physical, physiological and biological aspects; nature in all her manifestations of sound, in everything she reveals structurally... .[18]

During the 1960s and 1970s, Ohana showed a predilection for constructing symmetrical movement plans. Although this interest can be traced back to one of his earliest works, the Suite pour piano (constructed according to a simple five movement plan[19]), he began to explore the approach more thoroughly during the transitional period of the early 1960s, developing the principle further in several mature works before abandoning it in the middle 1970s. While these structures are untypical of the majority of his mature works, their presence suggests the need for a framework to provide stability for the quasi-improvisatory procedures which generate the inner material. Stage, as well as concert, works incorporate structural symmetries. Although drama and plot in themselves provide overall shape, the presence of symmetrical plans in the chamber operas *Syllabaire pour Phèdre* and *Autodafé*, indicates the necessity for a robust, basic structure to encase the succession of otherwise static, dramatic tableaux. That Ohana eventually turned away from symmetrical structures indicates not only a greater refinement of his techniques of variation and contrast which engender the internal sectionalism, but also a means of juxtaposing material that could give a work dynamic shape without the need for such large-scale architectural plans. Text also provides another convenient framework, and it is interesting to note that following Ohana's abandonment of symmetrical plans, his vocal works reveal a marked increase in the use of text. The refinement of form in the dramatic context is revealed in *Trois contes de l'Honorable Fleur*, as well as in Ohana's longest work, the opera *La Célestine*, neither of which require the additional support of a symmetrical plan to create unity or dynamic shape. In *La Célestine* the eleven tableaux of its two acts reveal a continuity of dramatic action, albeit articulated by textual narration and wordless vocalisations.

Ohana's symmetrical plans are found in works of both an odd and even number of movements. In those containing an odd number, the symmetry occurs around the central, pivotal movement, as would be expected. In those of an even number, a more subtle approach is involved; either central movements of similar musical character are paired to preserve an overall arch-type symmetry, or internal movements of like character are paired in an interlocking arch-form contained within the larger symmetry of the outer movements. While a number of Ohana's works reveal this basic structure, the symmetry represents an underlying scheme which is subordinate to the musical material itself. Internal movement structure is rarely affected by the architecture of the whole.

The first surviving work to experiment with this approach is *Tombeau de Claude Debussy,* composed according to a seven movement, symmetrical scheme; movements I, IV and VII include the solo voice, while II, III, V and VI are instrumental and of a different, musical character. Movements II, IV and VI also draw on images of nature as their compositional point of departure. Unusually, the internal structure of the pivotal movement, 'Autres soleils' is also symmetrical; two vocal sections embrace a central, solo piano cadenza. Completed the year after *Tombeau*, *Cinq séquences* follows a quinpartite plan (as the title suggests) which is symmetrical about the central, movement 'Tympanum'. Set in relief against the surrounding movements 'Tympanum' focuses on rhythm as distinct from other musical parameters and introduces Ohana's 'combinatoire-type' counterpoint. The remaining movements balance each other in terms of their contrasting approach to the organisation of texture: polyphonic versus homophonic; linear monody versus thickened monody; unmetred versus metred. The seven movement plan of *Si le jour paraît...* also reveals a symmetry about its central movement, 'Vingt avril'; based on the lament of Provençale 'Planh' (lament) of Troubadour poetry, it is the expressive heart of the work. It is enclosed by the outer movements in a broad arch scheme. While movements III and V are based on mythological stories, the surrounding movements balance each other in terms of musical character; the first three make use of stylistic features of traditional flamenco guitar playing, and the last three owe their inspirational source to nature. There is also a connection between movements based on certain types of Troubadour poetic forms, although these do not correspond with the larger symmetry. Table 8.1 illustrates the symmetrical movement plans of the transitional works while those in the mature works are shown in Table 8.2.

Table 8.1: Symmetrical schemes in the transitional works

Tombeau de Claude Debussy

I	Hommage – vocal
II	Soleils – Nature
III	Ballade de la Grande Guerre – – – – – – – – – – – |
	vocal sections – – – – – |
	/
IV	Autres soleils – – piano cadenza – – – – – – – – – – – Nature – – – vocal
	\
	vocal sections – – – – – |
V	Miroir endormi – – – – – – – – – – – – – – – – |
VI	Rose des vents et de la pluie – – – – – – – – – – – – – – – Nature
VII	Envoi – vocal

Cinq séquences

I	Polyphonie – – – – polyphonic
II	Monodie – – – – – – linear monody – unmetred
III	Tympanum – – – – – – – – rhythmic texture – – – – – – aleatory counterpoint
IV	Déchant – – – – – – thickened monody – metred
V	Hymne – – – – – – – homophonic

Si le jour paraît...

I	Temple – – – – – – – – – – – – – – – – – – – Flamenco
II	Enueg – – – – – – – Troubadour poem – – Flamenco
III	Maya-Marsya – – – – – – – – – – – – – – – – Flamenco – – myth
IV	Vingt Avril (Planh) – Troubadour poem – – – – – – – – – – – – – – – lament
V	La Chevelure de Bérénice – – – – – – – – – – Nature – – – myth
VI	Jeu des quatres vents – – – – – – – – – – – Nature
VII	Aube – – – – – – – – Troubadour poem – – Nature

Table 8.2: Symmetrical schemes in the mature works

Signes

I	'At Night'	ensemble	medium
II	'Alive with Birds'	flute	long
III	'Drowned with Rain'	percussion	short
IV	'Imprisoned with Spiders' Webs'	1/3-tone zither	short
V	'Beaten by the Wind'	piano	long
VI	'Burnt by the Sun'	ensemble	medium

Synaxis

I	Diaphonie	Medieval	monodic	short
II	Tympanum	Medieval	rhythmic textures	long
III	Sibile		rhythmic activity	medium
IV	Tropes	Medieval	reposeful	short
V	Clameur		rhythmic activity	medium
VI	Organum	Medieval	reposeful	short
VII	Antiphonie	Medieval	rhythmic textures	long
VIII	Maya		monodic	short

Syllabaire pour Phédre

Prologue – sop			short
Parodos	Coryphée		static
Episode I	Phèdre – Hippolyte	active	long
Stasimon – sop	Coryphée		static
Episode II – sop	Thésée – Hippolyte	active	long
Epilogue – sop			short

Cris

I	Générique	(material reworked in II, IV, V)
II	Délirante	extrovert / ritualistic
III	Debla	Cante Jondo monody – expressive
IV	Mémorial 44	(symmetrical internal form)
V	Slogans	extrovert / ritualistic

Autodafé

Prologue	---------------- vocal sound-mass	
Episode I	' '93' (French Revolution) -------------------	tableau
Stasimon I	------------------ vocal sound-mass	
Episode II	'Vitrail' (Albigensian Crusades) ---------------	tableau
Episode III	'Batouque, Són' (Victims of Spanish colonialisation) ----	tableau
Stasimon II	--------------- Prayer to God (Negro spirituals)	
Episode IV	'1914–18' (British-German trenches) -------------	tableau
Parodos	----------------- commentary on futility of war	
Stasimon III	------------------ vocal sound-mass	
Episode V	'Saturnale' (Museum of horrors) ---------------	tableau
Stasimon IV	----------------- commentary on Spanish Conquest	
Episode VI	'No pasarán' (Spanish Civil War) ---------------	tableau
Episode VII	'Leçon des ténèbres' (Napoleonic Wars) -----------	tableau
Episode VIII	'Mayas' (triumph of life) --- commentary on King Alphonso X	
Epilogue	(Death of death) --------- vocal sound-mass	

Office des oracles

I	Alpha -------- plainsong-like fragments --- short	
II	Oniracle ---------------- monodies (contemplative)	
III	Dragon à trois têtes ------ grotesque humour ------	rhythmic textures
IV	Minotaure aux miroirs	
V	Son Changó -------------------------	rhythmic textures
VI	Météoracle -------- very short	
VII	Tarots --------- very short	
VIII	Interrogation des oiseaux ------------------	rhythmic textures
IX	Ecriture automatique ---- satirical humour (mobile form)	
X	Oroscope ---------- satirical humour ------	rhythmic textures
XI	Pythié ------------------ monodies (contemplative)	
XII	Oméga ------- plainsong-like fragments --- short	

Although *Signes* was one of Ohana's first works to be conceived in a sequence of movements to be performed without a break, the movements clearly divide through their instrumentation and duration into a symmetrical scheme which radiates out from the central pair of movements. While the four inner movements are characterised by the prominence given to particular instrumental timbres, they balance each other in terms of length and complexity. The outer movements make equal use of the instrumental group as an ensemble, and although they contain different numbers of sub-sections, they are of equivalent overall duration (cf. Chapter 4). The symmetries involved in *Synaxis* are more complex; while the outer movements (I and VIII, and II and VII) balance each other in terms of musical character and duration, the inner movements are paired as interlocking arch-shape structures. (Like *Signes*, the movements are intended to proceed without a break.) Movements I and VIII are short, essentially monodic in character and act as a prologue and epilogue. Movements II and VII are the longest, balance each other with contrasting treatments of similar material and make use of spatial and antiphonal effects. The interlocking inner movements balance each other in musical character and length; IV and VI provide short contemplative interludes to the more extrovert rhythmic activity of III and V. Movements I, II, IV, VI and VII also allude to techniques borrowed from Medieval music; while these reflect a symmetry in relation to each other, there is no symmetry in relation to the overall structure.

Syllabaire pour Phèdre and *Autodafé* allude to the form of ancient Greek tragedy in which symmetry is also implicit: both are encased within a Prologue and Epilogue which stand outside the main action and both alternate Episodes with Stasimon. While Episodes are generally long and account for the action of the drama (albeit as relatively static tableaux), the Stasimon are short interludes which comment on the action in the manner of a Greek chorus. *Syllabaire pour Phèdre,* like *Synaxis*, dovetails pairs of internal movements within the overall symmetry of its outer movements, although the musical relationships are more superficial. *Autodafé* is symmetrical about its central Parodos, a commentary on the futility of war. (There are seven movements on either side of the Parodos.) The six inner movements of each half (Episodes and Stasimon) are contained within the outer frame of Prologue and Epilogue. The inner movements of the first half are also symmetrical; Episodes II and III form a central pair around which Stasimon I and II and Episodes I and IV are balanced. While Episodes I and IV are contrasted in subject matter, depicting the Terror of the French Revolution and human slaughter in the World War I trenches, respectively, Episodes II and III follow a greater dramatic continuity. Set at the time of the Albigensian Crusades, Episode II portrays the slaughter of the Cathars and all who died in the name of Christ at the hands of the Inquisition. Episode III continues the theme to depict the victims of Spanish colonialism in Central and South America many of whom also died in the name of Christianity. Although the inner movements of the second half of *Autodafé* are not strictly symmetrical, the long Episode V is balanced by the shorter and more dramatically integrated Episodes VI, VII and VIII. While Episode V depicts a nightmarish visit to a nocturnal museum of horrors, where the exhibits are living images of eternal torture, Episodes VI and VII integrate images of suffering in the Spanish Civil and Napoleonic Wars. Episode VIII continues the Spanish theme but in more optimistic vein; set in the time of King Alphonso X 'El Sabio', the triumph of joy and life is celebrated in a tableau depicting the arrival of spring. The concluding Epilogue comments on the death of death and all tyranny is consumed in the cleansing fires of the Autodafé itself.

In *Cris*, Ohana combined aspects of symmetry and dovetailed arch-shapes with a process of organic growth operating through, and directly linking, four out of the five movements. With the exception of the third movement, the remaining movements are interrelated through the reworking of material originally generated, as its title suggests, in the first movement, 'Générique'.[20] The third movement provides an interlude to the work as whole; alluding to the unaccompanied lament of the Cante Jondo, 'Debla' is monodic and improvisatory. Interlocking arch-shape relationships are strongest between movements II and V which balance each other in terms of their rhythmically active and ritualistic character, although not overall duration ('Délirante' is longer than 'Slogans'). Although movements I and IV are related through the detailed reworking of material, they are dissimilar in terms of overall musical character. The internal structure of the fourth movement of *Cris*, 'Mémorial 44', is unusual in that it conforms to a quinpartite, symmetrical pattern. A memorial to the victims of war, the central section recites the names of Nazi Concentration Camps 'ad libitum' in layered aleatory counterpoint, the rhythmic patterns being derived from the German text (see Ex. 8.1). Additional German text evokes the horror of abduction by night.

The surrounding, inner sections of 'Mémorial 44' are balanced in terms of respective duration and only indirectly through content as each re-works material derived from different sections of 'Générique'. The first contains melodic material suggestive of plainsong (derived from 'Générique' fig. 2), while the second contains rhythmic material (derived from Générique fig. 1) in which the phonetic material ('Tanng') is designed to suggest funerary bells. The second section also includes a fragment of Spanish text 'ya los llevan desnudos' (now they are carried away naked) which evokes not only the horrific images of piles of corpses in Concentration Camps but the brutality of war depicted in the etchings of Goya.[21] The isolated word 'Pourquoi?', which appears at the end of the movement, may refer to the nightmarish torture depicted in No. 32 (*'Por qué?'*) of Goya's *Disasters of War*. The material of the outer sections of 'Mémorial 44' is balanced in terms of texture and vocal effect. The first section exploits descending glissandi in a sound-mass of aleatory counterpoint in which approximate intonation and whistling evoke the sound of shells falling on a battlefield. The final section involves rising and falling glissandi (voiced through paper held to the lips) to create a sound-texture evocative of warning sirens. The 'cries' of the work's title refer to the exploration of a range of vocal effects from expressive song to percussive texture. While the 'cries' of 'Délirante' and 'Slogans' include war-cries, those of 'Debla' and 'Mémorial 44' represent the outpouring of personal grief. Apart from 'Mémorial 44', the only other movement to include recognisable text is 'Slogans' where isolated text fragments allude to the suffering of Christ on the Cross, the war-time codes broadcast to the French Resistance, and the political slogans of the Paris demonstrations of 1968.[22] The use of text sets these movement in relief from the rest of the work which otherwise employs onomatopoeic phonemes and morphemes.

The last of Ohana's works to incorporate structural symmetries is *Office des oracles*. As in *Synaxis, Syllabaire pour Phèdre* and *Autodafé*, the outer movements act as a prologue and epilogue to the main argument of the work, the alphabetic references of the titles supporting this function. Both involve

228   THE MUSIC OF MAURICE OHANA

Ex. 8.1: *Cris*, 'Mémorial 44' (fig. 34–67)

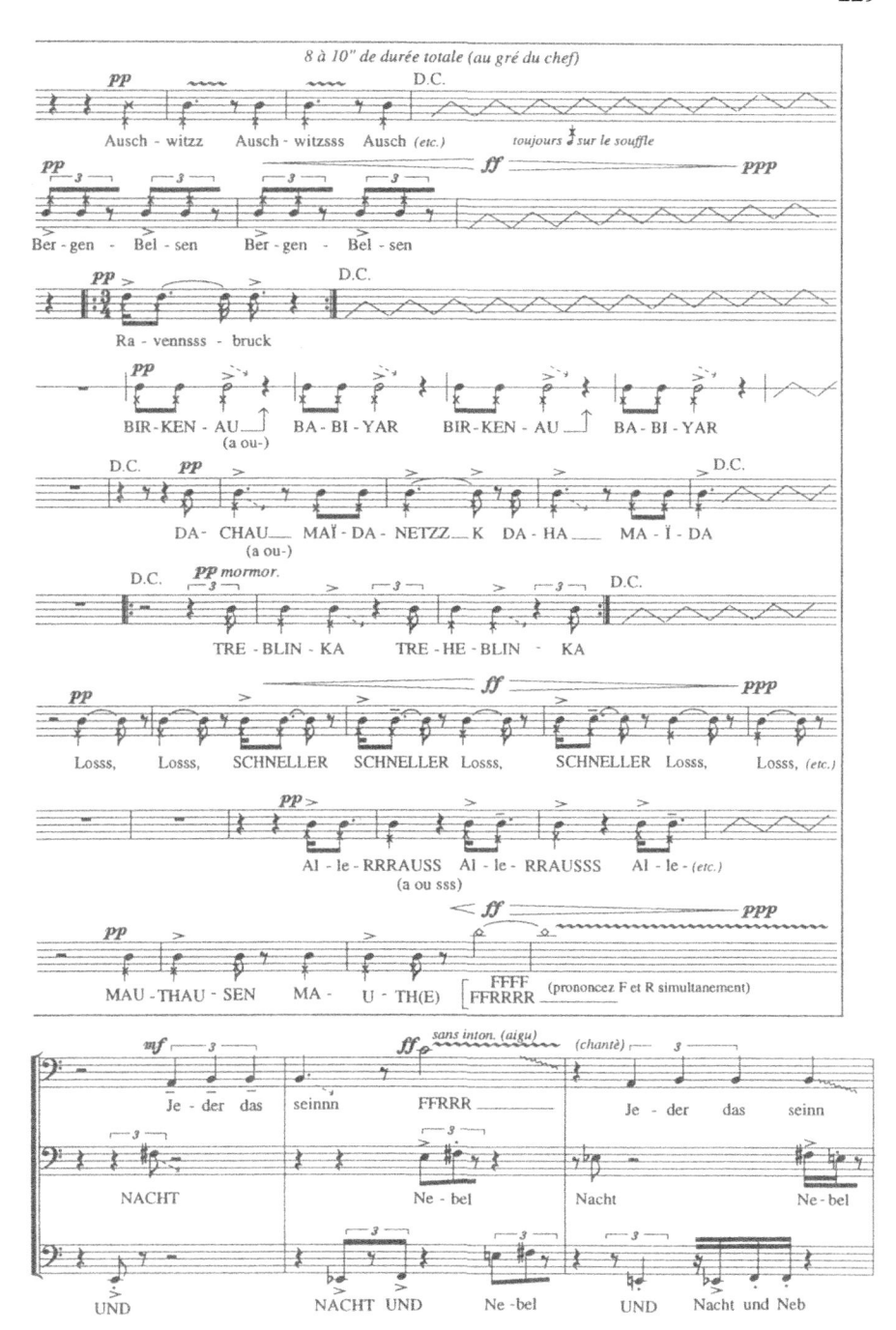

SYMMETRICAL STRUCTURES AND APPROACHES TO FORM 229

Reproduced by kind permission of Société des Editions Jobert, Paris / United Music Publishers Ltd.

plainsong-like melodic fragments, although treat the material in contrasting ways; 'Alpha' divides the material between a quartet of solo voices, while 'Omega' makes use of the full forces of all three choral groups in layers of aleatory counterpoint. (*Office* divides its forces into three independent instrumental and vocal groups each of which have their own conductor and are separated spatially.) Movements II and XI are similarly contemplative; 'Oniracle' juxtaposes melodic fragments in layers of aleatory counterpoint, while 'Pythié' presents an expressive monodic vocalisation. Movements III and X (like V and VIII) are concerned with rhythmic texture and subject the material to a variety of contrasting procedures. The central pivot is provided by movements VI and VII which effectively function as a single movement, the chorale-fragment of 'Tarots' acting as a postscript to the quasi-improvisatory, rhythmic textures of 'Météoracle'. Movements IV and IX are balanced only by virtue of their dissimilarity and complexity of internal structure. 'Minotaure aux miroirs' is divided into two main sections which are defined by the entry of the cantus firmus (on trombones) at fig. 19, this representing the appearance of the minotaur in the labyrinth. The 'mirrors' of the title refer to effects of echo and imitation which characterise the movements and are enforced by the spatial divisions of the respective instrumental and vocal groups. The first main section comprises three shorter sub-sections: the first is quasi-improvisatory and extends unmetred material according to Ohana's process of imitation, variation and addition; the second superimposes layers of aleatory counterpoint using all three instrumental groups; the third juxtaposes two monodic vocalisations by soprano soloists (from different vocal groups), suggestive of Ariadne's presence in the labyrinth. The second main section contains only two sub-sections; in the first, the measured, homophonic cantus firmus (played by group 3) provides an aural anchor-point for the fragmented, imitative rhythmic material of instrumental groups 1 and 2 which are juxtaposed against it; in the second, a female chorus imitates the material of the soprano soloists in a sequence of echoes.[23]

Movement IX is unusual in that aleatory procedures govern its internal structure. (Although there are earlier examples of mobile form, he did not experiment further with his procedure after *Office*.) With the somewhat tongue-in-cheek title of 'Ecriture automatique', the movement is intended to poke fun at this type of compositional approach (cf. Chapter 2). The movement consists of thirteen, contrasting episodes (indicated by box-notation) which are associated with particular instrumental or vocal groups. They can be played in any order (to be determined by the leading conductor), either individually or simultaneously, in which case they would be superimposed in aleatory counterpoint. One or more of the episodes can be omitted. The fourth episode is a duo for violin and viola; bearing the sub-title 'Trille du diable', it is intended as a satirical reference to the famous sonata of Tartini. Another of the thirteen episodes is also the tenth movement, 'Oroscope', this being required to occur approximately after half of the episodes have been played. This is the only episode which must not be combined with any other, as this movement is itself made up of layers of aleatory counterpoint. The only other requirement concerns the eighth episode which serves as a coda leading to the next movement, and is to be played last. *Offices des oracles* was intended as a series of humorous commentaries on contemporary, compositional trends; different 'oracles' are consulted in the quest to discover a future for musical composition (cf. Chapter 2). The penultimate movement refers to the oracle at Delphi where the high-priestess 'Pythié' gives an enigmatic 'answer' in a 'Sibylline' monodic vocalisation for contralto. The implication is that the expressiveness of the human voice is the way forward, the solution to contemporary problems of composition (see Ex. 8.2).

Ohana's earlier experiments with mobile form appear in *Chiffres de clavecin* and *Silenciaire* and are reserved to the internal structure of a particular section. In keeping with his desire to recreate the spontaneity of improvisation within a composed score, these sections are best described in terms of limited freedom, as the material itself is not left to chance. Even where mobile forms include the instruction to improvise on a given melodic or rhythmic cell, the intention is that the pitches of the particular cell should be repeated with free variation of rhythmic patterning, tempo and pitch-order. It does not require the performer to invent entirely new material (cf. Chapters 5 and 7). In *Chiffres de clavecin* (for harpsichord and orchestra) the 'Cadence' section of the fifth movement ('Cadence, Echos, Rumeurs') is a cadenza for the harpsichord soloist. The final section of the cadenza requires the soloist to decide which material is to be played and in which order. It is divided into a number of self-contained and contrasting blocks of material designated as 'refrains' and 'strophes'. The refrains comprise six elements; a complete statement of material, 'refrains entier' and five fragments derived from it. The four 'strophes' are longer and more melodic than the refrains, contrasting rhythmically and in terms of harmonic colour. To construct the end of the cadenza the soloist can alternate any number of the 'refrains' with any one of the first three 'strophes', in any order (none are to be played twice). All of the blocks may be played or the soloist can proceed directly to the fourth strophe after playing the 'refrain entier' once. Whatever combination of material is chosen, the fourth 'strophe' must be played last; like the eighth episode of 'Ecriture automatique' it functions as an obligatory coda leading into the next section of the movement 'Echos' and the entry of the orchestra at fig. 49.

Although *Chiffres de clavecin* is constructed according to a five movement plan (which proceeds without a break), there is no real symmetry inherent in the movement structure. The internal sectionalism of the individual movements (emphasised by the sub-titles given to each one) results from the procedures of contrasting instrumental and harmonic timbre, melodic and rhythmic texture and is both quasi-improvisatory and dynamic. The 'ciphers' of the work's title suggest that the individual movement titles are secret symbols, clues to understanding the compositional point of departure. There are references to technical procedures and styles (counterpoint, discant, chorale, passacaglia, cadenza), to architectural structures (columns and volutes), and to visions of nature and the universe (stars, clouds, echoes, deflagrations and chaos). The

232   THE MUSIC OF MAURICE OHANA

Ex. 8.2: *Office des oracles*, 'Pythié' (fig. 36–8)

Reproduced by kind permission of Société des Editions Jobert, Paris / United Music Publishers Ltd.

short, closely related third and fourth movements function as a single unit and are poetic essays in sound-texture. The shimmering, pointillist sounds of 'Etoiles-nuées' exploit a very high tessitura and comprise layers of aleatory counterpoint, while the more sombre resonances of 'Colonnes-volutes' explore low registers and are measured and vertically co-ordinated throughout. The contemplative mood of these sections is recalled in the delicate murmuring sounds of the closing section of the fifth movement 'Rumeurs'.

Silenciaire, for six percussionists and strings, is a single movement form conceived as a succession of sub-sections. Between figs. 22–26, there are four large sections called 'Aventures' (the only titled sections of the work) which may be played in any order or repeated 'ad libitum' according to the decision of the conductor. Each 'Aventure' presents a different type of aleatory counterpoint, combining the two instrumental groups (percussion and strings) in contrasting ways. Involving the full forces of the two groups, 'Aventure 1' comprises two blocks of material (one of strings, one on percussion) each of which is a sound-mass of aleatory counterpoint in which each part is given a different tempo indication; that on percussion comprises layers of fragmented but repetitive rhythms, while that on strings juxtaposes measured and unmeasured rhythms and both decide on dynamic nuance 'ad libitum'. The blocks of material may be played simultaneously or successively. 'Aventure 2' juxtaposes unmetred, fragmented rhythmic material (on percussion) with a block of homophonic material (on strings). A sustained chord in divisi upper strings provides background resonance, and the whole section is required to last no longer than two minutes. 'Aventure 3' freely combines a rhythmic-sound mass repeated 'ad libitum' (on wood percussion and sea-shells) with a series of metred chords (on strings). In 'Aventure 4' the material of both instrumental groups is metred although differently; there is vertical co-ordination within each group but not between them. To this is added a further layer; a quasi-improvisatory, unmetred monody on solo cello.

In No. 8 of the *24 Préludes*, the boxed-notation of the opening episodes (marked A, B, and C) appears to suggest a quasi-mobile form, although the order is, in fact, fixed. The three episodes present three different types of material each of which contains layered aleatory counterpoint. Once the material of each section has been played, more or less as written, the performer is required to vary the material freely in quasi-improvisatory fashion. While the order of the episodes is fixed, their respective duration is not. A similar device is used in *Autodafé* where the overall duration of the vocal sound-mass in Stasimon I is to be decided by the conductor.

Although several works composed in the years following *Office des oracles* were conceived in terms of individual movement structures, even superficial symmetries were abandoned in favour of juxtaposing material of different musical character (and technical procedure) according to Ohana's concept of 'tension by contrast'.[24] The approach could be applied as much to internal, sectional structures, as to formalised movement structures. Although *Lys de madrigaux* alternates five of its six movements (or madrigals) in a quasi-symmetrical succession of dovetailed arch-structures, any overall symmetry is avoided by the presence of a sixth madrigal and by the spiritual weight of the work occurring in the third movement 'Star Mad Blues'. The incorporation of an additional visual-spatial device underlines the progression of the work in terms of linear, rather than circular, direction. The twenty-four voices of the female chorus are divided into three groups which are positioned on three of the four 'corners' of the platform (back-stage left and right and front-stage right, the fourth 'corner' front-stage left being occupied by the piano) for the first two movements (or madrigals) and are required to come together as a single ensemble (to centre stage) in the final section of the second madrigal. During the sixth and final madrigal 'Miroir de Sapho' the chorus displaces once more, fragmenting itself into twelve couples dispersed equally to occupy the maximum space on the platform. In the final section of the last madrigal, a soprano soloist moves to an isolated position to sing the monody which brings the work to a close. The simplicity of the concluding monody and the 'Sibylline' associations of Ohana's treatment of the female voice are suggested in the work's title; 'lys' refers to the white, perfumed lily which has been symbolic of purity since the Middle Ages.

The first five madrigals of *Lys de madrigaux* alternate material of a contemplative character (movements I, III, V) with more dynamic rhythmic material (movements II and IV). In the first madrigal, 'Calypso', five sub-sections subject melodic ideas to a variety of treatments; a quasi-improvisatory monody is dispersed equally between the voices, is thickened as a homophonic, chorale-like texture, is superimposed on the homophonic material (no vertical co-ordination) and transformed to a plainsong-like melody thickened in note-for-note parallelism. The third madrigal, 'Star Mad Blues' is a setting of a Negro spiritual melody (cf. Chapter 5) and is the only movement to incorporate text. (All other movements make use of onomatopoeic phonemes and morphemes.) The fifth madrigal, 'Tropique de la Vièrge' disperses a melodic idea between groups of solo voices and explores sound-mass textures on which metred and unmetred monodies are superimposed. The contemplative character of the fifth madrigal is carried forward into 'Miroir de Sapho' which opens by building-up a shimmering sound-mass of melodic aleatory counterpoint (in twelve parts) in which the individual cells are repeated 'ad libitum' over a sequence of chords suggesting a modal F major. While movements II and IV balance each other in terms of more rapid tempi and their repetitive, motor rhythms, they are not comparable in terms of length or treatment of material. The range of procedures, techniques and vocal effects explored in 'Circé' makes it the longest and most complex movement of the work. Recalling rhythmic patterns in Stravinsky's *Les Noces* and Messiaen's *Cinq réchants*, homophonic quintuplets are set against triplet crotchets in 3:5 (cf. Ex. 7.1c). The 3+2 pattern of the opening quintuplets is alternated with 2+3 later in the first section. Subsequent sections explore melodic, rhythmic as well as percussive sound-mass textures and combine homophonic material with layers of aleatory counterpoint in a variety of densities. 'Parques' is a less complex and much shorter movement; in 6/8 it explores the very Spanish hemiola, superimposing homophonic melodic material over a repetitive, motor rhythm.

While many of Ohana's mature works are constructed in clearly defined movements, most are intended to proceed without a break, a feature which is emphasised by the through-numbering of figures. Other works, including many of the Sigma Series, the *24 Préludes, T'Harân-Ngô, Anneau du Tamarit,* the Piano Concerto and the second cello concerto *In Dark and Blue,* were conceived more as single structures divided into large, sometimes titled sections. This reflects the organic nature of the material employed in the internal structure of the sections themselves, although even works with clearly defined movements are often linked by a continuity of material: the plainsong parodies unify the movements of the Mass; the appearance of the Moon-Chorale in the Prologue and each of the three tales secures the overall unity of *Trois contes de l'Honorable Fleur* (cf. Chapter 2). Due to Ohana's paradoxical concept of organic sectionalism, where the musical material itself generates each successive section, there are many variations of structural detail from work to work.

> I consider myself to be in a pre-classical period, a chaotic period where form is determined by the germ of the musical material itself. Consequently form is very different from one work to another ... .[25]

In placing himself in an imagined 'pre-classical' period, Ohana not only underlined the importance of music of the Medieval and Renaissance periods, (particularly the sacred repertories), as an influence on his compositional style, but freed himself from any preconceptions of form which might be associated with the classical period and beyond. In terms of creative imagination he described himself as inhabiting an imagined, primeval world as yet untarnished by the discoveries and inventions of creators other than himself (cf. Chapter 2). The basic process generating internal structure in his mature music is that of continual extension by variation and addition; small cells create progressively larger sections, the individual character and length of a section depending on the type of material, as well as the instrumental or vocal forces, employed. His concept of 'tension by contrast' relates to the juxtaposition of sections and movements. While Ohana's forms are sectional, the material is generated organically, internal structures being therefore quite varied from work to work. In the opening of *Sibylle* (cf. Chapters 5 and 7), it was shown how cells combined to form sentences and sections which are consistent in terms of timbre and character of material. Overall unity is achieved through the interrelationships of similar material in different sections. While sections represent the largest sub-division of a movement, or work, cells are the smallest. The structural hierarchy which is contained within a section depends on the complexity of material and its treatment. If the section is short and the procedures involved are relatively simple, the component sub-divisions may be made up of sentences or merely phrases. If the section is long and the treatment of material more complex, the component sub-divisions may be better described in terms of episodes. Sections are usually defined by a fermata, rest, double bar and are combined with textural or timbral contrast.

The first movement of *Cris.* is a simple example of Ohana's internal sectionalism. Generating the main material for the work, 'Générique' is made up of eight short sections, only one of which is substantial enough to contain sentences. Essentially the material presented in this movement is not complex and consists of two main musical ideas (designated as 'A' and 'B', respectively) which are subject to continuous variation and extension from section to section. The first idea 'A' is chiefly characterised by cells of accented appoggiature (fig. 1) and is mainly, although not exclusively, homophonic. The second idea 'B' comprises layers of differing melodic cells and is essentially polyphonic. That 'B' is first heard in combination with 'A', the respective ideas being superimposed at fig. 2, underlines the essentially continuous and organic approach to the generation of material (see Ex. 8.3). Certain melodic cells within 'B' are themselves derived from material 'A'. As the movement progresses, the

Ex. 8.3: *Cris*, 'Générique' (fig.2, section 2, bars 13–14)

alternation of homorhythmic movement with polyphonic textures makes the sections easily identifiable. Some sections involve Ohana's 'combinatoire' technique and superimpose metred homophonic material with layers of unmetred aleatory counterpoint. Conveniently Ohana's positioning of figure numbers usually corresponds with the delineation of sections. Table 8.3 presents a formal scheme for the movement.

Table 8.3: *Cris*, 'Générique': formal scheme

Scoring: s = sopranos, ms = mezzo-sopranos, t = tenors, b = basses;
Rhythm: m= metered, u/m=unmetered, al = aleatory counterpoint, i.e. all unmetred, or metred and unmetred combined

Section & Figure		Sub-division	Scoring	Material and Character	Dynamic	Rhythm
1	0–2	3 phrases	s,ms	homophonic A	*f*	m
2	2–3	1 phrase	s,ms,t,b	polyphonic A + B		m
			s	A	*f*	m
			m	B	*mf*	m
			t	B	*p–f*	m
			b	B	*p–f*	m
3	3–5	3 phrases	s,ms,t,b	homophonic A	*f*	m
4	5–6	1 phrase	s,ms,t,b	homophonic B	*ff*	m
5	6–8	2 sentences	s,ms,t,b	polyphonic		al
		sentence 1	s	B sound-mass	*mf–pp*	u/m
			ms	A (cantus firmus)	*p–mf*	m
			t	B (cantus firmus)	*p*	m
		sentence 2	s	B sound-mass	*pp–ff*	al
			ms	A + B	*p–ff*	al
			t	B (cantus firmus)	*p–ff*	al
6	8–9	1 phrase	s,ms,t,b	polyphonic B	*p*	m
7	9–10	3 phrases	s,ms,t,b	homorhythmic A	*ff*	m
8	10–13	5 phrases	s,ms,t,b	polyphonic A + B	*ff–mf– f–ff*	al

Completed more than a decade later, *Livre des prodiges* has a more complex structure. Divided into two parts, as an allusion to *The Rite of Spring*, it is divided into titled sub-sections which proceed without a break (also in the manner of *The Rite*). Appearing in the first part after a short introduction, 'Cortège des taureaux ailés' comprises an internal structure made up of three, large inner sections, one of which is sufficiently complex to contain episodes. Table 8.4 presents a formal scheme for 'Cortège des taureaux ailés'. The first (and longest) section opens with homorhythmic material which defines the first episode (Ex. 7.1a) which, in subsequent episodes becomes a Stravinskian, rhythmic ostinato juxtaposed against contrasting material in different orchestral groups.[26] In this way, the new material of subsequent episodes creates variation

Table 8.4: *Livre des prodiges*, 'Cortège des taureaux ailés': formal scheme

Rhythm: m = metered.; ^{b} = bars (i.e. 5^{+6b} = 6 bars after fig. 5)

Section & Figure	Sub-division	Scoring	Material and Character	Dynamic	Rhythm
1 2–10					
2–4	episode 1	w.w.	homorhythmic	*mf*	m ♩=96
4–5^{+6b}	episode 2		layered		m ♩=120
		str.	ostinato	*mf*	
		brass	chordal idea	*mp – ff*	
		w.w.	melodic idea	*f*	
5^{+6b}–8	episode 3		polyphonic		m ♩=120
		str., pf.	ostinato	*p*	
		w.w., brass	melodic idea	*p*	
8–10	episode 4	tutti	homorhythmic	*mf – fff*	m animez progress.
10		tutti	climactic gliss.	*fff*	retenez
2 10–13					
10^{+2b}–12	sentence 1	str., low w.w.	chordal gliss.	*fff*	m 5/4 ♩=100
		hn., timp.	quintuplets	*mf*	
		high w.w.	melodic material	*mf*	
	final phrase		quintuplets	*f – ff*	
12–13	sentence 2	str., low w.w., brass, pf.	chordal idea (derived from section 1)		plus lent
3 13–16	3 phrases				m 5/8
13–14	phrase 1	tps.	quintuplet idea	*f*	
		w.w., pf.	new chordal idea	*ff*	
		str.	gliss.	*ff*	
14–15	phrase 2	tps.	quintuplets	*f – ff*	
		w.w., brass	chordal idea	*ff*	
15–16	phrase 3	tutti	homophonic (derived from section 1)	*ff*	très élargi

and contrast, while the ostinato provides continuity. The overall shape of the first section builds-up to a fortissimo climax where the homophonic rhythmic material predominates, finally culminating in a dramatic, fortissimo, tutti glissando. This gesture can be seen both as concluding the first section and opening the second, as part of the material of the second section is derived from it. The second section has, therefore, been taken as beginning at fig. 10, although it emerges definitively two bars later. (Fig. 10 and fig. 10+2 bars are both notated with double bars.) The chordal glissandi of the strings, with which the second section proper opens, are accompanied by the introduction of new material in the form of quintuplet crotchets. The overall gesture and combined instrumental texture would seem to allude to the 'Spring Rounds' section of Part One of *The Rite of Spring*, despite the rhythmic differences. (Although 'Spring Rounds' opens in 5/4, the ensuing 'sostenuto e pesante' section is in 4/4.) The opening of Ohana's second section on horns, low woodwind and strings is, as in 'Spring Rounds', followed by melodic material in wind, ornamented by Stravinskian *acciaccature*. The quintuplet 5/4 divisions of section two are extended into section three, although accelerated into a 5/8 (3+2). This has the effect of driving the whole section towards its conclusion in a rhythmically, dynamic way. Overall continuity between sections in Parts One and Two of *Livres des prodiges* is created by the progressive variation and extension of material from section to section; what was subordinate in one section becomes the main focus of the next. In this way, Ohana's compositional procedures, particularly in *Livre des prodiges*, are not only organic but have much in common with Dutilleux's concept of progressive growth.

To illustrate the behaviour of Ohana's sectionalism within an entire work, Table 8.5 presents a formal scheme for *Sibylle*. The material of this work has been identified in terms of two main, contrasting types (cf. Chapters 5 and 7); material that is chiefly melodic ('Melodic A', 'Melodic B') and material that is chiefly rhythmic ('Texture A' and 'Texture B'). 'Melodic A' is characterised by melodic cells of the pivotal-type, while 'Melodic B' is more lyrical and expressive, characterised by larger intervals (especially minor sevenths) and is usually associated with intervallic colour of Timbre II. 'Texture A' is characterised by dynamic rhythmic cells which often form regular patterns, and may involve some melodic interest, and 'Texture B' by textural or percussive rhythmic activity. While there are some occasional overlaps of melodic and rhythmic features between these main divisions, a phrase or section can be described in terms of its predominant material. The designation of material stems partly from the fundamental aim of the work to contrast, juxtapose and combine the voice, percussion and tape. Both soprano and percussion explore melodic, rhythmic and percussive capabilities. The incorporation of a pre-recorded tape enhances the timbral points of reference between the voice and the percussion. The blending and contrasting of vocal and percussion textures in *Sibylle* has much in common with many of the vocal and percussive effects found in Berio, in particular *Visage* and *Circles*.

Within Ohana's idea of 'tension by contrast' he sometimes freely adapts or alludes to formal procedures associated with different musical traditions. That his melodic style often suggests the atmosphere and shape of plainsong, has led to the free adaptation of the techniques of cantus firmus, discant, organum and conductus. In turn, the concept of antiphonal and responsorial singing, normally associated with psalmody, is fundamental both to his vocal and instrumental music, although is particularly exploited in the Mass. The alternation between soloists and chorus and between different choral groups, so prevalent in the internal structure of his vocal music, has been extended to apply to instrumental music where it is also one of his most important means of effecting textural contrast. As a consequence this led him in some works to explore the possibilities of spatial divisions, subdividing vocal and (or) instrumental forces into smaller groups such as in *Office des oracles* and *Lys de madrigaux*.

Table 8.5: *Sibylle*: formal scheme

Metrical type: m = metered, u/m = unmeterd, al = 'combinatoire'-type counterpoint)
Note: Ohana's tempo descriptions appear italicised under 'Metrical Type'.

Section & Fig.	Sub-division	Material	Character	Dynamic	Metrical Type
1 0–2	sentence 1	Melodic A	reposeful	*mf*	u/m–slow
	inserted phrase	Melodic B	expressive	*mf*	u/m–slow
	sentence 2	Texture A	active	*f*	m–faster
		Melodic B	expressive	*mf*	u/m–*lent*
2 2–3	phrase 1	Texture B	imitative	*f*	u/m–fast
	phrase 2	Melodic B	expressive	*p*	u/m–slow
		Texture B	homophonic	*p*	u/m–slow
		Melodic B	expressive	*p*	u/m–slow
	phrase 3	Texture B	active	*f–ff*	u/m–*vif*
	phrase 4	Melodic B	expressive	*p*	u/m–*lent*
3 3–4	4 phrases	Melodic A	expressive	*p–pp*	m–*mesuré*
4 4–6[+1b]					
	4–5 sentence 1	Melodic B	expressive	*p*	m–*lent*
	5–6[+1b] episode	Texture A + B	active	*ff*	al–*rapide, desordonné*
		Melodic B	homophonic	*ff*	u/m
		Texture A	homorhythmic	*mf*	u/m
		Melodic B	expressive	*mf*	u/m–*lent*
	inserted phrase	*text:* 'Sign'	spoken	*p*	m
5 6+1⁻⁹	sentence 1	Melodic A	reposeful	*mf–p*	m–*libre*
		Melodic B	reposeful	*f–mf*	*mesuré*
	sentence 2	Melodic A	energetic	*ff*	u/m–*animé*
	sentence 3	Melodic B	active	*mf*	u/m
6 9–12	sentence 1	Texture B	rhythmic canon	*f–fff*	u/m–*énergique*
		Melodic B	expressive	*pp*	m
	sentence 2	Texture A	reposeful	*pp*	u/m
		Melodic B	textural	*mf*	u/m
			expressive	*f*	u/m
	inserted phrase	*text:* 'Sigma, soles sed'	spoken	*p*	u/m

Section & Fig.	Sub-division	Material	Character	Dynamic	Metrical Type
12–18		entry of tape at 14			
12–14	episode 1	Melodic B + Texture B (in alternation)	expressive incantatory	*pp* *mf*	u/m–*lent* m– a bit faster
14–16	episode 2	Texture A + B Melodic A (combined & juxtaposed)		*mf*	al
16–18	episode 3	Texture A + B Melodic B (combined & juxtaposed)		*p–mp* *mf*	al
8 18–20		Disintegration of material		*ff–p*	al
18–19	phrase 1	percussive texture (perc. & tape)		*ff*	al
19–20	phrase 2	Texture A (against percussive texture)		*dim.*	al (rall.)
20–end	phrase 3	Melodic A (voice & tape)		*mf–p*	al–*détimbré*

While many of Ohana's allusions to formal procedures associated with different musical traditions are woven into the musical texture, others are highlighted by movement title. In *Cinq séquences*, the titles 'Polyphonie', 'Déchant' and 'Hymne' suggest the formal and stylistic models of Medieval music upon which this work was based. Similar models are evoked in both *Synaxis* and *Chiffres de clavecin* which contain the sub-titles 'Diaphonie', 'Trope' (as does the Mass), 'Organum', 'Antiphonie' (*Synaxis*), 'Contrepoints-Déchant-Choral' (*Chiffres*). The title 'Tympanum', which appears in both *Cinq séquences* and *Synaxis,* is also associated with the structures of Medieval architecture (as are 'Colonnes' and 'Volutes' in *Chiffres*); the space existing between arches, or straight lines in a Gothic Cathedral. It also refers to an ancient type of drum. Ohana alludes to certain forms associated with the Troubadour poets ('Eneug', 'Planh', 'Aube' and 'Alborada'), although the references are intended more as poetical evocations, rather than to suggest actual transcriptions.

Other musical traditions to which Ohana makes reference in repect of form and structure are those of Spanish, African and Afro-Cuban origin. Movements or works may refer to a specific dance or song-type, although again his aim is to evoke the character of the source, rather than to write pastiche. Thus 'Debla' of *Cris,* 'Mambo' of *Swan Song,* 'Conga' of *Deux pièces pour clavecin, So Tango* and the Rumba of 'Eros noir' in *Avoaha* are evocations of those song or dance types, rather than transcriptions. Ohana sometimes avoided using such titles in their exact form, changing them subtly to emphasise their poetic character: thus the second movement of *Cadran lunaire* is '...Jondo', not Cante Jondo; the final movement of the second String Quartet is 'Farân-Ngô', not 'Fandango'; the third string quartet is a more esoteric 'Sorgin-Ngô'. The most important aspect of Ohana's allusion to these traditions, however, is in terms of style, rather than structure.

Although Ohana apparently considered form 'unimportant' and an 'artificial problem', it would appear that it was an issue that he nevertheless addressed. With a musical language that is primarily horizontal and organic, where the driving force is 'tension by contrast', sectionalism at microcosm, as well as in macrocosm, is almost inevitable. The problem inherent in such a process is the difficulty of achieving dynamic shape or overall unity, particularly in a long work which may run the risk of seeming meandering. While these dangers are generally successfully avoided in Ohana's concert works, they are sometimes an issue in the dramatic music. It is interesting to note that, with the exception of the dramatic music, few of Ohana's works exceed much more than twenty minutes in duration. Although *Livre des prodiges* is one of the notable exceptions, unity is achieved through its use of melodic material, its tightly constructed form and a sense of driving motion in its powerful and dynamic approach to rhythm. Perhaps the most effective and tersely constructed of Ohana's dramatic works is *Syllabaire pour Phèdre* ; it is (for a dramatic work) relatively short, lasting little more than thirty minutes.

In single movement works, where the range of material is intentionally more limited, the problem of overall unity does not become an issue, even in large-scale works of this type such as *Anneau du Tamarit*, the Piano Concerto and Second Cello Concerto *In Dark and Blue*. In more complex, multi-movement works unity is achieved through the process of organic variation, as well as through stylistic reference and continuity of material between movements or subsections of similar character. Unity of musical material can also be enhanced by the presence of additional features; extra-musical argument and text both provide ready-made frames on which to hang a work. Text was the point of compositional departure not only for the Mass and *Trois contes de l'Honorable Fleur* but also for several of the late vocal works including, *Lux noctis - Dies solis*, *Tombeau de Louize Labé*, *Nuit de Pouchkine* and even *Avoaha*. As with most works of this genre, the text was chosen (or written) before embarking on the composition of the music. Although Ohana often made use of onomatopoeic phonemes and morphemes to articulate a vocal line, he frequently incorporated recited text, and sometimes a narrator, in his dramatic works. In this way he was able to account for the action while leaving the music free to serve more as commentary, than as the means of propelling the action forwards. While narrated text accelerates overall progress through a work it can create a sense of stasis. The device can detach the observer from the action, as in Stravinsky's *Oedipus Rex*. It is possible that Ohana's predilection for the device may have developed from the particularly French predilection for the extrinsic action of classical Greek tragedy. As in the plays of Racine, action rarely takes place on stage, the interplay of characters being more concerned with their respective responses to the action and resultant psychological states. The portrayal of drama as a succession of static tableaux, rather than as purely dramatic narrative, is highly suited to Ohana's sectional approach to form.

The danger of sectionalism is that of stasis. With the liberation of form from any harmonic implications and the liberation of harmony from function, it is difficult for a composer to discover a new and effective means of driving a work forward towards its conclusion. Sectionalism can not achieve this in itself but, combined with an organic process of continual variation, and the concept of textural and timbral contrast, such a method can give the impression of forward motion. It may well be that the concept of forward propulsion is itself a preconception more appropriate to music rooted in Austro-German traditions and not one of the same importance to music that is not.

Notes to Chapter Eight.

1 M. Ohana, interview (in English), M. Oliver (1984).
2 The present author in conversation with the composer in Paris, November 1982.
3 The present author discussing the sketches for the opera *La Célestine* during various conversations with the composer in the Autumn of 1982 and Spring 1983.
4 Ibid.
5 M. Ohana, interview (in English), M. Oliver (1984).
6 The present author in conversation with the composer in Paris, June 1988.
7 Ibid.
8 M. Ohana, interview (in English), R. Langham Smith (1993) p. 128.
9 M. Ohana, interview (in French), F.B. Mâche (1978) p. 113.
10 M. Ohana, interview (in English), M. Oliver (1984).
11 R. Howat, *Debussy in Proportion* (Cambridge, 1983) p. 162.
12 M. Ohana, interview (in French), F.B. Mâche (1978) p. 114.
13 It has been suggested by Harry Halbreich that Ohana experimented with Golden Section structures in *In Dark and Blue*. See booklet accompanying the recording Timpani CD1C1039 (1997).
14 Definition of impressionism in music by S. Jarocínski, *Debussy, Impressionism and Symbolism* trans. R. Myers (London, 1976) p. 11.
15 The report of the Secretary of the Académie des Beaux-Arts in 1887 in reference to *Printemps*.
16 'La Revue blanche: 1901', *Debussy on Music: The Critical Writings of the Great French Composer* trans. ed., R. Langham Smith (New York, 1977) p. 48.
17 R. Howat, (1983) op. cit.
18 M. Ohana, interview (in French), P. Ancelin (1964).
19 With the exception of the Toccata, Ohana later destroyed the *Suite pour piano*.
20 C. Rae, 'Cris: The Mature Vocalism', 'The Music of Maurice Ohana', (diss. U. of Oxford (1989)) Vol. 1, pp. 248–68.
21 The Spanish phrase suggests many of Goya's titles without actually being a citation.
22 P.A. Castanet, '1968: A Cultural and Social Survey of its Influences on French Music', *Contemporary Music Review* Vol. 8, 1, (1993) pp. 25–30.
23 C. Prost has suggestsed in her analysis of the movement that there are symmetries of pitch-structure. *La Revue musicale* (1986) pp.129–47.
24 M. Ohana, interview (in English), R. Langham Smith (1993).
25 M. Ohana, interview (in French), P. Ancelin (1964).
26 This material appears in embryonic form in *Stream* (1970).

CHAPTER NINE

Epilogue: Reception and Context

The music of Maurice Ohana has been unjustly neglected in Britain despite his work having long achieved recognition beyond our shores. In France, during his life-time, Ohana ranked among the leading figures of his generation for more than thirty years and received many of the highest official accolades.[1] Since his death, his music continues to be regularly performed, broadcast, as well as recorded, and a prize has been established to his memory, commemorating his contribution to French musical life as both composer and pianist.[2] Much of Ohana's music has found a permanent place in the French repertoire, most notably, the works for guitar, for percussion, for piano and for harpsichord, as well as many of those for choral forces. In Britain, the view of French music since 1945 has tended to be identified with the music of Olivier Messiaen and Pierre Boulez to the exclusion of other composers whose work has long been honoured in France, as well as in the wider, international arena. These others include, among the older generation, Maurice Ohana and Henri Dutilleux. Undoubtedly Boulez has been one of the most phenomenal figures in music since 1945 and the position of his erstwhile teacher Messiaen is secure as one of the giants of the twentieth century; yet however significant their respective contribution, they represent only part of the wider French, compositional mainstream.

Infamous insularity is to blame for the relative neglect of Ohana's music in Britain. Although his music, like that of Dutilleux, was innovative and forward-looking, he distanced himself from the preoccupations of his contemporaries involved at Darmstadt and proclaimed an iconoclastic rejection of serialism. Dutilleux, on the other hand, attended some of the Paris lectures of René Leibowitz during the immediate post-war years and also experimented with some serial devices (in the third song of *Trois sonnets de Jean Cassou*[3], as well as in the Second Symphony and *Métaboles*) but could never accept the basic principle of abolishing all hierarchy between the different degrees of the chromatic scale.[4] As Dutilleux has said of himself: 'Fundamentally I am not an atonal composer.'[5] Dutilleux and Ohana were among the composers excluded from representation at the Concerts du Domaine musical. Their distance from Boulez affected the promotion of their music in Britain throughout the years when the programming policies of Sir William Glock, Hans Keller (and others) were at their most influential, a period which extended well beyond Glock's retirement from the BBC in the 1970s.[6]

The readiness of those in Britain to accept the outmoded aesthetic of the Domaine musical resulted in a distorted view of contemporary French music which, in some quarters, still persists. As Controller of Music and Director of the Proms, Glock certainly promoted contemporary music at the BBC, including that of the French, but according to a supposed canon which posterity has shown not to be entirely representative. Clearly the revisionist approach of Glock, Keller and others, was well intentioned; with Britain suffering from its false reputation as 'The Land without Music',[7] one can understand that they wished to save Britain from what they perceived as its musical isolationism from the forces of European modernism. Certainly it was necessary to give exposure to significant, contemporary developments in continental Europe, but, as with all such swings, one imbalance was replaced by another. In 1972, Francis Routh drew attention to the dangers of presenting too narrow a view of contemporary music, and although he was considering the problem from the perspective of British music, his ungloved criticisms of the BBC monopoly could apply equally to the European composers similarly excluded at the time:

> The BBC Music Department has not kept pace with the enormously increased range of contemporary music ... an extreme instance of this limitation occurred in the 1960s when the newly appointed Head of Music, William Glock, exercised the power vested in his position to promote particular composers of the serialist and avant-garde school. Those who were not of this persuasion were disregarded, and their works not broadcast ... . A trend was thus set which was undesirable because it was lopsided and unrepresentative.[8]

Although Glock was frequently critical of what he considered to be a middle-of-the road approach to the programming of his predecessors, examination of the broadcasting archives reveals that music by living French composers was not ignored prior to his appointment in 1959 (Table 9.1).[9]

Table 9.1: BBC broadcasts of music by selected French composers 1945–69 [10]

(all networks)
Includes broadcasts of live concerts, recorded concerts, commercial recordings and repeat broadcasts.

	1945–49	1950–54	1955–59	1960–64	1965–69
Boulez	0	0	2	20	66
Constant	0	3	1	4	5
Dutilleux	4	1	6	2	6
Jolivet	0	14	16	6	9
Daniel-Lesur	4	2	2	0	1
Messiaen	4	25	16	86	231
Ohana	1*	0	4	5	2

(*) as a performer

During the period 1945–49, there were twelve separate broadcasts of works by Messiaen, Daniel-Lesur and Dutilleux on the Third Programme and Home Service, in addition to a broadcast recital of French and Spanish music by Maurice Ohana (then still active as a pianist).[11] During the 1950s there were thirty broadcasts of works by Jolivet, seven of Dutilleux, four of Ohana, Constant and Daniel-Lesur, and two of Boulez.[12] Broadcasts of music by Messiaen were more numerous, totalling forty-one, presumably as a result of the enthusiasm of Felix Aprahamian who was instrumental in introducing Messiaen's music to England during the 1930s.[13] Before 1959 there were also fourteen broadcasts of six works by Lili Boulanger (and two of a work by Nadia), more than twenty of works by Maurice Duruflé, seventeen broadcasts of fifteen works by Henri Sauguet, about a dozen of works by Jean-Michel Damase and at least two of Schaeffer and Henry's *Symphonie pour un homme seule*. This is still comparatively few if compared with the arguably more popular Francis Poulenc who received approximately 500 broadcasts. (It is interesting to note that during this period Poulenc's music was broadcast more often than that of either Offenbach or Liszt.)

The Ohana broadcasts of the 1950s included two performances of *Llanto por Ignacio Sánchez Mejías* (on consecutive days in November 1955) and one of *Cantigas* (January 1958), both works having then only recently been premièred in Paris and Hamburg, respectively. The remaining broadcast of the 1950s was also of a then recently premièred work, *Images de Don Quichotte*. Adapted from Cervantes, this work was one of several commissions Ohana received during the 1950s and 60s from French Radio for Dutilleux's 'illustrations musicales' (cf. Chapters 1 and 3). Ohana's BBC broadcasts of the 1960s took place largely early on in the decade and included: the première of the guitar concerto, *Trois graphiques* in 1961 with Narciso Yepez and the London Symphony Orchestra under Anthony Bernard; a recording of *Carillons pour les heures du jour et de la nuit* for solo harpsichord, broadcast the same year as its French première; and another performance of *Cantigas*. Ohana was also a featured composer in an episode of 'The Music Magazine' (19.11.61) which had a distinctly Franco-Spanish flavour; a talk on Ohana's music by Rollo Myers illustrated by extracts from the *Llanto*, *Sonatine monodique* and *Sarabande* for harpsichord and orchestra was followed by an item on Bizet's *Carmen* by William Mann.[14] Rollo Myers was one of the first British critics correctly to assess the importance not only of Ohana but also of Dutilleux both in his broadcasts and his writings on French music during the 1960s and 1970s. The two later Ohana broadcasts of the 1960s were both of recordings, *Tiento* for guitar and *Cris* for 12 unaccompanied mixed voices, the latter broadcast in Britain less than a year after its world première in Berlin.

Following Glock's appointment as Controller of Music in 1959, the influence of his collaboration with Boulez is reflected in the explosion of coverage that the music of Messiaen and Boulez received both on the airwaves and in the concert-hall. Broadcasts of their music during the 1960s were not only far more numerous than those of Ohana, Dutilleux and most other living French composers, but included numerous repeat broadcasts of their most recent works. The influence of the Glock–Boulez collaboration naturally extended to the Proms. Boulez was first represented on 29 August 1961 with a performance of 'Une dentelle s'abolit', the second of the *Improvisations sur Mallarmé*.[15] (It is interesting to note that the 1961 season also included the Proms première of Debussy's orchestral *Images* !) The following season included the Proms première of *Le Marteau sans maître* and the first representation of Messiaen (24 August 1962) with performances of *Cinq rechants* and *Oiseaux exotiques* (with Alloys Kontarsky as soloist). Dutilleux was not represented at the Proms until 1989 when *Métaboles* was performed twenty-four years after its world première in January 1965 by the Cleveland Orchestra under Georg Szell. At the time of writing, no work of Ohana, or of Marius Constant, has yet been represented at the Proms.

The dangers of promoting too narrow a view of contemporary music were recognised sooner in France than in Britain. In 1954, the same year that Boulez founded what were to become the Concerts du Domaine musical, the composer and conductor Marius Constant co-founded the French Radio specialist music programme, France-Musique. Another stylistically independent figure who later wrote, 'in the 1960s, not to be a serialist was like having some shameful disease',[16] Constant considered it unhealthy to allow a single musical aesthetic to be viewed as entirely representative. In 1963, he founded the Ensemble Ars Nova specifically to counteract the influence of the Domaine musical and revive the more pluralist policies associated with French music broadcasting of the immediate post-war years. (1963 was also the year that Dutilleux resigned his position at French Radio in order to devote more time to his own composition.) With Constant as their artistic and musical director, the Ensemble Ars Nova became the official new music ensemble of French Radio and performed a wide spectrum of new music, including the serial as well as the non-serial. They provided an important platform for disseminating the music of composers belonging to the 'other' French avant-garde who would otherwise have found difficulty in reaching a wider audience. The recognition and standing Ohana achieved in France was due very largely to the frequent broadcasts of his music as well as many commissions he received from French Radio throughout his lifetime.

Ohana's estrangement from Boulez also affected the promotion of his music in the United States. Any resentment Dutilleux may have felt as a result of his exclusion from the programmes and commissions of the Domaine musicale must have been countered by the recognition he received in the United States comparatively early in his career. Ohana was less fortunate. The success of Dutilleux's First Symphony quickly attracted the attention of Charles Münch and undoubtedly led to the Koussevitsky Foundation commission for the Second Symphony, premièred in Symphony Hall Boston on 11 December 1959 by the Boston Symphony Orchestra under Charles Münch. Other American commissions and performances followed.[17] Ohana's reputation in North America took longer to overcome the handicap of being overlooked by Boulez. Only in the late 1980s and 1990s did his music begin to be more regularly performed, his vocal and dramatic works being among those creating the greatest impact. His only American commission was for the ballet *Sundown Dances*, premièred by the Erick Hawkins Ballet at the Kennedy Center in Washington DC in May 1991.

Ohana's music became known in Germany and other countries in northern Europe during the 1950s. His recognition in Italy followed in the 1960s when he was awarded several prizes for his services to music, including the Prix Italia in 1969. He received the Laurenzo de Medici Prize in Florence in 1986. Ironically, his work took longer to achieve recognition in Spain. Neither the music of Ohana, nor much contemporary music in general, was well regarded in the Spain of General Franco. Political tensions resulted in the voluntary expatriation of many of their leading composers and consequent cultural isolation from the rest of Europe. Roberto Gerhard left Spain for England during the Civil War, settling in Cambridge in 1940. (Both Ohana and Gerhard were British citizens, albeit for different reasons.) Although Gerhard's position as an expatriate has parallels with that of Ohana, they are not entirely comparable; Ohana's move to Paris in 1932 before the Civil War was for the purpose of training and education rather than the result of political necessity. Of Swiss parentage, Gerhard's cultural background shared some of the cultural complexities of Ohana's. Although Gerhard, like Ohana, incorporated Spanish idioms into his music he was essentially attracted to the serial techniques of Schoenberg, with whom he studied in the 1920s.

That Ohana based several works on texts of Federico García Lorca, including the gargantuan *Llanto por Ignacio Sánchez Mejías*, may well have contributed to the view that his music was politically undesirable and even subversive. The Spanish conductor Arturo Tamayo,[18] a student of the Madrid Conservatoire during the 1960s, has described how, when Ohana's music was performed, the concerts were always eagerly attended, particularly by young musicians who sought the thrill of hearing music which was both good and not officially approved.[19] Not only were students of the Conservatoire struck by the chromaticism and brutal simplicity of Ohana's setting of the *Llanto*, but the guitar concerto *Trois graphiques* caused a public scandal when it was first heard in Spain due to its dramatic dissimilarity from Rodrigo's *Concerto de Aranjuez*.[20] Like the *Llanto*, *Trois graphiques* has more in common with the sombre brutality of Picasso's *Guernica* than with any conventional, picturesque impressions of the Iberian peninsular. The political constraints of Franco's Spain prevented Ohana's music from being widely disseminated until after 1975, although by 1977 Ohana was described as: '... without doubt the most prominent figure of the Spanish School...' .[21] Although Tamayo has indicated that Ohana's music influenced several Spanish composers, including Luis de Pablo, he has suggested that his influence would have been very great had his music been more widely available before the late 1970s.[22] It is interesting to note that the Basque composer Félix Ibarrondo left Spain in the late 1960s to settle in Paris where he subsequently became a student of both Ohana and Dutilleux. The Spanish critic Enrique Franco has long admired Ohana's music[23] and may well have been instrumental in disseminating his work in Spain. Ohana's recognition in Spain was confirmed in 1982 when he was awarded the Ritmo Prize of Madrid for his services to contemporary music.

That Ohana's recognition centred chiefly in France, where he is still considered one of the leading composers of his generation, was as much sociopolitical accident as cultural choice on behalf of the composer. In France he has long been defined as a French composer.[24] In his interviews and writings Ohana always acknowledged the importance of French training, education and culture as influences on his creative development, as much as enabling forces in the realisation of his musical career. In a country where acceptance of the eclectic and fascination for the exotic approaches tradition itself, the apparent cultural complexity of Ohana's roots and music provides a gateway to the understanding of his music. In Anglo-Saxon countries where the underlying homogeneity of Ohana's cultural context is less familiar, the predilection for nationalistic programming has frequently been an obstruction to his promotion. That Ohana's music was regularly performed, broadcast and available on commercial recordings throughout his life-time is testimony to his success, as is the critical attention that he received from the 1960s onwards. (He was also able to live almost exclusively from his compositional income from the late 1950s.[25]) That his music continues to be performed and recorded is confirmation of his position as one of the most distinctive and original musical voices in French music of the second half of the twentieth century. Writing in 1994 at the inauguration of a major retrospective of Ohana's music designed to mark what would have been his 80th birthday[26], Jean Roy said: 'With the death of Maurice Ohana on 13 November 1992, one of the leading figures of twentieth century music has departed ... he leaves an oeuvre which exerts an ever-growing influence on young musicians and composers, as on the public, perhaps because it casts a new light on future paths in music ... . After Messiaen and Boulez, he will become one of the pivotal figures of French music of our time.'[27] Even accounting for the enthusiasm such retrospectives engender, the implication is not only that Ohana achieved considerable recognition during his life-time, but that his work has influenced, and will continue to influence, others. Ohana's own view of his place in twentieth century music was, understandably, more modest:

> In my place and none other! Just for one single reason: that I wrote the music I wanted to write and none other. I never lent an ear to anything that could sort of entice me into somebody else's wealth ... . Nothing but bringing a certain truth which now in our day still appears still [sic] as a contradiction because it doesn't follow the reigning fashions. But with time I think my music will be just integrated in the big flow and will not appear as contradictory as it does now.[28]

Although Ohana taught at various musical institutions in Paris during the 1960s and 1970s (cf. Chapter 1), he avoided fostering an 'Ohana School', the concept being profoundly alien to him (and also to Dutilleux). Despite always claiming that he never had pupils, there were many young composers (and pianists) who visited him regularly for musical consultation and advice.[29] He encouraged young composers to follow their own instincts even if their ideas appeared contradictory or unfashionable, his example being that of his own approach to composition:

> We need to be Socratic today: see what you have in front of you and what it wants to be.... follow your instincts. There is no hierarchy between the popular and the learned: there is only one music (even Furtwängler said that). Always encourage diversity and contradiction ... . If I was to hazard advice to young composers it would be: wander the planet with your ear and take heed of the unity of music and of man beyond particularisms, nationalisms and racisms... there is not only one way of enriching music: do what you want to do.[30]

Ohana considered music itself to be the best form of instruction and, in his characteristically enigmatic way, stated that he was not interested in composers but only in music which should exist on its own terms.[31] The theme permeates many of his interviews and writings: 'In my humble opinion, composers don't exist. All that exists is the music itself and the inner revelation that it is capable of stimulating.'[32] The poetic declaration of Paul Verlaine, 'de la musique avant toute chose',[33] applies as much to Ohana's creative objectives as to those of his spiritual father, Debussy. Ohana's view of music as a spontaneous phenomenon, appearing independently of anyone who may have created it, was also expressed in a talk he gave for French Radio on the occasion of the centenary of the birth of Erik Satie. Ohana's assessment of Satie reflects many of his own compositional ideals and recalls his highly personal concept of 'immemorial memory' (cf. Chapter 2):

> Situated outside time and, in a way, outside the space of his particular epoch, the works of Satie seem to represent a clearing in the forest of art where aestheticisms have been abolished and where music alone exists without any reference to its creator... an anonymous and supreme wisdom. The psychological content has been purified to the extent that, rather than attribute these works to an individual, they belong to a sort of collective instinct of the human race.[34]

Ohana is a composer not easily compartmentalised. In emphasising the originality of his music, the definition of his position merely as independent may be too simplistic. Like Dutilleux, Ohana disliked the term for its implicit suggestion of compositional isolationism. Dutilleux prefers the expression 'authentic' to account for stylistic awareness and sincerity of personal expression and included Ohana among a list of composers (the others being André Jolivet, Olivier Messiaen, Serge Nigg, Pierre Boulez and Marius Constant) who, for him, exemplified that 'single worthwhile criterion [in music]'.[35] While Ohana certainly developed a compositional language independent of the Austro-German tradition and the predominant trends of the immediate post-war years, it would be wrong to surmise that he had nothing in common with his contemporaries, was not innovatory, or did not belong to the compositional mainstream. Many parallels can be drawn between his music and that of others. His predilection for referential notes, approach to instrumental colourism and love of jazz parallels similar preoccupations in Dutilleux. Some aspects of Ohana's harmonic language and his approach to aleatory counterpoint recall certain techniques in Lutosławski. His concept of sound-mass densities also has parallels in Xenakis and Ligeti. His life-long fascination with mythology and symbolism has parallels in Berio and Messiaen, as well as in Jolivet and Varèse. Like Berio,

Ligeti, Boulez and others, Ohana explored a new means of writing for the voice, extended the range of instrumental, performance techniques, experimented with the electro-acoustic medium and considered new ways of coordinating formal structures. While Ohana's works incorporating pre-recorded electronic tape are comparably few, his investigations in this medium influenced his approach in other contexts, particularly the independence of rhythm, as distinct from other parameters, and his innovations in terms of the sound-mass. Ohana, like Stockhausen (and others), explored the spatial dimension of music and eschewed the conventional divisions between performers and audience, particularly in his music-theatre works. His contribution to music-theatre as a whole belongs to the broader avant-garde repertoire in this genre; like Berio, Ligeti and Nono, Ohana also defined a means of revitalising the operatic form in a contemporary context. Ohana's recourse to plainchant, techniques of the Middle Ages and Renaissance, to folk music and to various non-Western musical traditions are also common preoccupations of many composers of the second half of the twentieth century.

In his interviews and writings Ohana always drew attention to his compositional forbears, Chopin, Falla, Debussy, Stravinsky and Bartók in particular. He gave his own music cultural and historical context by indicating the importance not only of the various folk music traditions which he had experienced from his youth, but of plainchant and the Medieval and Renaissance vocal repertories which also profoundly influenced his compositional style. He acknowledged his indebtedness to the achievements of the past but sought only that music which would nourish his own, music of other styles and traditions being something he might admire from afar:

> I know that, like everyone, I should genuflect in front of Bach, but I will not do it. He is one of the musicians who has given me the least. I admire him from afar, as one admires the Himalayas but without going there.... Mozart is another Himalaya who does not touch me.[36]

His rejection of what he once called 'bossy' Austro-German composers was less the result of disliking the music than because it was culturally foreign[37]:

> He [Bach] is an imposing composer...but he is not the sort of skies or landscape that I want to watch when I have to recharge my batteries with music. I think German music as such is enormous. It's one of the most colossal monuments in the human treasure of culture .... What I object to is the irresistible temptation in [sic] German composers and German teachers and in everything that comes from Germany, to impose that music as the sole truth in our world of expression ... that is unbearable ... their music to me is a sort of illness which I am not willing to accept.... They [Schoenberg and Webern] have been great composers and achieved great things which I admire, but you don't feed a bird as you would a tiger or a lion ...' [38]

Ohana's view of other composers was idiosyncratic and playfully tongue-in-cheek, reflecting his own tastes and temperament more than conventional historical assessment or even geographical boundaries. He sometimes liked to categorise composers according to an imagined north-south divide.[39] Ohana's 'northerners' obey strict dogmatic or academic disciplines and are usually, although not exclusively, Teutonic. They include not only Mahler, Wagner, the 'frightful Richard Strauss'[40] and Schoenberg, but also Vincent D'Indy and Palestrina. His 'southerners' have more freedom, are instinctive, draw on more ancient musical traditions and are usually, although not exclusively, Mediterranean. They include not only Falla, Albéniz, Debussy, Monteverdi, Domenico Scarlatti and Machaut, but also Purcell, Bartók, certain Russian composers, and even Japanese theatre music.[41]

> ... We people from the south have got such a past, such an enormous pedigree of art, of achievement going back to the Altamira caves, or the Lascaux caves ... why should we submit to the dogmatic teaching of people who rarely achieved anything of the same sort even many of thousands of years later ? We are a very old race of artists and I think ... conventional boundaries do not exist. Purcell to me is a man from the South, he thinks in this way, he is a man of my family. So of course is Monteverdi, so is Scarlatti. But I wouldn't put Palestrina among them. It's more a trend, a way of approaching art which is instinctive primarily, rather than speculative or bound by a system. In other words just as Purcell, Scarlatti and Monteverdi are most unacademic, Palestrina is an academic composer.[42]

Even if Ohana's creative universe embraced more than the strictly Mediterranean, the rich diversity of his Spanish roots provided the initial stimulus for his birth as a composer. Although Spanish sources, musical, literary and artistic, predominate in the early works, the importance of Spanish musical traditions as a technical quarry in his music as a whole has sometimes been over-emphasised. In discussing his Spanish origins, he was always at pains to draw attention to the melting-pot of temperaments, cultures and creeds which they represent; from the Greek and Roman, Arabic and Jewish, Christian and Byzantine, to the north African Berber and Indian Gypsy.[43] Certainly a remark attributed to Jean Cocteau suggesting that 'to sing well, poets must sing in their genealogical tree' found resonance with Ohana.[44] It should not suggest that his music was merely derivative, or overshadow the broader, cultural reference which his Spanish heritage was able to stimulate. Ohana's instinctive eclecticism was a natural consequence of his origins and led spontaneously to the exploration of other traditions which he considered to share similar preoccupations, most importantly the spontaneity of improvisation and the expressive lyricism of the human voice.

Ohana's early works sowed the seeds of a compositional style that would become less overtly derivative. *Cantigas* and the *Etudes chorégraphiques* opened the path of his subsequent technical development perhaps more than the *Llanto* or even *Trois caprices*. In the early 1960s, Ohana turned away from obviously Spanish subjects to explore a more ancient world where incantation and ritual could be celebrated in some imagined, archaic landscape. First glimpsed in the *Quatre improvisations* and *Carillons,* a larger window was opened onto the world of Ohanian antiquity by the *Tombeau de Claude Debussy*, which marks a turning-point in Ohana's compositional direction.[45] Despite the importance of *Tombeau* as the first work to begin to realise the compositional lessons of Debussy, Ohana's compositional language was still in a state of flux during the early 1960s, hence the works of this period being designated 'transitional' rather than 'mature'; the main technical procedures did not become fully established until the middle 1960s, notably with *Signes* and the works of the Sigma Series which followed. On the threshold of his new style, the works composed between 1962 and 1965 reveal a progressive retrieval of other compositional threads; the medievalism of *Cantigas* and percussive textures of *Etudes chorégraphiques* are investigated further in *Cinq séquences*, while *Si le jour paraît...* returns to a Debussian sound-world that is coloured with mythological allusion and Goyesque sombreness. Certainly *Si le jour paraît...* incorporates a number of performance techniques associated with the Spanish guitar, including the 'rasgueado' and 'tambora', but these are absorbed into a broader musical vocabulary which is no longer exclusively Spanish. By the middle of the 1960s Ohana had found a means of incorporating diverse cultural references into a more homogenous and distinctive language which could fuse the African, Afro-Cuban, Spanish and even the Japanese with jazz, Negro spirituals and plainchant. He thus established one of his prime compositional objectives which was the recreation of the spontaneity of improvisation within the confines of a composed score. Apart from the 'Debla' movement in *Cris*, which alludes to the vocal lament of the Cante jondo, Ohana's music of the 1960s includes few overt references to Spanish subjects or material. In the works of the 1970s Spanish sources only occasionally come to the fore: in the chamber opera *Autodafé,* and first cello concerto *Anneau du Tamarít,* composed to commemorate the fortieth anniversary of the death of Federico García Lorca.

During the 1980s Ohana was occupied with the largest and perhaps most Spanish of all his works, the opera *La Célestine*.[46] As a result, Spanish colour and reference infused other works of the same decade, many of which include material re-worked in the opera: the Second String Quartet, several pieces from the *Douze études d'interprétation, Cadran lunaire,* the harpsichord pieces *Wamba* and *Conga, Kypris* and *Quatre choeurs* for children's voices which includes his own arrangement of a traditional Asturian lullaby.[47] Written at the end of the fifteenth century when Spain was on the threshold of its Golden Age, reputedly by Fernando de Rojas, the dialogue-novel[48] *La tragicomedia de Calisto y Melibea* (first edition 1499) is central to Spanish literature and culture. In Rojas, Ohana found the ideal vehicle for the expression of another of his main compositional preoccupations: music as a dramatic form unfolding an archetypal, tragic action in which the human voice predominates. The title of the opera refers to the main protagonist around whom the action pivots, the worldly, witch-cum-whore Celestina (Célestine) who procures the naive Melibea (Mélibée) for the Don Juan-like lover Calisto (Calyx). For Ohana, Celestina personified the last remnant of the old Spanish world prior to the Fall of Granada where Jews, Arabs and Christians lived together in peace.[49] The dawning of the new age, after the death of all the main characters, is confirmed through the addition of a tableau (not in Rojas) depicting the triumphant return of Christopher Columbus to Seville.

Ohana's opera is a synthesis of all the main themes of his creative world, historical, mythological, supernatural, sacred and profane and represents the culmination of his works in the dramatic genre. In the 1950s his affection for the traditional Spanish puppet theatre resulted in his adaptation of Lorca's *Le Guignol au gourdin*, as well as his own production of Falla's *Tréteaux de Maître Pierre*. While Ohana's radiophonic scores of the 1950s and 1960s provided a valuable opportunity for experimentation, his approach to the dramatic medium was enhanced by his discovery of Chinese Opera and traditional Japanese theatre, including the Noh, Bunraku and Kabuki forms. These explorations bore fruit in the 1960s and 1970s with *Syllabaire pour Phèdre*, *Autodafé*, *Office des oracles* and *Trois contes de l'Honorable Fleur* and culminated in *La Célestine*. In the operatic genre, it is interesting to note Ohana's most admired works: in addition to Debussy's *Pelléas et Mélisande*, they include Mussorgsky's *Boris Godunov*, Gershwin's *Porgy and Bess*, Bartók's *Duke Bluebeard's Castle*, Britten's *Peter Grimes*, Puccini's *La Bohème* and Verdi's *Falstaff*.[50] Ohana's admiration for *Falstaff*, in particular, may reflect his own affinity with Shakespeare; he used a French translation of lines from a Shakespeare sonnet at the end of *Autodafé*[51] and set the original English text of King Lear's lament on the death of Cordelia in *La Célestine* ('Déploration du Père'). As in Lear, Melibea's father enters with his daughter dead in his arms, Shakespeare's text being sung against a recitation of Rojas' Spanish text, perhaps to suggest that Shakespeare may have been influenced by the earlier Spanish masterpiece.[52] Another Shakespearean reference occurs in the final section of *La Célestine* where a succession of famous lovers, including Romeo and Juliet, Calisto and Melibea, Pelléas and Mélisande, Tristan and Isolde, silently cross the stage. Ohana also alludes to King Lear in a sub-section of the monodrama for bass and string trio, *Stream*.

With a composer as prolific as Ohana, unevenness is inevitable. Preferring to move on to a new work rather than spend much time on correction or revision (in contrast to Dutilleux who works slowly and is fastidious in making corrections and revisions) his output over more than forty-five years was considerable. However accomplished the achievement of *La Célestine* (and some of the other dramatic works), or universal the human themes which it presents, Ohana's music is at its most eloquent in the more tersely constructed works on which his reputation will surely rest.[53] These include not only contributions to the repertoires for piano, for guitar, for harpsichord, for percussion and for cello (orchestral and chamber) which are among his most frequently performed works, but also his music for diverse chamber ensembles. Apart from the concertos, the orchestral works *T'Harân-Ngô*, *Livre des prodiges* and the more lyrically expressive *Tombeau de Claude Debussy*, considered by Ohana to be his most preferred work,[54] are central to his compositional legacy.

Ohana's paramount achievement and most enduring monument must be his contribution to the vocal and choral repertoire, this music representing the central focus of his work throughout his compositional life-time and the key to understanding his creative world. From *Cantigas* to *Avoaha*, Ohana's vocal music, in particular that for female voices, contains personal and expressive statements of the most refined eloquence. His declared aim was to liberate the human voice, enriching its means of vocal expression, timbre and agility through the discoveries he made not only in folk music, including African choral singing and the flamenco, but also in different plainsong repertories, Mozarabic as well as Gregorian.[55] In 1993 Dutilleux contributed to a memorial publication about Ohana and wrote:

> ... with its vital angularity and brilliant colours, bathed in light sometimes bright and dazzling, sometime coolly moonlit, his [Ohana's] music, blossomed magnificently in his vocal and choral works and I am envious that he was able to adapt his personal style so well to the requirements of the human voice. I have in mind pages of his *Office des oracles*, *Lys de madrigaux* and the startling discoveries of the final section of *La Célestine*.[56]

The final section of *La Célestine* to which Dutilleux refers, 'Rituel de l'Oubli', is an epilogue to the opera as a whole; 'pianissimo' wordless vocalisations are sub-divided between all the leading soloists and chorus in a rich web of aleatory counterpoint, repeated ad libitum. A similar effect appears in *Nuit de Pouchkine*, at the end of *Office des oracles* and is translated into an instrumental medium at the end of *T'Harân-Ngô*. Following the gargantuan effort of the opera which occupied Ohana for five years, and despite increasing ill-health, the works of his last four years bear witness to an Indian Summer of compositional activity in which he completed some of his most sublime vocal music. In these works, he also rediscovered a means of incorporating recognisable text far more frequently than in the works of the 1960s and 1970s, although phonetic articulation remains an important means of melodic articulation. It is not insignificant that Ohana chose twelve unaccompanied voices for *Swan Song*, composed, while he was still able, as a requiem for his own death. The two outer movements, 'Drone' and 'Mambo', evoke Afro-Cuban incantations to ward off evil spirits and death, while the more personal, prayer-like inner movements, 'Eléis' and 'Epitaphe' are based on Negro spiritual melodies and set original English text by the composer. Inspired by a late poem by the 16th century French poet Pierre de Ronsard, *A son âme*, Ohana's text for 'Epitaphe' paraphrases that of Ronsard both in its use of Scottish diminutives and its tenderly ironic tone (see Ex. 9.1). Addressing his departed soul, Ohana hopes that his music will survive on its own merits, although his suggestion that he did not achieve the breadth of international recognition he undoubtedly deserved during his life-time is, in part, poetic exaggeration reflecting a disillusionment that became very great at the end of his life.

> O soulie, my wee Ohanie / My honoured guest too soon departed / Now gone down there / Into the Night unknown / away from music, away from love / From sunny noons and seas, /Away! / Moonlight pale, fast fading /Into the dark /Yet in silence and regret without / Of glories once deserved / That never crossed your sky. / You, who linger on my tomb / Dream awhile, then go your way / Forget my name, but mind my song. / It's yours/If sung with gallant love / In timeless vigil awake, / A star that never dims. / While I sleep.[57]

256   THE MUSIC OF MAURICE OHANA

Ex. 9.1: *Swan Song*, 'Epitaphe' (bars 1–8)

Ex. 9.2: *In Dark and Blue* (fig. 29–30)

Reproduced by kind permission of Société des Editions Jobert, Paris / United Music Publishers Ltd.

In 1990 Ohana completed his second commission from Rostropovich, for the cello concerto *In Dark and Blue*. Whereas Ohana's first cello concerto, *Anneau du Tamarit* of 1976 was written to the memory of Federico García Lorca, and concerned Spanish themes, his second concerto reflected his fondness for jazz and blues and paid homage to Louis Armstrong. The second main section beginning at fig. 29 which functions as an expressive interlude, bears the inscription 'Here's to you Satchmo!' What follows is almost pure blues (see Ex. 9.2). Although *In Dark and Blue* was premièred by Rostropovich with Seiji Ozawa conducting a Japanese youth orchestra, the first performance was not a success, owing to lack of rehearsal.[58] Ohana's disappointment was very great.[59] The recording made in 1997, five years after Ohana's death, with Arturo Tamayo conducting the Luxembourg Philharmonic Orchestra and Sonia Wieder-Atherton, is considered by many as the realisation of the work in its full glory and a more fitting swan song to Ohana's contribution to the orchestral medium.

Despite rapidly deteriorating health, following the discovery of cancer and a brain tumour, Ohana managed to complete his last work *Avoaha* in 1991. It was premièred only nine months before his death.[60] Scored for the forces dearest to him (mixed chorus, two pianos and percussion) *Avoaha* draws the poetic themes of his final years together. Alluding to the destructive powers of Spanish colonialism, the slaves of the New World are shown to possess the true spiritual freedom. Implicit in the succession of twelve movements is the quest for spiritual regeneration, a theme common not only in the symbolic paintings of 'Le Douanier' Rousseau but much of the Spanish literature of the Magic Realists.[61] Reputedly derived from Afro-Cuban combat ritual[62] and magical in its associations, the title *Avoaha* is intended to allude to various tribal practices which, it is interesting to note, are also evoked in the novels of Alejo Carpentier. Through a series of conjurations, lamentations, songs of praise and more abstract sound-landscapes, the effect is of an imagined ritual ceremonial. The last movement of Ohana's last musical statement refers to the mythical city of 'El Dorado'. The polyglot text includes Spanish, African, English and French, the last section written in English being the most personal: 'O my crazy forgotten land of promis'd joy, when I dream of you my dark blood chants', the last word being perhaps a pun of the French verb 'chanter' meaning 'to sing'. With melodic inflections recalling his love of Negro spirituals and with jazz and blues-like interpolations on the piano echoed by 'pianissimo' Afro-Cuban rhythmic interjections on skin percussion, Ohana's last musical statement is both a contemplative hymn in praise of the lyrical beauty of the human voice and an assertion, by implication, that therein lies the promised land and the greatest treasures of music.

Notes to Chapter Nine.

1. Ohana's prizes and awards are listed in Chapter 1.
2. Established in 1994, the biennial 'Prix Maurice Ohana' is alternately awarded to a pianist and composer on a competitive basis. It is presently administrated by the Association des Amis de Maurice Ohana and SACEM (Société des auteurs, compositeurs et éditeurs de musique). The prize is intended to encourage outstanding young composers and pianists. The Composition prize has so far been awarded to F. de Orador and Jean-Christophe Marti. The next prize is scheduled for 2001. The Piano prize has been awarded to Fabio Grasso and Ricardo Martinez Descalzo. The next prize is scheduled for 2000 and will be awarded through the Concours International du Piano du XX siècle at Orléans.
3. J. Roy, 'Henri Dutilleux', *Présences contemporaines, musique française* (Paris, 1962) p. 417.
4. H. Dutilleux, *Mystère et mémoire des sons - entretiens avec Claude Glaymann* (Paris, 1997) pp. 47–8.
5. H. Dutilleux, interview 'Dutilleux at 75' (with Roger Nichols), BBC Radio 3 (1991).
6. These issues have also been examined in C. Rae, 'Henri Dutilleux and Maurice Ohana: Victims of an Exclusion Zone', *Tempo* (April, 2000) pp. 22–30.
7. O.A.H. Schmitz, *The Land Without Music*, Eng. trans. H. Herzel (London, 1925).
8. F. Routh, 'Cause for Concern', *Contemporary British Music* (London, 1972) p. 372.
9. The files of composers, performers and broadcast schedules 1945–69 at the BBC Written Archive Centre, Caversham, Reading.
10. Reproduced in C. Rae, (2000) op. cit. p. 28.
11. See Chapter 1.
12. The two Boulez broadcasts were in March 1957 – the first British broadcasts of *Structures I* and *Le Marteau sans maître*, fresh from the Domaine musical. It is almost certain that Glock had an input into this promotion given that the same year Boulez appeared in two concerts for the ICA while Glock was still chairman.
13. *Bien cher Félix: Letters from Olivier Messiaen and Yvonne Loriod to Felix Aprahamian*, ed. and trans. N. Simeone (Cambridge, 1998).
14. The rather un-French first item was a short talk by Ernest Bradbury about the Huddersfield Choral Society.
15. The work received its UK première at the Dartington Summer School in 1959. 1961 was also the year of the Proms débuts of Geneviève Joy, Dutilleux's wife, (4.8.61) and Yvonne Lefebure (14.8.61).
16. 'Portrait - Marius Constant', *Salabert-Actuel*, No. 5 (Paris, 1987) pp. 11–12.
17. *Métaboles* (1964) was dedicated to Georg Szell who conducted the first performance with the Cleveland Orchestra in 1965. *Ainsi la nuit* (1976) was commissioned by the Koussevitsky Foundation. *Timbres, espaces, mouvement* (1978, rev.1990) was commissioned by Rostropovich for the National Symphony Orchestra (Washington). *L'Arbre des songes* (1985) was composed for Isaac Stern's 60th birthday but commissioned by French Radio (Lorin Maazel conducted the first performance in 1985). *Le jeu des contraires* (1988) was commissioned by the Friends of the Maryland Summer Institute for the Creative and Performing Arts, the University of Maryland International Piano Competition and the William Kapell Piano Competition. *The Shadows of Time* (1997) was commissioned by Seiji Ozawa (also the dedicatee) for the Boston Symphony Orchestra with whom he gave the first performance in March 1998.

18	Arturo Tamayo conducted the première of Ohana's opera *La Célestine* in 1988 and has recorded the *Piano Concerto* and *T'Harân-Ngô*. He is a committee member of the Association des Amis de Maurice Ohana.
19	'Entretien avec Arturo Tamayo' in *La Célestine* programme of the Opéra de Paris Palais Garnier (June, 1988) p. 63.
20	Ibid.
21	Christiane Le Bordays, *La musique espagnole* (Paris, 1977) p. 123.
22	'Entretien avec Arturo Tamayo' in *La Célestine* programme of the Opéra de Paris Palais Garnier (June, 1988) p. 63.
23	*Le Monde de la Musique Maurice Ohana musicien de soleil*, Cahier No. 2 (Paris, 1994) (special number devoted to Ohana) p. 18.
24	J. Roy cites Claude Rostand as well as Antoine Goléa in this respect, *Présences contemporaines musique française* (Paris, 1962) p. 385.
25	M. Ohana, 'Les paradoxes de la musique contemporaine', *Musique en Questions* (SACEM, Paris 1980) p. 9.
26	Ohana would have been 81 in 1994 but French publications continue erroneouslyto state 1914 as the year of his birth.
27	*Le Monde de la Musique* , (1994) op. cit. p. 3.
28	M. Ohana, interview (in English) R. Langham Smith (1993) p. 129.
29	Listed in Chapter 1.
30	M. Ohana, interview (in French), J.C. Marti (1991) p. 15.
31	M. Ohana, 'Comment la musique', *Diapason* (September, 1980) p. 42.
32	M. Ohana, interview (in French), J.C. Marti (1991) p. 15.
33	Verlaine's poem entitled *Art poétique*.
34	M. Ohana, text of a talk on Erik Satie broadcast on French Radio in December 1966 for the centenary of the composer's birth, reproduced in *La Revue musicale* Nos 391–3 (Paris, 1986) p. 177–9. Translation of the extract (p. 178) by the present author.
35	C. Potter, (1997) op. cit. p. 182.
36	M. Ohana, interview (in French), with F.B. Mache *La Revue musicale* Nos 214–15 (1978) p. 112.
37	M. Ohana, interview (in English), M. Oliver (1984).
37	M. Ohana, interview (in English), R. Langham Smith (1993) pp. 126–7.
39	M. Ohana, 'Sud-Nord', *20ème siècle: images de la musique française* , (SACEM papiers, 1986) pp. 164–7.
40	M. Ohana, interview (in English), R. Langham Smith (1993) p. 127.
41	M. Ohana (1986) op. cit.
42	M. Ohana, interview (in English), R. Langham Smith (1993) p. 124.
43	M. Ohana, 'La géographie musicale de l'Espagne', *Journal musical français* (March, 1956) p. 1.
44	M. Ohana, 'Entretien avec Maurice Ohana' *La Célestine* programme of the Opéra de Paris Palais Garnier (June, 1988) p. 59.
45	M. Ohana, interview (in French), J.C. Marti (1991) p. 9.
46	The subject of a major study by Marie-Lorraine Martin, *La Célestine de Maurice Ohana* (Paris, 1999).
47	Other traditional Spanish melodies and dance forms appear in *La Célestine*.
48	Defined as a 'novel in dialogue' by Leslie Byrd Simpson cf. his preface to his English trans., *The Celestina* (U. California Press, 1955).
49	'Entretien avec Maurice Ohana' *La Célestine* op. cit. p. 59.
50	M. Ohana, interview (in French), J.C. Marti (1991) p. 10.
51	Sonnet No.146.
52	According to Ohana, Shakespeare knew of The Celestina via the early sixteenth-century French translation by King François I. 'Entretien avec Maurice Ohana'

EPILOGUE: RECEPTION AND CONTEXT 261

La Célestine, op. cit. p. 60. An English translation (James Mabbe) did not appear until 1631.
53 Following the six performances of *La Célestine* in June 1988, the opera has (at the time of writing) been neither revived nor recorded. *Autodafé* has suffered a similar fate. *Syllabaire pour Phèdre, Offices des oracles* and *Trois contes de l'Honorable Fleur* have, however, achieved a more lasting success.
54 M. Ohana, interview (in French), J.C. Marti (1991), p. 9.
55 Ibid. p. 11.
56 H. Dutilleux, *Le monde de la musique,* (1994) op. cit. p. 18.
57 Text from 'L'Epitaphe', *Swan Song.*
58 The present author in conversation with the composer in Paris, December 1991.
59 Ibid. and conversations in April, 1992.
60 Profoundly distressed by his condition, Ohana withdrew almost completely during the summer of 1992.
61 Notably in Alejo Carpentier's *Los pasos perdidos* (1953) Eng. trans. H. de Onis *The Lost Steps* (London, 1956).
62 M. Ohana's programme note for the first performance.

List of Works

The following list of works is in chronological order, except for arrangements which are listed immediately after the original version. The chronology is taken from the date of completion, but where it is known that a work was composed over a period of years the span of dates have been given. The list includes published, unpublished, withdrawn and destroyed works, as well as such details as are known relating to the incidental music. Although during his lifetime the composer did not wish to have details of withdrawn or destroyed works included in documents designed for commercial or publicity purposes, it has been thought of value in the present study to include such details as are still available. Information concerning works no longer extant has been obtained from a combination of secondary sources including concert programmes, newspaper reviews, writings on the composer published early in his career and descriptive catalogues. During his last years, Ohana deposited the manuscripts of some of his hitherto withdrawn or unpublished works with Jobert and Billaudot. Such relocations have been indicated. In order to avoid the need for a separate discography, details of recordings have been included. The composer's archive is presently administrated by the Association des Amis de Maurice Ohana, 5 Rue Andrieux, Paris 75008 of which Madame Solange Soubrane is the President. The Honorary President, at the time of writing, is the Director of SACEM. (Members of the Honorary Committee include: S. Caillat, S. de Castro, C. Chaynes, R. Cluzel, M. Constant, F. Derveaux, F. Deval, H. Dutilleux, J. Gottlieb, R. Hayrabedian, Mme Georges-Jobert, Mme N. Lainé, D.-Lesur, A. Meunier, A. Moen, J-C. Pennetier, A. Ponce, C. Prey, Y. Prin, G. Reibel, J. Roy, A. Tamayo.) The abbreviations used are those of The New Grove Dictionaries with the additions indicated below:

1/3-tone zith.	zither tuned to 1/3 tone micro-intervals
chr. zith.	zither tuned chromatically in semitones
choreog.	choreographer
arr.	arranged

La joie et le bonheur (1938)
orch (inst. unknown). incidental music for a play by Ives Regnier
Publisher: destroyed

Les fêtes nocturnes (1938)
orchestral suite extracted from *La joie et le bonheur*
Première: Paris, 1938
Publisher: destroyed

La venta encantada (1940)
orch (instr. unknown) based on an episode from Don Quixote
Première: Concert du groupe Zodiaque 29 April 1949, Salle Gaveau, Paris
Performers: Orchestre d'André Girard, cond. André Girard
Publisher: withdrawn

Suite pour piano (1940)
I Prélude, II Vespérale, III Fanfare, IV Cadence, V Toccata
Première: 12 June 1948, Paris Concert du groupe Zodiaque
Performer: Massimo Bogianckino
Publisher: destroyed, except Toccata which was withdrawn

Enterrar y callar (1944)
for pf, became No. 1 of the *Trois caprices* in 1955.
Première: 12 June 1948, Paris, concert du groupe Zodiaque
Performers: Maurice Ohana
Duration: *c.* 5' 20"
Publisher: Billaudot
Recordings: Boite à Musique BAM LT 5020 Maurice Ohana (re-issue BAM LT 5863); CD–ARN 68091 Jean-Claude Pennetier

Sonatine monodique (1944–45)
for pf
I Allegretto; II Vif (jota); III Andante; IV Animé (allegro)
Première: October 1947, first Concert du groupe Zodiaque
Performer: Massimo Bogianckino
Duration: *c.* 12'
Publisher: Billaudot
Recording: Boite à musique BAM LT 5020 Geneviève Joy (re-issue BAM LT 5863)

Sarabande (1947)
for two pfs
Première: October 1947, first Concert du groupe Zodiaque
Performers: Maurice Ohana and Massimo Bogianckino
Duration: *c.* 8'

Publisher: withdrawn
Revised 1950, as a Concerto for hpd and orch (222/2100/perc/86442)
Publisher: unpublished
Recording: Club français du disque no. 23 Denyse Gouarne (hpchd), Orchestre des Centi Solo; re-issued Record Society RS22, Musidisc RC 697

Les amants du décembre (1947)
for female voice and pf
Text: Claudine Chonez
Première: October 1947, first Concert du groupe Zodiaque
Performers: Geneviève Touraine (voice) Maurice Ohana (pf)
Publisher: destroyed

Concerto pour cuivres, percussion et cordes (1947)
for orch (instr. unknown)
Première: French Radio, Paris 1947, Concert du groupe Zodiaque
Performers: Orchestre d'André Girard, cond. André Girard
Publisher: destroyed

Don Juan (1947)
incidental music for orch (instr. unknown) for adaptation [French translation] of Tirso de Molina's play *El burlador de Sevilla y convidado de piedra*, collaboration with Daniel-Lesur
Publisher: destroyed

Deux mélodies sur des poèmes de Lorca (1947)
for mez-sop and pf (arr. gui / hpd)
Text: Federico García Lorca (in French translation) Chanson de la goutte de pluie, Nana (berceuse), No. 4 of *Huit chansons espagnoles*, a collection drawn together from Ohana's unpublished song arrangements by Christine Prost
Première: 12 June 1948, Paris Concert du groupe Zodiaque
Performers: Geneviève Touraine, Maurice Ohana
Publisher: unpublished

Tango el mariquita (1947)
for mez-sop and pf
Text: Federico Garcìa Lorca
No. 7 of *Huit chansons espagnoles*, a collection drawn together from Ohana's unpublished song arrangements by Christine Prost
Première: 11 June 1994, Auditorium St. Germain, Paris
Performers: Sylvie Sullé, Jay Gottlieb
Publisher: unpublished

Alborada (in memoriam Encarnación López 'La Argentinita')
arrangement of popular Spanish song for mez-sop and pf
No. 8 of *Huit chansons espagnoles*, a collection drawn together from Ohana's unpublished song arrangements by Christine Prost. This song may have been arranged from an earlier Alborada composed in 1937.
Première: 11 June 1994, Auditorium St. Germain, Paris
Performers: Sylvie Sullé, Jay Gottlieb
Publisher: unpublished

Duo pour violon et piano (1947–48)
Première: January 1948, Paris, Concert du groupe Zodiaque
Publisher: destroyed

Trois poèmes de Sadi (1947–48)
for bar and orch (instr. unknown)
I La sagesse, II Ode à un chat, III Le guerrier
Text: from *Jardin des roses* Shekh Muslihu'd-Din Sadi (trans. F. Toussaint)
Première: 6 March, 1948, Paris, French Radio, Le Club d'essai
Performers: Yvon le Marc-Hadour, Orch. Radio-symphonique, cond. Jean Giardino
Publisher: withdrawn

La peste (1948)
for orch (instr. unknown)
'Musique radiophonique' for Dutilleux's 'illustrations musicales' at French radio
Adaptation of Camus' novel by Claudine Chonez
Commission: Henri Dutilleux.
Première: 31 October 1949, French radio
Publisher: unpublished

Le damné par manque de confiance (1948)
for orch (instr. unknown)
'Musique radiophonique' for Dutilleux's 'illustrations musicales' at French radio
Adaptation of Tirso de Molina's *El condenado por desconfiado* (in French translation)
Commission: French radio
Première: 1948, French radio
Publisher: unpublished

Paso (1948)
for pf (No.3 of **Trois caprices**)
Première: 12 June, 1948, Paris, Concert du groupe Zodiaque
Performer: Maurice Ohana
Duration: *c.* 5'
Publisher: Billaudot

Recordings: Boite à Musique BAM LT 5020 Maurice Ohana (re-issue BAM LD 5863); CD-ARN 68091 Jean-Claude Pennetier

Llanto por Ignacio Sánchez Mejías (1949–50)
bar, narr, female chorus (8-12 vv), orch (1121/2100/timp/3 perc/hpd/66442)
Dedicatee: Alain Bermat
I La cogida y la muerte; II La sangre derramada; III Cuerpo presente;
IV Alma ausente
Text: Federico García Lorca
Commission: Cercle Culturel du Conservatoire, 1949
Première: 22 May, 1950, Amphithéâtre Richelieu, La Sorbonne, Paris
Performers: Bernard Cottret (bar), Maurico Mohlo (narr), Orchestre du Conservatoire, cond. Georges Delerue
Duration: *c.* 39'
Publisher: Billaudot
Recordings: Club française du disque No.23 Bernard Cottret (baritone), Mauricio Molho (narr) Orchestre et Choeur des Cento Soli, cond. Ataulfo Argenta. (re-issued Musidisc 697, CD Accord Musidisc 202482); Distex LP4 Buenos-Ayres, Manuel Cuadros (bar), Rafael Alberti (narr) Orchestre et Choeur cond. Jacques Bodmer; Erato STU 71136 Michel Jarry (bar) José-Luis Gomez (narr) Ensemble et Choeur Ars Nova, cond. Théodore Guschlbauer; CD–Caliope CAL 9877 Lionel Peintre (bar), Rodolpho de Souza (narr), Ensemble vocal et instrumental Musicatreize, dir. Roland Hayrabedian (to be re-issued by Opus 111)

Les représentations de Tanit (1951)
ballet, choreog. Maurice Béjart
Commission: Maurice Béjart
Première: 1956, Casino d'Enghien, Belgium
Performers: Le ballet de Maurice Béjart (cond. no longer known)
Duration: *c.* 30'
Publisher: Pierre Noël, withdrawn; since relocated with Billaudot
Arr: orch. suite (inst. unknown), pf, both versions withdrawn

Monsieur Bob'le (1951)
for chamber orch (1110/0100/perc/pf/10111)
incidental music for the play by Georges Schéhadé
Commission: French radio
Première: 30 January 1951, Théâtre de la Huchette
Performers: Orch. d'André Girard, cond. André Girard
Publisher: unpublished
arr. 1951 as **Suite pour un mimodrame**
suite for chamb. orch. extracted from the incidental music
Commission: French radio
Première: 29 May 1951, Concert du Club d'Essai de la Radiodiffusion Française

Performers: Ensemble de la Radiodiffusion française, cond. Georges Delerue
Duration: *c*. 15'
Publisher: Pierre Noël, withdrawn; since relocated with Billaudot (Ohana prohibited all concert/stage performances)

Concertino pour trompette et orchestre (1952)
orch (instr. unknown)
three movements
Première: 1952, Radio Morocco
Duration: *c*. 18'
Publisher: Pierre Noël; withdrawn and destroyed

Cantigas (1953–54)
for sop, mez-sop, child, SATB (26vv), ensemble (0312/0230/timp/4 perc/pf (or org)
Texts: Medieval and Renaissance Spanish
  I Cantiga de los Reyes Magos, text: José de Valdivielso (dedicatee José Bergamín); II Cantiga del destierro, text: Fray Ambrosio Montesino (dedicatee Sergio de Castro); III Cantiga de Vela, text: Gonzalo de Berceo (dedicatee Rafael Alberti); IV Cantiga del azahar, text: King Alfonso 'el Sabio'; V Cantiga de la Noche Santa, text: Fray Ambrosio Montesino (dedicatees Isabel and Fernando Pereda); VI Cantiga del Nacimiento, text: Juan Alvarez Gato (dedicatee Octavio Paz)
Commission: Norddeutscher Rundfunk, Hamburg
Première: 6 February 1957, Norddeutscher Rundfunk, Hamburg
Performers: Norddeutscher Rundfunk chorus & orch, cond. Heinz Freudenthal
Duration: *c*. 28'
Publishers: Billaudot (originally Schott)
Recordings: Erato STU 70443 Isabel Garcisanz (sop) Ensemble et Choeur Ars Nova, cond. Marcel Couraud; Erato STU 70544 Choeur de l'ORTF and Ensemble Ars Nova, cond. Marcel Couraud; CD-Pierre Verany PV 787032 Choeur and ensemble contemporain d'Aix-en-Provence cond. Roland Hayrabedian (to be re-issued by Opus 111)

La soirée des proverbes (1953–54)
incidental music for Georges Schéhadé's play of the same title for wind and perc (1201/0100/perc)
Commission: Jean-Louis Barrault
Première: 30 January 1954, Petit Théâtre Marigny, Paris
Performers: Renaud-Barrault theatre company, prod. J.L. Barrault, cond. Pierre Boulez
arr. 1954 for fl and perc
Publisher: unpublished (both versions)

Tableaux de l'héroïne fidèle (1954)
female and male solo voices, chorus, orch. (instr. unknown)
'Musique radiophonique' for Dutilleux's 'illustrations musicales' at French radio and also produced as a theatre work but details no longer extant.
Adaptation by Ohana of a tale from the Andalusian Romancero
Commission: French radio
Première: 1954, French radio, Paris
Duration: *c*. 1hr 10'
Publisher: destroyed

Hommage à Luis Milán (1954)
for pf (No.2 of **Trois caprices**)
Première: Maurice Ohana, in the 1955 recording below
Duration: *c*. 3'
Publisher: Billaudot
Recordings: Boîte à Musique BAM LT 5020 Maurice Ohana (re-issue BAM LD 5863); CD-ARN 68091 Jean-Claude Pennetier

Trois caprices (1954)
for pf
I Enterrar y callar, II Hommage à Luis Milán, III Paso
Duration: 13' 20"
Première complete: for 1955 recording by the composer BAM LT 5020
Publisher: Billaudot
Recording: CD-Arion ARN 68091, Jean-Claude Pennetier

La chanson du marin (1954)
incidental music (instr. unknown) for play of the same title by Georges Schéhadé
Commission: Jean-Louis Barrault theatre company
Première: 1954, Théâtre Marigny, Paris
Publisher: destroyed

Paso, Solea (1954)
for orch (instr. unknown)
ballet, choreog. Françoise Dominique
Commission: Opéra de Lyon
Première: 1954–55 season, Opéra de Lyon
Duration: *c*. 26'
Publisher: withdrawn

Deux dances - Tiento et Farruca (1954)
for solo perc (2 players)
Publisher: unpublished

Etudes chorégraphiques (1955)
for solo perc (4 players)
ballet choreog. Dore Hoyer
Commissioned: Norddeutscher Rundfunk and Hamburg State Opera, Dore Hoyer
Not premièred in this version, commission abandoned
arr. 6 players 1961–3
Commission: Groupe instrumental de percussions de Strasbourg, Ballet Municipal de Strasbourg
Ballet: choreog. Manuel Parrès
Première: 8 June 1963, Festival de Strasbourg
Performers: Ballet municipal de Strasbourg, Les Percussions de Strasbourg
Duration: *c.* 15'
Publisher: Schott
Recordings: Philips 836 990 DSY Les Percussions de Strasbourg (re-issue PH2 6718040) Grand Prix du Disque de l'Académie Charles Cros; Classic Produktions Osnabrück CD-CPO999 088-2 Cabaza Percussion Quartet; Philips CD PH442218-2 Les Percussions de Strasbourg

Les hommes et les autres (1956)
chr.zith, 1/3-tone zith., chamber ensemble (instr. unknown)
'Musique radiophonique' for Dutilleux's 'illustrations musicales' at French radio
Adaptation of Elio Vittorini's play *Uomini e no* by Alain Trutat.
Commission: French radio
Première: 1956 French radio broadcast
Duration: *c.* 22'
Publisher: unpublished

Médée (1956)
chamber ensemble (instr. unknown)
'Musique radiophonique' for Dutilleux's 'illustrations musicales' at French radio
Adaptation of Seneca by José Bergamín (in French translation)
Commission: French radio
Première: 1956 French radio broadcast
Publisher: unpublished

Images de Don Quichotte (1956)
chamber ensemble (1211/1100/2perc/pf/hpd/gui/vn/va/vc)
'Musique radiophonique' for Dutilleux's 'illustrations musicales' at French radio
Adaptation of Cervantes by Alexandre Arnoux, prod. Bronislaw Horowicz
Commission: French radio
Première: 1956 French radio broadcast; BBC radio broadcast Third Prog. 11.11.1957
Duration: *c.* 20'
Publisher: unpublished

Recording: Philips PH 0030 Compagnie Grenier-Hussenot, cond. Daniel Chabrun

Le Guignol au gourdin (1956)
ensemble (2101/0200/2 perc/pf/hpd/gui/vn/va/vc/db)
'Musique radiophonique' for Dutilleux's 'illustrations musicales' at French radio
Adaptation of Lorca's play *Tragicomedia de Don Cristobal y la seña Rosita* by Ohana
Commission: French radio
Première: 1956, Club d'Essai de la Radiodiffusion Française broadcast
Duration: *c.* 19' 25"
Publisher: unpublished
arr. 1958 as music-theatre (for puppets) for sop, bar, male chorus (6vv) ensemble (1211/0100/2perc/pf/hpd/22221)
Commission: Festival de Carcasonne
Première: Festival de Carcasonne July 1958, prod. Maurice Ohana, cond. Serge Baudo
Duration: *c.* 1hr 15'
Publisher: unpublished, since deposited with Billaudot

Prométhée (1956)
orch (2211/2210/3 perc/pf/66442)
Ballet: choreog. Maurice Béjart, scenario Pierre Rhallys
Commission: Festival de Lyon-Charbonnières
Première: July 1956, Festival de Lyon-Charbonnières. (1963–4 season repertoire Théâtre de la Monnaie, Brussells, Ballet of the 20th Century dir. Béjart)
Duration: *c.* 30'
arr. concert suite 1958
Première: NDR Hamburg, Orch NDR cond. Jean Martinon
Publisher: withdrawn, since deposited with Billaudot but Ohana prohibited all concert performances.

Tiento (1955–57)
gui (arr. hpd)
Commission: Narciso Yepes
Première: 1961, Paris
Performer: Narciso Yepes
Duration: *c.* 4' 30"
Publisher: Billaudot (arr. for hpd unpublished)
Recordings: Voix de son Maître CVB 2178 Oscar Ghiglia; DG139366 Narciso Yepes; CBS 30A064 Alberto Ponce; Barclay BAR 991031 Michel Dintrich; RCA RL 45548, RCA RS9014-5 Julian Bream; CD-Auvidis Astrée 8513 Stephan Schmidt

Fuentovejuna (1957)
SATB, wind and perc
incidental music for Lope de Vega's play
Première: 1957 Montauban Festival, cond. Louis Auriacombe
Publisher: unpublished

Goha (1957)
(instr unknown)
incidental music for a film dir. Jacques Baratier, scenario Georges Schéhadé
Publisher: unpublished

Trois graphiques (1950–57)
concerto for gui and orch (2222/2200/timp/4perc/88662)
Commission: Narciso Yepes
Dedicatee: Narciso Yepes
I Graphique de la Farruca et Cadences
II Improvisation sur Graphique de la Siguiriya
III Graphique de la Bulería et Tiento
Première: London, Radio broadcast BBC Third Programme, 20 November 1961
Performers: Narciso Yepes, London Symphony Orchestra cond. Anthony Bernard
Duration: *c*. 21' 16"
Publisher: Amphion-Durand
Recordings: Deutsche Grammophon DG 2530585 Narciso Yepez, London Symphony Orchestra cond. Raphael Fruhbeck de Burgos; Decca SLX 20515 Narciso Yepez, Orchestre Nacional d'España cond. Rafael Fruhbeck de Burgos; Arion ARN 38240 Alberto Ponce, Orchestre Philharmonico del Prado, cond. Daniel Chabrun

Farruca (1958)
hpd or gui
Publisher: withdrawn

Le Romancero du Cid (1958)
orch (instr unknown)
incidental music for a play by Alexandre Arnoux
Publisher: withdrawn

Recit de l'an Zéro (1958–9)
dramatic oratorio based on an allegorical poem by Georges Schéhadé
ten, bas, child, narr, SATB (16vv), ensemble (0211/0000/4perc/pf/ 1/3-tone zith/44321)
I Les Mages; II La chambre d' hôtel; III La Polka
Commission: French radio
Première: 11 April 1959, Paris

Performers: Gérard Friedman (ten) André Vessières (bas), Habib Benglia (narr)
orch de l'ORTF, cond. Daniel Chabrun, prod. Alain Trutat
Duration: *c*. 38'
Publishers: Billaudot

Le songe d'une nuit d'été (1959)
(inst. unknown)
incidental music for Shakespeare's play, adapt. Georges Neveu
Commission: French radio
Première: 1959 French radio broadcast
Publisher: withdrawn

Homère et Orchidée (1959)
solo 1/3-tone zith
incidental music for text by Bronislaw Horowicz
Commission: French radio
Première: 1959 French radio broadcast
Publisher: withdrawn

La Blessure (1960)
fl, 1/3-tone zith, pf, perc
incidental music for a film based on a novel by P. Moinot, dir. Edmond Lévy
publisher: unpublished

Chanson de toile (1960)
ensemble (instr. unknown)
incidental music for stage adaption of Tristan and Isolde legend by Yves Joly
    Puppet theatre; lib. Raphaël Cluzel
Publisher: withdrawn

Les dents du singe (1960)
chamber orch (inst. unknown)
incidental music for cartoon film by René Laloux
publisher: unpublished
Part of this score was reworked in **Tombeau de Claude Debussy**

La route qui poudroie (1960)
ensemble (1110/0000/perc/pf/1/3-tone zith/ vn.vc)
'Musique radiophonique' for Dutilleux's 'illustrations musicales' at French radio
Based on a text by Anne Marie Bauer, adapted by P.Barbier
Commission: French radio
Première: 1960 French radio broadcast
Duration: *c*. 15' 30"
Publisher: unpublished

Carillons pour les heures du jour et de la nuit (1960)
for hpd
Commission: Antoinette Vischer
Dedicatee: Antoinette Vischer
Première: 1961, French radio, Paris
Performer: Robert Veyron-Lacroix
Duration: *c.* 7'
Publisher: Billaudot
Recording: Erato STU 70513 Robert Veyron-Lacroix; CD–Erato MF 2292-45699-2, Elisabeth Chojnacka

Quatre improvisations (1960)
for fl
Dedicatee: Jean-Pierre Rampal
Première: 1962, French radio, Paris
Performer: Jean-Pierre Rampal
Duration: *c.* 7'
Publisher: Billaudot
Recording: ORTF Barclay BAR 995018, Michel Debost, awarded Prix de l'Académie du disque Français

Histoire véridique de Jacotin qui épousa la sirène des océans (1960–61)
5 singers, 2 narr, chamber orch (1111/0100/perc/1/3-tone zith/66442)
'Musique radiophonique' for Dutilleux's 'illustrations musicales' at French radio
Text [in French] by Camilo José Cela based on *Petit retable de Don Cristobal*
prod. Alain Trutat
Commission: French radio (Henri Dutilleux)
Première: 1961 Radiodiffusion Française cond. Daniel Chabrun
Awarded the Prix Italia in 1961
Duration: *c.* 35'
Publisher: unpublished but since deposited with Jobert
revised 1990 as **Le mariage sous la mer** a chamber opera for young performers
Commission: Conservatoire National de Région Boulogne-Billancourt, SACEM, Ministère de la Culture et de la Communication, Direction Régional des Affaires Culturelles d'Ile de France
Première: 18-19 April 1991, Conservatoire National de Région Boulogne-Billancourt
Performers: Solistes de l'Atelier Lyrique du CNR et de la Maîtrise de Versailles, Choeur d'enfants de la classe de CMI de l'école Castéja, ensemble instrumental 3e cycle, cond. Yves Lestang, prod. Antoine Campo, choreog. Nadine Praddaude
Duration: *c.* 50'
Publisher: unpublished but since deposited with Jobert

Tombeau de Claude Debussy (1961–62)
sop, pf, 1/3-tone zith, orch (1111/1100/6 perc/cel./66442)
Commission: French radio for Debussy Centenary
Dedicatee: Henri Dutilleux
I Hommage; II Soleils; III Ballade de la Grande Guerre; IV Autres soleils;
  V Miroir endormi; VI Rose des vents et de la pluie; VII Envoi
Première: 27 December 1962, French radio, Paris
Performers: Geneviève Roblot (sop), Monique Rollin (zith), Christian Ivaldi (pf)
  Orch. Philharmonique de l' ORTF, cond, André Girard
Première (concert performance): 4 January 1966, Théâtre des Champs-Elysées,
  same soloists and orch as above but cond. Charles Bruck.
Duration: c. 31'
Publisher: Amphion-Durand
Recording: Timpani CD-1C1044, Sylvie Sullé (sop), Christian Ivaldi (pf) Laure
  Morabito (zith), Orchestre Philharmonique de Luxembourg, cond. Arturo
  Tamayo

Cinq séquences (1963)
for str quartet
I Polyphonie; II Monodie; III Tympanum; IV Déchant; V Hymne
Première: 9 November 1964, Paris (also at 1964 Mexico Festival, Mexico City)
Performers: Quatuor Parrenin
Duration: c. 17'
Publisher: Jobert

Hélène (1963)
female chorus, ensemble (1110/0000/perc/1/3-tone zith/vn/va/vc)
'Musique radiophonique' for Dutilleux's 'illustrations musicales' at French radio
Adaptation of Euripides, trans. Gabriel Audisio
Commission: French radio
Première: 1963 French radio broadcast
Publisher: unpublished

Si le jour paraît... (1963–64)
for 10-string gui, (arr for 6 string gui)
I Temple (dedicatee Alberto Ponce); II Eneug; III Maya-Marsya (in memoriam
  Ramón Montoya); IV 20 avril (Planh); V La chevelure de Bérénice
  (dedicatee Ivo Malec); VI Jeu des quatre vents (dedicatee Ruiz Pipó);
  VII Aube
Première (complete): 28 June 1974, La Rochelle Festival
Performer: Alberto Ponce
Duration: c. 25'
Publisher: Billaudot (each piece also available separately)
Recordings: Arion ARN 31953, Arion 30S150, Arion 38240 Alberto Ponce;

(partial - Deutsche Grammophon DG 2530307 Leo Brouwer); CD-Auvidis Astrée 8513, Stephan Schmidt

Les Héraclides (1964)
for SATB, wind-band, pf, 1/3-tone zith, perc
'Musique radiophonique' for Dutilleux's 'illustrations musicales' at French radio
Adaptation of Euripides, trans. Gabriel Audisio
Commission: French radio
Première: 1964 French radio broadcast
Duration: *c.* 35'
Publisher: unpublished

Iphigénie en Tauride (1965)
for sop, mez-sop, con, ten, bar, bas, pf, 1/3-tone zith, perc
'Musique radiophonique' for Dutilleux's 'illustrations musicales' at French radio
Adaptation of Euripides, trans. Gabriel Audisio
Commission: French radio
Première: 1965 French radio broadcast
Duration: *c.* 45'
Publisher: unpublished

Neumes (1965)
for ob and pf
Commissioned: Paris Conservatoire, competition test piece
Première: 1965 'concours', Conservatoire de Paris (CNSM)
Duration: *c.* 8'
Publisher: Amphion-Durand
Recording: Caliope CAL 1816 René Daraux (ob.) Françoise Bonnet (pf.)

Signes (1965)
for fl, (picc), zith, (chr. and 1/3-tone) pf and perc (4 players)
Dedicatees: Michel Debost, Christian Ivaldi, Pierre Urban
Première: 23 May 1965, Mai Musical de Bordeaux
Performers: Michel Debost (fl.), Christian Ivaldi (pf.) Pierre Urban (zithers), Ensemble Ars Nova, cond. Marius Constant
Duration: *c.* 20'
Publisher: Amphion-Durand
Recordings: Erato STU 70443 Michel Debost (fl), Christian Ivaldi (pf) Monique Rollin (zith) Jean-Paul Drouet, Sylvio Gualda, Boris de Vinogradov, Geston Sylvestre (perc), dir. Marius Constant; (issued also on Musicipal Heritage Society 1087); CD-Erato MF2292-45503-2 Ensemble Ars Nova, dir. Marius Constant

Synaxis (1965–66)
concerto for 2 pfs, perc (4 players), orch (3343/4331/timp/4perc [excl. soloists]/ 2hp/1/3-tone zith/ 18.16.14.12.8)
Dedicatees and Commission: Groupe instrumental de percussions de Strasbourg
I Diaphonie; II Tympanum; III Sibile [sic]; IV Tropes; V Clameur; VI Organum; VII Antiphonie; VIII Maya
Première: 1966, Valdagno, Italy. Marzotto Prize concert
Performers: Geneviève Joy, Christian Ivaldi (pfs), Les Percussions de Strasbourg, Orch. du Prix Marzotto, cond. Ettore Gracis
Duration: *c.* 21'
Publisher: Amphion-Durand
Recording: Erato STU 70431 Geneviève Joy, Christian Ivaldi (pfs), Les percussions de Strasbourg, Orch. Philharmonique de l'ORTF cond. Charles Bruck

Hippolyte (1966)
sop, mez-sop, SATB, pf, hpd, chr-zith, 1/3-tone zith, perc
'Musique radiophonique' for Dutilleux's 'illustrations musicales' at French radio
Adaptation of Euripides, trans. Gabriel Audisio
Commission: French radio
Première: 1966 French radio broadcast
Publisher: unpublished

Syllabaire pour Phèdre (1966–7)
chamber opera based on Euripides
sop, mez-sop, 2 narr, SATB (12vv), ensemble (chr-zith, 1/3-tone zith, pf, hpd, hp, 4 perc, tape)
Dedicatee: Marius Constant
Libretto: Raphaël Cluzel
Prologue; Parodos; Episode I; Stasimon; Episode II; Epilogue
Première: 5 February 1968, Théâtre de la Musique, Paris
Performers: Solistes et chorale de Maurice Ravel de l'ORTF, Ensemble Ars Nova, cond. Marius Constant
Duration: *c.* 31'
Publisher: Jobert
Recordings: Erato STU 70443 Mady Mesplé (sop), Jean Marais (narr), solistes et choeur de l'ORTF, Ensemble Ars Nova, cond. Marius Constant; CD-Caliope Caliope CAL 9877 Marie-Françoise Lefort (sop) Felicitas Bergmann (mez-sop) Ensemble vocal et instrumental Musicatreize, dir. Roland Hayrabedian (to be re-issued by Opus 111)

Chiffres de clavecin (1967–68)
concerto for hpd, orch (1121/2110/3perc/hp/66442)
Dedicatee: Elisabeth Chojnacka

I Contrepoints – Déchant – Choral; II Déflagrations – Passacaille – Chaos d'accords; III Etoiles – Nuées; IV Colonnes – Volutes; V Cadence – Echos – Rumeurs
Première: 8 June 1969, La Chaux-de-Fonds, Switzerland
Performers: Elizabeth Chojnacka, L' Orchestre de chambre de Lausanne, cond. Jean-Claude Casadesus
Duration: c. 19'
Publisher: Jobert
Recordings: Erato STU 71548 Elisabeth Chojnacka, Nouvel Orchestre Philharmonique de Radio France, cond. Stanislaw Skrowaczewski; (re-issued Erato MF 2292-45699-2); Timpani, CD 1C1044, Elisabeth Chojnacka, Orchestre Philharmonique du Luxembourg cond. Arturo Tamayo (to be re-issued by Opus 111)

Sibylle (1968)
for sop, perc, tape (created by the composer)
Dedicatee: Isabel Garcisanz
Première: 5 May 1970, Atelier de Création Radiophonique de l'ORTF, Paris
Performers: Isabel Garcisanz (sop) Bernard Balet (perc), B. Leroux & G.N. Guyen (tape realisation)
Duration: c. 17'
Publisher: Jobert (tape also deposited with Jobert)
Recordings: Barclay BAR 995018 Isabel Garcisanz (sop), Bernard Balet (perc); (re-issued Musique Française d'Aujourd'hui CD-MFA ADES14.122-2)

Cris (1968–69)
for unaccompanied choir SATB (12vv)
Commission and Dedicatee: Marcel Couraud & solistes des choeurs de l'ORTF
I Générique; II Délirante; III Debla; IV Mémorial 44; V Slogans
Première: 1 February 1969, Berlin
Performers: Choeur de l' ORTF, cond. Marcel Couraud
Duration: c. 17' 30"
Publisher: Jobert
Recording: Erato STU 70544 Choeur de l' ORTF dir. Marcel Couraud

Silenciaire (1969)
concerto for perc and str (6 perc/33221)
Dedicatees: Jeanne and Norbert Pierlot
Commission: Lucerne Festival Strings
Première: 6 September 1969, Chateau de Ratilly, Lucerne Festival
Performers: Groupe instrumental des Percussions de Strasbourg and Lucerne Festival Strings, cond. Rudolph Baumgartner
Duration: c. 18' 20"
Publisher: Jobert
Recording: ORTF Barclay 995018 Les Percussions de Strasbourg, Ensemble

instrumental cond. Daniel Chabrun, awarded Prix de l'Académie du disque Français; Timpani CD 1C1044 Orchestre Philharmonique du Luxembourg cond. Arturo Tamayo.
Documentary: The rehearsals and first performance were recorded for a 1971 documentary film by Paul Seban entitled 'Maurice Ohana: Le Silenciaire' in which Ohana explains his conception of the work.

Stream (1970)
for bas, vn, va, vc
Commission and Dedicatees: Mario Haniotis, Trio de Cordes de Paris
Première: 21 January 1971, Angers
Performers: Mario Haniotis, Trio de Cordes de Paris (Charles Frey, David Bender, Jean Grout)
Duration: *c.* 16'
Publisher: Salabert

Syrtes (1970)
for vc and pf
Commission and Dedicatee: Mstislav Rostropovich
Première: 15 March 1972, Espace Cardin, Paris
Performers: Mstislav Rostropovich and Maurice Ohana
Duration: *c.* 16'
Publisher: Jobert

Sorôn-Ngô (1969–71)
for two pfs
Commission and Dedicatees: Geneviève Joy - Jacquéline Robin-Bonneau Duo
Première (1st version, 1970)): 25 Anniversary concert of the Joy-Robin Duo, 17 December 1970, Salle Gaveau, Paris
Performers: Geneviève Joy and Jacquéline Robin-Bonneau
Revised 1970–71 (extended beyond fig.12)
Première: 22 June 1971, Festival d'Aix-en-Provence (same performers)
Duration: *c.* 21'
Publisher: Jobert
Recording: Erato STU 70810 Geneviève Joy, Jacquéline Robin-Bonneau (pfs)

Autodafé (1971–72)
dramatic cantata for 3 choral groups SATB, ensemble (2121/2230/6 perc/pf/hp/tape), narr, puppets, 2 conductors
Text: by Ohana (multi lingual incl. French, English, Spanish, German)
Commission: Ministère des Affaires Culturelles, Choralies de Vaison-la-Romaine, Mouvement à Coeur Joie.
Première: 9 August 1971, Les Choralies, Théâtre ancien de Vaison-la-Romaine
Performers: L'ensemble vocal Musique Nouvelle, Les Percussions de Strasbourg, cond. Stéphane Caillat and Boris de Vinogradov

Publisher: withdrawn
Revised as chamber opera 1972
4 sop, 3 mez-sop, cont, 3 bar, bas, 2 narr (male and female), child, 3 choral groups SATB (I-12vv; II-32vv; III 60-80vv), tape, orch (2121/2230/5 perc/pf/hp/elec. gui/2221), mimes, puppets, shadow theatre
Prologue; Episode I '93'; Stasimon I; Episode II – 'Vitrail'; Episode III – 'Batouque, Són'; Stasimon II; Episode IV – 'Apocalypse de Saint-Loup (1914–1918)'; Parodos; Stasimon III; Episode V – 'Saturnale-musée nocturnel'; Stasimon IV; Episode VI – 'No pasarán'; Episode VII – 'Leçon des ténèbres-Caprichos'; Episode VIII – 'Mayas'; Epilogue
Commision: Opéra de Lyon
Première: 23 May 1972 Opéra de Lyon (8 performances 23 May to 4 June)
Performers: Soloists and chorus of Opéra de Lyon, prod. Jean Aster & Louis Erlo, Yves Joly Puppet Theatre, Orch. Philharmonique Rhône-Alpes, conds. Théodore Guschlbauer, Claire Gibault, prod. Jean Aster, Louis Erlo, Electro-acoustic realisation Gilles Fresnais
Duration: *c.* 1hr 20'
Publishser: Jobert
Recording: (excerpt only) ' Strophe' REM 311294XCD, Marie Kobayshi (mez-sop) Ensemble Triton

Sarc (1972)
for ob
Commission and Dedicatee: Jacques Vandeville
Première: 1 January 1973, French radio, France-Culture, Paris (Maison de l'ORTF)
Performer: Jacques Vandeville
Duration: *c.* 5'
Publisher: Billaudot

24 Préludes (1972–73)
for pf
Première (incomplete): 17 April, 1973, Festival de Royan
Performer: Gérard Frémy
Première (complete): 20 November 1973, Espace Cardin, Paris
Performer: Jean-Claude Pennetier
Duration: *c.* 42'
Publisher: Jobert
Recording: Arion ARN 38261 Jean-Claude Pennetier; CD-Arion ARN 68091, Jean-Claude Pennetier

T'Harân-Ngô (1973–74)
orch (3343/4431/timp/4perc/pf/2hp/16.14.12.10.8)
(conjuration, contemplation, glorification des forces premières de la Nature)

'Astres – lumière et nuit, Le feu – la terre, Les moissons et les arbres, L'air et l'eau – le silence et l'absence'
Commission: Orchestre national de Radio France
Première: 8 October 1975, Grand Auditorium de Radio France, Paris
Performers: Orchestre National de Radio France cond. Lucas Vis
Duration: *c.* 18'
Publisher: Jobert
Recording: Timpani 1C1039 M7 865 Orchestre Philharmonique du Luxembourg, cond. Arturo Tamayo

Office des oracles (1974)
music-theatre for 3 vocal groups (I, 2 sop, mez-sop, alt; II, SATB 32–40 vv; III, SATB 16 vv) ensemble (2020/0130/3perc/pf/org/vn/va) mimes, dancers and 3 conductors
Commission: J-P Armengaud, Président des Fêtes Musicales de la Sainte-Baume
Dedicatee: Boris de Vinogradov
I Alpha; II Oniracle; III Dragon à trois têtes; IV Minotaure aux miroirs; V Son Changó; VI Météoracle; VII Tarots; VIII Interrogation des oiseaux; IX Ecriture automatique; X Oroscope; XI Pythié; XII Oméga
Première: 9 August 1974, Fêtes Musicales de la Sainte-Baume
Performers: Jocelyne Taillon (contralto), Claude Meloni (baritone), l'Atelier Vocal, Ensemble instrumental de l' Itinéraire, conds. Boris de Vinogradov, Jean-François Monnot, Jean-Claude Pennetier, choreog. Wess Howard. (revived for Festival d'Avignon August 1975 and Festival Saintes Abbaye aux Dames July 1978)
Duration: *c.* 40–44'
Publisher: Jobert
Recording: CD Opus 111 OPS30246, Ensemble Musicatreize et Choeur Contemporain d'Aix-en-Provence, cond. Roland Hayrabedian; Excerpt 'Pythié' REM 311294XCD, Marie Kobayshi (mez-sop) Ensemble Triton

Sacral d' Ilx (1975)
for hpd, ob, hn
Dedicatee: Harry Halbreich
Commission: Festival international d'art contemporain de Royan
Première: 23 March 1976, Festival international d'art contemporain de Royan
Performers: Elisabeth Chojnacka (hpd), Jacques Vandeville (ob), Gilles Mahaud (hn)
Duration: *c.* 13'
Publisher: Jobert
Recording: CD-Erato MF 2292-45699-2 Jacques Vandeville (ob), Jens Mc Manama (hn) Elisabeth Chojnacka (hpd)

Noctuaire (1975)
for vc and pf
Commission: Ecole nationale de Musique de Boulogne-Billancourt
Dedicatee: Jean Brizard
Première: 1975 Festival de La Rochelle (also used as a Conservatoire test piece)
Performers: Jean Brizard (vc), Alain Louvier (pf)
Duration: *c.* 6'
Publisher: Amphion-Durand

Satyres (1976)
for 2 fls
Dedicatee: Pierre-Yves Artaud
Première: 15 March 1977, Studio 105 de Radio France, Paris
Performers: Pierre-Yves Artaud, Pierre Rouillier
Duration: *c.* 9'
Publisher: Jobert

Lys de madrigaux (1975–6)
female chorus (24vv) ensemble (pf/chr-zith, 1/3-tone zith/ org/perc)
Dedicatee: Guy Reibel
Commission: Radio France
I Calypso; II Circé; III Star Mad Blues; IV Parques; V Tropique de la Vièrge; VI Miroir de Sapho [sic]
Première: 1 June 1976, Grand Auditorium de la Radio France, Paris
Performers: Nicole Robin, Claude Lantony, Evelyne Horiot (sops), Anne Bartelloni (mez-sop), Françoise Gagneux (perc), Monique Rollin (ziths),Jean-Claude Pennetier (pf), Christian Villeneuve (org), choeur féminin de Radio France cond. Guy Reibel
Duration: *c.* 23'
Publisher: Jobert
Recording: Erato STU 71482 Choeur et Ensemble de la Radio France cond. Guy Reibel;CD-Opus 111 OPS 30-109 Ensemble vocal Musicatreize, Jay Gottlieb (pf), Roland Conil (org) Laure Morabito (zith) Georges van Gught (perc) cond. Roland Hayrabedian

Anneau du Tamarit (1976)
concerto for vc and orch (2222/2210/3perc/pf/86442)
Dedicatee: Alain Meunier
Première: 10 December 1977, Semaines musicales d'Orléans
Performers: Alain Meunier, Orchestre des Concerts Colonne, cond. Marius Constant
Duration: *c.* 22'
Publisher: Jobert
Recording: CD-Erato MF 2292-45503-2 Alain Meunier (vc) Orchestre National de France, cond. Marc Andrae

Messe (1977)
liturgical and concert versions
Commission: Festival d'Avignon
a) liturgical version
sop, mez-sop, SATB (second optional chorus ie congregation), ensemble (ob, tp, 2 perc, org)
I Entrée; II Prélude; III Kyrie; IV Gloria; V Epître; VI Alelluia; VII Psaume; VIII Trope (optional); IX Sanctus; X Agnus Dei; VIII Trope (after the Communion); XI Reprise de l'Agnus Dei (vocalisé)
Première: Eglise Saint Agricol, during the Avignon Festival, July 1977
Duration: *c.* 35–40'
Publisher: Jobert
b) concert version
sop, mez-sop, SATB, ensemble (ob, cl, bn, tp, trbn, 2 perc/org)
Numbers I, II, III, IV, VI, VIII, IX, X only.
Première: 31 July 1977, Eglise Saint-Agricol, Festival d'Avignon
Performers: Isabel Garcisanz (sop), Nicole Oxombre (mez-sop), Ensemble vocal et instrumental de Provence, cond. Daniel Chabrun
Duration: *c.* 28'
Publisher: Jobert
Recordings: CD Opus 111 OPS30246, Ensemble Musicatreize et Choeur Contemporain, cond. Roland Hayrabedian; Erato STU 71482 Choeur et Ensemble de la Radio France cond. Guy Reibel

Trois contes de l' Honorable Fleur (1978)
music-theatre for sop and ensemble (1111/0110/2perc/pf/1/3-tone zith/vc) mimes, puppets, shadow-theatre
Commission: France-Culture, Radio France for the 32nd Festival d'Avignon
Dedicatee: Michiko Hirayama
Lib: Odile Marcel based on original fairy-tales by the composer
Prologue (la jeune femme sous la lune); I Ogre mangeant des jeunes femmes sous la lune; II Le Vent d'Est enfermé dans un sac; III La pluie remontée au ciel
Première: 15 July 1978, Festival d'Avignon
Performers: Michiko Hirayama (sop), prod. Hubert Jappelle, ensemble cond. Daniel Chabrun
Duration: *c.* 56'
Publisher: Jobert
Recording: Philips PH6504 157 Michiko Hirayama (sop) Ensemble de solistes, dir. Daniel Chabrun

Livre des prodiges (1978–79)
orch (4444/6441/timp/4perc/2hp/pf/str)
Commission: Ministère de la Culture for 10th anniversary of the Orchestre de Lyon

Dedicatees: Serge Baudo, Orchestre de Lyon
Première partie: 1. Clair de terre; 2. Cortège des taureaux ailés; 3. Immémorial; 4. Hydre; 5. Clé des songes; 6. Clair de terre; 7. Soleil renversé
Deuxième partie: 1. Conjuration des sorts; 2. Alecto; 3. Son noir; 4. Jeu des masques; 5. Clair de terre; 6. Korô-Ngô
Première: 4 & 6 October 1979, Auditorium Maurice Ravel, Lyon; 9 October 1979 Théâtre des Champs Elysées, Paris
Performers: Orchestre de Lyon, cond. Serge Baudo
Duration: *c.* 29'
Publisher: Jobert
Recording: Erato MF 2292-45503-2 Orchestre National de France cond. Stanislaw Skrowaczewski

Deuxième quatuor à cordes (1978–80)
str quartet
Commission: Ministère de la Culture
I Sagittaire; II Mood; III Alborada; IV Faran-Ngô
Première: 27 February 1982, Studio 105 Maison de la Radio France, Paris
Performers: Arditti String Quartet (dissatisfied with the première, Ohana subsequently claimed a broadcast performance by the Talisch Quartet on 7 March 1983, Grand Auditorium de Radio France, as the official première).
Duration: *c.* 22' 30"
Publisher: Jobert

Crypt (1980)
str orch (66442)
Dedicatee: Claire Gibault
Commission: Orchestre de Chambéry et de la Savoie
Première: 24 October 1980, Théâtre Charles Dullin, Chambéry
Performers: Orchestre de Chambéry et de la Savoie, cond. Claire Gibault
Duration: *c.* 9'
Publisher: Jobert
Based on the fourth movement of the 2nd String Quartet

Wamba (1980)
carillon of bells
Commission: Renaud Gagneux, Eglise Saint-Germain-l'Auxerrois, Paris
Dedicatee: Renaud Gagneux
Première: 7 December 1980, Eglise Saint-Germain-l'Auxerrois, Paris
Duration: *c.* 9'
Publisher: unpublished
arr. for harpsichord 1982 as No.2 of **Deux pièces**

Concerto pour piano et orchestre (1980–81)
pf, orch (3343/4331/timp/3perc/hp/str)
Commission: Ministère de la Culture and Orchestre Philharmonique des Pays de Loire (on the occasion of its 10th anniversary)
Dedicatee: Jean-Claude Pennetier
Première: 26 and 27 June 1981, Nantes and Angers, respectively
Performers: Jean-Claude Pennetier, Orch Philharmonique des Pays de la Loire, cond. Marc Soustrot
Duration: *c.* 26'
Publisher: Jobert
Recording: Timpani 1C1039 M7 865 Jean-Claude Pennetier, Orchestre Philharmonique du Luxembourg, cond. Arturo Tamayo

Cadran lunaire (1981–82)
10-string gui
Dedicatee: Luis Martin Diego
I.....Saturnal; II......Jondo; III......Sylva; IV....Candil
Première: 9 December 1982, Rome
Performer: Luis Martin Diego
Duration: *c.* 20'
Publisher: Billaudot
Recording: CD-Auvidis Astrée 8513, Stephan Schmidt

Douze études d' interprétation (livre I) (1981–82)
for pf
Dedicatee: Paul Roberts
I Cadences libres; II Mouvements parallèles; III Agrégats sonores; IV Main gauche seule (in memoriam Maurice Ravel); V Quintes; VI Troisième pédale
Première: 8 April, 1983. Purcell Room, London
Performer: Paul Roberts
Duration: *c.* 30'
Publisher: Jobert
Recording: (complete) CD-REM 311114XCD: CDUR005 Dernièrs jours musique du XXème siècle (with livre II), Marie-Paule Siruguet; (partial) REM 311114XCD, Jeffrey Biegel; 1CD Harmonia Mundi HM 911569 Marie-Josèphe Jude; Harmonic Records H-CD 9354, Jean-Efflam Bavouzet (with livre II)

Deux pièces pour clavecin (1982–83)
for hpd
Dedicatee: Elisabeth Chojnacka
I Wamba (arr. from Wamba for carillons of bells); II Conga
Première: (Wamba only) 1 March 1982 Studio 105 de Radio France
Performer: Elisabeth Chojnacka

Première (complete) 4 January 1984, Studio 105, Radio France, Paris (same performer)
Duration: *c*. 12'
Publisher: Jobert
Recording: CD–Erato MF 2292-45699-2, Elisabeth Chojnacka

Kypris (1983-4)
for ob, va, db, pf
Commissioned and dedicatee: Opus ensemble
Première: 5 May 1985, Eglise des Billettes, Paris
Performers: Opus ensemble - Bruno Pizzamiglio (ob), Ana Bela Chaves (va), Alejandro Erlich-Oliva (db), Olga Prats (pf)
Duration: *c*. 11'
Publisher: Jobert

Douze études d' interprétation (livre II) (1983-85)
Nos. VII, VIII, IX, X, for piano, Nos. XI and XII for pf and perc
Dedicatees: Jay and Gordon Gottlieb
VII Septièmes (In memoriam Béla Bartók); VIII Secondes; IX Contrepoints libres; X Neuvièmes; XI Sons confondus; XII Imitations – Dialogues
Première (Nos. XI and XII): 8 January 1985, Salle Gaveau, Paris
Performers: Jay Gottlieb (pf), Gordon Gottlieb (perc)
Première (complete): 29 April 1986, Radio France, Paris
Performers: Jay Gottlieb (pf), Vincent Bauer (perc)
Duration: *c*. 40' (complete)
Publisher: Jobert
Recording: Audivis AV 4831 (Nos XI and XII) Jay Gottlieb (pf) Gordon Gottlieb (perc); (complete) CDUR005 Dernièrs jours musique du XXème siècle (with livre I), Marie-Paule Siruguet (pf) Vincent Bauer (perc); Harmonia Records H-CD 9354, Jean-Efflam Bavouet (pf) Florent Jodelet (perc)

Quatre choeurs (1987)
children's choir
Dedicatee: Christine Prost
I. Neige sur les Orangers (Asturian lullaby adaptation of traditional Spanish text); II. Mayombé (incantation afro-cubaine); III. Nuées; IV. Carillons
Duration: *c*. 10'
Publisher: Jobert

Huit chansons espangoles (*c*.1947–87)
mez-sop and pf
a collection of Ohana's unpublished song arrangements drawn together by Christine Prost

I Como la flor (*Cantares del querer lejos*); II Las mis penas (*Cantares del querer lejos*); III Cuando paso por el puente (*Cantares del querer lejos*); IV Nana (García Lorca); V Martinete; VI Que serenina (Austurian lullaby from *Quatre choeurs*); VII Tango el mariquita (Garcìa Lorca); VII Alborada (in memoriam Encarnación López 'La Argentinita')
Première: 11 June 1994, Auditorium St. Germain, Paris
Performers: Sylvie Sullé, Jay Gottlieb
Publisher: unpublished (extract of 'Martinete' reproduced in Longuemar, Geoffroy de, *Hommage à Maurice Ohana à l'occasion de son 75e anniversaire*, Programme of concert series 16–25 June, 1989)

La Célestine (1982–87)
Opera in 11 tableaux with prologue and epilogue
3 sop, cont, counter ten, ten, 2 bar, bas, narr, female chorus (22vv), SATB chorus, hpd, orch (2343/2231/5perc, pf, org/12.10.8.6.4., tape)
Commission: Radio France and Opéra de Paris
Libretto: Odile Marcel and Maurice Ohana after Fernando de Rojas
Première: 13 June 1988, Opéra de Paris (Palais Garnier)
Performers: [principal roles] La Célestine – Cathérine Ciesinski (cont), Jean-Luc Boutté (narr), Mélibée – Susan Roberts (sop), Calyx – Stephen Dickson (bar), Tristan – Bruce Brewer (ten); Elisabeth Chojnacka (hpd), chorus and orch. Paris Opera, cond. Arturo Tamayo, prod. Jorge Lavelli
Duration: *c.* 2 hr 30'
Publisher: Billaudot (formerly EFM)
Arr. 1989 **Trois Prophéties de la Sibylle**, 2 sops, pf, perc
Publisher: Billaudot
Arr. 1989–90 **Suite de Concert de la Célestine** for soloists, SATB ensemble
Duration: *c.* 15'
Publisher: Billaudot
Arr. 1989–90 **Miroir de Célestine**, hpd, perc
Première: 13 October 1990, Munich, (9.12.1996 Comédie des Champs Elysées, Paris)
Performers: Elisabeth Chojnacka (hpd) Sylvio Gualdo (perc)
Duration: *c.* 15'
Publisher: Billaudot

Lux noctis-Dies solis (1981–88)
4 choral groups (I, children's choir; II, SATB-16vv; III, SATB-32 vv; IV, SATB -64 vv) 2 org., perc,
Dedicatee: Stéphane Caillat
Texts: anon Latin texts and Catullus (adapted)
Première (Dies solis): 11 June 1983, Festival International de Lyon
Performers: Assocation d'Art Populaire, cond. Stéphane Caillat
Première (complete as dyptich): 8 December 1988, Festival d'Art Sacré, Luxembourg (same performers)

Duration (complete): *c.* 20'
Publisher: Jobert
Recording (complete): CD-Caliope CAL 9876 Les petits chanteurs de Paris, Ensemble vocal Musicatreize, Choeur contemporain d'Aix-en-Provence, Choeur de l'Université de Provence, Roland Conil, Jean-Marc Aymes (org), Jean-Paul Bernard (perc) cond. Roland Hayrabedian

Swan Song (1987–88)
for unaccompanied choir SATB (12vv)
Commission: Ministère de la Culture et de la Communication
Dedicatee: Roland Hayrabedian
I Drone; II Eléis; III Epitaphe (text by the composer after Ronsard); IV Mambo
Première (incomplete): 19 May, 1988 Auditorium des Halles Paris; (complete): 7 March 1989, Luxembourg Festival, Théâtre Municipal d'Esch
Performers: Groupe vocale de France, cond. Guy Reibel
Duration: *c.* 18'
Publisher: Jobert
Recording: CD Caliope CAL 9876 Ensemble vocal Musicatreize dir. Roland Hayrabedian (to be re-issued by Opus 111)

Anonyme XX siècle (1988)
for 2 gui
Dedicatees: Jean Horreaux, Jean-Marie Tréhard to whom the composer presented the work as a new year's gift for 1989.
Première: 6 June, 1989, Grand Auditorium de la Radio France, Paris
Performers: Jean Horreaux, Jean-Marie Tréhard
Duration: *c.* 4'
Publisher: Billaudot
Recording: CD-REM 311206 Jean Horreaux, Jean-Marie Tréhard

Sorgin-Ngô (1989)
3rd str quartet
Première: 13 February 1990 Prague (Paris 24 March 1990)
Performers: Talich Quartet
Duration: *c.* 22'
Publisher: Billaudot

Tombeau de Louize Labé 'O Beaux yeus bruns' (1990)
for unaccompanied chorus SATB (12vv)
Dedicatee: Roland Hayrabedian
Text: 'Tombeau' by Louize Labé adapted Ohana
Première: 22 December 1990, Moscow
Performers: Groupe Vocale Musicatreize, dir. Roland Hayrabedian
Duration: *c.* 6'
Publisher: Billaudot

Recording: CD Caliope CAL 9876 Ensemble vocal Musicatreize dir. Roland Hayrabedian

Nuit de Pouchkine (1990)
chorus SATB (12vv), counter tenor, viola da gamba (or vc)
Text: Pushkin (adapted)
Dedicatee: Mes amis de Musicatreize
Première: 16 November 1990, Chapelle Chorale Leningrad
Performers: Groupe Vocale Musicatreize, Marc Pontus (counter tenor) Sylvie Moquet (viola da gamba) dir. Roland Hayrabedian,
Duration: *c.* 7'
Publisher: Billaudot
Recording: CD Caliope CAL 9876 Ensemble vocal Musicatreize dir. Roland Hayrabedian

Sundown Dances (1990)
for seven instruments (fl, cl, tp, trbn, perc, vn, db)
Commissioned and Dedicatee: Erick Hawkins
Suite de ballet choreog. Erick Hawkins
Première: May 1991, Kennedy Center, Washington DC
Performers: Erick Hawkins Ballet Company
Duration *c.* 20'
Publisher: Billaudot

La Messe des Pauvres (1990)
orchestration of work by Erik Satie
Première: 15 December 1990, Eglise de St. Germain des Près, Paris, cond. Stéphane Caillat
Publisher: unpublished

Concerto pour violoncelle 'In Dark and Blue' (1988–90)
vc, orch (2221/2221/hp/2perc/str)
Commission and Dedicatee: Mstislav Rostropovich
Première: 13 May 1991, Festival d' Evian.
Performers: Mstislav Rostropovich, Toho Gakuen School Orchestra, cond. Seiji Ozawa
Duration: *c.* 20'
Publisher: Jobert (orchestral score); Billaudot (reduction vc and pf by Ton-That Tiêt with permission of the composer)
Recording: Timpani 1C1039 M7865, Sonia-Wieder-Atherton, Orchestre Philharmonique du Luxembourg, cond. Arturo Tamayo

So Tango (1991)
for hpd or pf
Commission: Elisabeth Chojnacka

Dedicatee: In memoriam Carlos Gardel
Première: 9 December 1996, Comédie des Champs Elysées Paris
Performer: Elisabeth Chojnacka
Duration: *c.* 4'
Publisher: Jobert
Recording: Auvidis-Valois no.V 4721 Elisabeth Chojnacka (hpd);CD Buda Record 926302 Alberto Neumann (pf)

Avoaha (1990–91)
for chorus SATB (36–48 vv) 2 pfs, 3 perc
Commission: Festival Olympique des Arts, Jeux Olympiques d'Albertville
Text: Ohana's arrangements of various Spanish, Latin, English and mystic African texts in various dialects (incl. Bantou, Dahomen, Yorouba)
I Iya-Ngô; II Igvodou; III A Yemaya; IV Refrain d'esclaves; V Iya; VI Eros noir; VII Conductus; VIII Aux Dieux du Vent et de la Foudre; IX Imprécations au Dieu Changó sourd aux sortilèges; X Eloge des héros et des ancêtres; XI Tiger Moon; XII El Dorado
Première: 14 February 1992, Palais des Congrès, Aix-les-Bains Festival, on the occasion ot the inauguration of the Jeux Olympiques d'Albertville and the Festival Olympique des Arts (other works formed in the same concert incl. Dutilleux *Mystère de l'Instant*, Florentz *Asmarâ- le livre des enchantements II*, Stravinsky *Les Noces*)
Performers: Eric Erikson Stockholm Chamber Choir, J.E. Bavouzet, J. Gottlieb (pfs), J.P. Bernard, F. Jodelet, T. Miroglio (perc), cond. Kent Nagano
Duration: *c.* 27'
Publisher: Billaudot
Recording: CD Opus 111 OPS 30-109, Jay Gottlieb, Roland Conil (pfs), Christian Hamouy, Georges van Gught, Jean-Paul Bernard (perc) ,Choeur Contemporain d'Aix-en-Provence, Ensemble vocal Musicatreize, dir. Roland Hayrabedian

Bibliography

Publications are chronological within each section

1. Writings by Ohana

'Alfredo Casella', *The Music Review*, viii (1947) p. 145, trans. M. Ohana for *Journal musical français* (9 April 1947)
'Deux oeuvres de Manuel de Falla', *Journal musical français* (22 October 1953)
'Sueño de una tarde de verano', unpublished poem (written in Spanish), November 1954 (copy in the archives of the present author)
'Chants espagnols', *Los Gitanillos de Cadiz*, Club français du disque G4188 (1955) (disc notes)
'La géographie musicale de l'Espagne', *Journal musical français* No. 47 (March 1956) pp. 1–8; No. 48 (April 1956) pp. 1–3
'Notes sur quelques formes du folklore espagnole', MS 1960s (copy in the archives of the present author)
'Erik Satie' in J. Roy: *Présences contemporaines: musique française* (Paris, Nouvelles Editions Debresse, 1962) pp. 387–9
'Horizons espagnols', Festival de Montauban, Cahier No. 6 (1962)
'*L'Amour sorcier* et les *Tréteaux de Maître Pierre* de Manuel de Falla', *Journal musical français* (22 October 1963)
'Béla Bartók', *Ujiras* (Budapest, July 1965), French orig. in *Nouvel observateur* (18 August 1965)
'Le Flamenco', MS of text written in Malaga, 1965 (copy in the archive of the present author)
'Prière 66', unpublished poem (written in French), November 1966 (copy in the archive of the present author)
'Erik Satie', text of French radio broadcast (December 1966) as part of centenary celebrations of birth of Satie, reproduced in *La Revue musicale* Nos 391–3 (Paris, 1986) pp. 177–9 (special issue devoted to Ohana)
'Etudes chorégraphiques', Philips DSY 836 990 (1967) (disc notes)
'Microintervals: Experimental Media II', *Twentieth Century Music,* ed. Rollo Myers (London, Calder and Boyars, rev. 2nd edn. 1968) pp. 147–50
'Syllabaire pour Phèdre' (written in English). Notes for opening of the 'Opera Forum' New York, 19 February 1973 (copy of the manuscript in the archives of the present author)
'Théâtre musicale ', MS 1970s (copy in the archives of the present author)
'La musique de notre temps ', MS 1970s (copy in the archives of the present author)
'Musica y sociedad', *Triunfo* No. 57 (November 1974)

'Je ne joue pas de guitare, mais je trouve à travers la guitare, *Diapason* (May 1974) p. 39

'En el centenario de Manuel de Falla: un revolucionario inconsciente', *Triunfo* No. 63 (November 1976)

'La Marionnette à l'Opéra', MS 1976 reproduced in *La Revue musicale* Nos 351–2 (Paris, 1982) p. 75 (special issue devoted to Ohana)

'Messe', programme notes for first performance at Festival d'Avignon 31 July 1977 (copy of the manuscript in the archives of the present author)

'Livre des prodiges', programme note for the première (copy in the archives of the present author)

'Les paradoxes de la musique contemporaine', *Musique en questions* No. 1 (Cahiers du SACEM, February 1980) p. 9

'La Niña de los Peines', *Le Chant du Monde*, Harmonia Mundi LDX 74859 CM340 (1980) (disc notes)

'L' ankylose du théâtre psychologique', *Aujourd'hui l'Opéra*, Recherches No. 42, (1980)

'Musique et poésie', *La Revue musicale* Nos 351–2 (Paris, 1982) pp. 75–6 (special issue devoted to Ohana)

'Au Service de la Musique', *La Revue musicale* Nos 361–3 (Paris, 1983) pp. 59–60 (special issue devoted to Sauguet)

'Sud-Nord', *20ème siècle: images de la musique française – textes et entretiens*, ed. J.P. Derrien (Paris, SACEM et Papiers, 1986) pp. 164–7

'Preface' to Deval, Frédéric, *Le Flamenco et ses valeurs* (Paris, Aubier, 1989)

2. Interviews with Ohana

Gavoty, Bernard, Daniel-Lesur, [Jean], 'Ecrire la musique', *Pour ou contre la musique moderne?* (Paris, Flammarion, 1957) pp. 248–50

Ancelin, Pierre, 'Pierre Ancelin avec Maurice Ohana', *Les lettres françaises, arts* (17 September 1964)

Vidal, Pierre, 'Rencontre avec Maurice Ohana et Narciso Yepes', *Musica* (June 1966)

Grunenwald, Alain, '*T'Harân-Ngô*: Conversation avec Maurice Ohana', *Arfuyen II* (Paris, 1975) pp. 58–63

Lyon, Raymond, 'Entretien avec Maurice Ohana', *Courrier musical de France* No. 62, 2e trimestre (Paris, April 1978) pp. 41–6

Mâche, François-Bernard, 'Les mal entendus, compositeurs des années 1970', *La Revue musicale* Nos 314–15 (Paris, 1978) pp. 109–15

Massin, Brigitte, 'Une musique ne serait plus représentation mais partage', *Le Matin de Paris* (20 July 1978)

Cadieu, Martine, 'Maurice Ohana: comment la musique', *Diapason* (September 1980) p. 42

Montrémy, J.M. de, 'Maurice Ohana, un moderne archaïque', *La Croix* (3 November 1981)

Bolbach, Pascal, 'Maurice Ohana et la guitare: entretien avec le compositeur', *Les Cahiers de la guitare*, 2e trimestre (1982) pp. 4–8

Paquelet, Christine, 'La percussion dans la musique d' Ohana', *Analyse musicale* No. 8, 3e trimestre (June 1987) pp. 56–8

Condé, Gérard, 'Autour de *La Célestine*: entretien avec Maurice Ohana', *Le Monde* (9 June 1988)

Mérigaud, Bernard, 'Ohana et la sorcière: entretien avec Maurice Ohana', *Télérama* No. 2004 (June 1988)

Drillon, Jacques, 'Une création mondiale au Palais-Garnier, le grand opéra de Maurice Ohana', *Le Nouvel observateur* (10 June 1988)

Gastellier, Fabienne, '*La Célestine*, ministre des plaisirs', *Le Quotidien de Paris* (13 June 1988)

Marti, Jean-Christophe, 'Anonyme XXe siècle', *L'Avant-scène opéra*, hors série No. 3 (Paris, 1991) pp. 4–15 (special issue devoted to Ohana)

Smith, Richard Langham, 'Ohana on Ohana: an English Interview', *Contemporary Music Review*, viii, 1 (1993) pp. 123–9

3. Writings on Ohana

Gide, André, *Journal 1939–49 Souvenirs* (Paris, Gallimard, Bibliothèque de la Pléiade, 1954) p. 286

Carpentier, Alejo, 'Revelación de un compositor', *El Domingo* (Caracas, 29 April 1956) reproduced in *Obras completas de Alejo Carpentier*, Vol. x, 'Ese músico que llevo dentro', (Mexico City, 1987) pp. 215–17

Rostand, Claude, *La musique française contemporaine* (Paris, Presses Universitaires de France, coll. 'Que sais-je?', 1952) pp. 123–6

Gavoty, Bernard, Daniel-Lesur, [Jean], 'Ecrire la musique', *Pour ou contre la musique moderne ?* (Paris, Flammarion, 1957) pp. 248–50

Roy, Jean, *Présences contemporaines. Musique française* (Paris, Nouvelles Editions Debresse, 1962) pp. 385–403

Samuel, Claude, *Panorama de l'art musical contemporain* (Paris, Gallimard, 1962) p. 334

Bernard, Robert, *Histoire de la musique*, Vol. ii (Paris, Nathan, 1963) p. 975

Darmangeat, Pierre, 'Le Concerto pour guitare et orchestre de Maurice Ohana', *Guitare et musique* (October–November, 1963)

Darmangeat, Pierre, '*Cantigas* de Maurice Ohana', *Guitare et musique* (January–February 1965)

Myers, Rollo, *Modern French Music: Its Evolution and Cultural Background from 1900 to the Present Day* (Oxford, Basil Blackwell, 1971) pp. 171–4, reprinted as *Modern French Music from Fauré to Boulez* (New York, Da Capo Press, 1984)

Cadieu, Martine, 'A l'Opéra de Lyon, *Autodafé* de Maurice Ohana', *Les lettres françaises* (7 June 1972)

Myers, Rollo, 'France', *Music in the Modern Age*, History of Western Music, Vol. v, ed. F.W. Sternfeld, (London, Weidenfeld and Nicolson, 1973) p. 271

Goldbeck, Frederick, *Twentieth Century Composers: France, Italy and Spain*, Vol. iv, (London, Weidenfeld and Nicolson, 1974) pp. 138–9

Roy, Jean, 'Les compositeurs français contemporains', *Diapason* No. 186 (April 1974) pp. 10–13 (the same issue includes a review of *Neumes*, p. 57)

Chameray, Claude, 'Biographie de Maurice Ohana', *Courrier musical de France* No. 51, 3e trimestre (Paris, 1975) pp. 9–12

Le Bordays, Christiane, *La Musique espagnole* (Paris, Presses Universitaires de France, coll. 'Que sais-je?', 1977) p. 123

Goléa, Antoine, *La Musique de la nuit des temps aux aurores nouvelles* (Paris, Leduc, 1977) pp. 844–5

Bayer, Francis, *Essai sur la notion d'espace dans la musique contemporaine* (dissertation, troisième cycle, Université de Paris X, 1977) pp. 154–7, published as *De Schoenberg à Cage: essai sur la notion d'espace dans la musique contemporaine* (Paris, Klincksieck, 1981) pp. 119–21

Riou, Alain, 'Le théâtre musical de Maurice Ohana', *Le Théâtre lyrique français 1945–1985*, ed. D. Pistone (Paris, Champion, 1978)

Richard, Jean-Vincent, '*Trois contes de l'Honorable Fleur*', *Diapason* (October 1978)

Dagan, Nicholas, '*Lys de madrigaux* de Maurice Ohana', *Panorama de la musique* (January–February 1978)

Bosseur, Dominique & Jean-Yves, *Révolutions musicales* (Paris, Le Sycomore, 1979) pp. 89–90

Wade, Graham, *Traditions of the Classical Guitar* (London, Calder, 1980) pp. 202 and 248

Massin, Brigitte, 'Ecrire aujourd'hui pour le piano', *Panorama de la musique* (March–April 1980) pp. 12–13

Prost, Christine, *Formes et thèmes: essai sur les structures profondes du langage musical de Maurice Ohana* (unpublished thesis, 3e cycle, Université de Provence, Aix-en-Provence, 1981)

Halbreich, Harry, 'Maurice Ohana à Nantes – création du Concerto pour piano', *Harmonie* (October 1981) p. 70

Bolbach, Pascal, 'Maurice Ohana et la guitare: analyse du *Tiento*', *Cahiers de la guitare*, 2e trimestre (Paris, 1982) pp. 8–10

Roy, Jean, ed. 'Maurice Ohana: essais, études et documents', *La Revue musicale* Nos 351–2 (Paris, 1982) (special issue devoted to Ohana, incl. J. Roy, 'Pour saluer Maurice Ohana' pp. 5–10; O. Marcel, 'L' Ibérisme de Maurice Ohana' pp. 13–26; C. Prost: 'Catalogue raisonné' pp. 29–67; M. Ohana,' Ecrits et paroles' pp. 69–76)

Bayer, Francis, 'Sous le signe de l'imaginaire: Maurice Ohana', *Esprit* No. 99 (March 1985) pp. 43–57

Bayer, Francis ed., 'André Gide et Maurice Ohana', *Bulletin des Amis d'André Gide* No. 71, xiv (1986) pp. 8–32

Prost, Christine, ed. 'Maurice Ohana: miroirs de l'oeuvre', *La Revue musicale* Nos 391–3 (Paris, 1986) (special issue devoted to Ohana, incl. H. Sauguet, 'Maurice Ohana' p. 5; C. Prost 'Introduction' pp. 7–9; R. Cluzel, 'Jeux de portraits' pp. 13–16; F. Ibarrondo, 'Sources d'avenir' pp. 19–26; P. Roberts, 'La musique de piano de Maurice Ohana' pp. 27–50; H. Halbreich, 'Harmonie et timbre dans la musique instrumentale' pp. 51–69; G. Reibel, 'La musique vocale et chorale de Maurice Ohana' pp. 71–85; O. Marcel, 'Usage de la parole – musique et théâtre dans l'oeuvre de Maurice Ohana' pp. 87–105; C. Prost, 'Poétique musicale de Maurice Ohana – statisme et dynamisme' pp. 107–27; C. Prost, 'Analyse: 'Minotaure aux miroirs' 4e pièce d'*Office des oracles*' pp. 129–47; A. Meunier, S. Gualda, L.M. Diego and E. Chojnacka, 'Témoinages' pp. 151–8; F. Bayer, 'Correspondance d'André Gide et Maurice Ohana' pp. 161–9; R. Cluzel, '*Syllabaire pour Phèdre* – pour et sur la musique de Maurice Ohana' pp. 171–5 (opera text); M. Ohana, 'Erik Satie' pp. 177–9; C. Prost, 'Catalogue raisonné' pp. 183–225)

Babin, Pierre, 'Le compositeur et le secret du temps', *L' Autre journal* No. 9 (23 April 1986)

Lacavalerie, Xavier, 'Ohana au plus haut des Cieux', *Télérama* no.1983 (26 April 1986)

Poirier, Alain, 'Maurice Ohana', *Guide de la musique de piano et de clavecin*, ed. F.R. Tranchefort (Paris, Fayard, 1987) pp. 555–7

East, Leslie, 'Late Arrivals', *Classical Music* (31 January 1987) p. 31

Beretti, Michel, *La Célestine – Programme de l' Opéra de Paris Palais-Garnier* (June 1988) (incl. J.P. Peter and M.C. Ponchelle, 'La Célestine, ou la faillite de l'entremise' pp.11–23; H. Halbreich, 'La Célestine, clef de voûte de l'oeuvre de Maurice Ohana' pp. 27–48; C. Prost,'Maurice Ohana' pp. 51–4; 'Entretien avec Maurice Ohana' pp. 56–60; 'Entretien avec Arturo Tamayo' pp. 62–4; 'Le monde comme combat – entretien avec Jorge Lavelli' pp. 67–9

Cadieu, Martine, '*La Célestine* – Maurice Ohana: une tragi-comédie de moeurs', *Opéra international* (June 1988) pp. 24–5

Rae, Caroline, '*La Célestine*: Maurice Ohanas Oper in Paris', *Die neue Zeitschrift für Musik*, Jg. 149, No. 10 (October 1988) pp. 35–6

Rae, Caroline, *The Music of Maurice Ohana*, 2 Vols (unpublished D Phil thesis, University of Oxford, 1989)

Halbreich, Harry, 'Maurice Ohana' *Guide de la musique de chambre,* ed. F.R. Tranchefort (Paris, Fayard, 1989) pp. 678–83

Longuemar, Geoffroy de, *Hommage à Maurice Ohana à l'occasion de son 75e anniversaire*, Programme of concert series 16–25 June 1989 promoted by French Ministère de la Culture, Spanish Ministerio de Cultura, UNESCO, SACEM, Association France-Espagne Meridiano, Musique et Vin. (incl. contributions by F. Bayer, E. Chojnacka, F. Deval, G. Condé, M. Ohana, J.P. Peter, C. Prost, N. Zourabichvili de Pelken. Extracts from MS scores include an arrangement by Ohana of a 'Martinete')

Pazdro, Michel, ed., 'Maurice Ohana: *Trois contes de l'Honorable Fleur, Syllabaire pour Phèdre, La Célestine*', *L'avant-scène opéra; opéra aujhourd'hui*, hors série No. 3 (special issue devoted to Ohana) (1991) (incl. H. Halbreich, '*La Célestine*' pp. 17–61; C. Prost, 'Deux opéras de chambre' pp. 62–79; S. de Castro, 'Pour Maurice Ohana' pp. 80–3

Rae, Caroline, 'Maurice Ohana: Iconoclast or Individualist?' *The Musical Times* cxxxii (February 1991) pp. 69–74

Deval, Fréderic, *De Federico García Lorca à Maurice Ohana: 'Llanto por Ignacio Sánchez Mejías'* (Paris, Actes Sud, 1992)

Rae, Caroline, 'Maurice Ohana', *Contemporary Composers* (Detroit, St James' Press, 1992) pp. 703–5

Rae, Caroline, 'Le symbolisme et l'archétype du mythe européen dans l'oeuvre de Maurice Ohana', *Cahiers du CIREM*, Nos 24–5 'Musique et Europe', (Tours, 1993) pp. 115–30

Bayer, Francis, 'Maurice Ohana sculpteur d'ombres', *Le Monde de la musique* No. 162 (January 1993) pp. 59–62

Halbreich, Harry, 'Maurice Ohana', *Guide de la musique sacrée et chorale profane de 1750 à nos jours*, ed. F.R. Tranchfort (Paris, Fayard, 1993) pp. 771–81

Castanet, Pierre Albert, '1968: A Cultural and Social Survey of its Influences on French Music', *Contemporary Music Review*, viii, 1, (1993) pp. 19–43

Rae, Caroline, 'Debussy et Ohana: allusions et références', *Cahiers Debussy* Nos 17–18 (1993–4) pp. 103–20

Rae, Caroline, 'L'Improvisation dans l'oeuvre de Maurice Ohana', *Actes du colloque international, 'l'improvisation musicale en question', tenu à l'Université de Rouen mars 1992* ed. J.P. Dambricourt (Rouen, 1994) pp. 73–85

Roy, Jean and Deval,Frédéric, eds. *Maurice Ohana le musicien du soleil, Le Monde de la musique* cahier No. 2 (1994) (special issue devoted to Ohana, contributors incl. F. Bayer, S. Bussotti, F. Deval, H. Dutilleux, H. Halbreich, B. Massin, K. Nagano, C. Prost, C. Rae, J.L Tournier, M. Weiss)

Rae, Caroline, 'The Piano Music of Maurice Ohana', *Revista Musica* Vol. 6 n.1/2 (São Paulo, Brazil, May–November 1995) pp. 44–74

Roy, Jean, 'Maurice Ohana la mémoire du piano', *Lettre du musicien - Piano* No. 10 (1996–7) pp. 72–3

Potter, Caroline, *Henri Dutilleux his Life and Works* (London, Ashgate, 1997) pp. 189–92

Rae, Caroline, 'Magic and Music, Alejo Carpentier and Maurice Ohana: Cross-Connections in 20th Century French Music and the South Americas', *Des Amériques impressions et expressions* (Paris, L'Harmattan, 1999) pp. 222–30

Martin, Marie-Lorraine, *'La Célestine' de Maurice Ohana: d'un mythe fondateur de la culture espagnole à un opéra-monde* (Paris, L'Harmattan, 1999)

Rae, Caroline, 'Henri Dutilleux and Maurice Ohana: Victims of an Exclusion Zone', *Tempo* No. 212 (April 2000) pp. 22–30 (the same issue includes reviews of *Office des oracles* and *Messe*, pp. 55–7)

Rae, Caroline, 'Ohana's *In Dark and Blue, Sorgin-Ngo* and other Music for Strings', *Notes*, Vol. 57, No. 2 (December 2000) pp. 464–68

4. Broadcasts - Documentaries, Features and Interviews

Myers, Rollo, 'Maurice Ohana', Music Magazine, BBC Third Programme (19 November 1961)

Bernard, Michel, 'Soirées musicales: Maurice Ohana au Festival d'Avignon', Radio France: France-Musique (26, 27 July, 1, 3 and 5 August 1975) (interviews with the composer by G. Aufray)

Ohana, Maurice, 'Concert lecture autour de *Sibylle* et *Lys de madrigaux*', Radio France: France-Musique (27 October 1979)

Barraud, Henri, 'Regards de la musique', Radio France: France-Musique (20 April, 1980) (interview with the composer by H.Barraud)

Texier, Marc & Prost, Christine, 'Maurice Ohana', Le Matin des musiciens, Radio France: France-Musique (14, 15, 16, 17 and 18 November 1982) (the composer in conversation with C. Prost)

Oliver, Michael, 'Maurice Ohana', Music Weekly, BBC Radio 3 (10 June 1984) (interview with the composer by M.Oliver)

'Maurice Ohana; à l'occasion de son 70e anniversaire', Radio France: France-Culture (29 September 1984)

Soumagnac, Myriam, 'Le Sacré dans la musique', Radio France: France-Musique (27 and 28 February 1986) (interviews with the composer)

'L' Oeuvre intégrale de piano de Maurice Ohana', Radio France: France-Musique (22, 29 April, 13 May 1986) (contributions by M. Ohana, P. Caloni, G. Condé, J. Doucelin)

Texier, Marc, 'Autour de *La Célestine*', Le Matin des musiciens, Radio France: France-Musique (20, 21, 22, 23, 24 and 25 June 1988) (contributions by M. Ohana, M. Beretti, J. Gilibert, C. Prost)

Smith, Richard Langham, 'Southerly Winds', BBC Radio 3, (1987, repeated 1989) (contributions by M. Ohana, G. Joy-Dutilleux, H. Halbreich, E. Kurtz, T. Murail, A. Myrat, P. Roberts)

Damien, Jean-Michel, 'Les imaginaires', Radio France: France-Musique (4 April 1992) (round-table with M. Ohana, E. Canat de Chizy, F. Ibarrondo, C. Rae, J. Gottlieb)

Larivière, Michèle, 'Hommage à Maurice Ohana', Intermezzo, Radio France: France-Musique (27, 28, 29 and 30 April 1994)

The Centre de Documentation de la Musique Contemporaine (Paris) completed a permanent 'Exposition-Ohana' in 1989. The CDMC has created permanent exibitions for other composers including Dutilleux, Françaix, Bayle, Reverdy, Philipot and others.

Several articles and recordings were consulted at the archives of the composer and at the Centre du Documentation de la Musique Contemporaine (CDMC) in Paris for which the complete source references are lacking.

Index

Accademia di Santa Cecilia 13, 72 *see also* Casella, Alfredo
African tribal music *see* folk music and *see* rhythm
Afro-Cuban music *see* folk music and *see* rhythm
Albéniz, Isaac xii, 3, 8–10, 12, 16, 75, 80, 153–4, 158, 187, 216–17, 252
Alberti, Rafael 10, 76, 81, 267, 268
aleatory techniques 60–2, 112, 125–6, 138, 140, 146, 163–8, 171–2, 185, 187, 196–213, 227–9, 230–4, 250, 255 *see also* combinatoire counterpoint and *see* form
Alfonso X 'el Sabio', King 34, 81, 225–6, 268
Alvarez Gato, Juan 81, 268
Antonio (Antonio Triana) 10, 28, 80
Apel, Willi 162
Aprahamian, Félix 246
Argentinita, La (Encarnación Júlvez López) 10–11, 13, 28nn, 68, 76, 80, 287
Armstrong, Louis 8, 257–8
Arnoux, Alexandre 22, 35, 270, 272
Association des amis de Maurice Ohana *see* Ohana, Maurice
Asturias, Miguel Angel 32, 64, 65–6n
Audisio, Gabriel 98, 275–7
Auric, Georges 21
Austro-German tradition 7, 16–17, 68, 75, 191, 220, 243, 250–1

Bach, Johann Sebastian 251
Backhaus, Wilhelm 8
Ballet Espagñol 10 *see also* López, Pilar
Ballet de Madrid 10
Ballet Municipal de Strasbourg 85
Barbier, Pierre 88, 273
Baroja, Pío 10
Barraud, Henry 20
Barrault, Jean-Louis 21, 268–9
Bartók, Béla 13, 20, 44–5, 116–17, 124, 128, 217, 221, 251–2

allusion to 117–19, 120–1, 123, 156
as dedicatee 117, 156–7, 286
Concerto for Orchestra 170n
Duke Bluebeard's Castle 170n, 254
Divertimento 118–19
Music for Strings Percussion and Celesta 116, 118–19
Basie, Count (William) 187
Bavouzet, Jean-Efflam 23, 285–6, 290
Bayer, Francis xiii, 23, 29n, 71
Bayonne Conservatoire 5, 7
BBC *see* British Broadcasting Corporation
Beethoven, Ludwig van 7, 210
Béjart, Maurice 10, 35, 81, 98, 267, 271
Benavente (y Martínez), Jacinto 10
Berber tribal music *see* folk music
Berceo, Gonzalo de 81, 268
Berg, Alban 20
Bergamín, José 10, 34, 35, 66n, 71, 76, 81, 98, 268, 270
Bernard, Anthony 246, 272
Berio, Luciano 31, 32, 46, 132, 250–1
Circles 132, 211, 239
Sequenza III 132
Sinfonia 31
Visage 132, 139, 239
Bermat, Alain 16–17, 100n *see also* Zodiaque, Le Groupe
Bigot, Eugène 9
Bizet, Georges (Alexandre Césare Léopold) 246
black sound (sonido negro) *see* Flamenco
Blake, William 45, 67n *see also* symbolism of opposites
blues *see* jazz
Bonnal *see* Ermend-Bonnal
Boulanger, Lili 246
Boulanger, Nadia 17
Boulez, Pierre xi, 20, 21, 29nn, 68, 99n, 193, 244–7, 249–51, 259n, 268

[Boulex *cont.*]
Le Marteau sans maître 109, 247, 259n
Improvisations sur Mallarmé 246
British Broadcasting Corporation 21, 244–7, 270, 272
Britten, Benjamin (Lord) 254
  Burning Fiery Furnace 138
  Curlew River 138–9
  Peter Grimes 254
Buñel, Luis 38
Bunraku *see* Japanese theatre
Busoni, Ferruccio Benvenuto 101n, 152

Cabasso, Laurent 23
Cage, John 152
Callimachus 66–7nn, *see also* Catullus
Campbell, Roy 12–13, 68
Camus, Albert 33, 34, 266
Cante Jondo *see* Flamenco and *see* Festival of Cante Jondo
cantus firmus *see* melody
Capdeville, Pierre 20
Carpentier, Alejo 6, 10, 27n, 28n, 31–2, 47, 64, 65nn, 66n, 76, 144, 214–15, 217, 258, 261n
Carrillo, Juan (Julián) 87, 152
Carter, Elliott 69
Casella, Alfredo 13–14, 29n,74
Castérède, Jacques 20
Castro, Sergio de 10, 17, 18, 21, 28n, 29nn, 68, 81, 263, 268 *see also* Zodiaque, Le Groupe
Catullus, Gaius Valerius 44, 67n, 287
Cela, Camilo José (Trulock) 10, 35, 38, 66n, 71, 88, 274
Cervantes (Saavedra), Miguel de 22, 33, 34, 70, 246, 270
Chinese instruments, allusion to 110–12, 122
Chinese theatre 22–3, 52, 84, 145, 161–2, 254
Chizy, Edith Canat de 23
Chojnacka, Elisabeth (Elzbieta) 139, 274, 277, 281, 285–90
Chonez, Claudine 18, 265–6
Chopin, Fryderyk xii, 3, 7, 8, 9, 12, 14, 37, 156, 251
Civil War, Spanish *see* Spanish Civil War
clusters, notation of 119, 181, 184
  see also harmony

Cluzel, Raphaël 90, 263, 273, 277
Cocteau, Jean 65, 252
combinatoire counterpoint 94, 99, 122, 125–6, 130–2, 142–3, 166, 199–204, 209–13, 222, 237
Concerts Colonne 8
Concerts de la Pléiade 20
Concerts du Domaine musical xi, 21, 132, 244, 247, 259n
Concerts Lamoureux 8, 9
Concerts Marigny 21
Concerts Pasdeloup 8
conductus *see* melody
Conrad, Joseph (Teodor Jósef Konrad Korzeniowski) 1, 8
Constant, Marius xi, xiii, 20, 21, 22, 23, 245–7, 250, 263, 276–7, 282
Corbusier, Le (Charles-Edouard Jeanneret) 8
Cossé, Laurence v, viii

Dalberto, Michel 23
Dali, Salvador 38
Dallapiccola, Luigi 13
Damase, Jean-Michel 246
Daniel-Lesur (Jean Yves) 11, 16, 20, 21, 32, 245–6, 263, 265
Darmstadt Summer School xi, 16, 21, 132, 244
Debussy, Claude Achille xii, 3, 7–9, 12–14, 22, 24, 35–7, 44–6, 66nn, 68, 88–90, 97, 99, 100n, 105, 109, 117, 128, 131, 145, 152, 158, 173, 178, 186, 189, 191, 220–1, 247, 250–2
  allusions to 91–4, 105–6, 142–3
  Children's Corner 156–7
  Concours international de piano de 24
  En blanc et noir 9, 36, 91, 93–5, 98, 184
  Estampes 'Jardins sous la pluie' 46, 91
  Etudes 9, 23, 91, 99, 116, 142, 150, 178, 184–5, 220
    'Pour les agréments' 220
    'Pour les quartes' 150, 177
    'Pour les sixtes' 150
  Nocturnes 90
  Pelléas et Mélisande 63, 91, 254
  Préludes 9, 91, 97, 185
    'Ce qu'a vu le vent d'ouest' 45, 97, 105–6
    'Feuilles mortes' 91–3

'La terrasse des audiences du clair de lune' 91–3, 178
Delerue, Georges 20
Denisov, Edison 141
Désormière, Roger 20
Dickens, Charles 8
D'Indy, Vincent 17, 20, 252
discant *see* melody
Dolin, Anton 18, 28n
Domaine musical, Concerts du *see* Concerts
drawings *see* Ohana, Maurice
duende *see* Flamenco
Dukas, Paul 20
Dufourt, Hugues 23
Duruflé, Maurice 246
Dutilleux, Henri xi–xiii, 17, 20–3, 29nn, 69, 90, 93, 99, 105, 115–16, 140–1, 144n, 145–6, 160, 171, 186, 192n, 244–50, 254–5, 259n, 263, 266–71, 273–7, 290
Deuxième Symphonie 'Le Double' 21, 244, 247
Figures de résonances 188–9
illustrations musicales *see* musique radiophonique
Métaboles 69, 171, 244, 247
Première Symphonie 247
progressive growth 146, 239
Tout un monde lointain 141–2, 144n
Trois sonnets de Jean Cassou 244

electro-acoustic music 22, 58, 131–2, 239–41, 251
Eliot T.S. (Thomas Stearns) 46, 63
Ellington, 'Duke' (Edward Kennedy) 8
Ensemble Ars Nova xi, 22, 98, 247, 267–8, 276–7 *see also* Constant, Marius
Ensemble intercontemporain xi, 21
Ermend-Bonnal (Joseph Bonnal) 7
Euripides 35, 54–5, 56, 98, 137, 275–7

Falla, Manuel de xii, 3, 8, 10, 12, 17, 23, 26–8nn, 37, 68, 74, 77, 80, 83, 86, 89, 117, 158, 187, 216–7, 251–2 *see also* Festival of Cante Jondo
Amor brujo, El 10, 154, 216
Fantasía Bética 9
Harpsichord Concerto 13, 23, 70, 77

Homenaje a Debussy 37, 72, 85, 87
Master Peter's Puppet Show see Retablo de Maese Pedro, El
Noches en los jardines de España 9, 77
Nuits dans les jardins d'Espagne see Noches en los jardines de España
Retablo de Maese Pedro, El 13, 23, 70, 77, 83–4, 254
Siete Canciones populares Españolas 74
Sombrero de tres picos, El 8, 10, 77
The Three Cornered Hat see Sombrero de tres picos, El
Tréteaux de Maître Pierre see Retablo de Maese Pedro, El
Festival of Cante Jondo 10, 80
Fischer, Edwin 8
Flamenco 10, 27–8nn, 37, 45, 47, 69–71, 74–5, 79, 86, 97, 101n, 162, 183, 187, 215, 217n, 223, 225
black sound *see* sonido negro
Cante Jondo 3, 26–7n, 37, 45, 59, 70–1, 75, 79, 86–7, 97, 100nn, 101n, 148, 152, 162, 183, 216, 227, 253
duende 47, 59, 76, 178, 192nn
Flamenco Competition (Cordoba) 24
Jota 10, 74
modal scales 75, 79, 100n, 216
Paso 74–5, 77, 100n (*see also* Plate No. 6)
performance techniques 37, 74, 79–80, 86–7, 97, 160–1, 192n, 196, 215, 253
percussive techniques 6, 86–7, 196, 215
rhythmic characteristics 6, 37, 74–5, 86, 97, 214–17, 234, *see also* rhythm
Saeta 74–5, 153
sonido negro 59, 76, 177–8
Tango 154
Florentz, Jean-Louis 23, 290
folk music 16, 117, 128, 193, 251
African tribal 5–6, 47–8, 52, 68, 71, 84–5, 89, 98, 125, 132, 140, 145, 196–7, 201–8, 213–15, 241–2, 253, 255
Afro-Cuban 6, 47–8, 52, 85, 140, 145, 196, 214–15, 241–2, 253, 255, 258

[folk music *cont.*]
  Berber 5, 152
  Cuban 6, 10, 47
  Spanish 5, 6, 8, 10–11, 47–8, 52, 68–71, 74–5, 80, 82, 84–6, 89, 98, 125, 132, 145, 148, 152–4, 196–7, 215–17, 241–2, 253
  relationships between Spanish and African 6, 47–8, 145, 196–7, 201–2, 214–15
Forest-Divonne, Pierre de la 16–17, 18 *see also* Zodiaque, le Groupe
form 80, 131, 219–43 *see also* spatial devices
  allusive titles 241–2
  coral-reef 146–50, 219–20
  mobile 61, 140, 230–3
  of Greek tragedy 56, 137–40, 226
  organic 116, 129, 131, 146–50, 220–1, 226–7, 235, 239
  proportional structures 221, 243n
  sectional 89, 99, 116, 129, 131, 142, 163, 193, 197–200, 219–22, 231, 233–43
  symmetrical 90, 95, 97, 115–16, 139–40, 221–33
Franco, Enrique 248
Franco, General 248
Freud, Sigmund 52
Furtwängler, Wilhelm 250

Gagaku *see* Japanese Court music
García Lorca, Federico 3, 10–13, 17–18, 22, 28–9nn, 33–4, 38, 53, 59, 67n, 70–1, 75–7, 80, 83, 99n, 178, 248, 253–4, 258, 265, 267, 271, 287
García Márquez, Gabriel 10, 64–5, 67n
Gato Alvarez, Juan *see* Alvarez Gato, Juan
Gerhard, Roberto 248
German (Nazi) Concentration Camps 37, 140, 227–9
Gershwin, George 254
Gide, André 1, 8, 14, 16, 26n
Gieseking, Walter 8
Girard, André 18, 264–5, 267, 275
Glock, Sir William xi, 21, 244–5, 259n
Gottlieb, Jay 23, 29n, 263, 265–6, 282, 286–7, 290

Goya, Francisco 33–8, 57, 59, 66n, 70–1, 80, 85–6, 97–8, 100n, 227, 243n, 253
  Los Caprichos (*The Caprices*) 34, 36, 38, 97
  Los Desastres de la Guerra (*The Disasters of War*) 34, 36, 72, 227
Granada, The Fall of 53, 253
Granados, Enrique 8, 9, 10, 12, 28n, 66n, 80
Greek epitrite rhythm *see* rhythm
Greek music (ancient), allusions to 35, 56–8, 86
Groupe musical le Zodiaque, Le *see* Zodiaque, Le Groupe
Guiraud, Ernest 152
guitar of 10-strings 24, 86, 97–8 *see also* Yepes, Narciso and *see* Ponce, Alberto
guitar writing 37, 85–7, 97–8

Hába, Alois 152
Habanera *see* rhythm
Halbreich, Harry 71, 281
Halffter, Ernesto 10
harpsichord writing 77–8, 86, 89, 166–7, 231–3
harmony 171–91
  added-resonance 187–8
  chords of Timbre I and Timbre II 179–83
  clusters 90, 107, 111, 119–20, 130, 142, 183–5
  colouristic devices 173, 181–2, 187
  Debussy, legacy of 178, 185–6
  harmonic schemes 108–9, 120, 125–7, 172–7, 179–89
  harmonic shadowing (thickened monody) 82, 87, 89–95, 124, 145, 150–1, 154–6, 163, 165, 169, 171–9, 186–7
  intervallic differentiation 74, 83, 87, 124, 172, 191
  microintervals 82, 84, 86–8, 90–1, 94–5, 106, 111, 124, 130, 142, 175, 189–91, 213
  modality 79–80, 82, 155–7, 234
  pianistic influence on 125, 174, 176, 180, 183–6, 219
  pseudo-tonality 155–6, 186–7, 234
  sound-masses 131, 140, 163–4, 167, 169, 171–3, 212–34, 237, 251
  Timbres I & II *see* harmonic schemes
  twelve-note chords 183–4

INDEX

Hawkins, Erick 248, 289
Hayrabedian, Roland viii, 263, 267–8, 277, 281–3, 288–90 (*see also* Plate No. 10)
Henry, Charles 9
Henry, Pierre 246
heterophony 131, 162
Hirayama, Michiko 64, 283
Hoffstein, Alexandre 9
Horowicz, Bronislaw 88, 270, 273
Horowitz, Vladimir 8
Hoyer, Dore 84, 270

Ibarrondo, Félix 23, 248
Imbert, Maurice 9, 18
improvisation 79, 82, 89, 119, 129–30, 142, 146, 150, 185–6, 197, 199, 210, 217, 220, 222, 231–3, 252–3
incidental music *see* 'musique radiophonique'
Inquisition, The Spanish 38, 60, 225–6
IRCAM (Institut de recherche et de co-ordination acoustique/musique) xi
Iturbi, José 10
Ives, Charles 152

Japanese Court music (Gagaku) 120
Japanese instruments, allusion to (45), 64, 110–12, 120, 162
Japanese theatre (Noh, Kabuki, Bunraku) 23, 44, 52, 62–4, 135–9, 145, 161–2, 252–4
Jarre, Maurice 20
Jarry, Albert 65
jazz 6, 52, 80, 127, 145, 155, 158, 178–9, 187, 197, 250, 253, 257–8
Jeune France, La 16, 20, 29n, 32, 65n
Jolas, Betsy 20
Jolivet, André 21, 23, 31–2, 65nn, 66n, 81, 89, 192n, 245–6, 250
Mana 32
Cinq incantations 89
Joly, Yves 84, 273, 280
Jota *see* Flamenco
Joy (Dutilleux), Geneviève xiii, 20–1, 23, 140, 264, 277, 279
Jung, Carl Gustav 42, 45, 51–2

Kabuki *see* Japanese theatre
Kazantzakis, Nikos 32–3
Keller, Hans 244–5

Kontarsky, Alloys 247
Korzeniowski, Jósef *see* Conrad, Joesph
Koussevitsky Foundation 21, 247

Landowski, Marcel 18, 24
Lazare-Lévy 8
legends *see* mythology
Leibowitz, René 21, 68, 244
Lesur, Daniel Jean Yves *see* Daniel-Lesur
Lévi-Strauss, Claude 31
Lévy, Edmond 88, 273
Lévy, Lazare *see* Lazare-Lévy
Ligeti, György 132, 152, 171, 184, 250–1
Aventures 132
Etudes 177, 179
Lux Aeterna 132
Lipatti, Dinu (Constantin) 8
Liszt, Franz 46, 246
Lockspeiser, Edward 191
Loftus, May (Mother Sheila) 7
López, Encarnación Júlvez *see* Argentinita, La
López, Pilar 10, 80
Lorca, Federico García *see* García Lorca, Federico
Lutosławski, Witold 69, 119, 184, 192n, 250
Chain 2 191
Concerto for Cello 144n
Five Songs 191
Jeux vénitiens 171
Symphony No.2 171
Trois poèmes d'Henri Michaux 171
Louvier, Alain 21, 282

Machado, Rogelio 10
Machaut, Guillaume de 212, 252
magic *see* mysticism and magic
Magic-Realism 31–2, 47, 64–5, 65–6n, 67n, 217, 258 *see also* Asturias, Miguel Angel *see* Carpentier, Alejo *see* García Marquez, Gabriel
Mahler, Gustav 251
Malec, Ivo 20, 97, 275
Mann, William 246
Maquis, The French 13
Marcel, Odile (Ohana's second wife) 24, 62, 99n, 283, 287
Marcel, Gabriel 24
Marcel, Jean-Marie 24

Márquez, Gabriel García, *see* García Márquez, Gabriel
Marshall, Frank 9
'masse-sonore' (sound-mass) *see* harmony and rhythm
Massine, Leonide 8, 10, 28n
melody 145–69
 Bartókian 3-note cells 118–19, 120–1, 125
 cantus firmus 81, 139, 165–8, 230, 237, 239
 conductus 81, 167–8, 239
 discant 95, 165, 168, 231, 239
 folk song 6, 70, 117, 154–7, 160
 incantatory 35, 57, 89–90, 116–18, 120–2, 142, 146–50, 152, 161
 melodic oscillation 118–19, 148, 160
 melodic parallelism (thickened monody) 124, 154, 165, 174–5, 178, 196
 microintervals 6, 22, 53, 69, 80, 82, 84, 86–9, 90–1, 94–5, 98, 106, 111, 122, 124, 130, 132, 142, 152–3, 213
 monody 74, 82, 89, 95, 97, 106, 145–69
 Negro spirituals 48, 80, 145, 155–6, 158, 186–7, 197, 234, 253, 255–6, 258
 pivotal melodies and referential notes 87, 117–18, 120–1, 148–50, 152–5, 157, 160, 239, 250
 plainsong parody 124, 162–9, 196, 235
 Sibylline monodies 58–9, 62, 146, 231–2, 234
 Spanish song-types 153–5
 Stravinsky, allusion to 46, 63, 116–18, 120–1, 149, 158–61, 163, 193
 trope 81, 139, 168–9
Mendelssohn (-Bartholdy), Felix 20
Menuhin, Yehudi (Lord) 24
Messiaen, Olivier xi, 16, 24, 31–2, 62, 68, 90, 93, 109, 140, 145, 156, 175, 186, 191, 193, 197, 219, 244–6, 249–50
 Cinq réchants 31, 214, 234, 247
 'Cloches d'angoisse et larmes d'adieu' (*Préludes*) 178
 Harawi 31
 Modes of Limited Transposition 178
 Oiseaux éxotiques 247
 Sept Haïkaï 112, 138
 Technique de mon langage musical 156, 188
 Visions de l'Amen 178
Meunier, Alain 22, 263, 282
Michelangelo (Buonarotti) 40
microintervals *see* melody and *see* harmony
Mihalovici, Marcel 21
Milán, Don Luis de 71, 81, 83 *see also Trois caprices*
Milhaud, Darius 20, 21
mobile form *see* form
Molina, Tirso de (Fray Gabriel Téllez) 33, 34, 70, 265–6
Montesino, Fray Ambrosio 81, 268
Monteverdi, Claudio 252
Montoya, Carlos 28n
Montoya, Ramón 10, 28n, 87, 97, 275
Mozart, Wolfgang Amadeus 7, 9, 14, 251
Münch, Charles 21, 247
music-theatre 22–3, 56, 61–4, 83–4, 88, 136–9, 167, 222, 251, 253–4, 271
musique radiophonique 22, 35, 69, 83, 105, 246, 266–71, 273–7
Mussorgsky, Modest 161, 254
Myers, Rollo xi–xii, 246
mysticism and magic 31–2, 38, 40–2, 47–9, 51–2, 53, 57, 61–5, 66n, 76, 81, 219, 235, 250, 258
mythical animals 38, 49–51, 53, 54–6, 57, 60–4, 143
mythical characters 38, 53, 54–6, 58–60, 62–4, 143
mythology, allusions to
 African 33, 40, 48, 56, 61
 Afro-Cuban 48, 56
 Buddhist 35, 36
 Celtic 40, 46, 51, 55
 Classical (Greek and Roman) 2, 6, 33–6, 44–5, 52–63, 97, 143, 160
 cosmogonic 18, 41, 44, 48–51, 55
 moon 44, 49–51, 64
 Oriental 44, 64
 pagan 35, 48, 49–54, 57, 63–4
 Phoenician 34
 South American (and Aztec) 33, 48, 54–5, 97
 Spanish 3, 33–5, 44, 48, 53, 56–7, 60–1, 70–1, 80–1, 143
 sun 40–1, 44, 45, 54, 63
 Teutonic 35, 254

Negro spirituals *see* melody
neumes *see* plainsong and rhythm
Nigg, Serge 20, 250
Niña de los Peiñes, La 59, 67n, 80
Noh *see* Japanese theatre
Nono, Luigi 251

Occupation of Paris 16, 20, 69
Offenbach, Jacques 246
Ohana, Albert (brother) 3,
Ohana, Fortuna Mercedes (née Bengio) (mother) 2, 3–4, 40 (*see also* Plate No. 7)
Ohana Isaac (brother) 3,
Ohana Jamu (grandmother) 2
Ohana, Maurice
Andalusian heritage 2, 3, 4, 6, 47
Association des amis de xii, 27n, 259n, 260n, 263
childhood 3, 4–5, 8
collaborations with Daniel-Lesur 11,
cultural roots 1–2, 13, 33–4, 47, 51–3, 68, 162, 252–3
date of birth 1, 26nn, 260n
death 1, 4, 25, 27n, 258
dispersal of ashes 6
drawings by 39, 41–3, 49–51, 60, 103, 105, 115–16, 138, 215 (*see also* Plate No. 6)
earliest memories 3
education (general) 4, 8
epitaph 44, 58, 145, 255–6 *see also* Compositions: *Swan Song*
family background 2, 3, 26n
first works 10, 11–12, 13, 16, 27n, 28n, 68
folk song collections 4, 27n, 128
founding of Le Groupe Zodiaque 16, 33 *see also* Zodiaque, Le Groupe
geographical influence 2, 6, 45, 51–3
his Paris flat 13, 25, 159
his Steinway piano 25, 174, 192nn, 219
incidental music 22, 34–5, 54, 56, 69, 70–1, 98–99, 105
involvement with French Radio 22, 23–4, 25, 29n, 88, 128
languages spoken by 4, 13
life in Paris pre 1940 8–10
marriages 16, 24, 30n
meeting and friendship with Dutilleux 20–1, 22
memberships (of juries and other committees) 24
military service 5, 12–14, 26n, 28–9n, 36, 40, 69, 93, 129 (*see also* Plate No. 4)
modification of date of birth 1, 26n
move to Biarritz 4–5
move to Paris 8, 11, 14, 16
name, correct spelling of 2, 26n, 41
name, origins of 2
name phonetically in Japanese 62, 135
nanny of (Titi) 3 (*see also* Plate No. 7)
nationality of composer 1, 24, 26n
nationality of composer's father 2–3, 26nn
performances with La Argentinita 10–11, 27n
piano recitals, concerts and tours 7, 8–9, 10–11, 12, 14–16, 23, 68
place of birth 1, 2
prizes and awards 24, 30n, 248
Prix 'Maurice Ohana' 259n
serialism, rejection of 13, 17, 32, 68, 244
signature (sun-burst) xv, 40–4, 49, 103
signs of destiny 10, 12–14
superstitions 1, 10, 173
teachers of piano 10, 12, 13, 14
teaching positions and methods 23, 249–50
ties with Britain 2–3, 12–14, 25, 26n, 66n
training, architectural 8, 18, 40, 221, 231
training, compositional 7–8, 11–12, 24–5
training, pianistic 3, 7, 8, 9
travels in Africa 4, 5–6, 9, 10, 12, 13, 24, 25
travels in Spain 4–5, 9, 10,11, 12, 25
writings 4, 13–14, 27nn, 31, 40, 47, 66n, 67nn, 88, 124, 143–4nn, 145, 152, 162, 169n, 251, 191–292
views about other composers 251–2
COMPOSITIONS:
Amants du décembre, Les (1947) 18, 265
Anneau du Tamarit (1976) 22, 53, 55, 57, 71, 142, 158, 201, 235, 242, 253, 258, 282

[Ohana, compositions *cont.*]
Anonyme XX siècle (1988) 44, 212, 288
Autodafé (1971–72) 22, 34, 38, 48, 55–6, 58–61, 65, 71, 116, 132, 137, 140, 142, 222, 225–6, 233, 253–4, 261n, 279–80
Avoaha (1990–91) 47–8, 56, 59, 98, 136, 145, 158, 194, 197, 212, 215, 241, 242, 254, 258, 290
Blessure, La (1960) 88, 106, 273
Cadran lunaire (1981–82), 44, 55, 60, 97, 165, 175, 209–10, 216, 241, 253, 285
Cantigas (1953–54) 22, 34, 68, 71–2, 81–2, 84, 87, 98, 95, 146, 169, 246, 252–4, 268
Carillons pour les heures du jour et de la nuit (1960) 88–9, 99, 246, 252, 274
Célestine, La (1982–87) 22, 34–5, 48, 56, 58–60, 71, 136, 146, 162, 165, 195, 197, 215, 218n, 222, 243n, 253–5, 260–1nn, 287
Chanson du marin, La (1954) 34, 269
Chanson de toile (1960) 35, 273
Chiffres de clavecin (1968) 55, 82, 139, 165–7, 231–3, 241, 277–8
Cinq séquences (1963) 35, 37, 54, 57, 89, 93–7, 99, 105, 125, 165, 169, 201, 207, 222–3, 241, 253, 275
Concerto for cello and orchestra No.1 *see Anneau du Tamarit*
Concerto for cello and orchestra No.2 *see In Dark and Blue*
Concerto for guitar and orchestra *see Trois graphiques*
Concerto for harpsichord and orchestra *see Chiffres de clavecin*
Concerto for two pianos and percussion *see Synaxis*
Concerto for percussion and strings *see Silenciaire*
Concerto for piano and orchestra *see Concerto pour piano et orchestre*
Concertino pour trompette et orchestre (1952) 70, 80, 268
Concerto pour cuivres, percussion et cordes (1947) 22, 75, 84, 265
Concerto pour piano et orchestre (1980–81) 41, 117, 158, 163, 165, 184–5, 201, 235, 242, 285
'Conga' *see Deux pièces pour clavecin*
Cris (1968–69) 37, 58, 132, 136, 139–40, 146, 165, 167, 215, 224–9, 235–7, 241, 246, 253, 278
Crypt (1980) 284
Damné par manque de confiance, Le (1948) 34, 70, 266
Dents du singe, Les (1960) 273
Deux dances - Tiento et Farruca (1954) 71, 84, 269
Deuxième quatuor à cordes (1978–80) 55, 158, 169, 253, 284
Deux mélodies sur des poèmes de Lorca (1947) 18, 34, 70, 75, 265
Deux pièces pour clavecin 'Wamba, Conga' (1982–83) 209–10, 241, 253, 285–6
Dies solis see Lux noctis - Dies solis
Don Juan (1947) 34, 70, 265
Douze études d'interprétation I (1981–82) 45–6, 49–51, 56, 150, 158, 163, 177–8, 192n, 209–10, 253, 285
  'Cadences libres' 153–5, 210, 215
  'Mouvement parallèles' 50, 174, 215
  'Agrégats sonores' 178
  'Main gauche seule' 50
  'Quintes' 51, 150–2, 165, 176–8
  'Troisième pédale' 42, 188
Douze études d'interprétation II (1983–85) 130, 253, 286
  'Septièmes' 117, 156
  'Contreponts libres' 187, 210–11
Duo for violin and piano (1947) 18, 75, 266
'Enterrar y callar' *see Trois caprices* (1954)
Etudes chorégraphiques (1955) 68, 71–2, 84–5, 93, 107, 196, 207–9, 252–3, 270
Etudes d'interprétation see Douze études d'interprétation
Farruca (1958) 71, 86, 272
Fêtes nocturnes, Les (1938) 11, 16, 264
Fuentovejuna (1957) 34, 71, 86, 272
Goha (1957) 272
Guignol au gourdin, Le (1956) 22, 34, 71, 83–4, 254, 271
Guitar Concerto *see Trois graphiques*
Hélène (1963) 29n, 35, 54, 98, 275

Héraclides, Les (1964) 29n, 35, 54, 98, 276
Hippolyte (1966) 29n, 54, 98, 277
Histoire véridique de Jacotin (1961) 29n, 35, 71, 88, 274
Homère et Orchidée (1959) 35, 88, 273
'Hommage à Luis Milán' *see Trois caprices* (1954)
Hommes et les autres, Les (1956) 22, 34, 69, 87, 270
Huit chansons espagnoles (1947–87) 10, 27n, 265–6, 286–7
Images de Don Quichotte (1956) 22, 34, 71, 83, 246, 270
In Dark and Blue (1988–90), 142, 212, 235, 242, 243n, 257–8, 289
Iphigénie en Tauride (1965) 29n, 35, 54, 98, 276
Joie et le bonheur, La (1938) 12, 264
Kypris (1983–84) 37, 56, 59, 117, 153–4, 158, 160–1, 253, 286
Llanto por Ignacio Sánchez Mejías (1949–50) 10–11, 13, 22, 34, 68–70, 72, 75–80, 82, 84, 87, 100n, 145, 179, 181, 246, 252, 267
Livre des Prodiges (1978–79) 46–8, 55, 59–60, 117, 160–1, 165, 194, 210, 215, 237–9, 242, 254, 283–4
Lux noctis - Dies solis (1981–88) 44, 56, 66–7nn, 212, 217n, 242, 287–8
Lys de madrigaux (1975–76) 55, 58–9, 132, 146, 156–8, 165, 183–4, 186–7, 189–90, 195, 214, 233–4, 240, 255, 282
Mariage sous la mer, Le (1991) *see Histoire véridique de Jacotin*
Mass *see Messe*
Médée (1956) 34, 71, 270
Messe (1977) 58, 82, 132, 146, 158, 164, 167–9, 177, 235, 239, 241–2, 283
Messe des Pauvres (1990) 289
Miroir de la Célestine (1990) 130, 287
Monsieur Bob'le (1951) 34, 267
Neumes (1965) 54, 57, 276
Noctuaire (1975) 42–3, 67n, 142, 282
Nuit de Pouchkine (1990) 42–3, 67n, 146, 212, 242, 255, 289

'O Beaux yeus bruns' *see Tombeau de Louize Labé*
Office des oracles (1974) 47, 55, 58, 60–2, 82, 116, 132, 136, 142, 146, 165, 167, 210–11, 215, 225–33, 240, 254–5, 261n, 281
'Paso' *see Trois caprices* (1954)
Paso, Soléa (1954) 71, 75, 269
Peste, La (1948) 34, 266
24 Préludes (1973) 37, 46, 142, 158, 162, 165–6, 175–8, 183, 185–7, 209–10, 233, 235, 280
Prométhée (1956) 34, 35, 81, 98, 271
Quatre choeurs (1987) 56, 253, 286
Quatre improvisations (1960) 35, 54, 57, 60, 88–90, 99, 116, 209, 252, 274
Récit de l'an Zéro (1958–59) 35, 72, 87–8, 272
Représentations de Tanit, Les (1951) 34, 35, 70, 80–1, 267
Romancero du Cid, Le (1958) 35, 71, 272
Route qui poudroie, La (1960) 29n, 88, 273
Sacral d'Ilx (1975) 55, 57, 129, 139, 142–3, 165, 167–8, 178, 281
Sarabande (1947) 18, 34, 37, 70, 72, 80, 246, 264
Sarc (1972) 55, 57, 129, 139, 142, 209, 280
Satyres (1976) 55, 57, 60, 129–30, 139, 142, 282
Sibylle (1968) 22, 55, 58, 129–30, 136, 139–41, 146–50, 197–201, 217n, 235, 239–41, 278
Signes (1965) 22, 38–40, 45–6, 54, 57, 68–9, 88, 105–30, 138, 140, 142–3, 162, 178, 181–2, 189–91, 194, 205, 209, 213–15, 222–5, 253, 276
Si le jour paraît... (1963–64) 35–7, 45, 54, 71, 86, 89, 97–9, 169, 178, 222–3, 253, 275
Silenciaire (1969) 55, 82, 85, 129–30, 140–1, 165, 167, 201, 205, 231, 233, 278–9
Soirée des proverbes, La (1953–54) 21, 34, 84, 268
Sonatine monodique (1945) 13, 16, 18, 70, 72, 74–5, 80, 246, 264
Songe d'une nuit d'été (1959) 34–5, 273

[Ohana, compositions *cont.*]
Sorôn-Ngô (1969–71) 21, 47, 55, 67n, 129–30, 140–2, 144n, 201, 215, 279
Sorgin-Ngo (1989) 47, 212, 288
So Tango (1991) 241, 289–90
String Quartet No. 1 *see Cinq séquences*
String Quartet No. 2 *see Deuxième Quatuor à cordes*
String Quartet No. 3 *see Sorgin-Ngo*
Stream (1970) 34, 129, 139–41, 254, 279
Suite de concert de La Célestine (1990) 287
Suite pour piano (1940) 12, 16, 18, 72, 100n, 221, 243n, 264
Suite pour un Mimodrame 34, 84, 267 see also *Monsieur Bob'le* (1951)
Sundown Dances (1990) 212–13, 247–8, 289
Swan Song (1987–88) 44, 58, 145, 158, 177, 212, 255–6, 261n, 288
Syllabaire pour Phèdre (1966–67) 22, 55–6, 58, 98, 129–30, 133–40, 162, 201–2, 204, 222, 224–7, 242, 254, 261n, 277
Synaxis (1965–66) 54, 57–8, 85, 129–30, 139–40, 144n, 165, 168–9, 201, 205–7, 210, 224–7, 241, 277
Syrtes (1970) 55, 129–30, 139–42, 279
Tableaux de l'héroïne fidèle (1954) 34, 71, 81, 83, 269
T'Harân-Ngô (1973–74) 42, 44–9, 55, 67n, 142, 210, 215, 235, 254–5, 280–1
Tiento (1955–57) 35, 37, 71–3, 85–6, 97, 98, 101n, 246, 271
Tiento et Farruca see Deux dances
Tombeau de Claude Debussy (1961–62) 9, 20, 35, 54, 69, 88–95, 97, 99, 105–6, 115, 132, 142, 159, 178, 221–3, 252, 254, 275
Tombeau de Louize Labé (1990) 146, 212, 242, 288–9
Tres graphicos see Trois graphiques
Trois caprices (1954) 34, 71–2, 80, 85, 97, 252, 269
No. 1 'Enterrar y callar' 13, 18, 34, 36–7, 70, 72–4, 264
No. 2 'Hommage à Luis Milán' 71–2, 81, 83, 89, 269
No. 3 'Paso' 70, 72, 75, 266
Trois contes de l'Honorable Fleur (1978) 44–6, 52, 55, 60–4, 117, 132, 135, 139, 146, 155, 159, 162, 165, 167, 222, 235, 242, 254, 261n, 283
Trois graphiques (1950–57) 35, 37, 71–2, 86–7, 98, 100n, 246, 248, 272
Trois poèmes de Saadi (1947–48) 18, 34, 70, 266
Trois prophéties de la Sibylle (1989) 56, 58, 147, 169n, 287
Venta encantada, La (1940) 11, 20, 28n, 34, 70, 264
Wamba (for carillon of bells) (1980) 89, 284
'Wamba' see *Deux pièces pour clavecin*
Ohana, Moses (grandfather) 2
Ohana, Noémi (sister) 3, 5, 7
Ohana, Olga (sister) 26n
Ohana, Rachel (sister) 3
Ohana, Semtob (brother) 3, 26n
Ohana, Simon David (father) 2–3, 8
Opera, Chinese see Chinese Opera
Ozawa, Seiji 258, 289

Pablo, Luis de 248
Palestrina, Giovanni Pierluigi da 252
Paris Conservatoire 8, 16, 23, 24
Pâris, Jéhanne 7–8
Parrès, Manuel 85, 270
Paz, Octavio 10, 81
Pedrell, Felipe 80
percussion, use of 45–6, 64, 74, 79, 84–5, 107–9, 111–12, 127–8, 130, 140, 150, 202–3, 205–9, 233, 239–41
Percussions de Strasbourg, Les 84, 130, 140, 270, 277–8
Pereda, Fernando 10, 81, 268
Petit, Pierre 20, 21
Petrassi, Goffredo 13
Philippot, Michel 20
piano writing 36, 45–6, 72–5, 83, 105–7, 127–8, 130, 140, 142, 165–6, 174, 176–7, 184–6, 188, 192n, 213–14
Picasso, Pablo 8, 38, 70, 99n, 248
Pincherle, Marc 18
plainsong (plainchant) 11, 57, 70, 77, 82, 89, 95, 98, 139, 145, 155–6,

162–9, 196, 227, 230, 235, 239, 251, 253, 255
political themes 140, 228–9
Ponce, Alberto 24, 86, 97–8, 263, 271–2, 275
Pool de percussion 23–4
Popol Vuh 32, 65n *see also* Asturias, Miguel Angel
Poulenc, Francis 246
Prey, Claude 20, 263
Prokofiev, Sergei 20
Prost, Christine 71, 169n, 243n, 265–6, 286
Proust, Marcel 8
pseudo-tonality *see* harmony
Puccini, Giacomo 254
puppet theatre 3, 24, 61, 64, 83–4, 254
Purcell, Henry 252

Racine, Jean 137, 242
Radio, French 16, 18, 20–2, 88, 90, 105, 128, 246–7, 250, 265–78, 280–8
Rameau, Jean-Philippe 9, 20
Ramirez, family *see* guitar, 10-string
Ravel, Maurice 7–10, 28n, 46, 88, 100n, 185, 189
  Académie de 24
  as dedidatee 285
  Concerto for piano Left Hand 8, 13
  Gaspard de la nuit 72, 100n, 184
  Jeux d'eau 46
  Piano Trio 156–7
  Sonatine 9, 16
Reibel, Guy 23, 169, 263, 282, 288
rhythm 193–17
  African 6, 47, 49, 85, 90, 127–8, 135, 196–7, 201–8, 213–15
  African drumming techniques 6, 47, 85, 205–7
  Afro-Cuban 7, 47, 49, 90, 127–8, 135, 196, 214–5, 258
  as texture 35, 84, 93, 124, 140, 193
  Greek epitrite 86, 154, 215–16
  Habanera 214–16, 217n
  homorhythm 93, 123
  layering of, 6–7, 45–6, 85, 93, 96, 111, 122, 125, 193–201, 205–7, 210–2, 234
  linear 193–4, 197–200
  metred versus unmetred 85, 93–4, 96–7, 119, 122, 148, 162, 165, 209–10, 237

motor 8, 194–5, 197, 214–15, 234
neutral 163–4, 195–6
ostinato 45, 46, 59, 72, 77, 85, 160, 208–9, 237
sound-masses (rhythmic) 113, 131, 140, 193, 201–5, 234
South American 48, 127
Spanish 6–7, 8, 72–5, 85–6, 90, 128, 183, 196–7, 201–2, 214–17
tempi, superimposition of 122, 201, 205–7, 210–2
Rimsky-Korsakov, Nikolay 10
ritualism 31, 46–51, 53, 64, 78, 80–1, 112, 129, 131, 140–3, 161, 194–5, 215, 252, 258
Roberts, Paul 23, 29n, 285
Robin (-Bonneau), Jacquéline 21, 140, 279
Rodrigo, Joaquin 248
Roland-Manuel (Roland Alexis Manuel Lévy) 20
Rojas, Fernando de 34, 253–4, 287
Ronsard, Pierre de 255
Rosenthal, Manuel 20
Rostropovich, Mstislav xi, 24, 141–2, 144nn, 258, 279, 289
Rousseau, Henri 'Le Douanier' 53, 62, 63–5, 258
Roussel, Albert 20
Routh, Francis, 245
Roy, Jean 28n, 249, 263
Rubinstein, Arthur 9, 28n
Ruiz Pipó, Manuel 97, 275

SACEM (Société des Auteurs, Compositeurs et Editeurs de Musique) 24, 259, 263
Saadi *see* Sadi, Shekh Muslihu'd-Din
Sadi, Shekh Muslihu'd-Din 18, 33–4, 70, 266
Saëta *see* Flamenco
Saguer, Louis 20
Saint-Exupéry, Antoine de 65
Sánchez Mejías, Ignacio 10, 76 *see also Llanto por Ignacio Sánchez Mejías*
Sappho 55, 58
Satchmo *see* Armstrong, Louis
Satie, Erik 178, 250, 289
Sauguet, Henri 246
scales of third-tone microintervals 153 *see also* harmony and melody
Scarlatti, Domenico 8–9, 12, 252
Schaeffer, Pierre 22, 128, 131, 246

Schéhadé, Georges 33–5, 88, 267–9, 272
Schoenberg, Arnold 20, 248
Schola Cantorum 11, 16–17, 20, 70, 81, 145, 162, 212
Schmitz, Oscar 245, 259n
Schnabel, Artur 8
Schöne, Lotte 9
Schulmann, Léa (Ohana's first wife) 16
Schumann, Robert 7
Second Viennese School 69, 251 *see also* Austro-German tradition
Seneca 34–5, 48, 71, 98, 168, 270
serialism, tyranny of 17, 32, 33
Shakespeare, William 33–5, 60–1, 67n, 254, 260–1n, 273
Sigma Series, The xii, 38, 53–4, 68, 88, 105, 116, 128–43, 207, 235, 253
Skrowaczewski, Stanislaw 17, 20, 21, 278, 284 *see also* Zodiaque, Le Groupe
'sonido negro' (black sound) *see* Flamenco
sound-mass *see* harmony and rhythm
Soubrane, Solange viii, xii, 27n, 263 *see also* Association des amis de Maurice Ohana
Spanish Civil War 9–10, 13, 66n, 226, 248
spatial devices 60–2, 211, 226, 230, 233–4, 240, 251
Stockhausen, Karlheinz 251
Strauss, Richard 252
Stravinsky, Igor 13, 20, 46–7, 56, 69, 83, 116–18, 128, 193, 251
allusions, quotations and paraphrases 46, 63, 117–18, 120–1, 125, 131, 149, 158–61, 163, 193, 237–9
Histoire du soldat 83
Noces, Les 46, 116–17, 120, 234, 290
Oedipus Rex 56, 242
Petrushka 184
Sacre du printemps, Le see Rite of Spring, The
Rite of Spring, The 46–7, 116–18, 159–61, 193, 214, 237
Symphony of Psalms 46, 116
string writing 18, 94–6, 131, 140–2, 233
surrealism 33, 36, 38, 65
symbolism 31–67

allegory 61–3
Christian 32, 48, 55, 74, 76
comic 33, 38, 45, 61–4
Death and Resurrection 40, 44, 46, 63, 83
in art 33–6, 64, 70
in literature 33–6, 64–5, 70
moon 44, 49, 51, 55
nature 44–6, 49, 53–6, 60, 105, 112, (219–21), 222–3, 231
of bulls and the bull-fight 60, 76, 78, 99n, 115–16, 138–9, 167
of opposites 42–3, 45, 53
of maturation 40
pre-Christian 32, 40, 53, 60
sexual 60–3
sun 40–4, 49, 55–6, 63
sun-moon 42–5, 55–6
tree 38–41, 49, 105, 129, 139, 221
Szalowski, Antoni 20
Szell, Georg 247

Tamayo, Arturo 248, 258, 260n, 263, 275, 278–9, 281, 285, 287, 289
Tartini, Giuseppe 62, 230
text, use of 9, 44, 48, 70–1, 76–7, 81, 88, 90, 133–7, 139, 158, 167–9, 222, 227–9, 234, 240, 242, 248, 255–6, 258, 279, 290
third-tone microintervals *see* harmony, melody and *see* scales of
Timbres I & II *see* harmony
Ton-That, Tiêt 23, 289
Troubadour poetry (and poetical forms) 35, 97, 169, 222–3, 241

Valdivielso, José de 81, 268
Valéry, Paul 9
Varèse, Edgard 31, 32, 46, 65n, 85, 101n, 171, 192n, 193, 250
Ionisation 207
variation 79, 89, 116, 131, 146–52, 197–200, 219, 222, 235–8
Vega (Carpio), Lope de 33, 71, 86, 272
Velasquez (Diego Velasquez de Silva) 36
Verdi, Giuseppe 254
Verlaine, Paul 250
Villon, François 93
Vïshnegradsky, Ivan 152
Vittorini, Elio 22, 34, 270
vocal style and techniques 22, 58–9, 76–7, 79–82, 90–1, 98, 130–7,

140–1, 145–6, 145–50, 201, 204, 227–30, 232, 239–42, 251–2, 254–5, 258

Wagner, Richard 251
Waller, Fats [Thomas Wright] 187
Webern, Anton 69
Wieder-Atherton, Sonia 258
Wittgenstein, Paul 8

Xenakis, Iannis 8, 24, 171, 250

Yepez, Narciso 24, 86–7, 98, 246, 271–2

Zarzuela 3–4
zither (chromatic and microinterval) 57, 64, 87–8, 90, 101n, 106–7, 111, 130, 152, 181, 189–91
Zodiaque, Le Groupe 16–21, 32, 65, 75, 100n, 264–6
  aims of 17–18
  concerts of 18–21
  cultural affiliations of 17
  demise of 21
  members of 16–17
  name, origin of 18

Printed in Great Britain
by Amazon